**Fighting Unemployment**

# FIGHTING UNEMPLOYMENT ———

## The Limits of Free Market Orthodoxy

*Edited by*
**David R. Howell**

OXFORD
UNIVERSITY PRESS

2005

# OXFORD

UNIVERSITY PRESS

Oxford   New York
Auckland   Bangkok   Buenos Aires   Cape Town   Chennai
Dar es Salaam   Delhi   Hong Kong   Istanbul   Karachi   Kolkata
Kuala Lumpur   Madrid   Melbourne   Mexico City   Mumbai   Nairobi
São Paulo   Shanghai   Taipei   Tokyo   Toronto

Copyright © 2005 by Oxford University Press, Inc.

Published by Oxford University Press, Inc.
198 Madison Avenue, New York, New York 10016

www.oup.com

Oxford is a registered trademark of Oxford University Press

Library of Congress Cataloging-in-Publication Data
Fighting unemployment : the limits of free market orthodoxy / edited by David R. Howell.
p.   cm.
Includes bibliographical references and index.
ISBN 0-19-516584-5; 0-19-516585-3 (pbk.)
1. Unemployment—Developed countries. 2. Free enterprise—Developed countries.
3. Labor market—Developed countries. I. Howell, David R.
HD5707.5.F54 2004
331.13'7'091722—dc22       2004049283

9 8 7 6 5 4 3 2 1

Printed in the United States of America
on acid-free paper

# Foreword

From about the mid-1980s through the 1990s, many policy analysts and economists concerned about excessively high unemployment in advanced European economies came to accept a particular view of the cause of joblessness—that it was the result largely of insufficient flexibility in the labor market in adapting to the changes brought about by technological progress and globalization. The inflexible culprits were welfare state and union policies intended to improve the economic position of lower-paid workers. The solution to joblessness was not higher growth rates (though everyone favors higher growth) but a range of changes to reduce the pay and economic security of lower-paid workers while lowering the taxes on higher-paid workers and deregulating business. In its 1994 *Jobs Study*, the Organization for Economic Cooperation and Development (OECD) encapsulated this perspective and called for market-oriented changes that many economies have indeed undertaken.

The evidence for the *Jobs Study* orthodoxy was and remains at best mixed. Many economists have known that the time-series and cross-country data on which some proponents of the view relied was of dubious value. Indeed, in various Employment Outlook analyses post-1994, OECD economists themselves made clearer the fragility of the empirical support for some of the orthodox claims. Other analysts, usually country specialists, have known that the simple flexibility story does not explain the good or poor performance of their national economies. How else to account for the success in employment of Scandinavian countries, the failure of New Zealand, which massively revamped its economic system along orthodox lines, the superior performance of Ireland compared to the

United Kingdom, and the success of the United States compared to economic near-clone, Canada?

But the orthodox message was a simple one that embodied virtues that
nearly everyone wants—economic flexibility and adaptability. With the
failure of communist command economies, the term "economic reform"
took on a distinct meaning—market-oriented reforms that freed business
decision makers from social regulation. Orthodox economic advisers declared that if more power were given to financial and global markets,
these same advisers could make the most magnificent economy that one
could imagine—outcomes of most beautiful colors and elaborate patterns.
Moreover, such markets, operating under their own rules, had the special power of being invisible to everyone who was stupid or not fit for his
post. Minister of finance, prime minister, president—can't you see the
power of the invisible hand to solve all problems? Are you stupid or not
fit for your post? Are you against reforms?

This volume brings together econometric analysis of the time-series
evidence on which the orthodox view of OECD joblessness has relied and
country case studies that make it clear that the emperor of orthodoxy is
not wearing the magnificent suit of policy panaceas claimed. The volume
deserves serious attention from researchers and policy makers, including
(perhaps most especially) those who believe in the orthodox view. The
book is chock full of facts and judicious interpretation that represent a
compelling challenge to orthodox thinking. There is none of the ideological ranting or raving or sound bite claims that often enter debate for or
against orthodox thinking. Rather, there is detailed objective analysis that
makes for the best economics. The message from the volume is a more
complex one than the simple structural reform story told in the OECD
*Jobs Study* and accompanying work. Ideally, adherents of the orthodox
view will respond to the facts and arguments given here, rather than repeat the mantra that the emperor's new clothes are indeed splendid. It is
through such dialogue that economists and policy makers will be able to
rethink the *Jobs Study* orthodoxy and find better solutions to our economic
problems.

At this writing, in a different area of economic policy, such a rethinking
is going on. The Washington Consensus view of globalization and development is in tatters, done in not by politics but by the cumulation of
evidence on the link between orthodox trade policies and economic success in less developed countries analogous to that given in this volume on
the link between orthodox reforms in OECD countries and employment
and growth. I believe that the orthodox analysis of labor market flexibility
and deregulation has a bit more clothing on than the Washington Consensus analysis of development. This is reflected in the judicious tone of
this volume, as opposed to the more raucous tone of critics of IMF and
Washington Consensus policies. But while Howell and his team are not
screaming "The emperor is naked"; they have mounted a major challenge

to orthodox thinking. Courtiers, lord high chamberlains, economic advisers, and ministers, pay attention. Marching down the street in your underwear is not a whole lot better than having nothing on at all.

Richard Freeman
London School of Economics

# Acknowledgments

This project grew out of my research on wage inequality in the United States. The mainstream view in the 1990s was that it was pretty self-evident that the explosion in U.S. earnings inequality was the result of a collapse in the demand for less-skilled workers, an outgrowth mainly of skill-biased technological change. This view never seemed very convincing. Rather, it seemed that ideological shifts toward market solutions and closely linked weakening of protective regulations and institutions (e.g., minimum wages and unions) were an important part of the story. A large and steady supply of foreign labor may also be important, at least in some regions. But this alternative view suggests a "European" type of solution—more regulations, more collective and coordinated bargaining, and more social protection spending—and therefore, according to the conventional wisdom, much higher unemployment! Did persistent high unemployment really follow ineluctably from a more regulated and sheltered labor market?

Work began on this "unemployment and labor market institutions" project in the mid-1990s. With a grant to David Gordon by the John D. and Catherine T. MacArthur Foundation to study the effects of globalization on the welfare state, the project came under the umbrella of the Center for Economic Policy Analysis (CEPA), which is affiliated with the New School University's economics department. I want to thank my colleagues at CEPA, Lance Taylor and Will Milberg, for their consistent support and good advice, and the MacArthur Foundation for its generous financial support.

While this project has produced wonderful collaborations (more on this later), it has endured the tragic, premature passing of two close friends, mentors, and colleagues. Shortly after establishing CEPA and writing the globalization grant proposal, David Gordon died. I owe a huge debt to him, as a teacher, mentor, employer, and colleague. This is a book that might be viewed as a sequel to his *Fat and Mean*, published just before his death, and I am sure it would have pleased him.

The initial stages of this project were shared with Bennett Harrison, who became a New School colleague in 1996. Bennett connected me to an exciting project on the development of new labor market statistics that he codirected with Barry Bluestone. He was passionate about the importance of challenging the conventional wisdom on "Eurosclerosis." Bennett passed away unexpectedly of cancer just before we began organizing the part of the project that would become the present volume. His contributions are greatly missed, as are his good humor and friendship.

While I take the usual responsibility for all errors and omissions, this volume reflects an extraordinary collaboration among all the authors of the chapters. This has truly been a collective effort. But most importantly, this book has benefited from the many contributions of Andrew Glyn and John Schmitt. Their own chapters are, of course, key contributions to the volume, but their insights, corrections, and advice have been invaluable, greatly improving what I have done, both as editor and as author. I also thank Marco Buti for his very useful comments. Eileen Appelbaum and Richard Freeman not only provided detailed comments and valuable suggestions on the manuscript but have been enthusiastic supporters of this project, which I greatly appreciate.

I thank Oxford University Press for agreeing to publish this volume, to my editors Steven McGroarty and Terry Vaughn for their helpful and friendly support throughout the process, and to Keith Faivre and his production team for their excellent and incredibly meticulous work. And many thanks go to Stephanie Fail for all her help with the final preparation of the manuscript at this end.

Most importantly, I thank my wife Lydia and daughter Sabrina. Lydia's support over the course of this project—indeed, over the course of my career—has been essential. Her moral outrage over the direction of U.S. social policy and its increasing influence abroad has helped keep the essential message of this project strongly stated: there are costs to free market prescriptions, and there is no single "correct" labor market model. It was she who came across the quote from John Maynard Keynes that seems so appropriate: "words ought to be a little wild for they are the assault of thoughts on the unthinking." A final note of appreciation goes to Sabrina (who is now taking her first economics course!) for help with everything from my computer to the book title—and just for being the lovely person that she is.

# Contents

# Contributors

**Dean Baker** is Co-Director of the Center for Economic and Policy Research (CEPR), Washington, D.C.

**Andrew Glyn** is Fellow and Tutor in Economics, Corpus Christi College, and University Lecturer in Economics, Oxford University.

**David R. Howell** is Professor and Associate Dean at the Robert J. Milano Graduate School at the New School and is Faculty Research Fellow at the Center for Economic Policy Analysis, also at the New School (New York City).

**Friedrich Huebler** is a doctoral student in economics at the Graduate Faculty, New School University.

**Per Kongshøj Madsen** is Associate Professor in Economic Policy at the Department of Political Science, University of Copenhagen.

**Rafael Muñoz de Bustillo Llorente** is Professor of Applied Economics, University of Salamanca.

**Peter Plougmann** is the Managing Director of New Insight A/S, Copenhagen.

**Ronald Schettkat** is a Professor at Bergische Universitat, Wuppertal, Germany.

**John Schmitt** is a Senior Research Associate, Center for Economic and Policy Research (CEPR), Washington, D.C.

**Jim Stanford** is an economist for the Canadian Auto Workers.

**Jonathan Wadsworth** is a Reader in the Economics Department at Royal Holloway College, University of London, and is a Senior Research Fellow, Centre for Economic Performance, London School of Economics.

**Fighting Unemployment**

# 1

## Introduction

DAVID R. HOWELL

*The strength of the self-adjusting school depends on it having behind it almost the whole body of organized economic thinking of the last hundred years. . . . [The heretics] believe that common observation is enough to show that the facts do not conform to the orthodox reasoning. . . . Now I range myself with the heretics.*

John Maynard Keynes

With much of the developed world plagued by high levels of unemployment since the 1980s, it has become widely accepted that the answer is "structural reform" of the labor market. It is said that only with the lower labor costs and greater flexibility that follows from labor market deregulation and a smaller welfare state can there be hope of achieving anything close to full employment. Mainstream economists and leading policy and banking institutions like the OECD, the IMF, and the ECB[1] have all strongly advocated such reforms, arguing that as firms are confronted by increasingly competitive, global markets, workers must adjust by accepting lower wages, stingier unemployment benefits, and less secure jobs. They have led the battle cry that policy makers must stand up to the insiders and special interests that ultimately undermine the employment-creating dynamism of free markets. Confronted by this conventional wisdom, policy makers have been caught between this "economic reality" and the popular and deeply embedded social norms that favor social regulation and the support of prevailing living standards, particularly concerning wages and job and income security.

This book takes a rather heretical view toward this orthodox free market prescription for good employment performance. The chapters that follow, authored by economists from seven European and North American countries, are unified by their focus on (and their answers to) several closely related questions: Does the available evidence really support the orthodox call for radical labor market deregulation? Is full employment really unattainable without American levels of wage inequality and job insecurity? And more generally, is there really no viable alternative to wholesale deregulation?

What unites all sides of the unemployment debate is the seriousness of the problem: unemployment in OECD-Europe ranged from 9–11% throughout the 1990s (OECD 2002: Appendix Table A). At mid-decade, 2.5 million jobless British workers were able, willing, and actively looking for work. Over 2.9 million French workers and about 3.6 million German workers were in similar straits. Among OECD countries, only Austria, the Czech Republic, Luxembourg, Japan, and Switzerland reported unemployment rates below 5% in 1995. Even the United States stood at 5.6%. While unemployment in OECD–Europe fell to 8.3% in 2001, it began rising again in 2002–2003. Unemployment in the United States fell sharply in the late 1990s, but has since risen just as sharply—from under 4% in 1999 to about 6% in 2003.

Although all developed countries have substantial benefits systems in place to reduce the costs of unemployment on individuals, families, and communities, redistribution never fully compensates for the material, social, and psychological costs of involuntary job loss. At the aggregate level, persistent high unemployment represents massive social inefficiency. How could high unemployment possibly persist over long periods in such wealthy, highly educated societies at the end of the twentieth century? After all, there have been no major "shocks" to the system since the 1979 OPEC oil price hike, and raw materials prices have since collapsed, to the great advantage of the wealthiest countries (and to the disadvantage of developing countries). And most importantly, after the sharp slowdown in the 1970s, productivity growth has improved. Indeed, the material well-being of working people in North America and Western Europe stands at unprecedented levels, sharply contrasting with the subsistence living standards that prevail in much of the rest of the world.[2]

All this wealth underscores the dark side of the recent economic performance of the world's richest nations—the dramatic rise in joblessness and economic insecurity since the late 1970s. While most workers can no longer expect a continuation of the 1950s–70s golden age of reliable growth in real wages and benefits, at the heart of the new insecurity is the fear of unemployment, which reached levels in the 1980–90s not seen since the great depression of the 1920s–30s. The affliction of high involuntary joblessness—which consists of the unemployed (who are still looking for work) and the discouraged (who have given up looking)—has been regularly referred to with terms like "crisis." A recent European Commission report is typical, asserting in its opening sentence that "Unemployment is the current European nightmare" (Buti, Pench, and Sestito 1998: i).

It is not always the case that the appropriate policy response to a major social problem requires addressing its root cause, or even having a good understanding of it. But this is certainly not the case with conventional wisdom about unemployment. In this view the cause is held to be the rigidity that comes with benefits and regulations that shelter workers from competitive labor market outcomes, and the cure must, it is argued, be wage and employment flexibility in the form of lower wages and greater job insecurity. As labor market rigidities are pared back, workers will get "priced" back into jobs. That this free market orthodoxy has come to completely dominate the academic and policy discussion of the unemployment crisis reflects a striking ideological shift towards pro-market (or "neo-liberal") policies that began to emerge in the late 1970s, a shift exemplified by the attack on the state and protective labor market institutions in the 1980s by the Thatcher (U.K.) and Reagan (U.S.) administrations. In economic thinking, there was a similar ideological shift toward theoretical and empirical work that presumed the superiority of reliance on individual incentives and free market forces, illustrated by the hegemony of the human capital revolution of the 1960s in labor economics and by the "new classical" thinking in macroeconomics since the 1970s.

In this increasingly market–friendly political and intellectual context, the major employment-related problems of the developed countries in the 1980s and 1990s—falling wages and rising earnings inequality in some labor markets and persistent high unemployment in others—has been explained with a "unified theory." In this account, inequality and unemployment are two sides of the same coin: fundamental economic forces (price, productivity, technology, and globalization "shocks") have produced a dramatic shift in demand against the least skilled, requiring either lower wages, as in the "flexible" labor markets of the United States, or higher unemployment, as in the more "rigid" welfare states of Europe. The solution to high joblessness is then quite straightforward: reduce the pay (and job security) of those already at the bottom of the pay distribution. The most recent and comprehensive case for the unified theory has been made by two leading liberal U.S. economists, Francine Blau and Lawrence Kahn (2002). As they put it,

> We hypothesized that the flexible U.S. labor market was able to accommodate these strains (shocks in the 1970s and 1980s) by letting absolute and relative real-wage levels adjust, thus permitting the unemployment rate to stay low. In contrast, according to this framework, in most other OECD countries, collective bargaining and other labor-market institutions and government regulations kept overall real wages rising and prevented the relative wages of unskilled workers from falling as fast as they did in the less-interventionist U.S. labor market or, in some cases, preventing any decrease at all in the relative pay of low-skilled workers. (255)

Among mainstream economists, it has been widely accepted that the crisis of high unemployment, and its persistence over time, essentially reflects a policy choice. Too often, the argument goes, policy makers and their political supporters chose to maintain institutional arrangements that furthered the interests of "insiders," harmed "outsiders," and resulted in sclerotic labor markets. In the words of Gregg and Manning (1997: 395), this stance may reflect less a balanced assessment of the evidence than the "touching faith that many economists have in the view that the deregulation of the labour market moves it towards the perfectly competitive ideal in which everyone who wants a job can find one at a wage equal to the value of their contribution to society."

While this "touching faith" has characterized the thinking of many academic economists,[3] it has been relentlessly promoted in the policy sphere by several leading international economic and financial organizations, most notably the OECD, the International Monetary Fund (IMF), the German Bundesbank, and the European Central Bank. Undoubtedly the most influential advocate of the labor market flexibility solution has been the OECD, in large part through its massive *Jobs Study* (OECD, 1994) and a series of follow-up implementation reports (OECD 1997, 1999) and country case studies. The International Monetary Fund (IMF) has followed the OECD's lead with several reports that have heralded the deregulation solution (IMF 1999, 2003). For this reason, "OECD-IMF orthodoxy" will be used in this volume as a shorthand label to describe the application of the orthodox free market view to the 1980–90s unemployment crisis. But it should be understood that this is only a term of convenience, since the view that deregulation is the only solution to the unemployment problem is widely accepted among economists and is, on the other hand, not necessarily shared by all individuals (or departments) within organizations like the IMF and OECD.

This book challenges this OECD-IMF orthodoxy. The unifying theme across the essays is that the free market case for blaming persistent high unemployment exclusively on the rigidities imposed by "employment unfriendly" labor market institutions cannot be sustained on the basis of the available evidence. This question has enormous policy significance. Since the individual, economic, and social costs of unemployment are so high, we need to fight unemployment as effectively as possible. At the same time, it is often forgotten (particularly by well-paid tenured economists— speaking of protective labor market institutions!) that eviscerating regulations and rolling back the welfare state can have high individual, economic, and social costs as well.

The chapters include both cross-country analyses (chapters 2 and 3) and individual country case studies (chapters 4–9). In different ways, each chapter calls into question the dominant policy prescription of recent years— that improving employment performance requires the adoption of the "American model" of deregulated and decentralized labor markets. The larger message is that very different labor market models, ranging from the relatively free market approach of the United States to the much more regulated and "universalistic" Scandinavian model, are capable of delivering low levels of involuntary joblessness. At the same time, these chapters suggest that these alternative models can have substantially different implications for the distribution of income and the economic well-being of the less advantaged. In short, the essays in this volume suggest that while protective labor market interventions can quite effectively reduce the incidence of low pay, income inequality, and poverty, they do not *necessarily* produce harmful employment effects. This may seem hopelessly naive, given what we hear over and over about the need for "tough choices" and the inevitability of tradeoffs. But the evidence is strongly suggestive—not a few strong welfare states have consistently outperformed even the United States.

A key implication of this critical assessment of the OECD-IMF orthodoxy is that its dominance has had the quite unfortunate effect of diverting the attention of researchers, policy makers, and the business media from other, better explanations of the unemployment crisis. While this volume does not attempt to provide the definitive alternative explanation (much less a solution) for persistent high unemployment, likely non-labor-market-related factors are considered in a number of the case study chapters, and I refer to them briefly in the final chapter of the book. It will be enough if this volume contributes to steering research and public opinion away from simpleminded free market prescriptions.

## 1.1 UNEMPLOYMENT AND THE WELFARE STATE

The developed countries have been hit with levels of unemployment not seen since the Great Depression. The policy response in the earlier episode was the creation, or vast expansion, of the welfare state. With the transformation from primarily agricultural and small-town economies, in which most families were at least partially self-sufficient, to urban industrial and service economies in which nearly all families are entirely dependent on wages, the state became the insurer of last resort. The growth of the welfare state has been a twentieth-century phenomenon, and its expansion has occurred in sudden spurts: after each of the two world wars, in response to the Great Depression, and during the unprecedented affluence of the 1960s and 1970s.

With high unemployment after World War I, the United Kingdom extended unemployment benefits in 1920, and by the mid-1930s both unemployment insurance and assistance programs were in place. As Nicholas Barr (1998: 28) writes, "Sixteen years after the end of the first World War, the UK had a system of unemployment relief which worked reasonably smoothly.... The main lesson for the future was that laissez-faire capitalism could not solve the problem of unemployment—in this area, too, state intervention was necessary." U.K. policy makers chose the more conservative path of unemployment insurance and assistance, not taking Keynes's advice that more aggressive state action to promote employment was necessary (Garraty 1979: 207).

In sharp contrast, the United States was among the last of the industrialized nations to establish a system of support for the unemployed and had no federal scheme until the 1935 Social Security Act. As an insurance scheme begun in the midst of the Depression, social security did not pay benefits to those unemployed at the time, and few had contributed enough to receive benefits before the end of the 1940s. With a negligible unemployment benefit fund and facing up to 16 million unemployed, the Roosevelt administration allocated $3.3 billion for public works in 1933–1934 and put 4 million people to work (Barr 1998: 30). The Swedish government followed the same public works route in 1933. But the most aggressive by far was the German (Nazi) government, whose public (military) spending had dramatically reduced unemployment by the mid-1930s (Garraty 1979: 206). The French, on the other hand, remained committed to laissez-faire policies, refusing to intervene in a substantial way either through public employment (the U.S. response) or unemployment relief (the U.K. response), preferring policies that attempted to discourage mechanization and diminish the pool of workers competing for jobs (e.g., through the repatriation of foreign-born workers) (Garraty 1979: 210–211).[4]

With the postwar boom, institutions, regulations, and policies designed to promote worker (and consumer) well-being became entrenched in one way or another in all the developed countries, even those—like the United States—most committed to a free market regime. This public commitment to the maintenance of a socially acceptable standard of living was clearly a reaction to the trauma of the Great Depression and World War II, but it also reflected shifting social norms as economic growth made the nations of North America and Europe dramatically richer over the course of a single generation. From the perspective of the entire world, this was a development limited to the rich Western nations. As Esping-Andersen (1994: 713) writes, "Even the poorest Third World nation has some form of social policy, but if by the welfare state we mean citizens' rights across a comprehensive array of human needs, the concept can hardly be stretched beyond the eighteen to twenty rich capitalist countries in the Organization for Economic Cooperation and Development area."

Notably, the case for the welfare state has been made on efficiency as well as equity grounds. The Great Depression helped teach the lesson that too much poverty, inequality, economic insecurity, and lack of access by large parts of the population to basic needs—food, health and safety, housing, and education—can cripple economic efficiency. The case for a healthy, safe, decently housed, and adequately educated workforce can be traced back to Alfred Marshall's *Principles of Economics* (1890) and even further back to Adam Smith's *Wealth of Nations* (1776). With the early postwar period, the efficiency implications of the argument were extended (see, for example, Gregg and Manning 1997; Agell 1999). The right to join a union and bargain collectively can increase worker voice, encourage stability in industrial relations, promote on-the-job training, and reduce the pressure on taxpayers to maintain acceptable standards of living by placing the responsibility for decent income and benefits on the firm (and consumer). The provision of unemployment insurance and assistance would not only help workers in time of need but would facilitate job search, and thereby potentially improve matches between jobs and worker skills and interests.

But, like the diversity in approaches to the unemployment problem in the interwar period noted earlier, developed countries have chosen sharply different welfare state models. In the late 1950s, Titmuss distinguished "residual" from "institutional" welfare states. The former, exemplified by the United States, is "distinct in its minimalist approach to welfare guarantees, its active encouragement of private welfare in the market, and its adherence to the traditional liberal view that social protections should be targeted to only those groups demonstrably incapable of working" (Esping-Andersen 1994: 715). The institutional model, exemplified by the Scandinavian countries, commits the state to a "system of social guarantees that, unconditionally, assures adequate living standards to all citizens" (Esping-Andersen 1994: 714).

In perhaps the most influential of such groupings, Esping-Andersen (1990) identifies Liberal (U.S., U.K.), Social-Democratic (Denmark, Sweden), and Conservative (France, Germany) models (see Hicks and Kenworthy [2003] for a recent critical assessment of the Esping-Andersen framework). In another typology, Visser focuses on industrial relations systems and identifies four categories (Auer 1999: 40). Visser's "Anglo-Saxon Pluralism" and "Northern Corporatism" groups overlap with Esping-Andersen's "Liberal" and "Social-Democratic" categories (and Titmuss's "Residual" and "Institutional" groups). But in the Visser scheme, "Central Social Partnership" countries (Austria, Germany, the Netherlands) are distinguished from "Latin Confrontation" countries (France, Italy, Spain). In the latter, bargaining is less well-coordinated between employers and unions; as a result, industrial relations tend to be more unstable and contested, with a greater role played by the state in the bargaining. Hall and Soskice (2001) simply distinguish "liberal market" from "coordinated market" economies.

## 1.2 THE NEW UNEMPLOYMENT CRISIS

While welfare state and industrial relations models differ significantly across the developed countries, rising unemployment in the 1980s and critically high unemployment rates in the 1990s struck almost all of them. Figure 1.1 shows the levels and spread of unemployment rates for 19 OECD member countries for each five-year period between 1960 and 1999 and adds figures for 2000 and the second quarter of 2002. As a reference, the line that runs from left to right marks the U.S. rate.

This figure highlights some key facts that are at the center of the unemployment policy debate. First, there was a general trend of increasing unemployment rates through the 1980s, and the median rate (half above, half below) peaked at 8.8% in 1990–1994. Second, the dispersion of rates moves with the median. The range of unemployment rates was extremely compressed in the four 1960–1979 periods (standard deviations range from 1.22 to 2.2). These rates became quite dispersed in the 1980s and 1990s (3.35 to 4.47) and then dropped sharply in 2000–2002 back to late-1970s

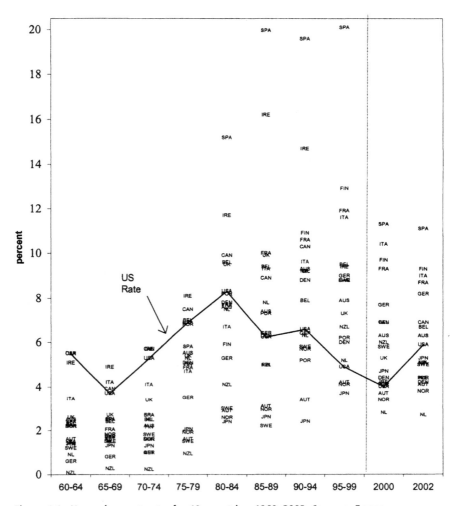

Figure 1.1. Unemployment rates for 19 countries, 1960–2002. Sources: 5-year unemployment rates, 1960–99: Baker et al., Appendix 3.2 (see chapter 3 of this volume). For 2000: OECD *Employment Outlook* (July 2002). For 2002: OECD online (www.oecd.org).

levels (2.24 in the second quarter of 2002). Third, the employment performance of the United States was among the very worst throughout the first two decades (1960–1979). Indeed, the U.S. unemployment rate did not drop below the median until the second half of the 1980s. And, fourth, while the United States performed strikingly well in the late 1990s, even in the 1995–1999 period three nations with a substantial commitment to social protection spending and regulation (Austria, Norway, and the Netherlands) performed as well or better using the unemployment yardstick. By the second quarter of 2002, fully 10 of the other 18 countries shown in figure 1.1 had unemployment rates below that of the United States. The latest data indicate that only five major OECD countries report substantially higher unemployment rates than the United States: Germany, Italy, France, Finland, and Spain.

An understanding of the unemployment crisis requires recognition of the variation across countries in unemployment by age and gender. Figures 1.2 (male) and 1.3 (female) show OECD standardized unemployment rates for two age groups, 15–24 and 25–54, for nine representative European and North American countries for 2001 (the most recent year available), organized roughly from the strongest welfare state on the left (Sweden and the Netherlands) to the most laissez-faire countries on the right (the United Kingdom and the United States), with the southern countries states in the middle (Spain and Italy). Germany and France are placed to the left of Spain and Italy, while Canada appears slightly to the right.

Figure 1.2 makes clear that for prime-age men, the Swedish and Dutch welfare states performed about as well (Sweden) or better (the Netherlands) than the U.S. and U.K. economies in 2001. On the other hand, Germany, France, Spain, Italy, and Canada all had prime-age male

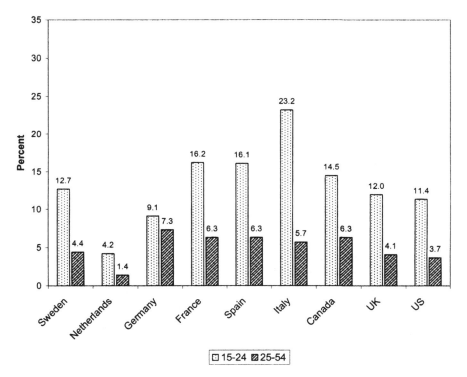

Figure 1.2. Male unemployment rates by age group for 9 OECD Countries, 2001.
Source: OECD *Employment Outlook* (2002), Statistical Annex, table C.

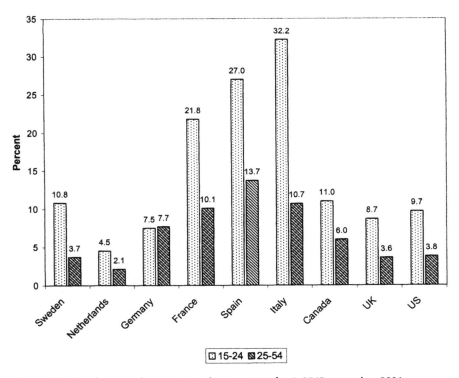

Figure 1.3. Female unemployment rates by age group for 9 OECD countries, 2001.
Source: OECD *Employment Outlook* (2002), Statistical Annex, table C.

unemployment rates between 5.7% and 7.3%, compared to the U.S.–U.K. range of 3.7%–4.1%. Male youth unemployment rates were particularly high in 2001 for France, Spain, Italy, and Canada. The results for women, shown in figure 1.3, were broadly similar. France, Spain, and Italy had by far the highest female unemployment rates for both youth and prime-age workers.

As a measure of labor market performance or worker well-being, the unemployment rate is well known to have drawbacks rarely considered in popular discussions. Statistical agencies have become quite skilled at improving comparability across countries, in the sense that similar surveys are used to calculate rates that are defined in similar ways. But it is difficult to account for the different ways people in different countries respond to the surveys and how they understand "employment." Young Mexican workers may think of any kind of low-paid informal employment as "working for pay last week." On the other hand, many young Spanish and southern Italian workers live at home (see chapter 7) with paid part-time, temporary, "under-the-table" jobs. If they believe that only "good" formal-sector jobs count as real "employment," they may respond that they are in fact "unemployed"—that they are not really working and that they are able, willing, and actively searching for a (real) job. The level of development and the nature of the social safety net will affect who can afford to drop out of the labor force altogether, again with potential implications for who is counted as unemployed. Schmitt and Wadsworth (see chapter 5) argue that this, rather than the 1980s–1990s neoliberal reforms, is the main reason for the decline in unemployment in the United Kingdom. A related problem is that the design and generosity of the unemployment benefit system can encourage workers to make sure they qualify to be counted as unemployed. As Gregg and Manning (1997: 407) put it, "The problem is that whether someone is classed as 'unemployed' on this definition is not likely to be invariant to the system of unemployment insurance." Given the differences in benefits systems, Spanish workers may have an incentive to meet the official criteria, unlike Mexican workers. Whatever the explanation, certainly the magnitude of unemployment rate differences between Spain and Mexico suggests that more than job availability (or labor market rigidities) is at work: standardized Mexican unemployment comes in below the U.S. rate, while Spanish unemployment has been three to four times higher, particularly for young women (see figure 1.3).

To avoid such measurement issues, another standard way to assess employment performance is to refer to the employed share of the working-age population—the employment rate. Figures 1.4 and 1.5 present this rate by age and gender for the same countries and year (2001) as the previous figures. Figure 1.4 shows that the employment rate for prime-age men is remarkably similar across these nine countries. With the exception of Italy (81.7%) and the Netherlands (92.7%), they range from 85.4% (Canada) to 88.1% (France). The U.S. prime-age male employment rate (87.9%) is nearly identical to that of France, Sweden, and Germany. Male youth employment rates show much more variation, from the Netherlands at the top (71.5%) to France and Italy (27.8% and 32.6%) at the bottom.

Female employment rates for prime-age workers (figure 1.5) show much greater variation across countries. But again, the United States does not stand out. While Sweden's prime-age female employment rate was 82.5%, far higher than the U.S. rate of 73.5%, which was in turn nearly identical to that of the Netherlands (72.6%), Germany (72.2%), Canada (74.3%), and the United Kingdom (73.6%). France's rate was slightly lower, at 70.8%, while the Spanish and Italian rates were far lower (52.8% and 49.5%). For female youth, figure 1.5 shows that the Netherlands had by far the highest rate (69.2%). The United States is in the next tier with Canada and the United Kingdom (52.2%–56.2%), followed by Sweden and Germany (48.5% and 43.9%). Far below are Spain (29.7%), Italy (22.1%), and France (20.7%).

These data (figures 1.2–1.5) suggest that much of the employment problem in the developed countries can be found in the high unemployment and low employment rates for youth in France, Spain, and Italy. But how big a problem is a high unemployment rate or a low employment

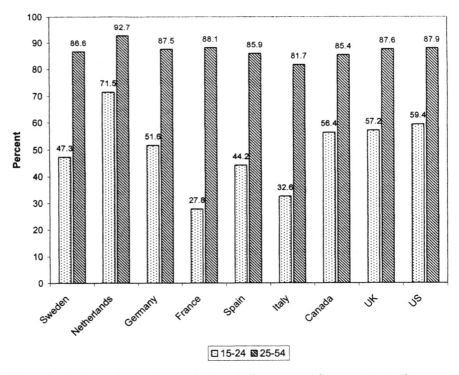

Figure 1.4. Male employment-to-population rates by age group for 9 OECD countries, 2001. Source: OECD *Employment Outlook* (2002), Statistical Annex, table C.

rate for young workers? To take an extreme example, assume that 90% of French persons ages 15–24 are in school and that the remaining 10% are either employed or unemployed. This 10% (employed and unemployed) is what would be tabulated as the "labor force" of 15- to 24-year-olds. If half of this labor force (5%) is unemployed, we get a huge 50% unemployment rate (5/10), and a very low 5% employment rate (5/100). These rates make the situation look catastrophic. But the incidence of unemployment in the youth population would actually be quite low; only 5% of the youth population in the example is unemployed.

Figures 1.6 and 1.7 contrast the standard unemployment rate with the much less commonly employed unemployment-population rate for 2001 for the same set of nine countries. Whereas male youth unemployment rates for the United States were lower than six of the other eight countries in the figure (the exceptions were Germany and the Netherlands), only three countries show higher unemployment to population rates: Spain, Italy, and Canada. Equally significant, the difference between the unemployment-population rates for these high youth-unemployment countries and the United States and the United Kingdom are surprisingly small (from .8 to 2.1 percentage points). Indeed, the incidence of male youth

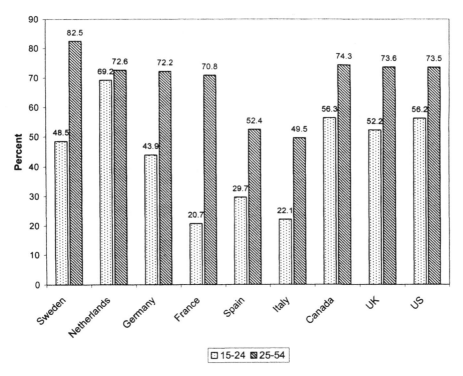

Figure 1.5. Female employment-to-population rates by age group for 9 OECD countries, 2001. Source: OECD *Employment Outlook* (2002), Statistical Annex, table C.

unemployment in 2001 was substantially higher in the United States (7.7%) than in France (5.3%), Germany (5.1%), and the Netherlands (3.2%). The results for female youth are similar, with only Spain, Italy, and Canada showing notably higher unemployment incidence. While France's unemployment rate for female youth was more than twice as high as the U.S. rate, the incidence of unemployment in the French female youth population was nearly identical (5.8% for France and 5.7% for the United States).[5]

In sum, figure 1.1 showed that, as measured by the standard unemployment measure, the decline in employment performance in much of the OECD relative to the United States took place in the 1990s, but by 2001–2002 national unemployment rates had substantially converged. As the more detailed data for 2001 show, much of the problem for the high unemployment countries (France, Spain, and Italy) can be found in high unemployment and low employment rates for youth (figures 1.2 and 1.3). The exception is Germany, whose unemployment rates were similar across age and gender groups. Employment rates produce broadly similar results: male prime-age employment rates are similar across countries, as are female prime-age rates except for Spain and Italy, but France, Spain, and Italy all show very low male and female youth employment rates (figures 1.4 and

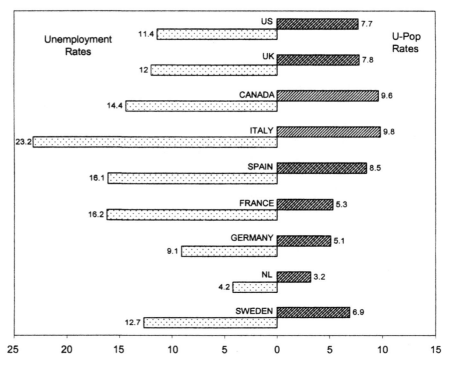

Figure 1.6. Male youth (16–24) unemployment and unemployment-to-population rates for 9 OECD countries, 2001. Source: OECD *Employment Outlook* (2002), Statistical Annex, table C.

1.5). However, when the incidence of unemployment in the youth population is considered, there is far less divergence across countries, and the United States does not stand out as particularly impressive (figures 1.6 and 1.7). This is an important alternative, if rarely used, measure for understanding the severity of youth unemployment (how many actually experience it), since schooling rates and social norms governing the appropriate age for entering the formal workforce vary widely across the OECD.

### 1.3 THE OECD-IMF ORTHODOXY

Despite the remarkable convergence in unemployment rates shown in figure 1.1, the largest countries on the European continent—France, Germany, Spain, and Italy—have continued to report much higher rates than the United States and the United Kingdom, and, in the conventional wisdom, sclerotic labor markets are the leading culprit (see for example Blau and Kahn 2002; Nickel et al. 2001; Heckman 2003). Leading policy and banking institutions like the OECD and the IMF have strongly advocated "structural reforms" in national labor markets. According to a recent IMF

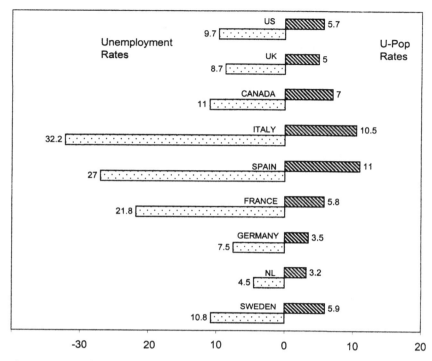

Figure 1.7. Female youth (16–24) unemployment and unemployment-to-population rates for 9 OECD countries, 2001. Source: OECD *Employment Outlook* (2002), Statistical Annex, table C.

survey paper, "the dominant view" holds that major structural labor market reforms are required for many OECD member countries and that particular attention should be focused on "the wage bargaining framework, the severity of various types of labor market regulations (job protection legislation, the flexibility of work arrangements), and the generosity of income replacement in unemployment benefit or welfare schemes" (IMF 1999).

The OECD-IMF orthodoxy has its roots in the basic supply-and-demand framework that assumes perfectly competitive markets (Gregg and Manning 1997). High minimum wages and widespread collective bargaining must raise wages and compress the wage structure, pricing less-skilled workers out of the labor market. The stakes are raised with demand shocks, such as productivity slowdowns, oil price hikes, significant technological changes, and intensifying trade competition, which may require downward wage flexibility, particularly for the less skilled. On the supply side, social spending that supports family income tends to reduce the incentive for family members to take available jobs. In sum, welfare state interventions raise both the wage floor (the lowest wages that can be paid) and the reservation wage (the lowest wage at which workers will be willing to work), necessarily reducing the demand for labor.

At the height of the mid-1990s European unemployment crisis, the OECD released *The Jobs Study* (OECD 1994), an ambitious and highly influential study of employment performance in the member countries. The recommendations of this report, known as "The Jobs Strategy," provide a "broad programme of action designed to improve labour-market performance in Member countries" (OECD 1997: 51). The *Jobs Study* (1994: 30) concluded that the source of OECD labor market problems could be found in the response on both sides of the Atlantic to the collapse in demand for less-skilled workers. Specifically, the problem was "the failure to adapt satisfactorily to change. In the U.S., workers have not upgraded their skills fast enough. In Europe . . . , by contrast, such low-wage jobs were, by and large, disallowed by society, whether through state-imposed or union-negotiated wage floors and employment protection." This reflected the views of most economists across the ideological spectrum.[6]

Table 1.1 presents what has become known as the Strategy's "Ten Commandments," whose theme is a call for less social protection spending and regulation and an increased reliance on competitive market forces. Our concern in this book is mainly with the fifth, sixth, seventh, and ninth recommendations: wages should be downwardly flexible, reflecting the demand for and supply of skill in local labor markets; employment protection legislation should be limited or eliminated altogether; and, similarly, social protection spending and regulations ("passive labor market policies") should be scaled back or eliminated. The only possible exception to a free market approach would be the promotion of job search and worker training ("active labor market policies"). Responding to an international unemployment experience that varied widely across OECD-Europe and that was, for most OECD countries, only noticeably worse than the United States for less than a decade (see figure 1.1), the Jobs Strategy nevertheless called on member countries to radically transform their labor market institutions along the laissez-faire lines of the American model.

If the OECD-IMF orthodoxy is correct, the extent to which flexibility-enhancing structural reforms have been implemented over the course of the past decade should go a long way toward explaining changes in the employment performance of OECD member countries in the 1990s. Indeed, this is precisely the contention of the OECD's *Member Countries' Experience* (OECD 1997), a follow-up report to the influential *OECD Jobs Study* (OECD 1994). According to the report, "Developments in structural unemployment over the 1990s to a large extent reflect the progress made in implementing the OECD Jobs Strategy." Again, in a 1999 assessment, the OECD confirmed the correctness of the Jobs Strategy path: countries "that have been most successful in curbing structural unemployment and improving overall labour market conditions . . . have been amongst the most determined in implementing the *Jobs Strategy*"(OECD 1999: 54).

Table 1.1. Main OECD Jobs Strategy Recommendations

| Area | Recommendations |
| --- | --- |
| 1. Macroeconomic policy | "Set macroeconomic policy such that it will both encourage growth and, in conjunction with good structural policies, make it sustainable, i.e., non-inflationary." |
| 2. Technology | "Enhance the creation and diffusion of technological know-how by improving frameworks for its development." |
| 3. Working time | "Increase flexibility of working time (both short-term and lifetime) voluntarily sought by workers and employers." |
| 4. Entrepreneurship | "Nurture an entrepreneurial climate by eliminating impediments to, and restrictions on, the creation and expansion of enterprises." |
| 5. Wages and labor costs | "Make wage and labor costs more flexible by removing restrictions that prevent wages from reflecting local conditions and individual skill levels, in particular of younger workers." |
| 6. Employment protection legislation (EPL) | "Reform employment security provisions that inhibit the expansion of employment in the private sector." |
| 7. Active labor market policies (ALMP) | "Strengthen the emphasis on active labor market policies and reinforce their effectiveness." |
| 8. Labor-force skills | "Improve labor force skills and competences through wide-ranging changes in education and training systems." |
| 9. Social security benefits | "Reform unemployment and related benefit systems—and their interaction with the tax system—such that societies' fundamental equity goals are achieved in ways that impinge far less on the efficient functioning of labor markets." |
| 10. Competition | "Enhance product market competition so as to reduce monopolistic tendencies and weaken insider-outsider mechanisms while also contributing to a more innovative and dynamic economy." |

Source: OECD (1997), Box 3: 51.

Despite this assessment by OECD experts, many countries have resisted the free market model. This hesitation is dismissed by the orthodoxy as a reflection of the power of self-interested "insiders" in maintaining the status quo. As leading OECD economists have put it, "the medicine prescribed under the OECD recommendations is bitter and hard for many countries to swallow, especially insofar as it appears to raise concerns about equity and appears to threaten some of the rents and privileges of insiders" (Elmeskov, Martin, and Scarpetta 1998: 30). The fact that the United States outperformed most European countries only for a relatively brief period, roughly the mid-1980s through the late 1990s and that this decade and a half coincided with unprecedented monetary and fiscal constraint in Europe (but not in the United States) has been largely ignored.

## 1.4 UNEMPLOYMENT, FLEXIBILITY, AND LABOR MARKET INSTITUTIONS

In the debate over job creation, nearly everyone agrees that flexibility is a good thing. It is certainly hard to argue with flexibility if the alternative is rigidity. But in the economist's lexicon, "flexibility" has a particular meaning: a market is flexible if short-run adjustments of prices and quantities (wages and employment) produce a match between demand and supply. In labor markets, this means that, with full information and negligible cost, workers should move quickly and smoothly from one job and employer to another to land the best job, while employers should hire and fire workers—again with full information and negligible cost—to maximize profits. But, as Schettkat points out in chapter 8, once it is recognized that the textbook assumptions of perfect competition do not (and could not) characterize developed world labor markets, the case for the efficiency of full wage and employment "flexibility" is substantially weakened, and labor market institutions (e.g., collective bargaining, unemployment benefits, and employment protection laws) may be preferred on both efficiency and equity grounds (Agell 1999). And, as Stanford points out (see chapter 4), for the purposes of achieving competitive advantage in real-world dynamic labor markets, a broader and perhaps more relevant understanding of flexibility is the *ability to quickly and effectively respond to change*. This kind of flexibility may require the kinds of skills and knowledge that come only with extensive organizational experience (Estevez-Abe, Iversen, and Soskice 2001). Successful, flexible organizations, in turn, may require longer-term planning, the antithesis of atomistic market flexibility.

Different labor market institutions, and different combinations of them, produce various kinds of rigidities and flexibility. To lay the groundwork for the chapters that follow, table 1.2 highlights some of the key indicators of institutions that have been most frequently singled out as the sources of the unemployment crisis. Alternative measures of the generosity of social protection spending are shown in columns 1–2. Cash transfers to the nonelderly population in the early 1990s ranged from 12%–15% in the Netherlands, Denmark, Sweden, and Finland, to just 3.7% in the United States and 1.9% in Japan. Such spending reduces the dependency of families on the paycheck and may therefore raise the reservation wages of the less-skilled, reducing their incentive to search for and take jobs (violating the ninth commandment of the OECD Jobs Strategy; see table 1.1). But this spending may also facilitate education, training, and job search and

Table 1.2. Selected Measures of Social Protection for OECD Member Countries, 1980–1995

| | Nonelderly Cash Transfers Share of GDP[1] (%) | Social Expenditure Share of GDP[2] (%) | Collective Bargaining Coverage[3] (%) | Unemployment Benefit Replacement Rate[4] (%) | | Unemployment Benefit Duration Index[4] | | Employment Protection Law Strictness Index[4] | |
|---|---|---|---|---|---|---|---|---|---|
| | 1992–95 | 1997 | 1994 | 1980–84 | 1995–99 | 1980–84 | 1995–99 | 1980–84 | 1995–99 |
| Australia | 6.2 | — | 80 | 22.3 | 26.7 | 1.02 | 1.02 | 0.5 | 0.5 |
| Austria | 8.9 | 26.2 | 98 | 33.2 | 31.0 | 0.75 | 0.75 | 1.25 | 1.3 |
| Belgium | 12.1 | 25.1 | 90 | 50.6 | 46.2 | 0.80 | 0.76 | 1.55 | 1.19 |
| Canada | 8 | 16.9 | 36 | 56.6 | 57.8 | 0.24 | 0.21 | 0.30 | 0.30 |
| Denmark | 12.4 | 30.8 | 69 | 69.0 | 60.8 | 0.62 | 1.00 | 1.10 | 0.74 |
| Finland | 15.3 | 29.5 | 95 | 32.5 | 58.6 | 0.66 | 0.54 | 1.20 | 1.08 |
| France | 10.7 | 29.6 | 95 | 62.5 | 57.9 | 0.32 | 0.51 | 1.30 | 1.50 |
| Germany | 8.4 | 27.7 | 92 | 38.8 | 36.3 | 0.62 | 0.60 | 1.65 | 1.41 |
| Ireland | — | 17.9 | — | 51.1 | 31.6 | 0.38 | 0.75 | 0.50 | 0.54 |
| Italy | 7 | 26.9 | 82 | 0 | 43.5 | 0.00 | 0.20 | 2.00 | 1.78 |
| Japan | 1.9 | 14.8 | 21 | 27.6 | 30.6 | 0.00 | 0.00 | 1.40 | 1.40 |
| Netherlands | 14.1 | 25.9 | 81 | 66.5 | 70.0 | 0.64 | 0.50 | 1.35 | 1.23 |
| New Zealand | — | — | 31 | 29.9 | 26.4 | 1.04 | 1.04 | 0.80 | 0.80 |
| Norway | 10.1 | 26.5 | 74 | 52.1 | 61.5 | 0.49 | 0.51 | 1.55 | 1.39 |
| Portugal | — | 19.1 | 71 | 34.3 | 65.0 | 0.02 | 0.38 | 1.93 | 1.91 |
| Spain | 6.8 | 20.9 | 78 | 76.9 | 65.0 | 0.19 | 0.28 | 1.91 | 1.62 |
| Sweden | 13.8 | 33.7 | 89 | 67.8 | 68.5 | 0.05 | 0.04 | 1.80 | 1.32 |
| Switzerland | — | 27.2 | 50 | 41.7 | 62.6 | 0.00 | 0.16 | 0.55 | 0.55 |
| United Kingdom | 9.4 | 21.9 | 47 | 27.6 | 21.6 | 0.70 | 0.73 | 0.35 | 0.35 |
| United States | 3.7 | 16.5 | 18 | 32.9 | 26.9 | 0.15 | 0.16 | 0.10 | 0.10 |

1. Smeeding et al., table 5a.2, in Danziger and Haveman (2001).
2. Public and mandatory private social expenditure as % of GDP; OECD Social Expenditure database.
3. OECD (1997: table 3.3).
4. See chapter 3, appendix 3.2.

promote both worker morale (and productivity) and the legitimacy of reliance on competitive market forces.

Collective bargaining (column 3) is often blamed not only for raising wages but for compressing the wage distribution and reducing employment flexibility (over time and across plants, firms, occupations, and industries), violating the fifth Jobs Strategy commandment. But unions can also increase worker voice, raise productivity (by helping to manage the workplace and reduce employer-worker conflict), and provide a vehicle to facilitate wage moderation. In the mid-1990s, the share of workers whose pay was determined collectively (but who may not be labor union members) ranged from 98% in Austria and 95% in France to 47% in the United Kingdom and 18% in the United States.

It is not just the breadth of coverage that matters for the way labor markets function, but the structure of bargaining. The industrial relations literature has focused on two dimensions of institutional structure—*centralization* (whether bargaining takes place at the national, industry sector, or firm level) and *coordination* (the extent to which individual employers and unions bargain as part of larger associations). Although the country scores on these two dimensions tend to be closely associated—highly centralized bargaining tends to be highly coordinated, and vice versa—this is not so in every case. For instance, Japan's strict pattern bargaining at the firm level gets a centralization score of 1 (most decentralized) and a coordination score of 3 (most coordinated). The fourth column of table 1.2 shows that the United States (2), New Zealand (2), and the United Kingdom (2.5) had the most "atomistic" bargaining arrangements, while Austria (5.25), Germany (5), and Norway (4.75) had the most coordinated industrial relations systems. It should be noted that, with the exception of postunification Germany, these coordinated market economies have consistently shown lower unemployment rates than their atomistic (free market) counterparts.

The unemployment benefit system can reduce the incentive to work, but it can also promote job training and search among workers (since they don't have to take an inappropriate job immediately) and can facilitate productivity improvements through enhanced employment flexibility, since employers in solidaristic societies will be more likely to fire workers (and workers will be more likely to accept working under this threat) if there is a substantial safety net, as in the Danish model (see chapter 9). Table 1.2 shows a wide range in benefit generosity across countries. The replacement rate (columns 4–5) measures the relative generosity of unemployment benefits in the first year. Table 1.2 shows that in the early 1980s, the most generous countries were Spain (77%), Denmark (69%), Sweden (68%), and the Netherlands (66.5%), while the United States, the United Kingdom, New Zealand, and Australia were least generous (22%–33%). As column 5 shows, these countries maintained their positions at the top and bottom of the generosity ranking throughout the 1980s and 1990s. France's replacement rate has been relatively high, dropping from 62% to 58% between the early

1980s and the late 1990s, while Germany's has been relatively low, declining from 39% to 36%. Both the United States and the United Kingdom substantially reduced their already low replacement rates.

The other key dimension of the unemployment benefit system is the duration of benefits. Columns 6–7 of table 1.2 report the OECD's unemployment-benefit duration index, measured as the weighted average of the benefits paid to unemployed workers from the second to the fifth year as a share of the first-year benefit level. The larger the number, the more generous the benefits in years 2–5 relative to those in the first year; a zero means that no benefits are paid after the first year. Interestingly, there is often an inverse relationship between the generosity of replacement rates and the duration of benefits. For example, the United Kingdom (.7–.73), Australia (1.02), and New Zealand (1.04) appear at the top of the duration ranking but are among those with the lowest replacement rates. Sweden, on the other hand, provides generous replacement rates (.04-.05), but only for a relatively short time. Notably, several countries with very different unemployment records increased their duration of benefits quite substantially: France, with already high unemployment (from .32 to .6); Denmark, with declining unemployment (from .62 to 1.0), and Ireland, also with sharply declining unemployment (from .38 to .75). Again, the United States (.15–.16) ranks at the bottom of the generosity ranking.

The last two columns report the OECD's employment protection law strictness index for the early 1980s and late 1990s. Strict regulations reduce the freedom to fire workers but also reduce the incentive to hire them. It should also be noted that there are longer-term effects—employers may make better hires in the first place if the freedom to fire is limited. Among the most strict are Italy (2.0 and 1.8), Spain (1.91 and 1.62), and Portugal (1.93 and 1.91). France and Germany are a notch below (1.3 and 1.5; 1.65 and 1.41). At the very bottom of the strictness ranking are the United Kingdom (.35) and the United States (.1).

In the world of the OECD-IMF orthodoxy, these vast differences in institutional frameworks largely explain the pattern of unemployment across the developed world and its change since the late 1970s. Chapters 2–10 critically assess this claim.

## 1.5 AN OVERVIEW OF THE CHAPTERS

The case for the OECD-IMF orthodoxy has been made most powerfully by reference to cross-country comparisons. The United States, with its minimalist welfare state, weak labor market institutions, and high and rising inequality, showed good employment performance in the 1990s, in sharp contrast to most European countries, which tend to do much more labor market regulation and redistribution. Chapters 2 and 3 take a look at the evidence.

Chapter 2 addresses the heart of the orthodox view—the belief that there is an ineluctable choice that must be made between employment and equality. Choosing equality, Europe has had to cope with high unemployment, whereas the high job growth of theUnited States reflects its willingness to accept high levels of earnings inequality. Howell and Huebler explore the evidence for a variety of tradeoffs: between unemployment rates and earnings inequality; between the change in unemployment rates and the growth in earnings inequality; between unemployment inequality (the ratio of high-skill unemployed to low-skill unemployed) and earnings inequality; and between employment rate inequality (again, high vs. low skill) and earnings inequality. In contrast to unified theory (and the OECD-IMF orthodoxy), they find little evidence for these predicted tradeoffs.

The tradeoff prediction follows directly from the simple competitive (supply/demand) model—constrain downward wage adjustments and employers will respond with fewer jobs. But, in fact, this model can also accommodate the evidence of little or no unemployment-inequality tradeoff. If OECD labor markets are fairly competitive in the textbook sense, differences in inequality across OECD member countries should reflect mainly differences in skill distributions. According to the "skill dispersion" view, institutions are not as responsible for high unemployment as the conventional wage rigidity view suggests, since the compressed wage distributions simply reflect compressed skill distributions. For example, it is Sweden's skill distribution, not necessarily the rigidities imposed by its welfare state, that accounts for the equality of its wage distribution. In the skill dispersion view, institutions may contribute to the unemployment problem by limiting incentives to hire (employment protection laws) and supply labor (generous unemployment benefits), but not because wages are too compressed. While there is some evidence for this skill dispersion effect, Howell and Huebler's results support other recent research that has found that differences in institutions, not skill distributions, are the main source of cross-country differences in the distribution of earnings.[7] They conclude that the failure of the data to show the predicted unemployment-inequality tradeoffs occurs not because competitive labor markets have ensured that wage distributions reflect productivity-related skill distributions but because the institutions that do in fact compress wages do not have a direct and necessary adverse effect on employment performance.

Still, even if wage compression per se is not the main source of the unemployment problem, "employment-unfriendly" institutions may be the main culprit, because they limit the necessary wage and employment adjustments to external shocks (Blanchard and Wolfers 2000), and perhaps because they have become increasingly restrictive in the face of the price and productivity shocks of the 1970s and 1980s. As Nickell et al. (2002: 19) put it, "broad movements in unemployment across the OECD can be explained by shifts in labor market institutions." Chapter 3 takes up the question of the robustness of the cross-country evidence for this claim. It is distinctive in a number of respects. Unlike much of the rest of this literature, Baker et al. begin from a skeptical stance, challenging the literature and the data to convincingly demonstrate the harmful effects of labor market institutions on employment performance across OECD member countries. Second, they offer the most comprehensive survey of the cross-country literature currently available. And third, they assemble a state-of-the-art data set (both from the generosity of other researchers whose papers they review and from the OECD) and employ these data in relatively simple, transparent regression tests of the institutions–unemployment relationship.

Baker et al. present simple scatter plots of unemployment against 6 standard measures of labor market institutions for five-year periods between 1980 and 1999. Only the unemployment replacement rate shows the predicted positive relationship, but even this is statistically insignificant and, it turns out, entirely driven by the outlying observations for Spain. The authors show that there is no relationship between the OECD's index of labor market deregulation and changes in the inflation-neutral unemployment rate (the NAIRU, as defined by the OECD) over the 1990s. In their multivariate tests, Baker et al. find weak and even perverse effects of the standard institutional variables and conclude that "the empirical case has not been made that could justify the sweeping and unconditional prescriptions for labor market deregulation which pervade much of the policy discussion."

Chapters 4–9 consist of country case studies and in almost every case (Spain is the exception) contrast the experiences of two countries. Like most of Europe, Canada experienced high levels of unemployment from the early 1980s through the late 1990s and responded by introducing significant labor market reforms aimed at implementing OECD-style flexibility. In chapter 4, Jim Stanford points out that, on the basis of labor force participation and employment rates, Canada's employment performance was even worse, particularly relative to the United States, than the unemployment data suggest. Was this a function of too little labor market flexibility? Stanford carefully distinguishes our common-sense understanding of flexibility as the "ability to change and respond to change" from its narrower meaning in conventional economic theory—as price and quantity adjustments to shifts in supply and demand.

Using standard indicators of this broader understanding of flexibility, Stanford shows that Canada actually scores quite highly. Shifts of employment across sectors and the responsiveness of employment (hiring and firing) and labor compensation to demand conditions have been higher in Canada than the United States. Similarly, the prevalence of both part-time employment and self-employment were higher in Canada in the 1990s. Among the most widely accepted measures of labor market rigidity is the lack of worker geographic mobility, and, according to Stanford, Canadians "have demonstrated themselves at least as able and willing to relocate in response to economic circumstances (positive or negative) as

Americans." Stanford also notes that unemployment remained high in the 1990s *after* major reforms in the unemployment benefit system were implemented at the beginning of the decade. Measured by flux and turbulence, the Canadian labor market has been as flexible as any.

This chapter suggests that the real objective of Canadian reforms has not been greater labor market flexibility per se but greater labor market *discipline*. When the labor market is deregulated, power shifts to employers as collective action is replaced by private contracting and as job insecurity increases. This promotes downward wage flexibility (and rising inequality), but other forms of flexibility are reduced, such as mobility between employers (a key, for example, to the success of the Dutch and Danish models). Stanford develops an index of regulation and finds, like Baker et al. (see chapter 3), that there is no statistical relationship between it and employment performance across OECD member countries. He finds that it is aggregate demand conditions, not labor market institutions, that best accounts for differences in labor market performance between Canada and the United States and concludes that "Canada experienced the 'worst of both worlds' during the 1990s: weak macroeconomic conditions combined with a movement away from interventionist labor and social policies. This combination produced both falling employment and rising inequality."

In chapter 5, John Schmitt and Jonathan Wadsworth investigate the extent to which the logic of flexibility that underpinned the OECD's *Job Study* can explain the labor-market performance of the United States and the United Kingdom. They focus on a central prediction of the OECD's theoretical model: that greater labor-market flexibility should be associated with relatively lower unemployment and higher employment of less-skilled workers, particularly young workers and those with lower levels of formal education. The reasoning is straightforward—downward wage and employment flexibility lowers the relative costs of hiring less-skilled workers, which is supposed to price them back into jobs.

Their principal findings call into question the orthodoxy's flexibility thesis. The international data for the end of the 1990s, as well as the data for Britain in the 1980s and 1990s, consistently demonstrate that labor market outcomes of both young and less-skilled workers in the flexible United States and United Kingdom are no better, and are frequently far worse, than those of their counterparts in most of the rest of the OECD. Regarding the United Kingdom, Schmitt and Wadsworth conclude that "the serious restructuring of the country's labor market since the early 1980s appears to have produced no noticeable improvement in the labor market prospects facing less-skilled workers in the 1990s relative to the 1980s." Indeed, they find that all of the improvement in U.K. unemployment rates is accounted for not by workers being priced into the labor market but by workers dropping out of the labor market, a result that "appears to contradict directly the logic behind much of the *Jobs Study* focus on flexibility."

Chapter 6 turns to Ireland and New Zealand, two small island nations on opposite sides of the globe, which have been acclaimed as 1990s success stories (OECD 1999; IMF 1999). Ireland's performance has been truly spectacular, with unemployment falling steadily from 15.6% in 1993 to 3.8% in 2001 (OECD 2002: table A). Andrew Glyn shows that Ireland achieved this extraordinary improvement in labor market performance without adopting the OECD's neoliberal labor market policy prescription. Employment took off, and unemployment collapsed, without an increase in wage inequality at the bottom (the d5/d1 ratio remained stable); without significant changes in employment protection regulations; and without major changes in the unemployment benefit system. Indeed, as Glyn puts it, "The precipitate fall in total and long-term unemployment during the 1990s, *without major reform of the benefit system*, makes wholly implausible the OECD's earlier claim that the benefit system was a major factor behind the extreme levels of joblessness in Ireland."

Glyn attributes Ireland's success not to increased decentralization and the freeing of the labor market but to cooperative and regulated wage bargaining. Responding in part to a large supply of relatively low-cost but well-educated workers, foreign direct investment poured into the country, which in turned spurred productivity growth. "Social-Partnership" agreements between trade unions and employers kept wage growth moderate, but take-home pay for workers increased because, as part of the bargaining, the state reduced the tax burden on workers. Glyn concludes that labor market deregulation "played no role in the employment boom of the 1990s."

Entirely unlike Ireland, New Zealand policy makers were early and enthusiastic converts to the OECD's labor market deregulation prescription, and the effects were substantial. As Glyn puts it, "The impact on trade unions was traumatic; union density and the share of workers covered by collective bargaining halved, the biggest fall in any OECD country." Not surprisingly, earnings inequality accelerated from already relatively high levels (see Howell and Huebler, chapter 2, figure 2.3). The OECD noted approvingly that New Zealand had substantially cut unemployment-related benefits and significantly tightened eligibility. At the same time, New Zealand followed the OECD's recommendation of balanced budgets and extremely tight monetary policy. But it turns out that New Zealand's unemployment performance has been quite mediocre, fluctuating between 7.8% and 10.3% between 1990 and 1994 and from 6.3% and 7.5% between 1995 and 1999, before falling to 5.3% in 2001 (OECD 2002: table A). The lesson Glyn draws from this Ireland–New Zealand comparison is that "extensive labor market deregulation is neither a necessary nor a sufficient condition for a radical improvement in employment."

Like Ireland, Spain experienced extremely high unemployment in the 1980 and 1990s and showed a sharp decline at the end of the 1990s. From a stunning 23.9% in 1994, Spain's unemployment rate fell to 13% in 2001 (OECD 2002: table A). In chapter 7, Rafael Bustillo challenges the conventional view that the main culprits were generous unemployment benefits, excessive wage rigidity, and strict employment protection legislation.

Bustillo argues that analysis of the benefit levels shows that they are not nearly as generous as many observers believe—about 30% of the average wage, one of the lowest in the European Union. He points out that "it is difficult to consider unemployment protection the culprit behind the high rate of unemployment in Spain when more than half of the unemployed workers are not eligible for UB, and when out of those who are eligible, more than half are eligible only for the much less generous (and means tested) unemployment assistance." As for wages, Bustillo demonstrates that Spain, while enduring high unemployment, has been characterized by wage moderation, relatively low labor costs, and relatively high earnings inequality. There is, in fact, little support for the wage rigidity story here. Nor are employment protection laws particularly onerous, despite the complaints of Spanish employers. The relatively high level of job security had its origins in the Franco period as a way to legitimate a system of low wages and an absence of the labor rights that had become standard throughout the OECD. Nevertheless, by the mid-1980s, dismissal rates were comparable to those of other leading OECD countries.

While Bustillo does not aim to provide a full explanation for the massive official unemployment levels reported since the early 1980s, he points to some prime suspects. The transformation from a highly agricultural to a service economy in a matter of a few decades in a period of political upheaval was probably important, as was the rapidly growing labor force and the persistence of extremely tight monetary policy. Bustillo also points to low R&D investment, a fairly ineffective system of active labor market policies (job training and placement), and limited geographic mobility, largely a result of high housing prices and high unemployment in all regions, which made it risky for workers to relocate.

Whereas Spain, with its high unemployment, is characterized by low levels of public social expenditure and relatively high wage inequality, the Netherlands and Germany are widely recognized as "corporatist" welfare states that rely on bargaining among employers, unions, and the state to ensure socially acceptable levels of employment and income. While the Netherlands experienced high unemployment in the late 1980s, it outperformed the United States in the early 1990s and again since 1997. Germany's high unemployment is entirely a postunification phenomenon— it was not until 1993 that Germany's unemployment rate was higher than that of the United States. In chapter 8, Ronald Schettkat assesses the employment performance of Holland and Germany in light of the OECD-IMF flexibility prescription.

The employment experience of the Dutch and the German economies contrasted sharply throughout the 1990s. This is often claimed to have been the result of deregulation in the Netherlands and overregulation in Germany (see, for example, OECD 1997). However, Schettkat argues that, despite Dutch reforms, by the late 1990s, their regulations still tended to be stronger, and their social protection spending more generous, than Germany's. For example, concerning employment protection regulations, "the Netherlands has the strictest regulations for regular employment, stricter than in Germany and far above the U.S. value." Nor can the answer be found in wage inequality. "If a compressed wage structure was the cause for high Dutch unemployment . . . one would expect that its rapidly improving employment performance would have been tied to rising wage dispersion. This, however, is not observed." Wage and skill dispersion are, in fact, quite similar in the two countries. And neither the tax nor the unemployment benefit systems can explain the higher unemployment rate in Germany.

According to Schettkat, the answer lies elsewhere. The Netherlands has been distinguished by high levels of part-time employment, particularly among women, which, in turn, facilitated a much more rapid growth in service-sector employment than in Germany. The Netherlands experienced substantially slower wage growth (at least partially compensated for by tax cuts), which contributed to an export boom. The key to the Dutch employment miracle has been a consistent mix of monetary, fiscal, and wage policies, in sharp contrast to Germany, whose policies since unification have been contradictory. The politics of the unification process (and of European integration) produced both huge public debts as funds flowed to the East and substantial growth in real wages. The response was fiscal austerity, tight monetary policy, and a rise in social security payments levied on both employers and employees, which may have hindered the growth of low-productivity service jobs (Manow and Seils 2000; Bibow 2001). The chapter concludes that the economic and political discussion has greatly overemphasized supply-side work incentives (regulations and benefits) and neglected the role of consistent wage bargaining practice and macroeconomic policy.

Chapter 9 considers Denmark and Sweden, two countries that exemplify the universalistic welfare state. If strong labor market regulation and high social protection spending necessarily produce high unemployment, the employment performance of these two countries should have been among the OECD's worst. As figure 1.1 shows, this has clearly not been the case. Denmark's five-year average unemployment rate was identical to that of the United States in the 1980s, rose above the U.S. rate in the 1990s, but by 2002 was again significantly below it; Sweden's five-year unemployment rates were far below those of the United States until the early 1990s, and, although unemployment shot up to almost 10% in 1997, by 2002 Sweden was again outperforming the United States (see figure 1.1). This vastly improved employment performance in both Denmark and Sweden has been achieved without changing the fundamentals of the Scandinavian model: high tax rates, a comprehensive social security system, a universal unemployment insurance benefit system, and among the lowest levels of wage and income inequality in the developed world.

In their chapter, Peter Ploughmann and Per Kongshøj Madsen argue that an important part of the explanation can be found in a strong commitment of both countries to active labor market policies—most important, job placement and work-related education and training programs. With the Netherlands and Ireland, Denmark and Sweden spend the most among OECD member countries in these areas, about 1.5% of GDP, which is three to four times greater than in the United Kingdom or the United States (see their figure 9.5). When linked to participation in effective job placement and training programs, relatively generous unemployment benefits (but of limited duration) can facilitate good matches of workers to jobs. The authors make the case that these government interventions actually facilitate labor market flexibility, as well as the transition to the "new economy" of services and high technology.

This reshaping of the Scandinavian welfare state to promote a flexible and innovative "high-road" economy appears to have been effective in both countries, even though in some respects they are quite different; Denmark is characterized by small firms, very low levels of employment protection, and high job turnover, while Sweden's economy is far more linked to the performance of multinational corporations, and its employment protection laws are much stronger. But, as the authors note, "The strong emphasis on life-long learning, new forms of work organizations, and the increasing use of e-learning are already key components of both the Danish and Swedish ALMP." The chapter concludes that the experience of these two countries shows that it is not necessary to embrace the American model of unregulated labor markets. While they face tough challenges, particularly the aging of the population and the growing presence of immigrant workers, Denmark and Sweden (and the Netherlands) show that impressive employment performance is possible without abandoning the universalistic welfare state.

Chapter 10 concludes the book with an overall assessment of the OECD-IMF orthodoxy. A consistent message of the chapters is that there is no simple explanation for high unemployment in the OECD area. Chapter 10 provides additional evidence that challenges the orthodox view, in part by focusing attention on the experiences of several important countries that were not the subject of our case studies—Austria, Belgium, France, and Italy. It notes that one of the consequences of the dominance of the free market orthodoxy is that other explanations have been given short shrift in the research and policy-related literature. Although an entirely convincing account of the high unemployment crisis of the past 25 years has yet to be written, this concluding chapter pulls together several elements of what such an account will likely have to include, all of which appear in one way or another in chapters 2–9.

The OECD-IMF orthodoxy is mistaken. The unemployment problem cannot be blamed on labor market rigidities imposed by the welfare state. The evidence simply does not support the free market view that convergence with the American model—reduced wages, increased inequality, and greater economic insecurity—is the only path to good employment performance. Markets are essential to the effective functioning of all modern economies, but they cannot function well without sensible regulation and strong social safety nets. The nature of these institutional constraints and supports varies widely across countries, reflecting different cultural values and institutional histories. Many of these "varieties of capitalism" can produce good employment performance, as the universalistic welfare states in northern Europe and Scandinavia have demonstrated. This book aims to help free the conventional wisdom from free market orthodoxy.

*Notes*

1. The Organization for Economic Cooperation and Development, the International Monetary Fund, and the European Central Bank.

2. National income per employed worker in 12 major Western European countries nearly doubled between 1973 and 1998, increasing from $28,100 to $43,100 (in 1990 dollars). This figure reached $55,600 for the United States. For purposes of comparison, this measure of national well-being was just $20,800 for Mexico, $14,500 for Brazil, $6,200 for China, and $4,500 for India (Maddison 2001: Table E-5 and E-6). In absolute terms, the level of worldwide inequality—explained mostly by cross-country inequality—has never been greater (Sutcliffe, 2003).

3. Gary Becker, perhaps the most prominent living economist, aptly summed up the orthodox view and the frustration of mainstream economists with European policy makers: "I argued in previous columns that rigid labor markets and high social security and other taxes on employed workers explain Europe's excessive unemployment. Yet, Helmut Kohl and the Christian Democrats took only modest actions to reduce labor taxes and give companies more flexibility over employees" (Becker, 1998).

4. According to Garrity (1979: 212), "The [French] state also devoted enormous energy to checking up on those who did qualify for aid—aid that amounted to only a few francs a day—to make sure that no undeserving person was feeding at the public trough. In 1935 some 323,000 francs were extracted from people found to have obtained relief improperly."

5. It might be argued that the similarity of the French and U.S. unemployment population rates in 2001 partly reflects the slowdown in the U.S. economy that year. In 1998, the male youth unemployment incidence was 6.7%, compared to the U.S. rate of 7.6%; the female youth rate was 7.4% for France and 6.5% for the United States.

6. On the right, the German economist Horst Siebert (1997) unhesitatingly placed the entire blame for high unemployment in Europe on labor market rigidities. Gary Becker spread the same message through his *Business Week* commentaries, pronouncing in one, for example, that "rigid labor markets and high social security taxes on employed workers explain Europe's excessive unemployment." Similarly, Robert Haveman (1997: 3), a prominent liberal economist who has specialized in the study of poverty, wrote that "a European-style policy package comprises generous and accessible social benefit programs, high minimum wage levels, and relatively stringent labor market regulations and constraints. It is accompanied by high unemployment and joblessness [and] slow employment growth."

7. See Bjorklund and Freeman (1997); Freeman and Schettkat (2000); Devroye and Freeman (2000); and Lucifora (2000).

## References

Agell, Jonas. 1999. "On the Benefits from Rigid Labour Markets: Norms, Market Failures, and Social Insurance." *Economic Journal* 109: F143–F164.

Auer, Peter. 1999. "Europe's Employment Revival: Four Small European Countries Compared." Geneva: International Labor Organization.

Barr, Nicholas. 1998. *The Economics of the Welfare State.* Stanford, Calif.: Stanford University Press.

Bertola, Giuseppe, and Pietro Garibaldi. 2002. "The Structure and History of Italian Unemployment." Manuscript prepared for the CESifo Conference on "Unemployment in Europe: Reasons and Remedies," Munich, December 6–7.

Bibow, Jorg. 2001. "The Economic Consequences of German Unification: The Impact of Misguided Macroeconomic Policies." Levy Economics Institute Public Policy Brief No. 67.

Bjorklund, Anders, and Richard B. Freeman. 1997. "Generating Equality and Eliminating Poverty, the Swedish Way." In Richard B. Freeman, Robert H. Topel, and Birgitta Swedenborg, eds., *The Welfare State in Transition: Reforming the Swedish Model.* Chicago: University of Chicago Press.

Blanchard, Olivier, and Justin Wolfers. 2000. "The Role of Shocks and Institutions in the Rise of European Unemployment: The Aggregate Evidence." *The Economic Journal* 110 (March): C1–C33.

Blau, Francine D., and Lawrence M. Kahn. 2002. *At Home and Abroad: U.S. Labor Market Performance in International Perspective.* New York: Russell Sage Foundation.

Brenner, Mats, and Torben Bundgaard Vad. 2000. "Sweden and Denmark: Defending the Welfare State." In Fritz W. Scharpf and Vivien A. Schmidt, eds., *Welfare and Work in the Open Economy, Vol. II: Diverse Responses to Common Challenges.* Oxford: Oxford University Press.

Buti, Marco, Lucio R. Pench, and Paolo Sestito. 2001. "European Unemployment: Contending Theories and Institutional Complexities." European Investment Bank, Chief Economist's Department, Report 98/01.

Card, David, Francis Kramarz, and Thomas Lemieux. 1995. "Changes in the Structure of Wages and Employment: A Comparison of the United States, Canada, and France." Industrial Relations Section, Princeton University Working Paper No. 355.

Cohen, Daniel, Arnaud Lefranc, and Gilles Saint-Paul. 1997. "French Unemployment: A Transatlantic Perspective." *Economic Policy* 25 (October): 267–291.

Devroye, Dan, and Richard B. Freeman. 2001. "Does Inequality in Skills Explain Inequality of Earnings Across Countries?" National Bureau of Economic Research Working Paper No. w8140, February.

Elmeskov, J., J. Martin, and S. Scarpetta. 1998. "Key Lessons for Labor Market Reforms: Evidence from OECD Countries Experience." *Swedish Economic Policy Review* 5(2): 205–252.

Esping-Andersen, Gosta. 1990. *The Three Worlds of Welfare Capitalism.* Cambridge: Cambridge University Press.

———. 1994. "Welfare States and the Economy." In N. J. Smelser and R. Swedberg, eds., *The Handbook of Economic Sociology.* New York: Russell Sage Foundation.

Estevez-Abe, Margarita, Torben Iversen, and David Soskice. 2001. "Social Protection and the Formation of Skills: A Reinterpretation of the Welfare State."

In P. S. Hall and D. Soskice, eds., *Varieties of Capitalism: The Institutional Foundations of Comparative Advantage*. Oxford: Oxford University Press.

Freeman, Richard B., and Ronald Schettkat. 2000. "Skill Compression, Wage Differentials and Employment: Germany vs. the U.S." Working paper No. 7610 (March), National Bureau of Economic Research.

Garraty, John A. 1979. *Unemployment in History: Economic Thought and Public Policy*. New York: Harper and Row.

Gregg, Paul, and Alan Manning. 1997. "Labour Market Regulation and Unemployment." In Dennis J. Snower and Guillermo de la Dehesa, eds., *Unemployment Policy: Government Options for the Labour Market*. Cambridge: Cambridge University Press.

Hall, Peter A., and David Soskice. 2001. "An Introduction to Varieties of Capitalism." In P. S. Hall and D. Soskice, eds., *Varieties of Capitalism: The Institutional Foundations of Comparative Advantage*. Oxford: Oxford University Press.

Haveman, Robert H. 1997. "Equity with Employment." *Boston Review*, Summer (http://bostonreview.net/BR22.3/haveman.html).

Heckman, James J. 2003. "Flexibility and Job Creation: Lessons from Germany." In *Knowledge, Information, and Expectations in Modern Macroeconomics: In Honor of Edmund S. Phelps*, ed. Philippe Aghion, Roman Frydman, Joseph Stiglitz, and Michael Woodford, 357-93. Princeton, N.J. Princeton University Press.

Hicks, Alexander, and Lane Kenworthy. 2003. "Varieties of Welfare Capitalism." *Socio-Economic Review* 1: 27–61.

Howell, David R. "Beyond the Unemployment Rate: Toward a New Summary Measure of Employment and Earnings Inadequacy." Unpublished manuscript.

International Monetary Fund (IMF). 1999. "Chronic Unemployment in the Euro Area: Causes and Cures." Chapter 4 in *World Economic Outlook* (May). Washington, D.C.: IMF.

Layard, Richard, Stephen Nickell, and Richard Jackman. 1991. *Unemployment: Marcroeconomic Performance and the Labour Market*. Oxford: Oxford University Press.

———. 1994. *The Unemployment Crisis*. Oxford: Oxford University Press.

Maddison, Angus. 2001. *The World Economy: A Millennial Perspective*. Paris: OECD.

Manow, Philip, and Eric Seils. 2000. "Adjusting Badly: The German Welfare State, Structural Change, and the Open Economy." In Fritz W. Scharpf and Vivien A. Schmidt, eds., *Welfare and Work in the Open Economy, Vol. II: Diverse Responses to Common Challenges*, pp. 264–307. Oxford: Oxford University Press.

Nickell, Stephen. 1997. "Unemployment and Labor Market Rigidities: Europe versus North America." *Journal of Economic Perspectives* 11(3) (Summer): 55–74.

Nickell, S., L. Nunziata, W. Ochel, and G. Quitini. 2001. "The Beveridge Curve, Unemployment and Wages in the OECD from the 1960s to the 1990s." CEP working Paper No. 502. London: London School of Economics.

Organization for Economic Cooperation and Development (OECD). 1994. *OECD Jobs Study*. Paris: OECD.

———. 1997. *Implementing the OECD Jobs Strategy: Member Countries' Experience*. Paris: OECD.

———. 1998. *Economic Outlook*, no. 64 (December). Paris: OECD.

———. 1999. *Implementing the OECD Jobs Strategy: Assessing Performance and Policy*. Paris: OECD.

Organization for Economic Cooperation and Development (OECD). 1994. *OECD Jobs Study*. Paris: OECD.

———. 2002a. "The Ins and Outs of Long-Term Unemployment." *Employment Outlook* (July).

———. 2002b. *Employment Outlook* Statistical Annex (July).

Siebert, Horst. 1997. "Labor Market Rigidities: At the Root of Unemployment in Europe." *Journal of Economic Perspectives* 11(3) (Summer): 37–54.

Sutcliffe, Bob. 2003. "A More or Less Unequal World? World Income Distribution in the 20th Century." Political Economy Research Institute Working Paper No. 54.

# 2

## Wage Compression and the Unemployment Crisis: Labor Market Institutions, Skills, and Inequality-Unemployment Tradeoffs

DAVID R. HOWELL
FRIEDRICH HUEBLER

It is the orthodox view that the persistence of high unemployment is explained by the rigidities imposed by labor market institutions such as centralized collective bargaining, legal minimum wages, employment protection laws, and unemployment benefit programs. Job creation is made less attractive for employers, whereas joblessness becomes more attractive for workers. These disincentives for employment growth may take place as direct effects of protective labor market institutions or indirectly through their effects on the wage structure—by raising wages at the bottom of the skill distribution, protective regulations and institutions price the less-skilled out of jobs. The policy response must be comprehensive labor market deregulation (OECD 1997; OECD 1999; IMF 1999; IMF 2003). This should be of particular importance in the aftermath of 1970s–80s productivity, energy price, technology, and trade shocks that are argued to have dramatically shifted the demand for labor away from the less-skilled. Because of the strong advocacy for this diagnosis and policy prescription by the Organization for Economic Cooperation and Development (OECD) and the International Monetary Fund (IMF), we refer to this widely accepted view as the "OECD-IMF orthodoxy."

This orthodox explanation for persistent high unemployment has two distinct variants. In the first, institutions may increase unemployment by blocking downward wage flexibility (the *wage compression* variant). In the second, institutions can undermine employment opportunities not through their direct effects on the wage structure but through non-wage-labor costs and work incentives, since competitive forces ensure that the skill distribution will determine the wage structure (the *skill dispersion* variant).

While the OECD-IMF orthodoxy points broadly at the problem of labor market rigidities, the wage compression version narrows the focus to wage rigidities, particularly at the bottom of the skill distribution.[1] As Horst Siebert (1997: 45) explains, "A lower degree of wage differentiation indicates that the wage rates do not completely fulfill their function of bringing about the necessary adjustments to a new equilibrium with more employment; then, as the alternative to adjusting the price of labor, adjustments take place via changes in the quantity of employment. A more differentiated wage structure has become more important in recent years." This simple textbook model has the great merit of accounting for both rising unemployment in Europe and rising wage inequality in the United States, and has been referred to as the "Unified Theory" (Blank, 1997; Blau and Kahn, 2002) and the "Transatlantic Consensus" (Atkinson, 1999). If this *wage compression* version of the OECD-IMF orthodoxy is right, there should be compelling evidence of tradeoffs between various measures of employment performance and earnings inequality.

But the OECD-IMF orthodoxy does not actually need a wage compression story. If OECD country labor markets are reasonably competitive, the skill distribution can be expected to trump the compressing effects of institutions in setting the earnings distribution.[2] In this case, there would be no necessary expectation of unemployment-inequality tradeoffs, since the skill mix and supply-demand forces will determine earnings inequality, and unemployment can then be explained by other institution-related effects, such as non-wage-related labor costs (e.g., taxes and the effects of employment protection laws) and work disincentives (e.g., unemployment benefits and other transfers). If this *skill-dispersion* variant of the OECD-IMF orthodoxy is right, we should not necessarily expect to find strong evidence of inequality-unemployment tradeoffs, since institutions do not have their employment-unfriendly effects mainly through the wage structure.

This chapter considers the institutions-unemployment question by focusing on the evidence for these wage compression and skill dispersion versions of the OECD-IMF orthodoxy. The first section explains the derivation of the necessity of inequality-unemployment tradeoffs from the simple demand-supply model. Section 2.2 turns to the data and describes recent cross-country earnings inequality trends, finding that large and persistent increases in equality over the past two decades are observed only in the United States, the United Kingdom, and New Zealand. Section 2.3 then addresses the empirical evidence for strong inequality-unemployment tradeoffs. We focus on a variety of possible measures of these tradeoffs: between unemployment rates and earnings inequality; between the change in unemployment rates and the growth in earnings inequality; between unemployment inequality (high skill vs. low skill) and earnings inequality; and between employment rate inequality and earnings inequality. We find little evidence for the predicted tradeoffs.

This lack of evidence for equality-employment performance tradeoffs is consistent with the skill dispersion variant of OECD orthodoxy—that it is the skill mix more than labor market institutions that determine the wage structure. Section 2.4 explores the empirical correspondence among earnings inequality, skill distributions, and labor market institutions across OECD countries. While we find little relationship between earnings inequality and skill dispersion as measured by education in the mid-1990s (consistent with Blau and Kahn's [1996] results), there is some evidence for the predicted positive relationship using test score data, which is clearly a superior measure of skills (consistent with Leuven, Oosterbeek, and van Ophem's [1998] critique of the Blau and Kahn study). But among the 14 countries for which we have data, the test score-based skills-earnings relationship is entirely driven by the two high and rising inequality countries, the United States and the United Kingdom. We also find that labor market institutions are at least as strongly linked to the structure of earnings as are skills. Indeed, in recent work that directly tests the skills versus institutions question, Bjorklund and Freeman (1997), Freeman and Schettkat (2000), Devroye and Freeman (2000), and Lucifora (2000) find that labor market institutions are far more important than skills in the explanation of cross-country differences in the distribution of earnings.

These results challenge both the wage compression and skill dispersion versions of the OECD-IMF orthodoxy. While institutions seem to matter a great deal for the wage structures of OECD countries, it seems increasingly clear that these same labor market institutions are *not* the main source of OECD employment problems (see also chapter 3). Our interpretation of the evidence suggests that the right kind and mix of labor market institutions can promote both egalitarian and full-employment objectives. This conclusion is buttressed by recent evidence that unemployment rates in the highly egalitarian countries of Sweden, Norway, the Netherlands, Denmark, and Austria are now at levels near to or below that of the United States. Policy makers should not assume that there is an unavoidable choice between low unemployment and high inequality.

## 2.1 DEMAND SHIFTS AND INEQUALITY-UNEMPLOYMENT TRADEOFFS

Underlying the orthodox Unified Theory explanation for sharply rising unemployment and inequality since the 1970s is the belief that there has been a massive shift in demand away from the less skilled, which has required substantial price (wage) or quantity (employment) adjustments. Among the more plausible explanations for the demand shock is skill-biased technological change.[3] As a recent IMF survey explains, "If the structure of relative wages is rigid, biased technical progress favoring the demand for skilled workers will lead to an increase in unemployment among the low-skilled workers" (IMF 1999: 102). In short, demand shifts in competitive markets require a choice for every country between lower wages and higher unemployment.

A convenient way to demonstrate this tradeoff appears in figures 2.1 and 2.2 (after Snower 1998). There are two categories of workers, those

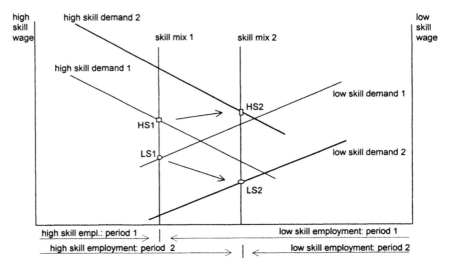

Figure 2.1. The conventional model: skill-biased demand shifts and rising earnings inequality in the United States.

with high skills (the left side) and those with low skills (the right side, read from right to left). The horizontal axis shows employment shares for these two groups. With no institutional barriers, there is no (voluntary) unemployment. The shift of the vertical line from "skill mix 1" to "skill mix 2" shows a movement toward greater "skill intensity."

At the same time, we know that in the United States during the 1980s, high-skill workers, defined as those with a college education or more, experienced a real wage increase of about 5%, while low-skill workers were faced with a much larger 20% wage decline (Gottschalk 1997). Within this simple supply-demand framework, these wage outcomes require sizable demand shifts: upward for high-skill workers and downward for the least skilled. With the high-skill wage on the left axis and the low-skill wage on the right, wage change for each group is depicted as an upward movement from point HS1 to point HS2 for high-skill workers and as a downward movement from LS1 to LS2 for low-skill workers. The growth in wage inequality is shown by comparing the gap between LS1 and HS1 at "skill mix 1" to that between LS2 and HS2 at "skill mix 2." Figure 2.1 depicts a substantial shift in the demand for skill, widely believed to reflect the spread of computer-based production technology. The significance of such demand shifts will be greater the more unequal the skill distribution and the greater the share of workers with low cognitive skills.

Figure 2.2 is similar, but here institutional barriers prevent wages from falling for the least skilled. Without downward wage flexibility, wages stay at LS1 and employers move up their demand curve (on this graph, to the right), reducing the number of jobs available to the least skilled. Thus,

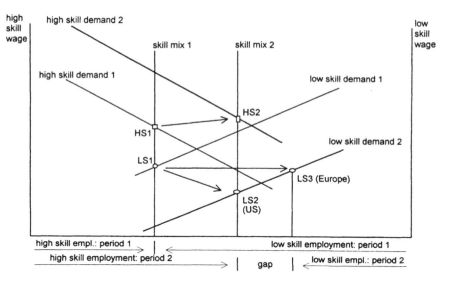

**Figure 2.2. The conventional model: skill-biased demand shifts and high unemployment in Europe.**

with a large skill-biased demand shift in an inflexible labor market, skilled workers remain fully employed, but a large share of the least skilled become redundant. This is, according to the *wage dispersion* variant of the OECD orthodoxy, precisely what explains the rise of European unemployment in the 1980s.

But this predicted tradeoff may not be observed for a variety of reasons. First, the conventional account of massive skill-biased demand shifts may be exaggerated. The growth in earnings inequality in the United States may have less to do with such demand shifts than with declining worker bargaining power, stemming from weakened institutions and shifts in social norms (Fortin and Lemieux 1997; Howell 1999, 2002). Similarly, high unemployment in Europe may also have had less to do with demand shifts than with tight macroeconomic policy and product market rigidities (Krueger and Pischke 1997; Akerlof 2002), in which case wage compression would not be closely linked to unemployment across countries.

Second, if labor markets are imperfect, some forms of monopsony characterize important parts of the economy and employers consequently have considerable bargaining power, and if institutions and social norms matter for wage setting, the responsiveness of employment to wage changes may be muted or nonexistent, even within countries with otherwise relatively competitive labor markets, like the United States (Akerlof 2002; Bhaskar, Manning, and To 2002). And these considerations may matter a great deal for cross-country comparisons. For example, consider the following hypothetical case, suggested by Bjorklund and Freeman's (1997) demonstration of the far greater inequality among otherwise similar Swedes in the United States compared to those in Sweden. We would expect pay inequality to be greater in the United States than in Sweden even for identical workers within identical assembly plants with the same total labor costs, simply because egalitarian outcomes are more highly valued in Sweden. In the U.S. plant, managers might earn much more, and shop floor workers much less, than their Swedish counterparts, so although total employment costs are the same in the two plants, inequality is far higher in the U.S. one. Lower wages would not be possible in the Swedish plant, both for morale reasons and because all the firms operate within the same set of social norms. Even among plants that could relocate, the same social constraints that keep managers' pay relatively low may also keep outsourcing (to the United States) to a minimum. This hypothetical case only suggests that even for countries with similar skill distributions, we may not observe the strong inequality-unemployment tradeoffs predicted by the simple textbook model (and by the Unified Theory).

A third issue concerns the direction of causation. For a variety of reasons that may be independent of the presence of labor market institutions, most regions tend to have a labor surplus.[4] Blanchflower and Oswald (1995) have provided substantial evidence for a "wage curve," in which wages tend to be lower in labor markets with higher unemployment. In contrast to the conventional view, their work suggests that it is unemployment that drives wage levels for a given skill group, not the reverse.[5] This may be a crucial distinction, for if the causality runs from unemployment to wage levels and if the wages of lower-skill (or lower-wage) workers are the most sensitive to local unemployment conditions, higher unemployment for the least skilled should lead to greater inequality. With more people pushed into the labor market by low wages (family members, typically women and teenage children, due to declining pay of the main earner in the household) and by welfare reform, and with the influx of low-skill workers from low-wage countries, the United States might be a good example: increasing labor supply contributing to relatively high unemployment among the less skilled. The empirical prediction that follows from this reverse-causation view is that there may be a *positive* correlation between earnings inequality and unemployment.[6]

Finally, weak evidence for inequality-unemployment tradeoffs may also reflect the possibility that labor market institutions not only compress the wage distribution but increase workplace efficiency (and employment) by encouraging trust and cooperation between workers and management and by promoting the development of firm-specific skills by less-skilled workers. Countries with institutions that reduce wage inequality and promote literacy among the least advantaged are likely to also have related institutions that promote cooperation and on-the-job training. Estevez-Abe, Iversen, and Soskice (2000) contend that higher levels of social protection—particularly employment protection, unemployment protection, and wage protection—provide workers with the insurance they need to invest in firm- and industry-specific skills. This "production regime" perspective on earnings and skill distributions represents a radical departure from the simple supply and demand stories of the Unified Theory. As Estevez-Abe et al. (2000: 7–8) put it, "Contrary to conventional neoclassical theory, which sees efforts to increase protection against job loss as an interference with the efficient operation of labor markets, measures to reduce future uncertainty over employment status—hence uncertainty over future wage premiums—can significantly improve firms' cost effectiveness" (see also Schettkat 1993).

In this alternative view, labor market institutions that are conventionally assumed to be the source of rigidities, and consequently unemployment, can be efficiency-enhancing by reducing insecurity and raising skill levels.[7] Estevez-Abe et al. argue that, with more to gain from access to good jobs or training slots, students in specific-skill production regimes have a greater incentive to perform well in school, raising the general skill levels of the least skilled and compressing the overall skill distribution. We would add that countries with more solidaristic traditions are also likely to invest more, and to do so more effectively, in education (and in health and housing) for those in lower-income communities. For both these reasons, we would expect relatively high literacy levels for those at the bottom of the skill distribution and a more compressed overall skill distribution in welfare states with more developed social protection programs. If countries with strong labor market institutions are likely to have a higher and more compressed skill mix, and if many of these same institutions tend to directly compress the earnings distribution, we should expect to see a correlation between the inequality of the earnings and skill distributions independent of the supply/demand mechanism of the textbook model. Institutions help determine the shape of both distributions.

In sum, if, independent of labor market institutions, labor markets are quite imperfect—employers have some flexibility (bargaining power) in wage setting—we might expect a positive relationship between unemployment and earnings inequality, not a tradeoff. Further, if labor market institutions compress the wage distribution while raising skill levels and increasing workplace and labor market efficiency (matching of workers with jobs), these institutions need not generate unemployment, and, again, inequality-unemployment tradeoffs will not be inevitable.

## 2.2 EARNINGS INEQUALITY IN THE OECD COUNTRIES

This section introduces the basic facts of earnings inequality, measured by the standard D9/D1 ratio (average earnings of the 90th percentile workers relative to those in the 10th percentile). Figure 2.3 shows male earnings inequality trends for the three countries with notable increases: an average annual rise of .043 percentage points for the United Kingdom, .063 points

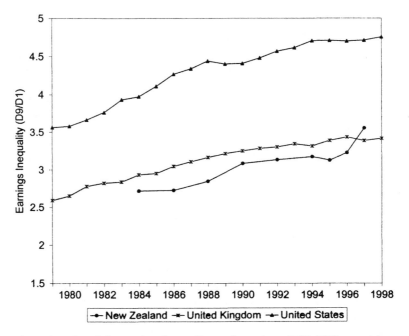

Figure 2.3. Trends in earnings inequality, male workers, 1979–1998: countries with increasing inequality. Source: See Appendix 2.B.

for the United States, and .064 points for New Zealand, much of it between 1995 and 1997). Figure 2.4 reports the trends for nine countries with little or no growth in inequality. These two figures indicate that the D9/D1 ratio for male workers in most developed countries has ranged from 2 to 3, far below the United States (4–4.5), followed by Canada (3.5–4), and France (3–3.5). It is worth noting that both Canada and France, despite these relatively high levels of earnings inequality, have been plagued by persistent high unemployment (see figure 1.1 of chapter 1).

Figures 2.5 and 2.6 show that female earnings inequality tended to be somewhat more compressed than the male earnings inequality, ranging from ratios of 2 to 3, with three major exceptions: the United States (figure 2.5) and Austria and Canada (figure 2.6), which ranged from 3.5 to more than 4. As in the case for males, the United States and the United Kingdom show the most conspicuous increases in female earnings inequality (figure 2.5). As figure 2.6 indicates, 10 of the 13 nations for which we had time series for female workers show stable or—in the case of Germany (1984–1995) and Italy (1979–1996)—declining earnings inequality. On balance, outside the United States, United Kingdom, and New Zealand, trends in both male and female earnings inequality appear fairly stable.

These data indicate that if wage compression is a key source of the unemployment problem, it is not because earnings have become more

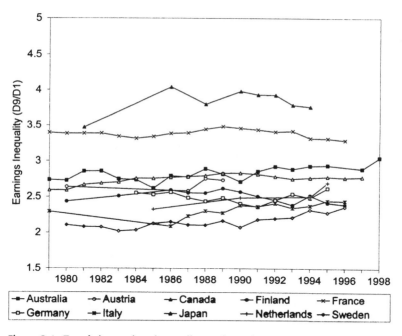

Figure 2.4. Trends in earnings inequality, male workers, 1979–1998: countries with stable or declining inequality. Source: See Appendix 2.B.

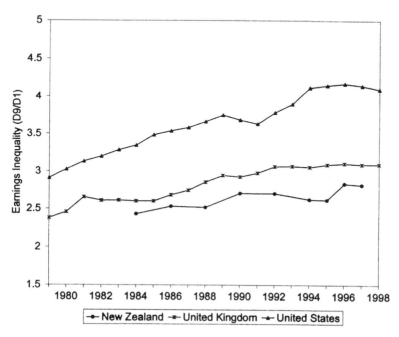

Figure 2.5. Trends in earnings inequality, female workers, 1979–1998: countries with increasing inequality. Source: See Appendix 2.B.

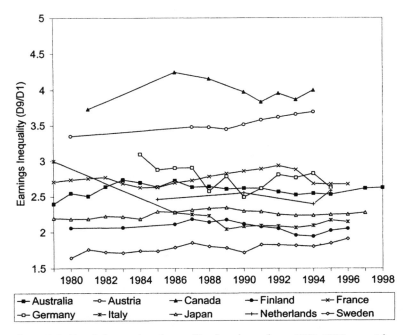

Figure 2.6. Trends in earnings inequality, female workers, 1979–1998: countries with stable or declining inequality. Source: See Appendix 2.B.

compressed since the late 1970s. In fact, the usual (Unified Theory) argument is just the reverse. In large part because of the increasing use of information technologies, skill-biased technological change is held to have reduced the relative demand for less-skilled workers. If this is so, we should observe a broad tendency toward *rising* earnings inequality, even in countries with strong labor market institutions designed to protect the less skilled from the worst effects of intense wage competition: as demand shifts toward those with the greatest cognitive skills, their earnings would be expected to rise relative to those with much lower levels of these skills, even if institutions helped set the wages of the latter above market-clearing levels. This suggests that countries with rapidly increasing diffusion of new technologies should show rising earnings inequality.

Figures 2.3 to 2.6 do not support this prediction. As a review by OECD staff (OECD 1996: 63) concludes, "the United Kingdom and the United States stand out as the only countries where there has been a continuation of a pronounced rise in earnings inequality." A leading expert on inequality, Anthony B. Atkinson (1998: 4), takes the same position: "It is misleading therefore to talk of a general 'trend' towards increased dispersion, and even in countries where dispersion has increased the historical record is better described as consisting of 'episodes' of widening income differences rather than as following an inexorable trend."

Still, it may be the case that, in the face of the presumed inexorable technology-driven demand shifts against the least skilled, countries with compressed and stable earnings distributions adjusted on the quantity side, through lower employment growth and higher unemployment. More specifically, it may be that stable D9/D1 ratios in the 2 to 3 range are simply too low to ensure that employer demand matches worker supply. Does the evidence show that higher levels of earnings inequality tend to be associated with lower unemployment and higher employment rates of the less skilled? We consider the evidence for this hypothesis in the next section.

## 2.3 EARNINGS INEQUALITY AND LOW-SKILL EMPLOYMENT OPPORTUNITIES

### 2.3.1 Unemployment Rates and Earnings Inequality

If the main source of the European unemployment problem is wage compression, we should observe a strong negative relationship between the growth in unemployment and both the level of earnings inequality and its change over time across countries. The standard is the D5/D1, the ratio of the median earnings (D5) to average earnings in the 10th percentile (D1) of the earnings distribution. Taking the average standardized unemployment rate and the D5/D1 inequality measure for four five-year periods (1980–1984, 1985–1989, 1990–1994, and 1995–1999) for 15 OECD countries for which data were available (55 country-time periods), we find a simple correlation coefficient of +.028, which has the wrong sign (a tradeoff would produce a negative sign) and is statistically insignificant by any conventional standard.

Figure 2.7 shows the 55 country-time points for unemployment and earnings inequality (D5/D1) levels that produced this positive coefficient. A tradeoff should appear as a downward sloping set of points, from the upper left to the bottom right. Clearly, the cross-country data for these 15 OECD countries show no pattern of this sort. On the other hand, the within-country evidence is mixed. The United States shows the clearest evidence of a tradeoff, with inequality increasing as unemployment fell between the early 1980s and the late 1990s. There also appears to be some evidence of a tradeoff for Finland, Germany, and France, and perhaps Japan and the Netherlands (in both cases the tradeoff appears over just two of the four periods). But other countries show a positive relationship between inequality and unemployment (Sweden and Belgium) or no clear pattern (Canada, the United Kingdom, and Denmark). While it is not surprising that the United States and Canada have the highest levels of D5/D1 inequality, it is notable that Canada has managed both higher earnings inequality and higher unemployment levels than the United States.

An alternative way to plot the data appears in figure 2.8, which shows the change in unemployment and earnings inequality between 1980 and 1995 for 16 OECD countries, with the inequality measure now defined as

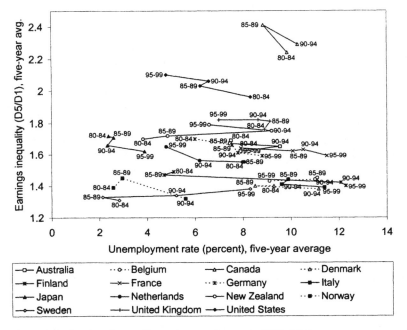

Figure 2.7. Earnings inequality and unemployment, 1980–1999.
Source: See Appendix 2.B; and Appendix 3.2 of chapter 3 of this volume.

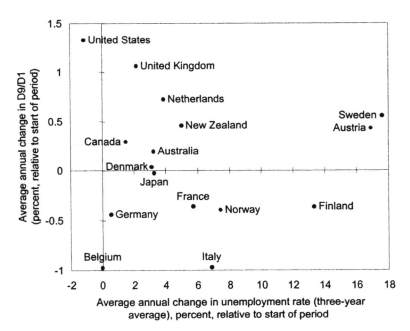

Figure 2.8. Unemployment rate and earnings inequality average annual change, all workers, 1980–1995. Source: See Appendix 2.B.

Table 2.1. Regression Results: Inequality and Unemployment

| Explanatory Variables | Unemployment Rate, 1995 Coefficient (Standard error) Adj. $R^2$ No. of countries | | Change in Unemployment Rate, 1980–95 Coefficient (Standard error) Adj. $R^2$ No. of countries | |
|---|---|---|---|---|
| | All countries | Without U.S. | All countries | Without U.S. |
| Earnings inequality | −0.319 | 0.340 | −0.130* | −0.091 |
| D9/D1, 1995 | (1.107) | (1.319) | (0.074) | (0.094) |
| | −0.06 | −0.06 | 0.11 | −0.005 |
| | 18 | 17 | 17 | 16 |
| Change in earnings inequality | −79.30** | −90.80* | −2.32 | 0.491 |
| D9/D1, 1980–95 | (35.39) | (45.72) | (2.91) | (3.57) |
| | 0.20 | 0.16 | −0.02 | −0.07 |
| | 17 | 16 | 17 | 16 |

* significant at the 0.10 level.
** significant at the 0.05 level.
Each cell shows the result of a separate OLS regression test. In many cases, the D9/D1 ratio was not available for 1980 or 1995; for those countries, the inequality and unemployment figures for the nearest year were used. See Appendix 2.A for the data and Appendix 2.B for data sources.

the D9/D1 (the average earnings at the 90th decile relative to those at the 10th decile). Again, there is no obvious tradeoff between unemployment and earnings inequality trends across this set of OECD nations over the 1980–1995 period.[8] Some countries show substantial percentage increases in unemployment and declining inequality (France, Norway, Italy, and Finland), but others show substantial increases in both unemployment and inequality (the United Kingdom, the Netherlands, New Zealand, Austria, and Sweden). It is also worth noting that among countries with growing unemployment, there were countries with highly compressed skill distributions among those with rising inequality (Sweden and the Netherlands) and declining inequality (Norway and Finland).

Although we have only a limited number of country observations, evidence of unemployment-inequality tradeoffs can also be found by regressing unemployment on inequality. To the extent that countries have constrained earnings inequality and its growth, we should expect to observe high and rising unemployment, particularly in a period of major skill-biased demand shocks. The first row of table 2.1 (column 1) shows no statistical association between unemployment and earnings inequality (D9/D1) in the mid-1990s across the 18 OECD nations for which we have data. On the other hand, moving across row 1 to column 3 shows the expected negative relationship between the level of earnings inequality and the change in unemployment—higher earnings inequality is associated with a smaller increase in unemployment. But this relationship is

Table 2.2. Regression Results: Inequality and Unemployment, Controlling for Skill

| Explanatory Variables | Unemployment Rate, 1995 Coefficient (Standard error) | | Change in Unemployment Rate, 1980–95 Coefficient (Standard error) | |
|---|---|---|---|---|
| Change in earnings inequality | −92.98* | −90.33* | −0.112 | −0.231 |
| D9/D1, 1980–95 | (49.01) | (46.83) | (4.864) | (4.626) |
| Literacy ratio | 1.598 | | −0.173 | |
| 95th/5th percentile test scores, 1994–98 | (2.518) | | (0.250) | |
| Low literacy share | | 0.105 | | −0.012 |
| Percent at level 1, 1994–98 | | (0.167) | | (0.017) |
| Adj. R² | 0.14 | 0.28 | −0.11 | 0.08 |
| Number of countries | 13 | 13 | 13 | 13 |

* significant at the 0.10 level.
Each column shows the result of a separate OLS regression test. In many cases, the D9/D1 ratio was not available for 1980 or 1995; for those countries, the inequality and unemployment figures for the nearest year were used.
See Appendix 2.A for the data and Appendix 2.B for data sources.

only barely significant by conventional standards and, as column 4 shows, disappears entirely without the United States. In sum, this top row indicates little or no negative relationship (tradeoff) between earnings inequality levels and the level or change in unemployment in the post-1980 period.

The results shown in the first cell of Row 2 (table 2.1) suggests that unemployment levels in the mid-1990s were negatively related to the change in earnings inequality since 1980 (statistically significant at the 5% level). Without the United States, the negative relationship remains, but the significance falls to just the 10% level. But the right side of row 1 shows that there was no relationship between changes in earnings inequality and the change in unemployment over the 1980–1995 period, particularly when the United States is excluded. Taken together, the results in row 2 suggest that countries with more flexible wage structures, as measured by the relative change in inequality, may have tended to have lower *levels* of unemployment, but there is no evidence that they tended to experience a lower *growth* in unemployment since 1980.

These are simple univariate tests. Controlling for other factors might help produce stronger support for the tradeoff prediction. With so few country observations, the ability to include additional measures is limited, but table 2.2 shows the results of experimenting with one potentially important control—the country's skill mix. Since labor market institutions designed to prevent extremely low wages would be expected to have less harmful employment effects in countries with low shares of very-low-skill workers (such as Sweden) than in countries with relatively high shares (say, France), controlling for skill mix might strengthen the effect of earnings inequality on unemployment.

We use two measures of skill mix—the 95/5 literacy ratio (those scoring in the 95th percentile relative to those in the 5th percentile) and the share of those scoring in the bottom literacy category in total employment. Given the difficulty of comparing education levels across countries, it is almost certainly better to compare earnings and skill dispersion with "direct" test score measures. The final report of the International Adult Literacy Survey (OECD 2000b) contains prose, document, and quantitative literacy scores for countries at the 5th and 95th percentiles of the skill distribution. We first calculate mean values across the three literacy variables and then a ratio of the mean score at the 95th percentile over the mean score at the 5th percentile. Our low-literacy variable is a measure of the share of workers scoring in the lowest (level 1) literacy category.

Rows 2 and 3 of table 2.2 show that neither of these skill measures has a significant effect on unemployment or its change in any of the four regressions. The first two columns indicate that taking into account the skill distribution makes no difference for the relationship between the change in earnings inequality and the 1995 unemployment rate; as in table 2.1, the coefficient on the change in earnings inequality is negative but barely significant at the 10% level. The right panel of the table (columns 3 and 4) shows that including the skill measures actually tends to reduce the already quite weak statistical relationship between the change in inequality (relative wage flexibility) and the change in unemployment. With or without accounting for the skill mix, our simple regression results show little or no tradeoff between levels/changes in inequality and levels/changes in unemployment in the post-1980 period.

### 2.3.2 Earnings Inequality and Unemployment by Skill Level

Another way to examine the tradeoff hypothesis is to compare levels and changes in inequality with levels and changes in *relative* unemployment rates—the ratio of unskilled to skilled unemployment. These relative unemployment rates may be a better way to gauge the employment consequences of rigid wages. Since labor market institutions (e.g., wage floors, unemployment benefits, employment protections, and employment taxes) mainly affect the least skilled, the gap between low- and high-skill unemployment rates should provide a good measure of the effects of this rigidity. At the same time, comparing *relative* unemployment rates by education level helps control for the effects of differences across nations in macroeconomic policy, the business cycle, and particular national institutional and cultural characteristics.

The conventional hypothesis is that countries with flexible labor markets show higher earnings inequality but lower unemployment inequality: the ratio of low- to high-skill unemployment will be lower in flexible labor markets since adjustments to adverse demand shifts against the least skilled can occur through wage flexibility. On the other hand, with extensive

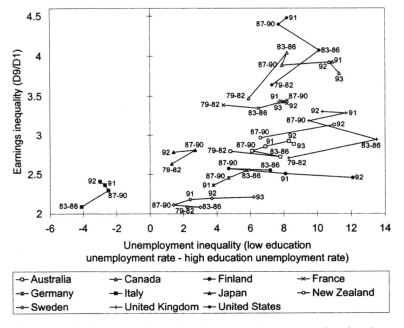

**Figure 2.9. Earnings inequality and relative unemployment rates by education level, male workers, 1979–1993. Source: See Appendix 2.B.**

shelters from wage competition, adjustment in European markets occurs on the quantity side: employment declines, unemployment rises. So, across skill groups we should observe a tradeoff between relative wage inequality and relative unemployment inequality—again, the plot should show points ranging from the upper left to bottom right.

Figure 2.9 shows earnings inequality, defined as the ratio of the wages of the average 90th percentile worker to that of the 10th percentile worker (D9/D1) plotted against unemployment inequality (the difference between low- and high-skill unemployment rates) for male workers over the 1979–1993 period. The United States appears in the upper right corner with the highest earnings inequality *and* the highest unemployment inequality. That is, compared to skilled workers, *low-skill workers in the United States fare the worst in terms of both relative earnings and the probability of being unemployed.* Indeed, the trend for the United States shows rapidly growing earnings inequality with no improvement in unemployment inequality. Canada experienced comparable levels of unemployment inequality but somewhat lower earnings inequality. The United Kingdom did somewhat worse than the United States on unemployment inequality but much better on earnings dispersion. On the other hand, France, Germany, Sweden, Japan, Australia, and Italy were all superior on both dimensions of inequality.

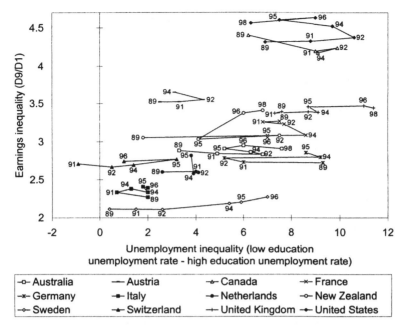

Figure 2.10. Earnings inequality and relative unemployment rates by education level, all workers, 1989–1998. Source: See Appendix 2.B.

Figure 2.10 also compares these two measures of inequality, but does so for all workers (male and female) for a more recent period (1989–1998) using a different measure of unemployment inequality.[9] The pattern is similar. Again, the United States and Canada have the highest levels of both earnings and unemployment inequality. Germany, France, and the United Kingdom share similarly high unemployment inequality but show much lower earnings inequality. Austria, Switzerland, the Netherlands, and Italy are superior on both measures. The patterns shown in figures 2.9 and 2.10 directly challenge the conventional tradeoff view: countries with lower earnings inequality also tend to have lower unemployment inequality. Low-skill workers do not tend to show a lower likelihood of unemployment in countries where their wages are relatively low.

### 2.3.3 Employment Rates and Earnings Inequality

If wage rigidity is a major source of the unemployment problem, the underlying reason may be that the absence of downwardly flexible wage rates has undermined *employment* growth. Inadequate job opportunities can be expected to raise unemployment by increasing the number of workers without jobs looking for work, but poor employment prospects may also lead workers to drop out of the labor market altogether. For this reason, employment rates are a broader measure of the employment consequences of a country's wage-setting system. But the orthodox prediction is the same: if demand shifts have been strongly biased against low-skill workers throughout the developed world, these workers should have paid the price in lower relative wages (producing higher inequality) in nations with greater wage flexibility; in contrast, in the more rigid European labor markets, lower-skill workers should have experienced lower employment rates as they were priced out of the labor market. So again there is a tradeoff, this time between earnings inequality and employment rate inequality.

Comparing employment rates by skill across different OECD countries using different methodologies, Nickell and Bell (1995) and Card, Kramarz, and Lemieux (1995) find no support for the tradeoff prediction. In their study of the United States, Canada, and France, Card et al. leave no doubt about the lack of support for the conventional view:

> Consistent with the view that French labor market institutions restrict relative wage flexibility, we find that wage differentials between skill groups held constant or narrowed slightly over the 1980s. As in Canada, however, we find little evidence that this apparent rigidity in relative wages translated into greater employment losses for less-skilled workers. Indeed, the pattern of employment-population growth rates across age-education cells in France is almost identical to the pattern in the United States. Taking the evidence for the United States, Canada, and France as a whole, we conclude that it is very difficult to maintain the hypothesis that the 'wage inflexibility' in Canada and France translated into greater relative employment losses for less-skilled workers in these countries. (Card et al. 1995: 3)

Similar results were found for Sweden (Edin, Harkman, and Holmlund 1996) and Germany (Krueger and Pischke 1997).[10]

The most common approach to measuring the dispersion of employment rates by skill is to use educational attainment data. For 25- to 64-year-old males, Glyn and Salverda (2000) calculate employment rates for the top and bottom quartile of the educational distribution for 15 OECD nations. Using their data, figure 2.11 shows a plot of the difference between the top and the bottom education quartiles (Q4-Q1) against the standard D9/D1 measure of earnings inequality for 1994 (the only year for which data were available).[11] The predicted tradeoff should again show a downward sloping relationship, with the United States and other Anglo-Saxon countries in the upper left and the northern European welfare states in the bottom right. Clearly, there is no support for such a relationship in these data. If anything, there is an upward sloping trend. In Glyn's data, Ireland has the highest level of earnings inequality, followed by the United States, whose employment rate inequality (which should be very low according to the tradeoff view) is greater than that of West Germany, Austria, Australia, Sweden, Japan, and Switzerland.

We should also observe a tradeoff between the *change* in earnings inequality and the *change* in employment rate dispersion by skill: as demand

Figure 2.11. Earnings inequality and employment rate inequality, Male workers, 1994. Source: See Appendix 2.B.

shifts work against the least skilled, countries that respond with wage flexibility (rising earnings inequality) can avoid paying the price of declining demand in the form of declining employment (falling relative employment rates for the less skilled). Again, with change in earnings inequality on the vertical axis and change in employment rate dispersion on the horizontal, nations should be arrayed from upper left to bottom right, from those with the most flexible wage setting institutions to those with the least flexible.

With data from Glyn (2000), figure 2.12 shows average annual percentage changes for both earnings and employment rate inequality for 16 OECD nations. For most, we plot two points, one for the 1980s, another for the 1990s. Data limitations resulted in just a single decade observation for five nations (Japan, Switzerland, Norway, Ireland, and Denmark). As in the earlier figures on unemployment, this figure offers no suggestion of a tradeoff: since 1980, declining relative wages have not produced relatively higher employment rates for lower-skill men across these sixteen developed countries.

Indeed, what is most striking is the concentration of points in the upper right quadrant. In most countries over these two decades, lower-skill workers experienced both declining relative earnings *and* declining relative employment rates. Among the 27 country-decade points shown in figure 2.12, only Canada in the 1990s achieved declines in both earnings and employment rate inequality. Countries with the highest growth in

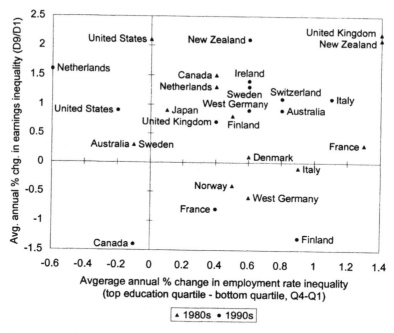

Figure 2.12. Changes in earnings inequality and employment rate inequality, male workers, 1980s and 1990s. Source: See Appendix 2.B.

earnings inequality ranged from the Netherlands in the 1990s, with sharply falling employment rate inequality, to New Zealand and the United Kingdom in the 1980s, which had, with France, the highest growth in employment rate inequality.

The data indicate that the relative position of the least skilled has tended to decline over these two decades. But again, if the explanation is skill-biased demand shifts in labor markets in which institutions have disallowed wage flexibility, we should observe a tradeoff pattern (upper left to bottom right), even within the upper right quadrant. There is no such pattern.

Finally, regression tests offer another angle to view the association between wage dispersion and employment rate inequality for the highest and lowest educated workers. According to Glyn and Salverda (2000: 11), their tests show that "greater wage dispersion is not associated with higher employment at the bottom end of the labour market, given both the overall employment level and the educational level of the bottom end of the labour force."

In sum, available cross-national data provide no support for the orthodox view that the employment problems of the developed (OECD) countries are systematically linked to the adoption of relatively egalitarian wage-setting mechanisms.

## 2.4 SKILLS, INSTITUTIONS, AND EARNINGS INEQUALITY

In a textbook competitive world, across countries, earnings inequality should mirror skill inequality. We would expect to see little evidence of inequality-unemployment tradeoffs because institutions do not (by definition) greatly affect the skill-determined earnings distribution. At least concerning the wage distribution, competitive forces trump institutional constraints (Nickell and Layard 1997: 64).

Assuming that competitive forces ensure that the skill distribution dominates the effects of institutions (and social norms) in determining the wage structure, we can explain the failure of the data to confirm a tradeoff between earnings inequality and unemployment. But this skill dispersion variant of the OECD-IMF orthodoxy requires that developed world labor markets produce textbook-like outcomes and assumes that efforts to produce more egalitarian outcomes will be achieved much more effectively by equalizing the skill distribution than directly through institutional constraints. The answer to low wages is not interference with market outcomes but skill upgrading. Indeed, the main complaint by the OECD *Jobs Study* (1994: 30) about U.S. labor markets concerns skills: in the face of collapsing demand in the United States, "workers have not upgraded their skills fast enough."

While the preceding section presented evidence that challenges the conventional view that labor market institutions raise unemployment by compressing the wage distribution, does the evidence also suggest that the reason is that competitive forces dominate the effects of institutional differences across countries in the setting of relative wages?

Nickell and Layard (1997) make their case for a skill dispersion explanation for the cross-country pattern of earnings inequality on the basis of evidence for six countries: Germany, the Netherlands, Sweden, Switzerland, Canada, and the United States. Using literacy scores from the OECD's 1994 International Adult Literacy Survey, they show graphically that relative earnings appear to correspond to relative test scores for workers with high and low levels of educational attainment for these six countries. We begin by extending the analysis of Nickell and Layard (1997) by including additional countries, using the OECD's original 1994 literacy survey and two more recent surveys (from 1996 and 1998), also produced by the OECD.[12] We use the quantitative literacy test scores to calculate a measure of skill inequality by educational attainment group (those with completed tertiary education relative to those with less than upper-secondary education).

These test score ratios are combined in figure 2.13 with the OECD's (2000a) measure of earnings inequality for 1996–1998 and are based on the same educational attainment groups as those used to measure skill inequality (tertiary education, less than upper-secondary education). The figure suggests a positive correlation ($R^2 = 0.36$), but it is not particularly strong. For example, 4 of the 16 countries have identical earnings inequality scores (Czech Republic, the United Kingdom, Hungary, the United States) but

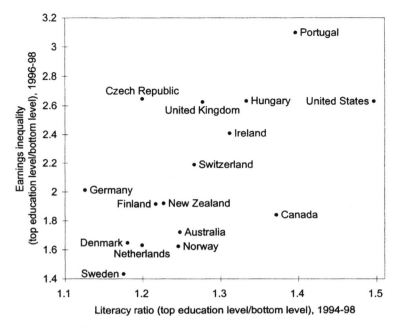

**Figure 2.13. Skill dispersion and earnings inequality (education ratios), all workers, 1994–1998. Source: See Appendix 2.B.**

range from the bottom to the top of the skill dispersion scale—from 1.2 for the Czech Republic to 1.5 for the United States. At a lower level of earnings inequality, the same can be said for Germany, Finland, New Zealand, and Canada, which have literacy ratios that range from the lowest (most equal) to the third highest. A lack of correspondence can also be read along the vertical axis: the Netherlands and the Czech Republic have the same literacy ratio but dramatically different levels of earnings inequality.

An alternative approach to the measurement of skill inequality is to simply take a ratio of top to bottom percentiles of the literacy distribution (rather than taking test scores by education category, as in figure 2.13). Figure 2.14 plots earnings inequality and this measure of skill inequality for 14 OECD countries. It appears to highlight two sets of nations. Among the more "laissez-faire" and largely Anglo-Saxon countries—New Zealand, Ireland, Australia, the United Kingdom, Canada, and the United States— there is a strong positive relationship between earnings inequality and skill dispersion. On the other hand, among the central and northern European nations—Denmark, Germany, the Netherlands, Finland, Sweden, Norway, Belgium, and Switzerland—there is no apparent relationship. Another way to read these results is that the United States, Canada, Ireland, and the United Kingdom have high earnings and skill inequality, but for the countries with moderate to low earnings inequality (a D9/D1

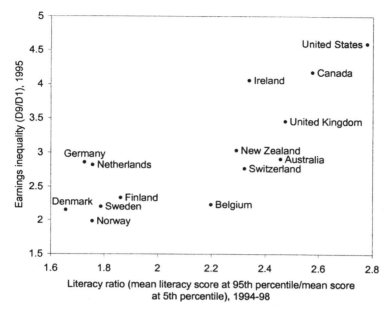

Figure 2.14. Skill dispersion and earnings inequality (percentile ratios), all workers, 1994–1998. Source: See Appendix 2.B.

ratio below 3), six countries have very compressed skill distributions and four show considerable skill inequality (New Zealand, Australia, Switzerland, and Belgium).

In the orthodox world of the Unified Theory, collapsing demand for the least skilled describes the post-1980 period in the OECD, and in this setting we should observe earnings inequality rising most dramatically for countries with the greatest skill inequality. Figure 2.15 is based on the same sources of data as figure 2.14 but relates skill inequality to the *change* in earnings inequality for the 1980–1995 period. Again, if there is a positive relationship between the skill mix and earnings inequality growth, it appears to be limited to the Anglo-Saxon countries. Indeed, figure 2.15 suggests that any positive association between skill dispersion and the change in earnings inequality is driven almost entirely by the presence of the United States, which appears here as a clear outlier. Mos of the countries are distributed across the figure horizontally. Thus, countries with low skill inequality (Denmark and Sweden), moderate skill inequality (Switzerland and New Zealand), and high skill inequality (Australia and Canada) all show slight increases in earnings inequality.

The regression results in rows 1 and 2 of table 2.3 show a strong and statistically significant relationship between our two skill measures and the level and change in earnings inequality for the 13 to 14 countries for which we had data. While the literacy ratio can account for 61% of the

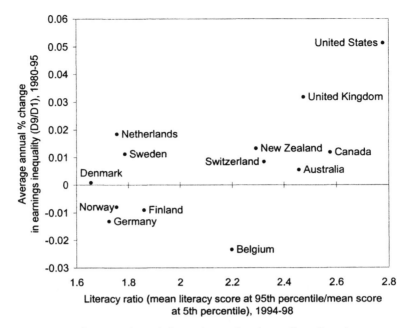

Figure 2.15. Literacy ratio and change in earnings inequality, all workers, 1980–1995. Sources: See Appendix 2.B.

variation in mid-1990s earnings inequality across 14 OECD countries, from figure 2.14 we know that these apparently strong results reflect an averaging of the strong association that exists for Anglo-Saxon countries and the lack of any association for the European countries. Column 2 reports that the literacy ratio can account for 30% of the differences in earnings inequality changes in the 1980s and 1990s, and figure 2.15 suggests that result depends entirely on the presence of the United States. Indeed, dropping theUnited States reduces the literacy coefficient from .03 (significant at the 5% level) to an insignificant .002, and its explanatory power drops from 30% to 7% (not shown in table 2.3).

The last five rows of table 2.3 report the results of separate regression tests of conventional measures of the institutions that figure most prominently in the cross-country literature on unemployment. All have statistically significant negative effects on earnings inequality; all but the unemployment protection index and the summary unemployment benefits indicator have highly significant negative effects for the change in earnings inequality (column 2). In each case, scatterplots (similar to figures 2.13–2.15, but with measures of institutions on the horizontal axis) show that the association between the change in earnings inequality and labor market institutions is a result of the location of the the United States and the United Kingdom in the upper left corner of the graph. These two

Table 2.3. Univariate Regression Results: Skills, Institutions, and Earnings
Inequality

| Explanatory Variables | Earnings Inequality (D9/D1), 1995 Coefficient (Standard error) Adj. $R^2$ No. of countries | Change in Earnings Inequality, 1980–95 Coefficient (Standard error) Adj. $R^2$ No. of countries |
|---|---|---|
| Literacy ratio 95th/5th percentile test scores, 1994–98 | 1.76*** (0.383) 0.61 14 | 0.031** (0.012) 0.30 13 |
| Low literacy share Percent at level 1, 1994–98 | 0.106*** (0.026) 0.55 14 | 0.002** (0.001) 0.24 13 |
| Employment protection index 0–1, 1990s | −1.72*** (0.627) 0.28 18 | −0.042** (0.017) 0.24 17 |
| Unemployment protection index 0–1, 1990s | −1.26** (0.574) 0.18 18 | −0.018 (0.017) 0.01 17 |
| Unemployment benefits Summary indicator, 1995 | −0.029** (0.011) 0.26 18 | −0.0004 (0.0003) 0.04 17 |
| Bargaining coverage Percent, 1994 | −0.014** (0.006) 0.26 17 | −0.0004*** (0.0001) 0.30 17 |
| Bargaining coordination 1–3, 1994 | −0.461* (0.248) 0.14 16 | −0.016** (0.006) 0.29 16 |

* significant at the 0.10 level.
** significant at the 0.05 level.
*** significant at the 0.01 level.
Each cell shows the result of a separate OLS regression test. In many cases the D9/D1 ratio was not available for 1980 or 1995; for those countries the inequality figures for the nearest year were used.
See Appendix 2.A for the data and Appendix 2.B for data sources.

countries consistently provide the least shelter from labor market forces and show the highest increases in earnings inequality.

As we noted in section 2.1, there is good reason to expect a strong link between labor market institutions and the skill composition of the workforce. Skill formation is closely linked to social protection. Workers face risks when they invest in specific skills and thus need insurance in the form of employment or unemployment protection. In countries where firm-specific and industry-specific skills are important (such as Japan and Germany), the transition from education to work is relatively institutionalized, for example in the form of vocational training systems. Estevez-Abe et al. (2000: 31) find that "earnings dispersion . . . is closely related to particular skill systems as well as the wage bargaining institutions that tend to go with these systems."

The real test for the competitive hypothesis that institutions play a decidedly secondary role in explaining the pattern of earnings inequality across countries is whether this association between earnings inequality and skill dispersion holds independent of the institutional context. It seems unlikely—and it is difficult to test—because the standard institutional variables are so highly correlated with the best measures of skill mix. For example, our skill inequality measure shows a correlation of .88 with employment protection, .694 with unemployment benefits, and .747 with bargaining coverage (all significant at the .001 level).

The univariate regression results shown in table 2.4 make clear that countries with strong protective labor market institutions tend to have low skill inequality and low shares of very-low-skilled workers. Indeed, the relationship is so strong that the institutional variables could serve well as proxies for skill inequality. The relationship between the literacy ratio and the employment protection index constructed by Estevez-Abe et al. (2000) is particularly strong (adj. $R^2 = 0.75$). Measures of bargaining coordination and coverage are also closely correlated with measures of skill inequality.

This evidence suggests that support for strong egalitarian educational and labor market institutions tends to be closely linked across countries. Both wage compression and skill compression reflect the extent to which a society has made strong institutional interventions in the labor market and in the education and training sector. Countries with institutions designed to shelter workers from labor market competition also establish institutions to promote skill equality. On the basis of our data, we cannot say which is more important for the wage structure, the skill mix or labor market institutions. But the answer given by Devroye and Freeman (2000) is clear: protective labor market institutions are substantially *more* important than the skills distribution. On the basis of their examination of the pattern of skills, institutions, and relative earnings in Germany, Holland, Sweden, and the United States, they conclude that "differences in skill dispersion across countries explain only a modest proportion of differences in the dispersion of earnings across countries." Recent work by Blau and Kahn comes to a similar conclusion (2002). We conclude that, at a minimum, labor market institutions matter a great deal for the earnings distribution, both by directly compressing the wage structure and by helping to determine the level and mix of worker skills.

Table 2.4. Univariate Regression Results: Skills and Institutional Characteristics

| Explanatory Variables | Literacy Ratio, 1994–98 Coefficient (Standard error) Adj. $R^2$ No. of countries | Low Literacy Share, 1994–98 Coefficient (Standard error) Adj. $R^2$ No. of countries |
|---|---|---|
| Employment protection index 0–1, 1990s | −1.315** (0.205) 0.75 14 | −19.95** (3.716) 0.68 14 |
| Unemployment protection index 0–1, 1990s | −0.931** (0.241) 0.52 14 | −13.6** (4.190) 0.42 14 |
| Unemployment benefits summary indicator, 1995 | −0.018** (0.005) 0.44 14 | −0.256* (0.094) 0.33 14 |
| Bargaining coverage percent, 1994 | −0.011** (0.003) 0.52 13 | −0.154** (0.044) 0.48 13 |
| Bargaining coordination 1–3, 1994 | −0.492** (0.107) 0.63 13 | −6.86** (1.633) 0.58 13 |

* significant at the 0.05 level.
** significant at the 0.01 level.
Each cell shows the result of a separate OLS regression test.
See Appendix 2.A for the data and Appendix 2.B for data sources.

## 2.5 CONCLUSIONS

In this chapter we evaluated alternative explanations of recent trends in earnings and employment outcomes across OECD countries. On one side, the *wage compression* version of the OECD-IMF orthodoxy blames a variety of welfare state institutions for compressing the wage distributions and effectively "disallowing" low-wage jobs in an economic environment in which demand is shifting strongly away from the least skilled. The consequence of this wage rigidity should be a substantial inequality-unemployment tradeoff. The *skill dispersion* variant, on the other hand, suggests that, while welfare states try to compress the earnings distribution, in the end markets ensure that this distribution closely mirrors the skill distribution. These market pressures help explain the failure of earnings inequality/unemployment rate tradeoffs to appear in the data. In sum, orthodox supply and demand stories produce contradictory accounts of the role of institutions: on the one side, institutions are the culprits in the battle against unemployment because they cause "too much" wage compression; on the other, they may play a key role in raising the inflation-steady level of unemployment, but not mainly via wage compression.

In this orthodox world, the labor market produces a determinate set of wage-employment equilibria. We suggest an alternative institutionalist vision of the labor market, one in which wage setting is characterized by a meaningful range of indeterminacy. Within this feasible range, social norms and labor market institutions play key roles in determining where the wage is actually set. Under these circumstances, institutions may strongly influence the pattern of wages across countries but need not necessarily be a key determinant of persistent differences in unemployment (or employment) rates.

We addressed three empirical predictions that follow directly from the orthodox supply and demand model and reflect the conventional wisdom. First, if increasing earnings inequality in the United States is caused mainly by technology-driven, skill-biased demand shifts, we should observe a tendency for rising inequality across all developed countries. In fact, we find that only the United Kingdom, the United States, and New Zealand have experienced strong and persistent rises in earnings inequality over the past two decades. It seems clear that other OECD countries have adopted similar technologies without experiencing comparable relative earnings outcomes.[13]

In the wage compression (Unified Theory) view, the failure of more countries to substantially increase the dispersion of earnings (by allowing the relative wages of the least skilled to fall) explains the widespread experience of high unemployment in the 1980s and 1990s. We find no evidence of meaningful tradeoffs between earnings inequality and either employment or unemployment rates (or between changes in them) across OECD countries. These results challenge the orthodox view that too much wage compression is the main source of European employment problems.

It is possible that the reason for the absence of an unemployment-earnings inequality tradeoff is that it is differences in skill dispersion, not in institutions, that mainly determine national differences in earnings inequality. We find support for such a positive link between skill dispersion and earnings inequality. But our results also suggest a more complicated view. First, for whatever reason, the correspondence appears to exist only among Anglo-Saxon countries (the United States, the United Kingdom, New Zealand, Australia, and Canada). Indeed, without the United States and the United Kingdom, there is little or no association between our two measures of skill dispersion and the *change* in earnings inequality. Second, a number of measures of labor market institutions (employment and unemployment protection, bargaining coverage, and bargaining coordination) are also closely associated with earnings inequality trends. Third, the high correlation between skill dispersion and

institutional variables lends support to the view that labor market institutions and social policies jointly determine both the skill mix of the
workforce *and* earnings inequality. Underlying a country's skill mix and
labor market institutions are policies and programs that in turn reflect
ideologies and social norms, and it is these that ultimately determine the
patterns of earnings inequality that we observe. Countries that protect
low-skill workers from extremely low wages also provide more and better
education and training for them. And countries with relatively literate
"low-skill" workers (Sweden, Denmark, Germany) tend to set wages collectively through highly centralized and coordinated bargaining systems.

A convincing explanation for differences in earnings and employment
trends across developed countries requires moving beyond simple supply
and demand stories. Real-world wage setting is best characterized as taking
place within a feasible range set by supply and demand, so labor market
institutions can be expected to play important and complicated roles, with
outcomes not always consistent with the predictions of the textbook supply-
demand model. Our conclusions regarding earnings inequality and unemployment trends across the OECD are illustrative. As Freeman (2000: 1)
has put it, "The institutional organization of the labour market has iden-
tifiable large effects on distribution, but modest hard-to-uncover effects on
efficiency." Our survey of the evidence suggests that, while labor market
institutions and related government policies are central to both skill formation and wage setting (and therefore earnings inequality), they are not
the main source of the recent European unemployment problem.

*Acknowledgment* This is a substantially revised version of CEPA Working Paper
2001–02 (May 2001). The authors thank CEPA and the MacArthur Foundation for
their support, and John Schmitt and Andrew Glyn in particular, for both valuable
comments and data.

*Notes*

1. A recent paper by Bertola, Blau, and Kahn (2002) illustrates this. The authors
point out that, according to the Unified Theory, "the United States allowed real
and relative wages to adjust, while, in Europe and other Western nations, employment took the brunt of the shocks" (Bertola et al. 2002: 164). They interpret
their results to support this view, concluding that "The relevant shifts are partly
common across industrial countries, and, while essentially unobservable, they may
correspond to the popular notion that globalization and new technologies make it
increasingly difficult for OECD countries to deliver favorable employment and
wage opportunities to some of their workers. Thus, the same flexibility that allows
the U.S. labor market to absorb macroeconomic shocks with smaller changes in
unemployment than occur in other countries also makes for more flexible real
wages and relative wages" (Bertola et al. 2002: 206).
2. Nickell and Layard (1997: 64), for example, make the case for "the very
simple hypothesis that variations in earnings distributions across countries

correspond rather closely to variations in true skill distributions. Thus, Sweden has a very compressed earnings distribution relative to the United States, because it has a very compressed skill distribution. There is no need to wheel on the all-purpose 'European institutions' to explain the differences—supply and demand does fine."

3. According to Freeman and Katz (1994: 46), "In the 1980s, the increased use of microcomputers and computer-based technologies shifted demand toward more educated workers. . . . Whether because of computerization or other causes, the pace of relative demand shifts favoring more skilled workers accelerated within sectors." Similarly, Bound and Johnson (1995: 13) write that "Our suspicion is that a secular shift in production functions in favor of workers with relatively high intellectual as opposed to manual ability—a process that accelerated during the 1980s because of computers—is responsible, in concert with the slowdown of the growth in the relative supply of skilled labor, for most of the wage phenomena that have been observed." For a critical assessment of this skill-biased technological change explanation of earnings inequality, see Howell (1999).

4. It seems reasonable to assume that low-skill labor markets tend to be characterized by persistent labor surplus. For instance, shifts in product mix (agriculture to manufacturing to services), technological change, and firm failures ensure some regular worker displacement. At the same time, there is generally imperfect information about opportunities, work conditions, and pay levels. Closely related, there is limited mobility among those already established (jobless workers stay when they "should" leave). On the other hand, given large inequalities in earnings opportunities across regions, there is also substantial migration to richer regions that already have a labor surplus. And if wages rise sufficiently over the reservation wage, labor market participation in the region will rise.

5. As David Card notes in his review (1995: 785), "causality is to be thought of as running from the amount of joblessness to the level of wages."

6. This alternative view is consistent with recent work by Galbraith, Conceição, and Ferreira (1999: 29–30), who find that "wage-rate inequality, in manufacturing at least, has risen and fallen *in step with* changes in unemployment in America . . . over virtually the entire century . . . [and] the same appears to be true for Europe in recent years."

7. Estevez-Abe et al. (2000: 10) conclude that "institutionally we would expect to find coordinated wage bargaining systems in economies in which specific skills are important, and non-coordinated systems where they are not. And in terms of outcomes we would expect to find stable distributions of earnings across occupations in the first, but not necessarily the second case."

8. It should be noted that these results are in some cases extremely sensitive to the years chosen as endpoints, although we tried to compensate by using three-year averages for the unemployment rate. Sweden, for example, has cut its unemployment rate in half (from more than 10% to 5.3%) since the mid-1990s, which would put it far to the left of its position in these figures. Interestingly, far from a tradeoff, both earnings inequality and unemployment increased from 1990 through 1997. We thank John Schmitt for this point.

9. Figure 2.9 uses unemployment data by skill for males from Nickell and Bell (1995), who define skill categories differently for different countries (e.g., across educational attainment categories in some cases, across high- and low-skill occupations in others). In contrast, for all workers, figure 2.10 uses data from the OECD

in which skill categories are defined consistently across countries according to educational attainment.

10. "If demand fell for less skilled workers, we would expect to find employment declining most among the lowest wage groups; instead, there appears to be little relationship" (Krueger and Pischke 1997: 13).

11. The ratio of the top to the bottom quartile produces broadly similar results. Andrew Glyn has convincingly argued that the absolute difference is the better measure.

12. The results of all three studies were published in the final report of the International Adult Literacy Survey (OECD 2000b).

13. Nor do relative unemployment rates by education level show the predicted pattern: rather than rising, the ratio of low-skill to high-skill unemployment rates has tended to be stable or fall since the early 1980s (Howell 2002).

## References

Akerlof, George A. 2002. "Behavioral Macroeconomics and Macroeconomic Behavior. *American Economic Review* 92(3) (June): 411–433.

Atkinson, Anthony B. 1998. "The Distribution of Income in Industrialized Countries." Paper presented at the Symposium on Income Inequality: Issues and Policy Options, sponsored by the Federal Reserve Bank of Kansas City, Jackson Hole, Wyoming, August 27–29.

———. 1999. "Is Rising Inequality Inevitable?: A Critique of the Transatlantic Consensus." WIDER annual lecture, presented at University of Oslo, November 1.

Bertola, Giuseppe, Francine D. Blau, and Lawrence M. Kahn. 2002. "Comparative Analysis of Labor Market Outcomes: Lessons for the United States from International Long-run Evidence." In *The Roaring Nineties: Can Full Employment Be Sustained?*, edited by Alan Krueger and Robert Solow. New York: Russell Sage Foundation.

Bhaskar, V., Alan Manning, and Ted To. 2002. "Oligopsony and Monopsonistic Competition in Labor Markets." *Journal of Economic Perspectives* 16(2) (Spring): 155–174.

Bjorklund, Anders, and Richard B. Freeman. 1997. "Generating Equality and Eliminating Poverty, the Swedish Way." In *The Welfare State in Transition: Reforming the Swedish Model*, edited by Richard B. Freeman, Robert H. Topel, and Birgitta Swedenborg. Chicago: University of Chicago Press.

Blanchflower, David G., and Andrew J. Oswald. 1995. "International Wage Curves." In *Differences and Changes in Wage Structures*, edited by Richard B. Freeman and Lawrence F. Katz. Chicago: University of Chicago Press.

Blank, Rebecca M. 1997. *No Easy Answers: Comparative Labor Market Problems in the United States versus Europe.* Working Paper No. 188, Northwestern University/ University of Chicago Joint Center for Poverty Research.

Blau, Francine D., and Lawrence M. Kahn. 1996. "International Differences in Male Wage Inequality: Institutions versus Market Forces." *Journal of Political Economy* 104(4): 791–837.

Blau, Francine D., and Lawrence M. Kahn. 2002. *At Home and Abroad: U.S. Labor Market Performance in International Perspective.* New York: Russell Sage Foundation.

Bound, John, and George Johnson. 1995. "What Are the Causes of Rising Wage Inequality in the United States?" *Economic Policy Review* 1(1) (January): 9–17.

Card, David. 1995. "The Wage Curve: A Review." *Journal of Economic Literature* 33(2) (June): 785–799.

Card, David, Francis Kramarz, and Thomas Lemieux. 1995. *Changes in the Relative Structure of Wages and Employment: A Comparison of the United States, Canada, and France.* Working Paper 355, Industrial Relations Section, Princeton University, December.

Devroye, Daniel, and Richard Freeman. 2000. "Does Inequality in Skills Explain Inequality of Earnings across Countries?" Unpublished manuscript, Harvard University, April 19.

Edin, Per-Anders, Anders Harkman, and Bertil Holmlund. 1996. "Unemployment and Wage Inequality in Sweden." Mimeo, Uppsala University.

Estevez-Abe, Margarita, Torben Iversen, and David Soskice. 2000. "Social Protection and the Formation of Skills: A Reinterpretation of the Welfare State." Paper presented at Wiener Inequality and Social Policy Seminar, Harvard University, March 13.

Fortin, Nicole M., and Thomas Lemieux. "Institutional Changes and Rising Wage Inequality: Is There a Linkage?" *Journal of Economic Perspectives* 11(2) (Spring): 75–96.

Freeman, Richard B. 2000. *Single Peaked vs. Diversified Capitalism: The Relation between Economic Institutions and Outcomes.* Working Paper 7556, National Bureau of Economic Research, February.

Freeman, Richard B., and Lawrence Katz. 1994. "Rising Wage Inequality: The United States vs. Other Advanced Countries." In *Working under Different Rules,* edited by Richard B. Freeman. New York: Russell Sage Foundation.

Freeman, Richard B., and Ronald Schettkat. 2000. *Skill Compression, Wage Differentials and Employment: Germany vs. the U.S.* Working Paper 7610, National Bureau of Economic Research, March.

Galbraith, James K., Pedro Conceição, and Pedro Ferreira. 1999. "Inequality and Unemployment in Europe: The American Cure." *New Left Review* 237 (September–October): 28–51.

Glyn, Andrew. 2000. "Unemployment and Inequality." In *Readings in Macroeconomics,* 2nd ed., edited by Tim Jenkinson. Oxford: Oxford University Press.

Glyn, Andrew, and Wiemer Salverda. 2000. "Employment Inequalities." In *Labor Market Inequalities: Problems and Policies of Low-wage Employment in International Perspective,* edited by M. Gregory, W. Salverda, and S. Bazen. Oxford: Oxford University Press.

Gottschalk, Peter. 1997. "Inequality, Income Growth, and Mobility: The Basic Facts." *Journal of Economic Perspectives* 11(2) (Spring): 21–40.

Howell, David R. 1999. "Theory-driven Facts and the Growth in Earnings Inequality." *Review of Radical Political Economics* 31(1) (March): 54–86.

———. 2002. "Increasing Earnings Inequality and Unemployment in Developed Countries: Markets, Institutions and the 'Unified Theory.'" *Politics and Society* 30(2) (June): 193–243.

International Monetary Fund (IMF). 1999. "Chronic Unemployment in the Euro Area: Causes and Cures." Chapter 4 in *World Economic Outlook* (May). Washington, D.C.: IMF.

Krueger, Alan B., and Jörn-Steffen Pischke. 1997. *Observations and Conjectures on the U.S. Employment Miracle.* Working Paper 6146, National Bureau of Economic Research (August).

Leuven, Edwin, Hessel Oosterbeek, and Hans van Ophem. 1998. *Explaining International Differences in Male Wage Inequality by Differences in Demand and Supply of Skill.* Discussion Paper 392, Centre for Economic Performance, London School of Economics and Political Science, May.

Lucifora, Claudio. 2000. "Wage Inequalities and Low Pay: The Role of Labor Market Institutions." In *Labor Market Inequalities: Problems and Policies of Low Wage Employment in International Perspective,* edited by Mary Gregory, Wiemer Salverda, and Stephen Bazen. Oxford: Oxford University Press.

Nickell, Stephen, and Brian Bell. 1995. "The Collapse in Demand for the Unskilled and Unemployment across the OECD." *Oxford Review of Economic Policy* 11(1) (Spring): 40–62.

Nickell, Stephen, and Richard Layard. 1997. *Labor Market Institutions and Economic Performance.* Discussion paper, Centre for Economic Performance, University of Oxford.

Organization for Economic Cooperation and Development (OECD). 1994. *OECD Jobs Study: Evidence and Explanations, Part II: The Adjustment Potential of the Labor Market.* Paris: OECD.

———. 1996. *Employment Outlook* (July). Paris: OECD.

———. 1997a. *Employment Outlook* (July). Paris: OECD.

———. 1997b. *Implementing the OECD Jobs Strategy: Member Countries' Experience.* Paris: OECD.

———. 1999. *OECD Economic Outlook,* no. 66. Database. Paris: OECD.

———. 2000a. *Education at a Glance: OECD Indicators.* Paris: OECD.

———. 2000b. *Literacy in the Information Age: Final Report of the International Adult Literacy Survey.* Paris: OECD.

Schettkat, Ronald. 1993. "Compensating Differentials? Wage Differentials and Employment Stability in the U.S. and German Economies." *Journal of Economic Issues* 27(1) (March): 153–170.

Siebert, Horst. 1997. "Labor Market Rigidities: At the Root of Employment in Europe." *Journal of Economic Perspectives* 11(3) (Summer): 37–54.

Snower, Dennis J. 1998. "Causes of Changing Earnings Inequality." Paper presented at the Symposium on Income Inequality: Issues and Policy Options, sponsored by the Federal Reserve Bank of Kansas City, Jackson Hole, Wyoming, August 27–29.

# Appendix 2.A

Data Used for Regressions in Tables 2.1, 2.2, 2.3, and 2.4

| Country | Period Start | Period End | Start D9/D1 | End D9/D1 | D9/D1 Change | Start Unemp. Rate | End Unemp. Rate | Unemp. Rate Change | Literacy Ratio 95th/5th | Low Literacy Share | Emp. Protectn. Index | Unemp. Protectn. Index | Unemp. Benefits | Bargain. Coverage | Coordination | Centralization |
|---|---|---|---|---|---|---|---|---|---|---|---|---|---|---|---|---|
| Australia | 1980 | 1995 | 2.83 | 2.91 | 0.0055 | 5.98 | 8.87 | 0.1925 | 2.46 | 16.93 | 0.27 | 0.22 | 27.3 | 80 | 1.5 | 1.5 |
| Austria | 1980 | 1994 | 3.44 | 3.65 | 0.0148 | 1.79 | 6.03 | 0.3026 | — | — | 0.84 | 0.81 | 25.8 | 98 | 3 | 2 |
| Belgium | 1986 | 1993 | 2.40 | 2.24 | −0.0234 | 11.76 | 11.72 | −0.0055 | 2.20 | 16.80 | 0.56 | 0.82 | 41.6 | 90 | 2 | 2 |
| Canada | 1981 | 1994 | 4.02 | 4.18 | 0.0119 | 8.71 | 10.37 | 0.1277 | 2.58 | 17.23 | 0.30 | 0.30 | 27.3 | 36 | 1 | 1 |
| Denmark | 1980 | 1990 | 2.15 | 2.15 | 0.0008 | 7.35 | 9.62 | 0.2275 | 1.66 | 7.87 | 0.53 | 0.91 | 70.3 | 69 | 2 | 2 |
| Finland | 1980 | 1995 | 2.47 | 2.34 | −0.0089 | 5.17 | 15.51 | 0.6892 | 1.86 | 11.33 | 0.64 | 0.43 | 43.2 | 95 | 2 | 2 |
| France | 1980 | 1995 | 3.25 | 3.08 | −0.0116 | 6.49 | 12.04 | 0.3702 | — | — | 0.61 | 0.54 | 37.5 | 95 | — | 2 |
| Germany | 1984 | 1995 | 3.00 | 2.86 | −0.0131 | 7.95 | 8.41 | 0.0415 | 1.73 | 10.03 | 0.86 | 0.77 | 26.4 | 92 | 3 | 2 |
| Ireland | — | 1994 | — | 4.06 | — | — | 14.20 | — | 2.34 | 24.23 | 0.36 | 0.37 | 26.1 | — | — | — |
| Italy | 1979 | 1995 | 2.85 | 2.41 | −0.0276 | 5.52 | 11.54 | 0.3766 | — | — | 0.81 | 0.18 | 19.7 | 82 | 2.5 | 2 |
| Japan | 1980 | 1995 | 3.01 | 3.00 | −0.0007 | 2.10 | 3.13 | 0.0684 | — | — | 0.76 | 0.33 | 9.9 | 21 | 3 | 1 |
| Netherlands | 1980 | 1995 | 2.54 | 2.82 | 0.0185 | 4.49 | 7.10 | 0.1739 | 1.76 | 10.30 | 0.80 | 0.89 | 45.9 | 81 | 2 | 2 |
| New Zealand | 1984 | 1995 | 2.89 | 3.03 | 0.0133 | 4.42 | 6.84 | 0.2198 | 2.29 | 20.07 | 0.29 | 0.27 | 29.8 | 31 | 1 | 1 |
| Norway | 1989 | 1993 | 2.02 | 1.99 | −0.0079 | 4.45 | 5.77 | 0.3293 | 1.75 | 8.27 | 0.66 | 0.64 | 38.8 | 74 | 2.5 | 2 |
| Sweden | 1980 | 1995 | 2.03 | 2.20 | 0.0113 | 2.17 | 7.90 | 0.3819 | 1.79 | 6.77 | 0.94 | 0.63 | 27.3 | 89 | 2 | 2 |
| Switzerland | 1991 | 1995 | 2.71 | 2.77 | 0.0085 | 1.38 | 4.54 | 0.7899 | 2.32 | 16.93 | 0.49 | 0.86 | 29.5 | 50 | 2 | 2 |
| United Kingdom | 1980 | 1995 | 2.98 | 3.46 | 0.0318 | 6.54 | 8.65 | 0.1413 | 2.47 | 22.77 | 0.25 | 0.11 | 18.1 | 47 | 1 | 1.5 |
| United States | 1980 | 1995 | 3.83 | 4.60 | 0.0513 | 6.88 | 5.69 | −0.0788 | 2.78 | 21.80 | 0.14 | 0.10 | 11.8 | 18 | 1 | 1 |
| Mean | | | 2.85 | 2.99 | 0.0044 | 5.48 | 8.77 | 0.2558 | 2.14 | 15.10 | 0.56 | 0.51 | 30.9 | 68 | 2.0 | 1.7 |
| Standard deviation | | | 0.57 | 0.75 | 0.2 | 2.74 | 3.33 | 0.23 | 0.37 | 5.93 | 0.25 | 0.29 | 14.05 | 27.7 | 0.72 | 0.44 |

Data sources: See Appendix 2.B.

# Appendix 2.B: Data Sources

Bargaining coverage, 1994: OECD (1997a): table 3.3, p. 71.

Centralization, 1994: OECD (1997a): table 3.3, p. 71.

Coordination, 1994: OECD (1997a): table 3.3, p. 71.

Earnings inequality (D5/D1), 1980–1999 (fig. 7): OECD statistics (personal communication from Paul Swaim, OECD, Paris).

Earnings inequality (D9/D1), 1979–1998 (figs. 3–6, 8–10, 14, 15): OECD database on earnings dispersion, 1999.

Earnings inequality (D9/D1), 1980s and 1990s (fig. 12): Glyn (2000).

Earnings inequality (D9/D1), 1994 (fig. 11): Glyn and Salverda (2000).

Earnings inequality (top education level/bottom level), 1996–1998 (fig. 13): OECD (2000a): table E5.1, p. 297.

Employment protection index, 1990s: Estevez-Abe et al. (2000): table 1.

Employment rate inequality (top education quartile–bottom quartile), 1994 (fig. 11): Glyn and Salverda (2000).

Employment rate inequality (top education quartile–bottom quartile), 1980s and 1990s (fig. 12): Glyn (2000).

Literacy ratio (mean literacy score at 95th percentile/mean score at 5th percentile), 1994–1998 (fig. 14 and 15): OECD (2000b): table 2.1, pp. 135–136.

Literacy ratio (top education level/bottom level), 1994–1998 (fig. 13): OECD (2000b) table 2.4, pp. 138–139.

Low literacy share (percent at literacy level 1), 1994–98: OECD (2000b): table 2.2, pp. 136–137.

Relative unemployment rate by education level (low education unemployment rate–high education unemployment rate), 1979–1993 (fig. 9): Nickell and Bell (1995): table 2a, pp. 47–48.

Relative unemployment rate by education level (low education unemployment rate–high education unemployment rate), 1989–1998 (fig. 10): Education at a glance: OECD Indicators 1993, 1995, 1996, 1997, 1998, 2000.

Unemployment benefits (summary measure), 1995: OECD (1997b): table 5, p. 54.

Unemployment protection index, 1990s: Estevez-Abe et al. (2000): table 2.

Unemployment rate (three-year average), 1980–1995 (fig. 8): OECD (1999).

# 3

## Labor Market Institutions and Unemployment: Assessment of the Cross-Country Evidence

DEAN BAKER
ANDREW GLYN
DAVID R. HOWELL
JOHN SCHMITT

The rigidities imposed by labor market institutions and policies are widely held to play a key role in the explanation of the European unemployment crisis of the 1980s and 1990s. This was the central message of the OECD's *Jobs Study* (1994), and a recent follow-up report on the implementation of the *Jobs Study*'s recommendations confirms that this rigidity explanation remains the conventional wisdom: "Previous OECD work ... and a growing body of academic research suggests a direct link between structural reform and labor market outcomes (see Box 2.3)" (OECD 1999: 52–53). A recent paper in the *Swedish Economic Policy Review* by three noted OECD researchers (Elsmeskov, Martin, and Scarpetta 1998) provides a good example of the broad consistency between OECD and academic research on the determinants of OECD unemployment. Comparing their results with Nickell and Layard (1998), a prominent academic paper, they conclude that "Both studies assign significant roles to unemployment benefits, collective bargaining structures, active labor market policies ... and the tax wedge—even if the variables in question are defined somewhat differently between the two studies." The International Monetary Fund has weighed in as well, making the case for labor market deregulation in two recent reports (IMF 1999, 2003). This consensus—which we will term the OECD-IMF orthodoxy—contends that labor market institutions and policies lie at the heart of the unemployment problem.

This chapter evaluates the empirical evidence for this orthodox view. Our approach is distinctive in that we begin from a skeptical stance and ask whether the available evidence, from both the literature and our own analysis of the standard data, can provide a compelling case for the conventional account. In the first section we set the macroeconomic and institutional stage. Section 2 then takes an initial look at the data, by presenting simple scatter plots in which conventional measures of the most commonly referenced labor market institutions are set, one at a time, against the standardized unemployment rate for 19 OECD countries for the 1980–1999 period. These figures show that standardized rates over time by country show little or no statistical association with conventional measures of institutions and policies.

Such straightforward statistical evidence appears rarely in the leading papers. Rather, empirical support for the orthodox explanation comes almost exclusively from multivariate analyses that have become increasingly complex since the pioneering work of Layard, Nickell, and Jackman (1991, 1994). In section 3, we survey the leading papers in this literature. While these studies tend to conclude that institutions are a key part of the story, the actual empirical results appear far less robust and uniform across studies than is commonly believed. Indeed, while the OECD policy position has stressed the "direct links" between labor market institutions and the unemployment problem, a close reading of its own survey of the cross-country evidence turns up "no evidence" for the negative employment effects of union density and only "mixed evidence" for the effects of unemployment benefits and employment protection laws (OECD 1999: 55, box 2.3). At the same time, the standard interpretation systematically downplays the empirical support that exists for a beneficial role of collective-bargaining coordination (typically large effects) and active labor market policies (mixed effects). It should also be noted that an important part of the explanatory power of the institutional approach, in fact, derives from these two institutions' apparent ability to *reduce* unemployment.

We then present, in section 4, our own multivariate results. With data for 20 OECD countries organized into five-year periods and extended to 1999, we present results of regression tests of the effects of institutions on unemployment across different time periods with different combinations of variables. We show, first, how sensitive one of the best-known results in the literature is to the particular set of institutional measures used. We then show that the most comprehensive available measures of institutions and policies can account for only a minor part of the differences in the evolution of unemployment across these 20 OECD countries over the past 40 years and that the impacts of institutions on unemployment are strikingly unstable over time. The upshot is that our multivariate results provide no more support for the labor market rigidity explanation than did our simple scatter plots. These results lend support to Tony Atkinson's (2001: 48–49) view that "Aggregate cross-country evidence, interesting though it may be, cannot on its own provide a reliable guide to the likely consequences of rolling back the welfare state."

## 3.1 MACROECONOMIC AND INSTITUTIONAL SETTINGS

### 3.1.1 Unemployment and Inflation

As the first columns of table 3.1 show, both the average rate of unemployment and its dispersion increased dramatically from the early 1970s to the early 1990s, a pattern that many comparative studies of OECD unemployment have attempted to explain. The unweighted average unemployment rate quadrupled between the late 1960s and the early 1990s and dispersion (as measured by the standard deviation) rose practically as fast, a development reflected in the fanning out of the country points in figure 1.1 clearly illustrates. The second half of the 1990s saw modest declines in both average unemployment and its dispersion, falling even more sharply in 2000–2001. Thus, after peaking at 10.9% in 1994, unemployment in OECD-Europe fell to 7.6% in 2001. This compares to a decline in U.S. unemployment from 7.5% in 1992 to 4.0% in 2000; it then rose sharply to 4.8% in 2001 (OECD 2002: table A).

The course of inflation shows a striking contrast to that of unemployment. Average inflation rates (again with annual fluctuations smoothed out) began rising earlier than unemployment and reached their peak in the late 1970s, with a great deal of variation across countries. As table 3.1 shows, inflation then subsided, at first slowly and then precipitately during the 1980s. By the late 1990s, the inflation rate was half the level prevailing in the early 1960s, and dispersion was lower, as well.

This broad pattern for inflation trends has been widely interpreted as supporting a view that the economy has an equilibrium unemployment rate, or NAIRU, which has fluctuated both across time and across countries over the past four decades. Factors other than the labor market are involved in determining inflation, notably prices of imports from outside the OECD. However, the rising inflation from the late 1960s through to

**Table 3.1. Unemployment and Inflation Trends for 19 OECD Countries, 1960–99**

|         | Unemployment Rate | | Inflation Rate | |
|---------|-------------------|-----------|----------------|-----------|
|         | Mean              | Std. Dev. | Mean           | Std. Dev. |
| 1960–64 | 2.1               | 1.7       | 3.6            | 1.3       |
| 1965–69 | 2.1               | 1.3       | 4.1            | 1.0       |
| 1970–74 | 2.5               | 1.7       | 8.2            | 1.9       |
| 1975–79 | 4.3               | 2.3       | 10.1           | 4.3       |
| 1980–84 | 6.9               | 3.9       | 9.0            | 3.6       |
| 1985–89 | 7.7               | 4.8       | 4.0            | 2.6       |
| 1990–94 | 8.8               | 4.1       | 3.6            | 1.3       |
| 1995–99 | 8.2               | 4.0       | 1.8            | 0.8       |

Source: see Appendix 3.2.

the end of the 1970s is broadly consistent with unemployment having been typically below the NAIRU, with the subsequent disinflation suggesting that unemployment had overshot and was somewhat above the NAIRU. By the turn of the century, inflation was both low and generally steady. The continued high degree of dispersion of unemployment, therefore, suggests corresponding variations in country level NAIRUs. In terms of explaining cross-country patterns of unemployment, the change in inflation is frequently taken as a rough indicator of how far each economy is away from equilibrium unemployment.

Within the NAIRU framework, the experience just reviewed is interpreted as showing that increases in the NAIRU up to the early 1990s differed greatly across countries and that there were some interesting decreases in the NAIRU in the 1990s. Two sets of influences have been suggested to explain these patterns—macroeconomic developments and labor market institutions.

### 3.1.2 Macroeconomic Developments

A number of macroeconomic influences can affect equilibrium unemployment. These revolve around the "space" for real wage gains. The essential point is that if real wages have to decline—or, more plausibly, have to rise more slowly than the rate to which workers have become accustomed—then a higher level of unemployment will be required to weaken workers' bargaining power and thus prevent "excessive" wage increases and rising inflation. A host of complicated issues surround the form and permanence of such effects. Does a slower growth of "feasible" real wages lead to a temporarily higher NAIRU until workers' expectations have adjusted? Or, is the effect much longer lived as expectations adjust very slowly or if the higher level of unemployment itself generates other labor market changes that perpetuate the higher joblessness? The literature contains a range of views on the subject. Blanchard and Wolfers (2000) treat the "shocks" such as slower productivity growth as having permanent effects, whereas Nickell et al. (2001) explicitly model most of these shocks as having only a temporary impact.

The favorite candidate for a macroeconomic shock, or change in trend, is indeed the slower productivity growth after 1973, which reduced the extent to which real wages could grow without reducing profitability. Table 3.2 shows the sharp deceleration in Total Factor Productivity (TFP) growth through the 1970s and the first half of the 1980s. But this slowdown in productivity growth could contribute to explaining high unemployment in the 1990s only if real wage bargaining was very slow to adapt.

The feasible growth of real wages also depends on the country's terms of trade. An increase in the real cost of imports relative to domestic output squeezes the feasible growth of real wage increases (table 3.1 shows the impact of the terms of trade on living standards). The terms of trade of most OECD countries deteriorated in the first half of the 1970s and again in the first half of the 1980s (associated with the two oil shocks), and this

**Table 3.2. The Macroeconomic Background**

| | Total Factor Productivity Growth %pa | | Impact of Terms of Trade %pa | | Tax Wedge (% of Incomes) | | Real Interest Rates % | | Structural Budget Balance % GDP | |
|---|---|---|---|---|---|---|---|---|---|---|
| | Mean | St. Dev. | Mean | St. Dev. | Mean | St. Dev. | Mean | St. Dev. | Mean | St. Dev. |
| 1960–64 | 4.0 | 1.6 | 0.7 | 0.6 | 19.2 | 5.5 | 2.1 | 1.4 | N/A | N/A |
| 1965–69 | 3.8 | 1.6 | 0.5 | 0.5 | 21.7 | 6.8 | 2.2 | 0.9 | N/A | N/A |
| 1970–74 | 3.1 | 1.3 | −0.7 | 0.6 | 25.5 | 8.2 | −0.2 | 1.9 | 0.6 | 3.1 |
| 1975–79 | 2.0 | 1.0 | 0.4 | 0.5 | 28.7 | 8.8 | 0.4 | 3.0 | −2.6 | 3.6 |
| 1980–84 | 1.6 | 0.9 | −0.5 | 1.2 | 31.0 | 7.7 | 4.4 | 2.2 | −4.0 | 4.3 |
| 1985–89 | 1.5 | 0.9 | 1.3 | 0.9 | 31.4 | 7.7 | 5.2 | 1.4 | −3.0 | 3.5 |
| 1990–94 | 1.5 | 0.9 | 0.7 | 0.7 | 31.9 | 7.6 | 5.9 | 1.6 | −3.8 | 2.9 |
| 1995–99 | 1.5 | 0.9 | 0.1 | 1.0 | 31.9 | 7.5 | 3.7 | 1.4 | −1.4 | 1.8 |

Source: see Appendix 3.2.

factor played a major role in the pioneering account of rising unemployment by Bruno and Sachs (1985). However, as table 3.2 shows, the terms of trade for OECD countries improved after the mid-1980s, so it would require very strong persistence mechanisms from earlier negative shocks for this factor to continue to explain the high unemployment in the 1990s.

The "tax wedge" on average incomes means that real take-home pay is lower than the pretax real wage; if that wedge increases, then take-home pay and thus the feasible growth of real consumption grow more slowly. Changes in the tax wedge may affect not only the bargaining stance of organized workers but also individual labor supply decisions, since a high tax level may decrease the incentive to work, particularly if unemployment benefits are generous. Table 3.1 indicates that there were substantial increases in the tax wedge in the 1970s, followed by relative stability in the 1980s and 1990s.

Finally, among the widely used macroeconomic variables is the real interest rate. High real interest rates may raise unemployment through several possible channels. Most obviously, higher real interest rates can increase unemployment by depressing aggregate demand. However, the underlying cause of the higher unemployment could still lie elsewhere, with higher real interest rates simply the weapon used by the authorities to ensure that unemployment adjusts to a rise in the NAIRU—which, for instance, may have occurred because of developments in the labor market, as suggested by Blanchard (1999). Second, higher real interest rates may signal cases where the government deliberately pushes unemployment above the NAIRU in order to reduce the inflation rate. Finally, there are ways in which high real interest rates can affect the NAIRU itself. For example, higher real interest rates may push up profit markups as firms seek to maintain profits after interest payments. Higher markups mean lower real wages, and higher unemployment may then be required to achieve a corresponding reduction in wage pressure (a higher NAIRU). The pattern shown in table 3.2 is of modest real interest rates in the 1960s, very low or zero rates in the 1970s, followed by real interest rates averaging 5% or more through to the early 1990s, and some decline at the end of the decade. So higher real interest rates could help explain the persistence of high unemployment through the 1990s, though the difficulty in unraveling their causal role should be kept in mind.

The movements in the structural budget balance could also affect the unemployment rate, although the primary impact would be from a traditional Keynesian demand-side perspective. Other things equal, a smaller deficit would be associated with less demand and higher unemployment. Table 3.2 shows a large rise in the structural deficits in the 1970s and then a sharp falloff in the deficit in the 1990s. The latter was associated with the Maastricht accord, which laid down strict deficit limits as a condition for being admitted into the euro zone. The rapid pace of deficit reduction required by this agreement could partially explain high unemployment in the 1990s.

In considering the deficit figures shown in the table, it is important to keep in mind that they are based on an estimate of the deficit, *at the NAIRU*. This point is important, because if the NAIRU is itself misestimated, then the measures of the structural deficit would be wrong, as well. Much of the increase in the structural deficit from the early 1970s to the 1980s coincided with a rise in the estimated NAIRUs for most countries. A higher unemployment rate is, of course, associated with a higher deficit. If the NAIRU did not rise as much as the OECD assumed, then the structural deficits did not increase as much as is indicated in the table. In other words, the assessment of fiscal policy over this period is itself dependent on the view one holds of the NAIRU.

### 3.1.3 Institutions

In the orthodox view, it is institutional rigidities, not macroeconomic developments, that cause persistent high unemployment. A standard set of "institutional variables" has been developed in the literature to capture various aspects of the labor market that affect either collective wage setting (for example, union strength) or individual labor-supply conditions (such as active labor market policy) or both (unemployment benefit levels, for example). Because of the constraints of data availability and comparability across countries, this set of measures is not usually claimed to be comprehensive.

Union strength is a notoriously difficult variable to capture quantitatively, and this problem is compounded in cross-country studies by the differing national contexts. The most commonly cited variable is the proportion of employees in unions—union density. The data for the 19 OECD countries considered (see table 3.3) suggest modestly rising density from the early 1960s until the early 1980s. By the late 1990s, average density had

Table 3.3. Measures of Union Strength and Bargaining Stance

|  | Union Density % | | Bargaining Coverage % | | Bargaining Coordination (1–3) | |
|---|---|---|---|---|---|---|
|  | Mean | St. Dev. | Mean | St. Dev. | Mean | St. Dev. |
| 1960–64 | 38.8 | 14.2 |  |  | 2.21 | 0.65 |
| 1965–69 | 39.1 | 14.2 |  |  | 2.21 | 0.64 |
| 1970–74 | 41.4 | 15.2 |  |  | 2.24 | 0.60 |
| 1975–79 | 44.8 | 18.0 | 71.4 | 21.9 | 2.29 | 0.50 |
| 1980–84 | 44.6 | 19.8 | 71.6 | 22.7 | 2.16 | 0.55 |
| 1985–89 | 42.2 | 20.3 | 70.6 | 23.8 | 2.03 | 0.57 |
| 1990–94 | 41.2 | 21.1 | 69.2 | 25.5 | 2.01 | 0.66 |
| 1995–99 | 38.7 | 22.5 | 68.5 | 27.2 | 1.92 | 0.65 |

Source: see Appendix 3.2.

fallen back to its original level, though the variability in union membership across countries has considerably increased. In some countries, many more workers are covered by collective agreements than belong to unions, and this extension of union agreements should strengthen unions' bargaining position. But data for the coverage of collective bargaining agreements are much patchier, especially for the earlier periods. The available data suggest a fairly small decline in collective bargaining coverage since the early 1980s.

Finally, much attention since Calmfors and Driffil (1988) has been devoted to the degree of centralization of bargaining, later adjusted to coordination in wage bargaining by unions and by employers (Soskice 1990). A great deal of effort has been devoted to constructing internationally comparable measures of coordination, which try also to reflect variations within a country over time in bargaining practices (examples of this appear in later chapters, notably the cases of Ireland and Netherlands, two of the "success stories" of the 1990s). The most comprehensive coordination index, reported by Nickell et al. (2001), suggests some slight increase up to the late 1960s, with a definite decline subsequently. This movement was far from uniform, however. In five countries (Ireland, the Netherlands, Finland, Italy, and Portugal), bargaining coordination is shown as increasing between the early 1980s and the late 1990s.

Overall, then, the bargaining variables tell a pretty consistent story, in which union strength and bargaining coordination rise until the end of the 1970s or the early 1980s, followed by a rather modest decline on average. It is important to appreciate that the radical reductions in union strength seen in some countries (the United Kingdom and New Zealand, for example) are not typical for OECD countries.

Two measurable dimensions of unemployment benefits, the replacement rate and the duration of benefits, are widely seen as affecting labor

Table 3.4. Measures of Labor Market Policies

|  | Employment Protection Legislation | | Unemployment Benefit Replacement Ratio (%) | | Duration of Benefits (index 0–1) | | Active Labor Market Policies (% of GDP) | |
|---|---|---|---|---|---|---|---|---|
|  | Mean | St. Dev. | Mean | St. Dev. | Mean | St. Dev. | Mean | St. Dev. |
| 1960–64 | 0.79 | 0.62 | 28.0 | 11.1 | 0.34 | 0.40 |  |  |
| 1965–69 | 0.85 | 0.61 | 31.0 | 15.8 | 0.35 | 0.39 |  |  |
| 1970–74 | 0.99 | 0.59 | 34.6 | 18.2 | 0.37 | 0.35 |  |  |
| 1975–79 | 1.09 | 0.59 | 43.2 | 20.3 | 0.42 | 0.34 |  |  |
| 1980–84 | 1.11 | 0.59 | 45.4 | 21.4 | 0.45 | 0.34 |  |  |
| 1985–89 | 1.11 | 0.58 | 48.1 | 21.9 | 0.46 | 0.33 | 0.78 | 0.48 |
| 1990–94 | 1.05 | 0.53 | 48.5 | 20.0 | 0.49 | 0.32 | 0.97 | 0.60 |
| 1995–99 | 0.92 | 0.43 | 47.9 | 17.5 | 0.53 | 0.33 | 0.99 | 0.54 |

Source: see Appendix 3.2.

supply decisions and therefore (voluntary) unemployment. The data in table 3.4 show the average (pretax) replacement ratio for the first year of unemployment, together with an index for duration based on the proportion of these benefits still being received in later years of unemployment. The average replacement ratio increased by one-half between the early 1960s and late 1970s, after which there were further small increases before the hint of a decline at the end of the 1990s. The duration index shows a rather steady rise throughout the whole period. It is well recognized that these measures should be supplemented by data on eligibility, since the harshness of work tests and other requirements vary widely across countries.

The second set of institutional variables is more focused on the microeconomic conditions in the labor market. First, there is employment protection legislation, which has many dimensions (see OECD 1999) and which is the central target in many discussions of labor market flexibility. A high degree of employment protection is widely thought to inhibit hiring, though the parallel constraints on firing make the overall impact on unemployment somewhat ambiguous. The data in table 3.4 suggest a steady rise in the index until the early 1980s, after which there was a slow decline, reversing about one-third of the earlier increase.

Finally, unemployment rates may be affected by a range of active labor market policies, which include the provision of information, counseling, and training to the unemployed. The OECD has gathered data on expenditure on these policies since the mid-1980s. Table 3.3 shows some increase in this spending in the 1990s, with divergences between countries tending to increase.

### 3.1.4 Assessment

This discussion of institutions and macroeconomic background suggests plenty of candidates that could help to explain the trend in OECD unemployment over recent decades. The macroeconomic environment deteriorated after 1974 with consistently slower TFP growth and periodic terms of trade shocks. Higher real interest rates took over as a depressing factor in the 1980s, with a modest reversal at the end of the period. The continued rise in the share of taxation until the early 1980s put further pressure on take-home pay. Union strength increased noticeably until the end of the 1970s, after which there was some reversal, but this coincided with a declining degree of coordination within the bargaining process, which could have brought adverse bargaining outcomes, including higher unemployment. Employment protection legislation strengthened until the early 1990s, after which there was a partial reversal; replacement ratios rose until the late 1980s, and the duration of benefits seems to have increased rather steadily. Rising inflation until the late 1970s is consistent with the view that unemployment was somewhat below the NAIRU in the 1970s. The trend toward lower inflation thereafter suggests actual unemployment somewhat above the NAIRU.

This broad story has appealed to a wide range of economists who have approached these issues from a variety of perspectives (see Bruno and Sachs [1985], Layard, Nickell, and Jackman [1991, 1994], OECD [1994], and Siebert [1997]). However, as noted, there are significant differences within the empirical literature over the exact ways and extent to which different sources of labor market rigidity are believed to have increased the unemployment rate. The third section of this chapter examines this literature in more detail. In order to provide background for this more detailed empirical work, the next section relates unemployment levels for OECD countries to six standard measures of labor market institutions and policies.

### 3.2 INSTITUTIONS AND UNEMPLOYMENT: AN INITIAL LOOK

If a "direct link" exists between labor market institutions and policies and unemployment (OECD 1999: 52–53), a first place to look for it is in the simple correlations between the variables. Figures 3.1–3.6 present scatter plots of six conventional measures of institutions against the OECD's standardized unemployment rates for 20 countries (see Appendix 3.2 for definitions and sources). Since these institutional measures tend to show little annual change and we are interested in longer-term determinants of the pattern of unemployment, the data are organized into five-year averages—a common practice in this literature (see Nickell 1997; Elsmekov et al. 1998; and Blanchard and Wolfers 2000). We focus on the past two decades (1980–1984, 1985–1989, 1990–1994, and 1995–1999), the period during which unemployment reached extremely high levels in many OECD member countries.

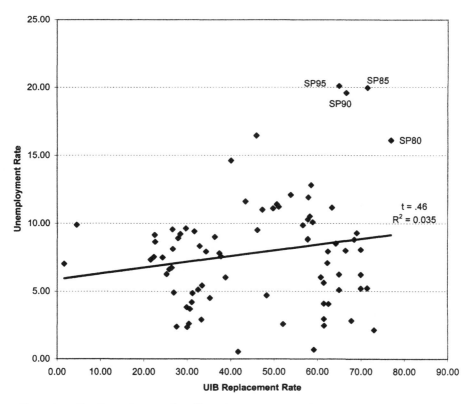

Figure 3.1. The Unemployment benefit replacement rate and unemployment, 1980–1999 (20 countries, 4 five-year periods). Source: See Appendix 3.2.

We begin with the two commonly used, OECD-derived measures of the generosity of the unemployment benefits system, the replacement rate (the level of benefits relative to earnings) and the index of duration of benefits for which averages across countries were shown in table 3.4. Among the institutions held to have the greatest adverse employment effects, these measures of benefit generosity are also among the least controversial. As a follow-up report to the *Jobs Study* (OECD 1997a: 52) puts it, "There is broad consensus that unemployment rates across time and countries are related to the generosity of income support available to the unemployed." It is worth noting that there may be a problem of reverse causation in simple tests of association between unemployment and unemployment benefit generosity, since governments are likely to respond to higher unemployment with greater generosity of benefits.

Despite both the widely accepted view that unemployment benefit generosity lies at the heart of the unemployment problem and the likelihood of at least some reverse causation, figures 3.1 and 3.2 show little association between the standard measures of unemployment benefit

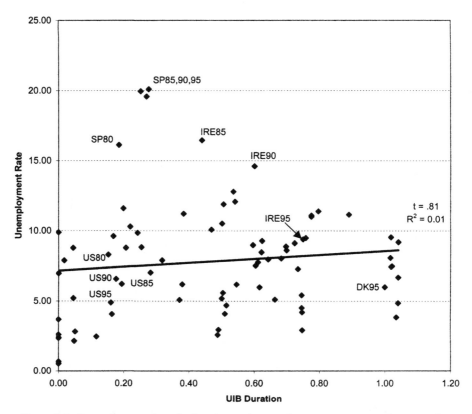

Figure 3.2. **Unemployment benefit duration and unemployment, 1980–1999 (20 countries, 4 five-year periods). Source: See Appendix 3.2.**

generosity and unemployment over the 1980–1999 period. Figure 3.1 shows a slight positive relationship between the unemployment rate and the replacement rate (the coefficient of the regression line is not statistically significant at the 10% level [t = 1.5], and this measure accounts for less than 3% of the variation in the unemployment rate over these 20 countries and four periods). Spain is an outlier, and without it, the trend line is absolutely flat. Directly below the four Spanish points are those for Sweden; while both countries had similar replacement rates (ranging from 65%–76%), the five-year average unemployment rates in Spain ranged from 16%–20%, while Swedish unemployment rates ranged from 2%–8%. Another example of the lack of correspondence between replacement rates and unemployment can be seen with France and the Netherlands. While French replacement rates were about 58% from 1980 to 1999 and Dutch rates were much higher, at 70%, French unemployment rose from 8% to 12%, while Dutch unemployment fell from 8% to 5%. Nor do differences in the duration of benefits appear to explain the perverse (from

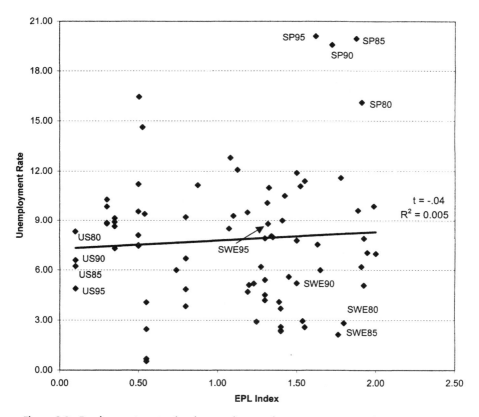

Figure 3.3. Employment protection laws and unemployment, 1980–1999 (20 countries, 4 five-year periods). Source: See Appendix 3.2.

the rigidity-view perspective) replacement rate unemployment trends for France and the Netherlands; the duration of benefits was substantially higher in the Netherlands for the first three periods (1980–1995) and about the same in the last (1995–1999).

Indeed, as figure 3.2 shows, there is also no simple association between unemployment benefit duration and unemployment levels across these 20 countries and four time periods. With similar unemployment rates, New Zealand (1.04) and the United States (.15–.19) are at opposite ends of the spectrum on this measure of duration. On the other hand, the quintessential welfare state, Sweden, with a strong commitment to active labor market policies (training and job placement services), gets a duration score (.04–.05) that is far smaller than that of even the United States. Spain's duration score since 1985 (.25–.28) is slightly above that of the United States, but far below that of the United Kingdom (.70–.73); nevertheless, Spain has had unemployment rates two to three times higher than those in the United Kingdom (20.1% vs. 7.3% for 1995–1999).

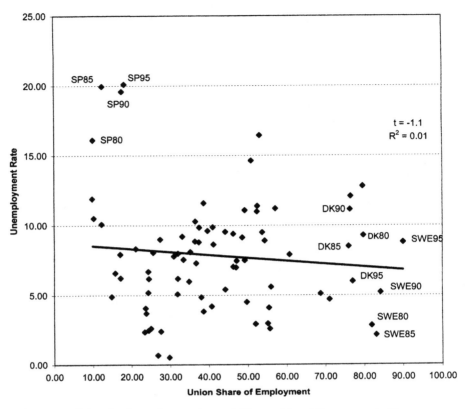

Figure 3.4. Union density and unemployment (20 countries, 4 five-year periods).
Source: See Appendix 3.2.

An index of the strength of employment protection laws is plotted against unemployment in figure 3.3. An OECD survey (1999) found that "empirical results are somewhat mixed.... Bertola (1992), Nickell and Layard (1997), and OECD (1999b) were unable to find a statistically significant relationship between EPL and the unemployment rate." This is, indeed, precisely what figure 3.3 indicates. With similar unemployment rates, at least through 1994, Sweden and Portugal had far higher EPL scores than the United States. Spain, however, had much higher official unemployment rates than Portugal (and Sweden), despite similar EPL scores.

Figures 3.4 and 3.5 present plots of union density and bargaining coordination against unemployment, both of which again show no statistically meaningful relationship. As the OECD (1999: 55, box 2.3) concludes, "Notably there is little evidence of an effect of union density . . . on unemployment once other features of the collective bargaining system are taken in to account." In fact, our figure 3.4 shows no effect even *without*

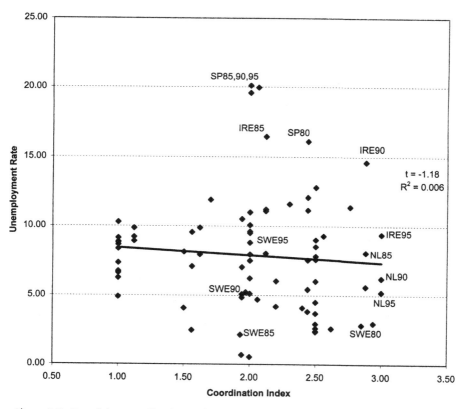

Figure 3.5. Bargaining coordination and unemployment (20 countries, 4 five-year periods). Source: See Appendix 3.2.

taking these other features into account. One of the key collective bargaining features is coordination, which appears in figure 3.5. Bargaining coordination is often found to be among the stronger variables in cross-country multivariate tests—the more coordination (greater institutional intervention), the *lower* the unemployment rate. Our simple plot does not indicate this for the full set of country-time points, but it is worth noting that both Ireland and the Netherlands do show both greater coordination and lower unemployment over time.

On the role of taxes, the OECD (1999: 55, box 2.3) concludes that "Recent studies seem to suggest a significant effect of taxes on labor on unemployment." Again, no simple bivariate relationship appears in our data. Figure 3.6 shows that Sweden had extremely high tax levels and relatively low unemployment (although the latter increased substantially in the 1990s), whereas Spain reports fairly low taxes but extremely high unemployment. Ireland is again of interest: relatively low taxes and very high unemployment, which fell sharply in the second half of the 1990s.

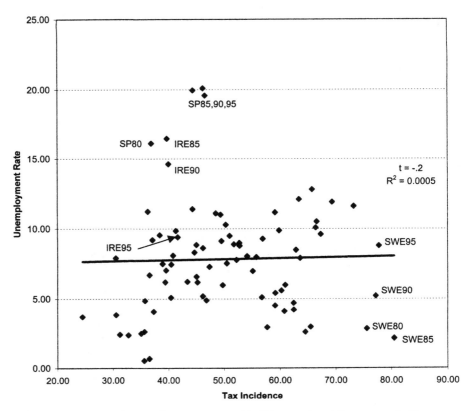

Figure 3.6. Taxes and unemployment, 1980–1999 (20 countries, 4 five-year periods).
Source: See Appendix 3.2.

France and Belgium also show high and rising unemployment at the same time that tax levels were relatively high and rising. So, while no cross-country relationship appears in figure 3.6, the tax-unemployment relationship, like that of coordination, may be more consistent with conventional expectations (coordination lowers unemployment, taxes raise it) over time for particular countries (effects that are picked up in multiple regressions, discussed later, once country dummy variables are included).

In sum, figures 3.1–3.6 offer no hint that labor market institutions and policies could explain even a small part of the post-1980 pattern of unemployment for these 19 countries.

We conclude this section by focusing on the relationship between labor market deregulation (sometimes referred to as "structural reform") and declining structural unemployment (measured by the NAIRU) in the 1990s. An enumeration of reforms was carried out by the OECD as part of its follow-up to *The Jobs Study* (OECD 1994). Their 1999 survey (OECD 1999b) provides an extremely comprehensive listing of changes in the generosity of unemployment benefits, the strictness of employment protection laws, the level of minimum wages and the like, focusing on the period from 1995 but also with summary data from the early 1990s. The OECD listed all the reforms suggested for each country in its labor market reviews, developed a weighting system for assessing their significance, and then analyzed whether the recommended reform had been fully implemented, partially implemented, ignored, or even flouted (in the sense that policy had moved in the "wrong" direction).

The OECD found a significant positive relation between their measure of "follow-through" by countries in response to OECD recommendations and the extent to which the NAIRU fell in the 1990s (OECD 1999b: figure 2.7). But such a measure ignores the very different number of recommendations for labor market reforms that countries received from the OECD (varying from 4 in the case of the United States and Australia to 21 for Finland and 23 for Germany). The effect of reforms on unemployment should presumably depend on how many were implemented, not simply

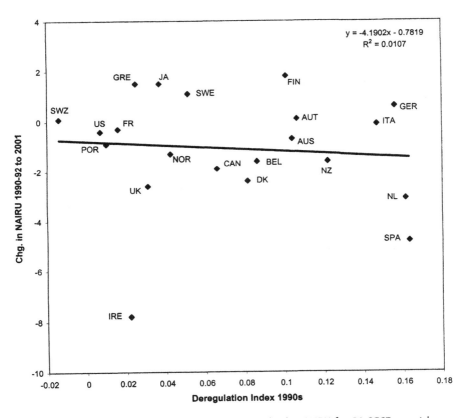

Figure 3.7. Labor market deregulation and changes in the NAIRU for 21 OECD countries in the 1990s. Source: See Appendix 3.2.

on the *proportion* of OECD suggestions that were followed. Accordingly, we constructed an alternative index showing the "volume" of labor market deregulation recommendations that were actually carried out, which depends on both the number of measures advocated by the OECD and their "follow-through" by the countries (see Data Appendix). We focused our index on reforms connected with the benefits, employment protection, and wage bargaining systems, as these constitute the core of labor market deregulation.

Figure 3.7 compares this index of labor market deregulation in the 1990s with the OECD's estimate of the change in the NAIRU over the same period for 21 OECD member countries. It is clear that there is no significant relationship between these measures of deregulation and the change in unemployment across OECD countries. Obviously Ireland is an extreme case with the most dramatic fall in the NAIRU accompanied by rather little labor market reform. However, even if Ireland is excluded (and this would be hard to justify), the relationship between deregulation efforts and structural unemployment across countries still appears very weak (only about one tenth of the variance in the NAIRU change being "explained"). By this measure, changes in structural unemployment that have occurred across the major OECD member countries in the 1990s are not associated with the extent of labor market reform.

### 3.3 INSTITUTIONS AND UNEMPLOYMENT: THE RECENT CROSS-COUNTRY LITERATURE

Since the late 1980s, a considerable literature has developed on the extent to which differences in unemployment rates between nations and over time can be explained by labor market institutions. This section examines some of the most influential of these studies. We do not present an exhaustive review of the literature. Our goal is to present some of the main findings of this research and to highlight the main methodological issues that have arisen.

To facilitate our assessment of these papers, table 3.5 presents the results from six representative studies of a set of regressions designed to measure the relationship between labor market institutions and unemployment. The key differences in the structure of the regressions are noted later. The construction of the variables, which differs somewhat across regressions, is explained more fully in Appendix 3.1.

#### 3.3.1 Nickell

Building on his earlier work with Layard and Jackman (Layard et al. 1991), Nickell (1997) lays out a clear and simple framework for examining the link between institutions and unemployment with a sample of 20 OECD countries for two six-year periods, 1983–1988 and 1989–1994. The study calculates the average rates of unemployment, long-term unemployment, and short-term unemployment for each country in each period,

**Table 3.5. Summary of the Implied Impacts of Differences in Labor Market Institutions on Unemployment**

| | Nickell 1997[1] | Elmeskov 1998[2] | Belot & van Ours 2002[3] | Nickell et al. 2001 | Blanchard & Wolfers 2000 | Bertola et al. 2001 |
|---|---|---|---|---|---|---|
| *Institutions* | | | | | | |
| EPL (1 unit increase) | No effect | 1.43 | 0.87 | 4.45 | 0.24 | 0.20 |
| UB Repl. Ratio (+10 PP) | 0.88 | 1.29 | 0.10 | 1.24 | 0.70 | No effect |
| UB Duration +1 yr | 0.70 | — | — | 0.88[4] | 1.27 | 1.43 |
| ALMP +10 PP | −1.92 | −1.47 | — | — | No effect | No effect |
| Union Density +10 PP | 0.96 | No effect | −1.06 | No effect | 0.84 | No effect |
| Union Coverage +10 PP | 3.60[5] | — | — | — | No effect | No effect |
| Co-ordination +1 unit | −3.68 | −1.48[6] | −0.70 | −11.64 | −1.13 | −1.11 |
| Taxes +10 PP | +2.08 | 0.94 | 1.79 | 1.69 | 0.91 | 0.97 |
| *Macroeconomic shocks* | | | | | | |
| Δ inflation +1 PP | −1.36 | — | −0.48 | — | — | −3.06 |
| GDP Gap | — | −1.25 | — | — | — | |
| TFP slowdown −1 PP | — | — | — | 0.86 | 0.73 | No effect |
| Real interest hike +1 PP | — | — | — | — | 0.47 | 0.63 |
| Labor demand fall −1 PP | — | — | — | 2.54 | 0.18 | 0.12 |
| Money supply | — | — | — | No effect | — | — |
| Real Import/Oil Price Rise +1 PP | — | — | — | 0.52 | — | — |
| Youth share | — | — | — | — | — | No effect |
| *Interactions* | | | | | | |
| Institutions w/macro | No | No | No | No | Yes | Yes |
| Institutions w/ institutions | No | Yes | Yes | Yes | No | No |
| *Fixed Effects* | | | | | | |
| Country | No | Yes | Yes | Yes | Yes | Yes |
| Time | Yes | No | Yes | Yes | No | No |
| Country trend | No | No | No | Yes | No | No |
| *Sample* | | | | | | |
| Period | 1983–94 | 1983–95 | 1960–95 | 1961–92 | 1960–95 | 1970–96 |
| Periodicity | 6-year | Annual | 5-year | Annual | 5-year | 5-year |

(*Continued*)

which then appear (in log form) as the dependent variables in a set of regressions. The independent variables intended to capture the impact of key labor market institutions and regulations are employment protection (rank 1–20), the replacement rate (percentage of working wage), unemployment benefit duration (years), active labor market policy (spending

Table 3.5. (*Continued*)

|            | Nickell 1997[1] | Elmeskov 1998[2] | Belot & van Ours 2002[3] | Nickell et al. 2001 | Blanchard & Wolfers 2000 | Bertola et al. 2001 |
|------------|---------|----------|-----------|-------------|-------------|-------------|
| Countries  | 20      | 19       | 18        | 20          | 20          | 20          |
| Data Set   | Nickell | OECD     | Belot & VO | Nickell et al. | Nickell/ BW | Nickell/ BW |

Source: Column (1) is based on Nickell (1998) table 2: column 1; Column (2): Elmeskov et al. (1998), table 2, column 1; Column (3): Belot and van Ours (2002), table 7, column 5; Column (4): Nickell et al. (2001), table 13, column 1; Column (5): Blanchard and Wolfers (1999), table 5, column 1; Column (6): Bertola et al. (2001), table 9, column 1. "No effect" means not statistically significant; —means variable not included.

1. Shows the impact of differences in the independent variable on a country with the mean unemployment rate for the sample.

2. Shows impact of a change of one standard deviation in the independent variables.

3. The calculation of the change in EPL assumes a 10-unit increase in the index. Effects shown include the effect of the interaction terms, under the assumption that the interacted institutional variable is set at the sample mean for the last period.

4. Assumes an increase of 0.12 in the duration index, which is equivalent to adding an additional year of benefits at a replacement rate of 40%.

5. Assumes a rise of one unit in an index that ranges from 1 to 3.

6. The effect of being a country with either a low or a high degree of coordination and centralization, compared to a country with intermediate levels for these measures.

per unemployed worker as a percentage of GDP per employed worker), union density (percent), union coverage (index 1–3), bargaining coordination (2–6), and the total tax rate (percent). The regressions also include the change in the average inflation rate during the period and a dummy for the second time period. The regressions were run using generalized least squares, allowing for random effects of country variables.

The first column of table 3.5 shows the projected impact of the specified changes in the institutional variables, based on Nickell's regression results. Since the dependent variable is the log of the unemployment rate, rather than the unemployment rate itself, the results imply that the effect of each institution will be proportionate to the unemployment rate in a particular country at a given point in time. The results show the effect on a country that has an 8% unemployment rate, approximately the average for the sample period. All of the variables are significant with the expected sign, with the exception of employment protection legislation.

The implied impact of the hypothetical changes in some of the institutional variables on the unemployment rate is quite large. For example, the regression results imply that an increase of 1 unit in the 3-unit index used to measure union coverage would lead to a 3.6 percentage point rise in the unemployment rate. Similarly, the results imply that an increase of 1 unit in the 4-unit index measure of bargaining coordination would lead to a 3.7 percentage point drop in the unemployment rate. The estimated impact of active labor market policy also appears quite large, with an increase of 10 percentage points in the measure of spending on active labor market policy leading to a 2.4 percentage point drop in the unemployment rate. The impacts of the other labor market institutions implied by the regression results are also substantial, although for the policy changes specified in the table, they are smaller than for these three measures.

Despite the apparent strength of these results, Nickell's interpretation is cautious; he comments at the outset that the labor market rigidities explanation for high European unemployment "is not *totally* wrong." His concluding discussion points out that many of the institutional features that are thought of as labor market rigidities are no more prevalent among the group of high unemployment countries than among the low unemployment countries. He also points out that some of these features, such as bargaining coordination, appear to reduce unemployment. The paper closes with the warning that "the broad-brush analysis that says that European unemployment is high because European labor markets are too 'rigid' is too vague and probably misleading."

### 3.3.2 Elmeskov, Martin, and Scarpetta

"Key Lessons for Labor Market Reforms," by Elmeskov, Martin, and Scarpetta (1998) (hereafter EMS), is an assessment of the effectiveness of the recommendations from the OECD *Jobs Study* [OECD 1994] by three OECD economists. The methodology of the tests run by EMS differs in several important ways from that used by Nickell (1997), the most significant of which is that it uses annual data, which is central to the purpose of the paper: explaining the recent declines in unemployment rates in many OECD nations. EMS also use a different data set, relying on OECD measures for the labor market institutions. The second column of table 3.5 shows projections of the impact of the specified changes in the institutional variables based on the regression results from the study.

EMS's results differ from those obtained by Nickell (1997) in several noteworthy ways, even though the period covered is almost identical. They find a large significant positive relationship between employment protection and unemployment. The results indicate that an increase of 4.3 units (one standard deviation) on an index with a possible range from 0 to 18, is associated with a 1.4 percentage point rise in the unemployment rate, which contrasts with Nickell's finding that there was no relationship between employment protection legislation and the unemployment rate. This result may reflect the fact that the employment protection legislation index in EMS is quite different from the one used in Nickell. The EMS measure assigns values for several different features of the employment protection legislation, while the Nickell measure is a simple ranking. Similarly, the coefficients of the coordination variables, while highly significant, are considerably smaller in absolute value than the estimates reported in Nickell. This result could be in part attributable to the difference between the OECD coordination index and the Nickell index. EMS also use a separate index of centralization, which refers to the level at which bargaining takes place (firm, industry, or nationwide).

Unlike Nickell (1997), EMS do not find a statistically significant relationship between union density and unemployment, and their estimate of the impact of taxation is only half as large. In other tests, EMS estimate the impact of bargaining coordination more carefully, distinguishing between coordination among workers and employers and centralization in the bargaining process. They also interact these measures with other labor market variables. A finding that shows up in a variety of specifications is that countries with intermediate levels of coordination and centralization tend to have the highest rates of unemployment and that countries with highly coordinated and centralized bargaining tend to have even lower unemployment rates than those with the most decentralized and least coordinated bargaining systems. The regressions with interacted terms also show this pattern (EMS 1998: tables 2 and 4). Through both direct and interacted effects, their results show that the effects of employment protection legislation and taxes on increasing unemployment are concentrated in countries with an intermediate level of coordination.

The use of annual data allows for a test of Granger causality from unemployment rates to benefit generosity and the tax wedge. The causality issue is important because, if countries are raising their benefits as a result of high unemployment, or increasing taxes to cover the cost of providing benefits to a larger population of unemployed workers, this *reverse causation* might also result in a significant relationship between higher benefits or tax rates and higher unemployment. While the authors make little note of it, the reported test results show solid evidence of Granger causality from higher unemployment to higher unemployment benefits for three of the countries with high levels of unemployment during this period, Belgium, France, and Italy, as well as for two countries with lower unemployment levels, the United Kingdom and the United States (EMS 1998: table A.3). They also find evidence for Granger causality from higher unemployment to higher tax rates in 3 of the 19 countries examined. While clearly not universal, this evidence of reverse causation provides serious grounds for viewing with caution test results that show a correlation between high unemployment and long benefit duration.

Using their regression results, EMS examine the extent to which changes in the unemployment rates in the OECD countries over this period can be explained by the changes in labor market institutions. They find that for most countries, the vast majority of the change in the unemployment rate can be attributed to country-specific effects, rather than to any identified change in labor market institutions (EMS 1998: table 3). For example, according to their estimates, institutional changes can account for only 0.3 percentage points of a 2.1 percentage point drop in the structural rate of unemployment in Ireland, 1.3 percentage points of a 4.2 percentage point increase in the structural unemployment rate in Sweden, and −0.2 percentage points of a 2.2 percentage point rise in the structural unemployment rate in Spain. EMS explicitly acknowledge this limitation of their model: "it should be stressed at the outset that an important fraction of the structural change in unemployment cannot be accounted for by changes in the explanatory variables included in our analysis" (11).

Yet, in spite of these rather weak findings, particularly in comparison with Nickell (1997), EMS are much less cautious and strongly argue for the importance of labor market institutions in the explanation for high unemployment in the OECD. They conclude by urging nations to reform their labor markets along the lines recommended by the OECD:

> Some of the medicine prescribed under the OECD recommendations is bitter and hard for many countries to swallow, especially insofar as it appears to raise concerns about equity and appears to threaten some of the rents and privileges of insiders. As a result, there is a natural tendency in many countries to delay needed reforms in certain areas and/or search for alternative, 'sweeter' remedies. It requires strong political will and leadership to convince electorates that it is necessary to swallow all of the medicine and that it will take time before this treatment leads to improved labor market performance and falling unemployment. But the success stories show that it can be done!

### 3.3.3 Belot and van Ours

Belot and van Ours (2002) extend the approach of EMS (1998) by exploring a wider set of interactions between variables. They also extend the period of analysis, using five-year periods from 1960 to 1996. The study reports the results of four regressions that test the direct impact of institutions on unemployment over this period. The only regression in which most of the direct effects of the institutional variables have significant coefficients with the expected sign does not include time or country fixed effects. In this "successful" regression, the coefficient for the tax rate, the replacement rate, and union density variables are all positive and statistically significant, as the conventional labor market rigidity view predicts. On the other hand, the coefficients on the coordination and employment protection variables are negative and significant, the latter being a perverse result for the conventional view, since it implies that employment protection legislation lowers the unemployment rate.

The authors then present the results of a number of alternative specifications. When fixed effects and a time variable are included, the coefficients of all the institutional variables become insignificant, although the coefficient for the change in the inflation rate is negative and significant in every specification. In a regression that includes interacted variables, a positive and significant interaction is found between the tax rate and the replacement rate, implying that taxes will have a larger effect on the unemployment rate if the replacement rate is high and that raising the replacement rate will have a larger impact on the unemployment rate if the tax rate is high. Both high replacement rates and high tax rates reduce the gap between take-home pay and the benefits available to unemployed workers. The implication of this finding is that increasing either the replacement rate or the tax rate has a larger impact on the unemployment rate if the other one is already high.

Ultimately, these regressions produce largely inconclusive results about the impact of the interactions. For example, an interaction variable between employment protection and centralized bargaining has a significant positive coefficient in one regression (table 7, column 5), but the coefficient of the employment protection variable becomes negative and significant in a regression in which bargaining is held at a decentralized level (table 7, column 6). The coefficient of an interacted union density variable and centralization variable is negative and significant in one regression (table 7, column 5), implying that higher unionization rates are associated with lower levels of unemployment. However, this coefficient also changes sign in the case of decentralized bargaining. The only variable to have a significant coefficient for its direct effect in the preferred regression (table 7, column 5) is the replacement rate. However, the estimated effect of the replacement rate is negative, suggesting the surprising conclusion that in low tax countries, raising the replacement rate would actually lead to lower unemployment (table 4, column 3).

Like Nickell (1997), and in sharp contrast to EMS, Belot and van Ours are cautious in their interpretation of these results. They conclude by noting that "institutions matter and institutions interact" (18), warning that policies that lead to lower unemployment in some countries may not have the same effect on countries with a different institutional structure.

### 3.3.4 Nickell et al.

Like Belot and van Ours (2002), the Nickell et al. (2001) study tries to explain trends in unemployment rates in the OECD over the longer period, in this case from 1961 to 1995. But, like EMS, this paper uses annual data and takes into account the interactions between institutions. The interacted institutions include coordination and employment protection, benefit duration and the replacement rate, coordination and union density, and coordination and the tax rate. Like Blanchard and Wolfers (2000), this study also measures the effects of several macroeconomic shocks, including changes in labor demand, total factor productivity growth, real import prices, the money supply, and the real interest rate. Nickell et al. also look at a broader set of labor market outcomes, including regressions for the inflow into unemployment (proxied by short-term unemployment), real compensation growth, and employment-to-population rates as dependent variables, in addition to the regressions with the unemployment rate as the dependent variable.

Nickell et al. are quite explicit about their goal: "our aim is to see how far it is possible to defend the proposition that the dramatic long term shifts in unemployment seen in the OECD countries over the period from the 1960s to the 1990s can be explained by changes in labor market institutions in the same period" (1). This is clearly a far less agnostic starting point on the importance of labor market institutions than that taken in Nickell's earlier paper (1997).

Before directly assessing the study's results, it is worth noting several unusual features of the Nickell et al. analysis. First, the regressions in this paper all include country-specific time trends. While none of these time trends is close to being statistically significant, they do explain a large portion of the changes in unemployment over this period. This point may not be readily apparent because the estimated coefficients are generally small (the largest in absolute value is Portugal's—0.107). But, because the regressions include a lagged dependent variable that is estimated at between 0.86 and 0.87, the full effect of the time trend is more than seven times what it would be in the absence of the lagged dependent variable. This means, in the case of Portugal, that its country-specific time trend implies a decline in its unemployment rate of 9.6 percentage points over a 20-year period. While the estimated time trends for the other countries are smaller, 11 of the 20 countries have time trends that imply a change in the unemployment rate of at least 3.5 percentage points over a 20-year period. One implication of these estimated time trends is that, if institutions had remained unchanged, the unemployment rate would have been *negative* in several countries by the end of the period. By definition, the changes in the unemployment rate attributable to the time trends are independent of the labor market institutions included in the regression.

A second notable feature is that, while most of the cross-country studies have used data grouped in five- or six-year periods, Nickell et al. make use of annual data. There must be some question about how much extra precision is really bought with the apparent increase in degrees of freedom gained by using annual data, especially when most of the relevant institutions change slowly and several of the institutional measures are essentially interpolated from a few benchmark observations (especially EPL and coordination).

Nickell et al. finds that most of the institutional variables and the macro shock variables are statistically significant with the expected sign. The replacement ratio, benefit duration, and employment tax variables all have positive significant coefficients in the two unemployment regressions that appear in the paper (see column 4 of table 4). However, both the employment protection and union density variables have insignificant coefficients. The size of coefficient of the tax variable is comparable to the estimates in the other models; however, the estimated impact of the benefit duration is much larger than in the other studies, and the impact of the replacement rate is considerably smaller.

Consistent with much of this literature, Nickell et al. finds that bargaining coordination is negative and significant in both of the unemployment regressions. But the effects implied by their coefficients are far too large to be plausible, implying that the direct effect of an increase of one unit in the coordination index is associated with a percentage point decline of between 6.4 and 7.2 in the unemployment rate (table 13, columns 1 and 2). Taking interactions into effect, the total decline in the unemployment rate that would result from an increase in bargaining coordination implied by these regressions would be even larger (since interaction terms with employment protection and union density both had highly significant negative coefficients). The coefficients of the inter-acted variables show that coordination offsets much of the impact of taxation in raising the unemployment rate and, combined with higher union density, leads to a lower unemployment rate. The interaction terms also show that higher replacement rates amplify the impact of benefit duration in raising the unemployment rate (or vise versa), an effect also found in Belot and van Ours (2002).

The impact of the macroeconomic variables is largely consistent with standard theory. The labor demand shock, total factor productivity shock, and real import price shock variables were all highly significant with the expected signs. However, the money supply shock term was not signifi-cant. The real interest rate variable was significant with the expected sign, but the estimated impact was small.

Nickell et al. find that only the coefficients of the replacement rate and employment tax variables are significant in regressions that have the employment to population (EPOP) rate as the dependent variable. The coordination variable is again highly significant with a positive coeffi-cient, suggesting that greater coordination increases the EPOP. While the study correctly notes that the determinants of the EPOP and unemploy-ment rates are likely to be different, the inclusion of country fixed effects should account for much of these differences. Insofar as the institutional variables included in this analysis affect the unemployment rate in a way that has no effect on the EPOP, the impact of changes in these institutions is substantially different than is generally recognized. Specifically, the im-plication is that a change in a labor market institution that lowers the unemployment rate (e.g., weakening employment protection legislation) will not increase employment levels. Instead, it will simply encourage people to leave the labor market altogether. While Nickell et al. make little of this result, it can be interpreted as challenging the conventional rigidity view, since there seems little reason to weaken labor market protections if the main outcome is to drive people out of the labor force, rather than to increase the percentage of the workforce who hold jobs.

We should also point out that this paper has been revised and that there are some notable differences between the results presented in the 2002 version and those that appear in the earlier (2001) draft. The main difference seems to be that the more recent one extends the data from 1992 to 1995. In the 2001 version, the employment protection legislation vari-able was highly significant in all three of the published unemployment regressions (table 13) and quite large in its economic impact. In contrast, the coefficient of this variable in the regressions in the more recent version is not close to being significant. The additional three years also seems to have a substantial affect on the coefficients of other variables as well.

In the 2002 version, the effect of higher taxes is more than 30% lower, the effect of coordination is nearly 40% lower, and the effect of benefit duration is cut by more than 50%. The additional three years of data also now make the coefficient of the interest rate variable significant. It had been very close to zero and not close to significant in the earlier regressions. The fact that the inclusion of three additional years leads to substantial changes in the regression results raises serious questions about the robustness of the conclusions.

Nevertheless, Nickell et al. conclude that their results show that "broad movements in unemployment across the OECD can be explained by shifts in labor market institutions." Indeed, they contend that "with better data, e.g. on union coverage or the administration of the benefit system, we could probably generate a more complete explanation. To be more precise, changes in labor market institutions explain around 55 percent of the rise in European unemployment from the 1960s to the first half of the 1990s" (19). Much of the rest of the increase is attributed to the recession of the early 1990s.

### 3.3.5 Blanchard and Wolfers

An innovation of Blanchard and Wolfers (2000) is their emphasis on the interaction of institutions and macroeconomic shocks, represented by the slowdown in total factor productivity growth, trends in long-term real interest rates, and shifts in labor demand. These macro-institution interactions are central to the study, since Blanchard and Wolfers, in direct contrast to Nickell et al. (2001), explicitly rule out the possibility that institutions alone, or the change in institutions over time, can explain the evolution of OECD unemployment. The authors point out that the same supposedly employment-unfriendly institutions were present in the 1970s, when the unemployment rate was low. As Blanchard and Wolfers put it, "while labor market institutions can potentially explain cross country differences today, they do not appear able to explain the general evolution of unemployment over time" (2). The authors instead pursue the hypothesis that certain labor market institutions inhibit the ability of economies to respond to adverse shocks, thereby leading to higher unemployment.

The Blanchard-Wolfers study uses 8 five-year periods from 1960 to 1996 (the last two years are treated as a full period). In some regressions, some of the institutions vary over the period, but in most cases labor market institutions are held fixed. The regressions use nonlinear least squares to estimate the coefficients of the interaction terms, allowing for the simultaneous estimate of coefficients for the macro shock terms and the institutional variables.

The results provide some evidence for the proposition that labor market institutions, in the presence of adverse shocks, lead to higher unemployment. Column 5 of their table 5 shows the impact of differences in labor market institutions on unemployment assuming that the values for the macroeconomic shocks variables were at their levels for the period 1991–1995. Most of the coefficients are significant and have the expected sign. The sizes of the implied effects are generally comparable to those in Nickell (1997), EMS, and Nickell et al. (2001), although the impact of differences in employment protection legislation variable and taxes is somewhat smaller than in the other studies. The results imply that even a 10 percentage point rise in the tax rate would lead to just a 0.9 percentage point rise in the unemployment rate.

Blanchard and Wolfers hold that their results provide support for the view that the combination of macroeconomic shocks over the past three decades and the rigidity in the labor markets in some countries helps to explain both the general increase in the unemployment from the 1960s to the 1990s and the variation across countries. However, the study also notes that their findings are sensitive to changes in specification. For example, in a regression that uses alternative measures of the replacement rate, the employment protection and tax wedge variables become insignificant, while union density is significant at only a 10% confidence level (Blanchard and Wolfers 2000: table 6, column 1). Further, when a time-varying measure of the replacement rate is used (as it clearly should be), all three of these variables become insignificant, as do the replacement rate variables (table 6, column 2). In regressions that use an alternative or time-varying measures of employment protection, this variable is insignificant, although the replacement rate, benefit duration, tax wedge, and union density variables are all highly significant (table 6, columns 3 and 4). It is worth emphasizing that only bargaining coordination (a "good" labor market institution) has a significant coefficient in every regression, regardless of the specification.

The fact that the inclusion of time-varying institutions weakens the results leads Blanchard and Wolfers to be cautious in assessing their evidence about the links between institutions and unemployment. They conclude by noting that institutions are becoming more "employment-friendly" and that "further improvements should help reduce unemployment—although the poor results obtained using time-varying institutions make us reluctant to push this position strongly, at least based on the evidence in this paper" (19).

### 3.3.6 Fitoussi, Jestaz, Phelps, and Zoega

Like Blanchard and Wolfers (2000), Fitoussi et al. (2000) try to explain unemployment with a model that emphasizes the interaction of macroeconomic shocks and institutions. More specifically, they run tests with country fixed effects, a country-specific persistence parameter (which measures the persistence of unemployment levels through time), a country-specific sensitivity parameter (which measures the extent to which the unemployment rate responds to contemporaneous shocks), and a series of macroeconomic shocks over the past three decades. Although Fitoussi et al. view their results as confirming the theory that the interaction of shocks and institutions explains much of the variation in unemployment rates over the past three decades, there are problems with this conclusion, some of which are noted in the study. The biggest problem is that the estimates of the sensitivity parameter, which is supposed to measure the extent to which shocks lead to higher unemployment, are highest in the countries that are thought to have relatively few labor market rigidities. For example, the United States, the United Kingdom, Canada, Ireland, and the Netherlands are five of the seven highest-ranking countries by the estimated sensitivity parameter (Fitoussi et al.: table 2). This implies that macroeconomic shocks lead to more unemployment in these five countries than they do in most other OECD countries. This result appears to be directly at odds with the view that the interaction of macroeconomic shocks and the labor market rigidities characteristic of continental Europe is the source of high European unemployment.

The paper examines the extent to which the country fixed effect and the country-specific sensitivity parameter can be explained by differences in labor market institutions. Fitoussi et al. find that the replacement ratio (albeit very small), union density, and union coverage have positive and statistically significant effects on the size of country-specific fixed effect, which should imply that they lead to higher unemployment, whereas coordination has a negative and statistically significant effect. Benefit duration and union density have a positive and statistically significant effect on the size of the country-specific sensitivity parameter, while coordination and active labor market policies have a statistically significant negative effect. The other labor market variables are insignificant in these regressions. Given the weakness of these results, these somewhat unusual regressions can be seen as, at best, providing only modest support to the labor market rigidities view.

The authors then present regressions that test more directly the extent to which changes in labor market policies, monetary policy, and national differences in asset prices explain trends in unemployment in the 1980s and 1990s. A regression that essentially replicates Nickell (1997) for six years in the 1980s finds that labor market institutions (including country fixed effects) can explain nearly 80% of the variance in national unemployment rates over the years from 1983 to 1988 (Fitoussi et al.: table 6). However, when changes in the unemployment rate from the 1980s to the 1990s are regressed against changes in institutions, most of the coefficients become insignificant (Fitoussi et al.: table 7).

Fitoussi et al. test the monetary policy hypothesis by using a set of variables intended to capture the effect of monetary policy in a simple cross-section regression, with the difference between the country unemployment rates in the 1990s and the 1980s as the dependent variable. These regressions provide some support for the view that monetary policy is at least partly responsible for higher unemployment in the 1990s. A test that includes only real interest rate variables and the country average unemployment rate in the 1990s explains nearly 40% of the variance in unemployment among the nations tested (Fitoussi et al.: table 10, column 1). The coefficient on the real interest rate variable implies that a one percentage point rise in the real interest rate is associated with a 0.84 percentage point increase in the unemployment rate.

Fitoussi et al. accept that labor market institutions can explain the persistence of high unemployment in at least some nations but conclude that "institutional reforms in the OECD" can explain only a small portion of the divergent trends in unemployment (257). The study then points to the success of many countries, most notably Ireland, which have seen large reductions in their unemployment rates with little or no reform of their labor market institutions (see also chapter 6). This study examines the extent to which monetary policy and asset price fluctuations can explain recent patterns in unemployment rates, precisely because it views the explanatory power of the labor market institutions view to be limited. Fitoussi et al. conclude that "the labor market reforms advocated by the OECD Secretariat, although helpful in some cases, leave us far short of explaining why the countries that recovered in the 1990s did so, and by the amounts they did" (276).

### 3.3.7 Bertola, Blau, and Kahn

Bertola, Blau, and Kahn (2001) (BBK) also attempt to explain trends in unemployment rates by the interaction of macroeconomic shocks and labor market institutions. One notable difference in the BBK analysis is its inclusion of demographic variables, specifically variables intended to measure the percentage of young workers in the labor force, in regressions examining differences in unemployment rates across countries and through time. In most other ways, the core analysis follows closely the methodology used by Blanchard and Wolfers.

The additional hypothesis that BBK examines is that differences in the youth share of the population partly explain differences in national unemployment rates and that the rigidities created by various labor market institutions make some countries less able to employ young workers. The evidence reported in the study on this issue is ambiguous, with the youth variables statistically insignificant in several specifications and, in one case, statistically significant with the wrong sign (e.g., table 9, columns 1 and 5).

The study also presents rather ambiguous evidence on the larger hypothesis that labor market institutions explain national differences in unemployment rates. Column 6 of table 4 shows the impact on the unemployment rate of differences in each of the institutional variables, implied by the estimated coefficients in the regression whose results are shown in BBK (table 9, column 1). This calculation uses the size of the macroeconomic shocks in the period 1991–1995. The tax variable is significant and consistent with the size of the estimates produced in other studies, implying that a 10 percentage point decline in the tax rate is associated with a decline of 1.0 percentage points in the unemployment rate. Benefit duration is positive and significant, although the implied effect is somewhat larger than in other studies, with the regression result implying that a one-year increase in benefit duration is associated with a 1.4 percentage point rise in the unemployment rate. The employment protection legislation variable has a positive and significant coefficient, although it is worth noting that this variable is a straight ranking of the OECD countries. While Nickell (1997) used the same variable for employment protection legislation, subsequent research has relied on indexes that assigned values for different types of employment protection. The study does not provide a rationale for returning to this cruder method of measuring the strength of employment protection legislation.

The coordination variable has a negative and significant coefficient similar in size to the results found in other studies. The replacement rate, union density, union coverage and active labor market variables are all insignificant in this regression, as is also the case in most of the other regression results shown in the study.

In our view, this regression result, coupled with the others shown in the same table, provides little basis for accepting the labor market institutions explanation. In these regressions, none of the institutional variables consistently have significant coefficients, with the results very sensitive to the specification used in the specific regression. (It should be noted that BBK assess their results quite differently, by emphasizing that the institutional variables are jointly significant using an F-test.)

In spite of the mixed nature of their regression results, BBK are quite unambiguous in assessing their findings, which they take as confirmation of the "Unified Theory," commenting that "we find the superior overall performance in the United States since the 1970s is largely due to the interaction between macro shocks and our laissez-faire labor market institutions" (52). Summarizing its findings, the study asserts that "high wage inequality and low wage levels are associated with low unemployment" and "that 'globalization' and 'new technologies' make it increasingly difficult for OECD countries to deliver favorable employment and wage opportunities to some of their workers" (53).

### 3.3.8 Assessment

While this literature is widely viewed to provide strong evidence for the labor market rigidity view, a close reading of the leading papers suggests that the evidence is actually quite mixed, as several of the studies explicitly acknowledge.

Even when we focus only on the most supportive results from each study, we see a disconcerting range of estimates of the impact of institutions. Only the tax and unemployment benefit duration variables are significant in all the regressions in which they appear, although two of the regressions did not include a duration measure. Even with these variables, the range of the estimated coefficients is sufficiently large to raise questions about the structure of the tests. The implied impact of a 10 percentage point increase in the tax-rate variable ranges from an increase in the unemployment rate of 0.9 percentage points (EMS 1998) to an increase of 2.1 percentage points (Nickell 1997). The implied impact of a one-year increase in benefit duration in the five regressions in which it appeared ranges from an increase in the unemployment rate of 0.7 percentage points (Nickell, 1997) to an increase of 1.4 percentage points (Bertola et al. 2001).

The employment protection legislation (EPL) variable is positive and significant in five of the six regressions in which it appears, although the impact of an increase of one unit in the EPL index ranges from a 0.2 percentage point increase in the unemployment rate (Bertola et al. 2001) to a 4.45 percentage point increase in the unemployment rate (Nickell et al. 2001). While some of this difference can be explained by the different indexes used in the regressions, there would still be a substantial range of estimates even after taking these into account.

The unemployment replacement rate is positive and significant in five of the six sets of regression results shown in table 3.5. But here also the range of the estimates is striking. The implied impact of a 10 percentage point increase in the size of the replacement rate variable ranges from a 0.1 percentage point rise in unemployment (Belot and van Ours 2002) to a 1.3 percentage point increase (Elmeskov et al. 1998). The range of the estimated coefficient for the variables that were generally found to have a significant relationship with the unemployment rate is sufficiently large to both raise questions about the robustness of this result and to obscure the potential tradeoffs for policy makers.

A second point is that some of the explanatory power of the regressions comes from "good" institutions—those that lower unemployment. The coefficient of the coordination variable is negative and significant in five of the six sets of regression results shown in the table, although the size of the effect implied by two of the estimates is too large to be plausible. Also, the active labor market policy variable is negative and significant in two of the four regressions results shown in table 3.4, suggesting that a greater commitment to retraining unemployed workers and matching them to jobs may be an effective method of lowering the unemployment rate. While the OECD has actively promoted ALMP as one solution to high unemployment, the organization has been almost silent about the one labor market policy that consistently shows the largest promise in reducing unemployment: bargaining coordination. Indeed, the OECD has consistently advocated decentralization of wage bargaining.

Third, it is worth repeating that there are features of many of these studies that raise serious doubts about the labor market institutions explanation of unemployment. The sizes of several of the coefficient estimates in Nickell (1997) are clearly implausible, such as the implied result that an increase of one unit in the bargaining coordination variable is associated with a 3.7 percentage point decline in the unemployment rate, while an increase of one unit in the union coverage index is associated with a 3.6 percentage point increase in the unemployment rate. The EMS study (1998) finds that most of the changes in the unemployment rate from the 1980s to the mid-1990s are explained by country-specific effects, rather than by the institutional variables used in the regressions. It also found significant evidence of reverse causality in the case of the replacement rate and the unemployment rate, suggesting that the strength of the correlation found in these regressions may be at least partly explained by the fact that countries tend to increase benefits when they have high rates of unemployment.

The Nickell et al. (2001) study also reports implausible coefficient estimates. As is noted in the study itself, the structure of the regressions is highly unusual, including a lagged dependent variable. In addition, the fact that labor market institutions show almost no effect on the employment-to-population ratio raises serious questions over how these institutions can be responsible for unemployment. The Fitoussi et al. (2000) effort to explain unemployment through the interaction of shocks and institutions had the peculiar finding that most of the "success" stories appeared among the list of nations most vulnerable to macroeconomic shocks. The Bertola et al. (2001) study mostly finds weak results, although their discussion implies otherwise.

The Blanchard and Wolfers (2000) study also shows mixed results, as they note. The results are highly sensitive to specification, and regressions that use time-varying measures of institutions produce weaker results than regressions that assume that these institutions never change. Assessing the research on institutions and unemployment, the authors note:

> One must worry however that these results are in part the result of economic Darwinism. The measures used by Nickell have all been constructed ex-post facto, by researchers who were not unaware of unemployment developments. When constructing a measure of employment protection for Spain, it is hard to forget that unemployment in Spain is very high.... Also, given the complexity in measuring institutions, measures which do well in explaining unemployment have survived better than those that did not. (18)

Blanchard and Wolfers rightly stress the importance of ensuring that results are robust to variations in variable specification, time period, and estimation method. Our interpretation of this literature is that the results are decidedly not robust to such variations. Our own analysis of the cross-country data is presented in the next section.

## 3.4 REGRESSION RESULTS

In this section, we produce our own empirical estimates of the effects of labor market institutions on unemployment rates across OECD member countries, using a data set that spans the full 1960–1999 period. Our data, which build primarily on those constructed by Nickell et al. (2001) but which include variables from Blanchard and Wolfers (1999), Belot and van Ours (2001), and other sources, have several advantages over those that have been analyzed to date. Our data are augmented, mainly from OECD sources, to cover the late 1990s, when unemployment rates fell sharply in many of the OECD countries. At the same time, we have filled some gaps for the 1960s that are present in other data sets. We have also been able to combine what appear to be the most appropriate variables from different, previously published sources. To preview the results, our analysis reinforces the conclusions we drew from our review of earlier research. Using simple and transparent models, our results provide little support for the widely accepted labor market rigidity view.

Table 3.6 presents our main results. Columns 1 and 2 conduct a simple test of the robustness of the main results in Nickell's influential (1997) paper. Our basic approach is to test the sensitivity of the initial Nickell results by using new versions of the institutional variables produced for Nickell et al. (2001). As in Nickell (1997), the regression in column 1 attempts to explain the standardized unemployment rate in 20 OECD countries, using data on each country's level of employment protection, replacement rate, benefit duration, union density, bargaining coordination, and tax wedge. Nickell's original regression spanned two six-year periods (1983-1988 and 1989–1994), while our regressions cover two five-year periods (1985–1989 and 1990–1994). Following Nickell (1997), we have estimated the relationship using generalized least squares random effects. Since the Nickell et al. (2003) data set does not include information on union coverage or active labor market policies because of lack of data for the 1960s and 1970s, the regression in column 1 excludes these variables, which did appear in the original Nickell specification (we add these variables, from other sources, in column 2).

Using the Nickell et al. (2001) data in the Nickell (1997) regression produces results that differ markedly from those obtained in the original study. In Nickell (1997), seven of the eight institutional variables had the correct sign and were statistically significant at standard levels. The only exception was the employment protection variable, which was close to zero and not statistically significant. Using the Nickell et al. data, however, three of the six institutional variables have the wrong sign (employment protection, union density, and the tax wedge), and none are statistically significant. These initial results reinforce the conclusions we drew from our literature review: the strong policy recommendations often associated with the rigidity view appear to flow from empirical analyses that are not particularly robust.

Of course, it may be that the exclusion of two important variables that appeared in the original Nickell specification—union coverage and active labor market policies—explains the poor results in column 1. To explore this possibility, the regression in column 2 reintroduces the two variables into the analysis, using data on union coverage from Blanchard and Wolfers (2000) and data on active labor market policies from the OECD. The inclusion of the two missing variables does little to rescue the rigidity story. The union coverage variable is significant at the 10% level, but

Table 3.6. Determinants of the Standardized Unemployment Rate

| Period | (1) 1985–94 | (2) 1985–94 | (3) 1960–99 | (4) 1960–84 | (5) 1980–99 |
|---|---|---|---|---|---|
| EPL | −0.117 | −0.737 | −0.009 | 0.199 | −0.317* |
|  | (2.157) | (2.715) | (0.506) | (0.389) | (1.444) |
| Replacement rate | 0.064 | 0.052 | −0.610** | −0.058** | 0.012 |
|  | (0.050) | (0.065) | (0.009) | (0.015) | (0.018) |
| Duration | 3.955 | −0.138 | −5.174** | −6.685** | −5.100 |
|  | (2.950) | (3.495) | (1.024) | (0.814) | (0.144) |
| Union density | −0.009 | −0.027 | −0.599 | 0.014 | 0.021 |
|  | (0.056) | (0.065) | (0.428) | (0.052) | (0.055) |
| Coordination | −1.587 | −2.795 | −4.793** | 1.663 | −7.043** |
|  | (1.623) | (1.764) | (1.091) | (1.674) | (1.327) |
| Tax wedge | −0.039 | −0.147 | −0.023 | 0.185** | −0.097 |
|  | (0.101) | (0.107) | (0.065) | (0.069) | (0.072) |
| Union coverage | — | 5.540# |  |  |  |
|  |  | (2.963) |  |  |  |
| ALMP (inst'd) | — | −0.013 |  |  | — |
|  |  | (0.080) |  |  |  |
| Rep Ratio* Duration |  |  | 0.126** | 0.167** | 0.096# |
|  |  |  | (0.027) | (0.027) | (0.059) |
| Union Den* Coord |  |  | 0.076** | 0.011 | 0.071** |
|  |  |  | (0.020) | (0.026) | (0.025) |
| Tax* Coord |  |  | 0.020 | −0.067** | 0.058* |
|  |  |  | (0.024) | (0.023) | (0.048) |
| Change inflation | −1.841* | −1.830# | −0.451** | −0.315** | −0.277 |
|  | (0.769) | (0.997) | (0.151) | (0.083) | (0.220) |
| Time effects | Yes | Yes | Yes | Yes | Yes |
| Country effects | No | No | Yes | Yes | Yes |
| Obs | 40 | 37 | 156 | 96 | 80 |
| Countries | 20 | 19 | 20 | 20 | 20 |

Columns (1) and (2) estimated using random effects ("xtreg, re" in Stata 6.0). ALMP in column (2), following Nickell (1997), is instrumented using countries' average ALMP value over the 1985–1999 period. Column (3) estimated using feasible generalized least squares, correcting for panel heteroscedasticity ("xtgls, p(h)" in Stata 6.0).
Standard errors in parentheses.
# significant at the 10% level.
* significant at the 5% level.
** significant at the 1% level.
Source: see Appendix 3.2.

ALMP is not significant, and the introduction of these variables does not alter the signs or statistical significance of the original institutional variables. This second set of results, then, further confirms the sensitivity of the empirical support for the rigidity view to reasonable alterations in the definitions of the institutional variables.

As our earlier review of the literature indicated, after Nickell (1997), research in this area generally headed in the direction of greater complexity. Researchers have expanded the time period analyzed, allowed for interactions between institutions (Bertola, Blau, and Kahn 2001 and

Nickell et al. 2001, for example) and between institutions and macroeconomic shocks over time (Blanchard and Wolfers 2000), and deployed increasingly sophisticated econometric techniques (see section 3). Policy discussions based on these analyses, however, have been much less conditional in their thrust than would be justified by the findings of most of this new underlying research. The suggestion that countries cut replacement ratios, for example, has not been made conditional on the existence of a negative productivity shock or adverse turns in the terms-of-trade.

In this context, it is worth using the available data from the past four decades to see to what extent labor market institutions, in and of themselves, can account for the evolution of national unemployment rates. We do this by extending the simple model in column 1 to data for 20 OECD countries over eight five-year periods spanning the years 1960–1999. We also include the interactions between institutions that have entered into the mainstream of the discussion (allowing that unemployment replacement ratios may have a bigger effect when the duration of benefits is long, for example), as well as country effects (which implies that we are examining the extent to which changes in institutions over time affect the evolution of unemployment over time) and time effects common to all countries (which means that our results explain deviations from the evolution over time of the average OECD unemployment rate). The macroeconomic situation is represented by the change in inflation. One interpretation of the results of this procedure is that it estimates the "average"effect of institutions on unemployment, independent of particular macroeconomic shocks.

The results of estimating this model for the whole period are reported in column 3 of table 3.6. They provide little support for those who advocate comprehensive deregulation of OECD labor markets. Employment protection legislation has no systematic effect at all. A higher replacement ratio is associated with lower unemployment unless benefit duration is extremely high; conversely, longer duration of benefits reduces unemployment unless benefits are at very high levels. Coordination has a very large effect in reducing unemployment (lessened if union density is very high). Taxation has no effect. The time dummies are very large and significant (with 5.5% more unexplained unemployment on average in 1995–1999 than in 1960–1964), and some of the country effects are enormous (to take the extreme cases, Spain has unemployment on average 15% higher than that in Austria, a fact unexplained by the institutional variables).

There are further revealing results if the 40 years are split into the period up to the early 1980s, which includes most of the overall rise in unemployment (column 4) and the period since the early 1980s, during which unemployment rates continued to diverge but without a strong average trend (column 5). The effects of benefits appear weaker in the second period, and EPL now reduces unemployment. The impact of coordination in reducing unemployment is much stronger in the second period, though the effect is lessened at higher levels of either unionization or taxation. Whereas taxation increases unemployment in the first period, it had no systematic impact in the second (column 5). If anything, the results for the more recent period offer even weaker support for the deregulationist position than does the 1960–1984 period.

The results reported here serve to underline the lack of robustness in the estimates of the impact of labor market institutions; these seem dependent on the particular measures of the institutions used and on the time period covered. Certainly, there is little evidence here of the consistency of results that could convincingly underpin sweeping recommendations for labor market reform.

## 3.5 SUMMARY AND CONCLUSIONS

This chapter has examined the evidence for the OECD-IMF orthodoxy— the widespread belief that labor market rigidities are responsible for the high unemployment experienced by many developed countries in the 1980s and 1990s and that labor market deregulation is therefore the best route to reducing unemployment and raising employment rates. As Elmskov et al. (1998) put it, all of the "bitter medicine" prescribed by the OECD's recommendations must be swallowed—including greater wage flexibility, reduced unemployment benefits, and weaker employment protection. We find little convincing support in the cross-country evidence for this orthodox policy prescription.

Simple cross-section plots presented in section 2.2 show no correlation whatever between the six most commonly employed institutional variables and levels of unemployment. Nor is there any obvious link between the pattern of deregulation in the 1990s and trends in unemployment rates. In support of its case for labor market deregulation, the OECD has attempted to link the degree to which countries have followed their prescriptions for labor market deregulation with the extent to which structural unemployment (the NAIRU) has declined (see, for example, OECD 1999). We constructed from OECD sources an index of the extent of labor market deregulation in the 1990s and found no meaningful relationship between this OECD measure of labor market deregulation and shifts in the NAIRU.

We surveyed in section 2.3 the increasingly sophisticated empirical literature that has attempted to statistically link these institutions with the pattern of unemployment across the OECD. On the one hand, we found that these studies are far from unanimous in their estimates of the impact of the standard institutional variables on unemployment and that a number of the prominent papers explicitly refer to this lack of robustness of their own results across specifications and variable definitions. On the other hand, these studies generally share the conclusion that the statistical evidence provides reasonably strong support for the OECD-IMF orthodoxy—labor market institutions can be shown to be an important part of the explanation for the cross-country pattern of unemployment from the 1960s through the 1990s.

We presented econometric results of our own using an expanded data set, which relies mainly on the most current standard OECD measures and, in contrast to other available studies, additional observations for the 1960s and the late 1990s. Our results offer a sharp contrast to the generally supportive assessments in the cross-country literature we surveyed. In short, we found no empirical support for the OECD-IMF orthodoxy. In a first test, we found that the strong cross-sectional relation between unemployment and institutions found by Nickell (1997) for the mid-1980s to the mid-1990s is not robust to alternative definitions of the variables—better measures of "employment-unfriendly" institutions (including those employed by Nickell et al. [2001]) were found to have no statistical effect on the pattern of unemployment in tests otherwise similar to those in Nickell (1997).

We then ran tests with conventional specifications on our extended (1960–1999) data set, and again the results offered little support for the orthodox view. The strongest result was for bargaining coordination, particularly for the period since the early 1980s—a "good" institutional variable, since it tends to reduce unemployment, but one that rarely features in the OECD's policy advice. High taxation seems to have been associated with high unemployment up to the early 1980s, but the relationship appears much weaker subsequently. Two leading "bad" institutions, employment protection and unemployment benefits, have perverse or weak effects.

Our results suggest a yawning gap between the confidence with which the case for labor market deregulation has been asserted and the evidence that the regulating institutions are the culprits. It is even less evident that further weakening of social and collective protections for workers will have significant positive impacts on employment prospects. The effects of various kinds of deregulation on unemployment are very hard to determine and may be quite negligible. Moreover, such effects as there are may influence labor force participation rather than employment (e.g., lower wages and greater employment insecurity may lead workers to opt out of the labor force altogether, which could contribute to lowering the unemployment rate).

It is easily forgotten that labor market institutions act as a form of social insurance that can make these markets function not just more equitably but more efficiently. The generosity of unemployment insurance, the level of the minimum wage, and the extent of employee rights in case of dismissal have direct impacts on large numbers of people, whether at work or not, and reflect a long process of struggle by citizens and the labor movement. This, of course, helps to explain the continued overwhelming popularity of these sheltering institutions throughout much of Europe. Too often, such benefits are not incorporated into the policy discussion to be set against potential costs and are simply dismissed as the unjustified gains of "insiders." Deregulation is promoted by the OECD-IMF orthodoxy as though the employment costs of protective labor market institutions are self-evidently greater than their efficiency and equity benefits. In our view, the empirical case has not been made that could justify the sweeping and unconditional prescriptions for labor market deregulation that pervade much of the policy discussion.

*Acknowledgments* We thank the MacArthur Foundation and the Center for Economic Policy Analysis of New School University for financial support. We are greatly indebted to Michèle Belot, Olivier Blanchard, Steve Nickell, Luca Nunziata, Justin Wolfers, and Jan C. van Ours for making their data and documentation available to us, and to Laura Bardone, Andrea Bassanini, Dominique Parturot, Stefano Scarpetta, and Paul Swaim for OECD data and for their advice about them. We are also grateful to Wendy Carlin, Andrew Martin, John Martin, John Morley, Vincente Navarro, Steve Nickwell, and Luca Nunziata for their most helpful comments and discussion. None of the colleagues named are responsible for the results and interpretations reported in this essay. Our data are available on request.

*Notes*

1. Box 2.3 is titled "Recent Cross-Country Evidence on the Determinants of Structural Unemployment." The OECD's use of the term "structural reform" refers to liberalization of labor market institutions and policies: improving the effectiveness of collective bargaining arrangements to maintain wage moderation, and scaling back unemployment benefit systems, employment protection legislation, and "taxes on labor" (1999: 55).

2. For simplicity, we will use "labor market institutions" to refer to both institutions (e.g., union density) and policies (e.g., employment protection laws).

3. As might happen, for example, when those made long-term unemployed become decreasingly effective as part of the reserve army in holding down wages—an example of "hysteresis."

4. The growth of TFP shows how far real wages can grow, allowing for an equal proportionate change in the rate of profit; the more intuitive measure of the growth of labor productivity shows how far real wages can grow while maintaining the share of profits in national income. In both cases, any faster growth of consumer prices compared to the GDP deflator reduces the "space" for real wage increases.

5. We have not included regression results from a seventh study discussed in this section, Fitoussi et al. (2000), in table 3.5 because the main findings cannot be directly compared to the other studies using the framework in the table.

6. The study also includes a set of employment measures, reflecting labor force participation, which appear as dependent variables in another set of regressions. Measures of employment are generally not included in subsequent research within this framework, although they are of considerable interest, since institutions that may affect unemployment are usually thought of as doing so by affecting numbers of people in work, rather than by causing people to drop out of the labor force.

7. It is important to note that active labor market policy is measured as spending per unemployed worker. This means that a 10 percentage point increase in this variable incorporates the fact that higher active labor market policy is

associated with lower rates of unemployment. The regressions all use instrumental variables to control for this problem of endogeneity.

8. The labor demand variable seems problematic in a regression with unemployment as the dependent variable, since it can be seen as being equivalent to regressing unemployment on employment. Nickell et al. (2003) justify the use of this variable by defining it as the residual of a labor demand model, where a positive residual can be seen as evidence of a shift in technology towards one that uses relatively more labor. The obvious danger in this method is that if the labor demand model is misspecified, then this term is effectively just a measure of employment. In the regressions in the paper the labor-demand variable always appears with a very large and extremely significant coefficient (t-statistics over 19), which suggests that this term is in fact simply measuring employment.

9. The real interest rate variable uses a long-term interest rate, so it is not directly testing the effect of monetary policy on unemployment.

10. The new version also includes a change in the union density variable, which is found to be highly significant. Since these regressions all include country dummies, this term should be thought of as a measure of the change in the change (the second derivative), since the regression would be picking up differences from the mean rate of change. In other words, if a country consistently experienced a decline of 0.5 percentage points in its unionization rate, this would have no effect on the unemployment rate. The regression results imply that the unemployment rate would rise if the rate of decline in the unionization fell to zero and that the unemployment rate would fall if the rate of decline in the unionization rate rose to 1.0 percentage point annually. There is no obvious theoretical explanation for this pattern, and it is not obvious why the union density variable was included in this form.

11. In contrast to earlier studies, this study has interacted variables in which the coefficient is estimated separately. In other words, the NLS method combines productivity growth and employment protection legislation, producing coefficients for each that minimize the error in the regression. In the other papers with models that included interactions, the interacted terms were entered in exactly the same way as any other variable and had only a single coefficient. For example, the benefit duration and replacement rate variable in Nickell et al. (2001) entered the regression in exactly the same way as either the benefit duration or replacement rate variable. Only a single coefficient is estimated for this interacted variable.

12. The study then examines the extent to which higher stock prices may explain a reduction in unemployment rates in a series of regressions using annual data from 1960–1998, which the authors regard as the main contribution of this paper. These regressions provide some evidence for this view, with the stock market variables having significant negative coefficients. Fitoussi et al. interpret this result as suggesting a supply-side phenomenon: firms are willing to invest in hiring more workers when they anticipate larger profits in the future, as evidenced by rising share prices. It is worth noting that the study's findings are also consistent with a demand-driven reduction in unemployment rates, as higher stock prices lead to more consumption through the wealth effect.

13. BBK also include a novel test of the underlying hypothesis of the labor market institution explanation for unemployment—that compression of wage inequality is responsible for high unemployment. They construct predicted unemployment rates for each time and country, using a regression with unemployment as a dependent variable and time and country variables as the independent variables. They similarly construct predicted levels of wage inequality. Finally,

they regress the residuals against each other. While the study treats the results as confirming the labor market institution explanation, it is worth noting that only these tests—which regress residuals against each other—produce significant results. The study does not find a statistically significant relationship between inequality and unemployment when a direct test is used.

14. This sort of ranking is problematic because it can easily result in an inaccurate ordering, due to errors in judgment. More important, it misrepresents differences in the strength of protection. For example, if five countries have almost identical levels of employment protection, they will be separated by 5 units with a ranking measure (e.g., the lowest ranked 9, the highest ranked 14). By contrast, they would have almost the same number if an index were used.

15. When assessing the coefficients shown in table 3.5, it is important to keep in mind that we have attempted to focus on the preferred regression in each study. In each of the studies, results were shown from other regressions that provided less support for the rigidity account.

16. The benefit duration variable is measured somewhat differently across the studies. See Appendix 3.2 for a more precise description of each of the variables.

17. All variables are five-year averages from the 1960–1995 version of the Nickell et al. (2001) data set. The only exception is the tax wedge variable, which we have modified slightly, relying on OECD sources. First, we have filled in gaps for New Zealand and Australia for the 1990 period; second, we have altered what we believe may be minor data errors for Japan and the Netherlands in the 1990s. Neither set of data changes has any effect on the qualitative results in table 3.6.

18. One additional difference between Nickell (1997) and the regressions in columns 1 and 2 is that Nickell (1997) uses the log of unemployment, while we use the level (in the line with most other studies). Using the log of the unemployment rate does not change qualitatively the results in table 3.6.

19. The Blanchard and Wolfers union coverage variable is the same in both periods, as we believe was the also case in the original Nickell (1997) analysis. It takes the values 1, 2, or 3, based on whether coverage was low (less than 25%), medium (25%–70%), or high (more than 70%).

20. We use the data set on expenditures on ALMP as a share of GDP per unemployed person, provided to us by the OECD. In the regression analysis, following Nickell (1997), we instrument the potentially endogenous ALMP variable using the average level of expenditures over the full 1985–1999 period for which we have data.

21. The regression in column 2 has three fewer observations than column 1 because the OECD does not have data on ALMP for Portugal, or for Italy for the 1985–1989 period. Running the regression in column 1 on the sample in column 2 does not alter qualitatively the results in column 1.

22. Following Nickell et al. (2001), we incorporate country effects and a full set of time dummies and estimate the model using feasible generalized least squares, allowing for panel heteroscedasticity.

23. Some experiments that include some of the macroeconomic shocks noted in the literature suggest that their inclusion has rather limited impact on the results for institutions.

24. The interacted variables are introduced as deviations from the sample mean so that the coefficients of the "uninteracted" variables in the top rows of the table show the impact of the variable given average values of the of those variables with which it is interacted.

*References*

Armstrong, P., A. Glyn, and J. Harrison. 1991. *Capitalism since 1945*. Oxford: Blackwell.

Atkinson, A. B. 2001. *The Economic Consequences of Rolling Back the Welfare State.* Cambridge, Mass.: MIT Press.

Belot, M., and J. van Ours. 2000. "Does the Recent Success of Some OECD Countries in Lowering Their Unemployment Rate Lie in the Clever Design of Their Economic Reforms?" Institute for the Study of Labor (IZA) Discussion Paper No. 147.

Bertola, G. M., F. D. Blau, and L. M. Kahn. 2001. "Comparative Analysis of Labor Market Outcomes: Lessons for the United States from International Long-Run Evidence." In National Bureau of Economic Research Working Paper #w8526, October.

Blanchard, O. 1999. Comment on L. Ball. "Aggregate Demand and Long-Run Unemployment." *Brookings Studies on Economic Activity* 2.

Blanchard, O., and J. Wolfers. 2000. "The Role of Shocks and Institutions in the Rise of European Unemployment: The Aggregate Evidence." *Economic Journal* 110 (March): C1–C33.

Bruno, M., and J. Sachs. 1985. *Economics of Worldwide Stagflation*. Basil Blackwell.

Calmfors, L., and J. Driffil. 1988. "Centralisation of Wage Bargaining, Corporatism and Macroeconomic Performance." *Economic Policy* 3: 14–61.

Elmeskov, M. J., and S. Scarpetta. 1998. "Key Lessons for Labor Market Reforms: Evidence from OECD Countries Experience." *Swedish Economic Policy Review* 5(2): 205–252.

Fitoussi, J.-P., D. Jestaz, E. Phelps, and G. Zoega. 2000. "Roots of the Recent Recoveries: Labor Reforms or Private Sector Forces?" *Brookings Papers on Economic Activity* 1: 237–309.

International Monetary Fund (IMF). 1999. "Chronic Unemployment in the Euro Area: Causes and Cures." Chapter 4 in *World Economic Outlook* (April). Washington, D.C.: IMF.

———. 2003. "Unemployment and Labor Market Institutions: Why Reforms Pay Off." Chapter 4 in *World Economic Outlook* (May). Washington, D.C.: IMF.

Layard, R., S. Nickell, and R. Jackman. 1994. *The Unemployment Crisis*. Oxford: Oxford University Press.

Nickell, S. 1997. "Unemployment and Labor Market Rigidities: Europe versus North America." *Journal of Economic Perspectives* 11(3) (Summer): 55–74.

Nickell, S., L. Nunziata, W. Ochel, and G. Quitini. 2001. *The Beveridge Curve, Unemployment and Wages in the OECD from the 1960s to the 1990*. London: CEP, LSE. Revised version, 2002.

Nickell, S., L. Nunziata, and W. Ochel. 2002. "Unemployment in the OECD since the 1960s: What Do We Know?" *Bank of England.*

Organization for Economic Cooperation and Development (OECD). 1994a. *OECD Jobs Study, Evidence, and Explanations, Part I: Labor Market Trends and Underlying Forces of Change.* Paris: OCED.

———. 1994b. *OECD Jobs Study, Evidence, and Explanations, Part II: The Adjustment Potential of the Labor Market.* Paris: OCED.

———. 1995. *OECD Jobs Study, Taxation, Employment, and Unemployment.* Paris: OCED.

———. 1996. *OECD Employment Outlook.* Paris: OCED.

————. 1997. "Economic Performance and the Structure of Collective Bargaining." *OECD Employment Outlook* (July). Paris: OCED.

————. 1999b. *Implementing the Jobs Study*.

————. 2002. *OCED Economic Outlook*. Paris: OCED.

Siebert, H. 1997. "Labor Market Rigidities: At the Root of Unemployment in Europe." *Journal of Economic Perspectives* 11(3) (Summer): 37–54.

Soskice, D. 1990. "Wage Determination: The Changing Role of Institutions in Advanced Industrialised Countries." *Oxford Review of Economic Policy* 6(4): 36–61.

# Appendix 3.1

**Definition of Labor Market Institution Variables Shown in Table 3.4**

| | Nickell 1997 | Elmeskov 1998 #4 | Belot & van Ours 2002 | Nickell et al. 2001 | Blanchard & Wolfers 2000 | Fitoussi et al. 2000 | Bertola et al. 2001 |
|---|---|---|---|---|---|---|---|
| Dependent Variable | ln (unemployment rate) | Unemploy rate PP | Unemploy rate PP | Unemploy rate PP | Unemploy rate PP | Unemploy rate PP | Unemploy rate PP |
| *Institutions* | | | | | | | |
| EPL | Ranking 1–19 | Index 0–16 | Index 0–1 | Index 0–2 | Ranking 1–19 | Index 0-2 | Ranking 1–19 |
| *Unemployment Benefits* | | | | | | | |
| Replacement ratio | RR in first year | Index (RR*Duration) | RR in first year | RR in first year | RR in first year | RR in first year | RR in first year |
| Duration | Years | — | Index 0–2 | Index based on RR in years 2–5 | Years | Index based on RR in years 2–5 | Index 0–4 |
| ALMP | Ratio of government expenditures per unemployed worker to output per worker | — | — | — | Same as Nickell '97 | — | Same as Nickell '97 |
| *Unionization* | | | | | | | |
| Density | PP | PP | PP | PP | PP | PP | PP |
| Coverage | Index 1–3 | — | — | — | Index 1–3 | — | PP |
| Coordination | Index 2–6 | Index 1–3 | Index 1–3 | Index 1–3 | Index 2–6 | Index 1–3 | Ranking 1–19 |
| Taxes | PP | PP | PP | PP | PP | PP | PP |

Source: Column (1) is based on Nickell (1998), table 2; column 1; Column (2), Elmeskov, Martin, and Scarpetta (1998), table 2, column 1; Column (3), Belot and van Ours (2002), table 7, column 5; Column (4), Nickell et al. (2001), table 13, column 1; Column (5), Blanchard and Wolfers (2000), table 5, column 1; Column (6) Fitoussi et al. (2000), table 6; Column (7), Bertola et al. (2001), table 9, column 1.

# Appendix 3.2

Our data set is based on data covering 1960–1995, assembled by Nickell and Nunziata (NN) and prepared as an update to the data set used in Nickell et al. (2001). For the regression in column (1) of table 3.6, we used the NN data without alteration; for regression (2), we added ALMP and union coverage as described here. For regression (3) and for the other tables and charts in sections (1) and (2), we amended or added to the NN data as described here.

*Unemployment Rate.* For 1980–1999, we assembled series for the standardized unemployment rate from OECD *Economic Outlook* for December 2001, which we linked back to 1980 using earlier issues and OECD *Labour Force Statistics* data on unemployment rate, following national definitions for countries where earlier series on the standardized rate was not available. This was combined with NN data for 1960–1979.

*Inflation.* Private Consumption Deflator from OECD *Historical Statistics* database on OECD *Statistical Compendium* (2000), no. 2 (missing data filled in using OECD *National Accounts*).

*Total Factor Productivity.* NN series updated for 1995–1999 using data from OECD Working Paper No. 248 (2000) and updates from OECD. For Austria, New Zealand, and Switzerland, average five-year growth for 1995–1999 was assumed to be same as in previous decade.

*Impact of Terms of Trade.* NN series updated for 1995–1999 using data on import prices, GDP prices, and import share from OECD *National Accounts*.

*Tax Wedge.* NN series updated for 1995–1999 using series from the OECD.

*Revenue Statistics.* 1965–1999 CD (2000) for the sum of individual (income) tax, social security contributions (employer and employee), payroll taxes, VAT, sales taxes, excise taxes, and customs duties, all as a share of GDP. Gaps in data filled in using OECD series for share of government receipts as a percentage of GDP (from OECD *Historical Statistics*).

*Real Interest Rates.* NN series updated for 1995–1999 from OECD *Economic Outlook* series for long-term interest rates and consumer price deflator. Gaps in data for earlier years filled from IMF *International Financial Statistics*.

*Structural Budget Deficit.* Series from OECD *Economic Outlook* (December 2001) linked to earlier data from *Economic Outlook* database in *Statistical Compendium* and to actual deficits, if structural deficit not available.

*Union Density.* NN series updated for 1995–1999 from Ebbinghaus and Weber 2000 (European countries), *U.K. Labour Market Trends, Japan Statistical Yearbook*, Australian Bureau of Statistics website (1995 Nickell figure adjusted), and New Zealand Statistics website. Ireland figure kindly supplied by H. Perry, UCD.

*Union Coverage (of collective agreements).* From Belot and van Ours (2001).

*Bargaining Coordination.* NN provide two series, one created for Nickell et al. and one from Belot and van Ours. We followed them in using the latter for regressions (1) and (2) and the former, which we prefer because it incorporates more variation over time and is updated in Nickell et al. (2002), for regression (3)–(5).

*Employment Protection Legislation.* We used NN's series, which was derived from Blanchard and Wolfers and updated for Nickell et al. (2002).

*Benefit Replacement Ratio.* We followed NN, using the updated OECD database on replacement ratios (kindly provided by the OECD); very minor modifications were made to their procedure for three Scandinavian countries in the 1970s.

*Benefit Duration.* As for the benefit replacement ratio; this measure is a weighted average of benefits in force in the second to fifth years of benefit as a percentage of the first-year benefits.

*Active Labor Market Policies.* Authors' calculations from database on ALMP spending kindly supplied by the OECD.

*Labor Market Deregulation.* The OECD's report *Implementing the Jobs Study* (1999b) lists five areas of labor market reform: including unemployment and non-employment benefits (12 subsections, including replacement rates, duration, and eligibility), wage formation (6 subsections, including bargaining decentralization, minimum wages), and EPL and working time arrangements (10 subsections, including authorization for dismissals, constraints on part-time work). They also include active labor market policies (ALMP) and the tax wedge. We did not include the latter two areas in our analysis. ALMP does not really fall in to the heading of labor market deregulation (its "active" nature reflects the need to overcome market failures rather than widening the scope for market forces). The overall tax wedge, while it may be important for employment, can hardly be considered to be determined primarily on labor market grounds and it seems arbitrary to examine it in relation to the rather few countries on the receiving end of OECD recommendations for tax wedge reduction. We did, however, include in our analysis two minor elements classified under the tax wedge—targeted reductions in social insurance and the taxation of low income earners—as these are explicitly aimed at increasing wage flexibility by "making work pay." The importance of each of the 30 policy subcategories was weighted following the OECD's rating of their importance. We used a numerical version of this weighting constructed by Van Ploek and Borghijs (2001) with minor modifications. The country's response to the OECD's suggestions (weighted 1.0 for "sufficient action," 0.5 for "more action needed," 0 for "no action," and −0.5 for "opposite action") were taken from OECD's Appendix tables (1999b). A country that had been recommended to implement every one of the 30 policies and that had fully carried them out would have an index of 0.64. Thus a low number for the index reflects either few recommendations or a low rate of compliance.

# 4

## Testing the Flexibility Paradigm: Canadian Labor Market Performance in International Context

JIM STANFORD

The paradigm of "labor market flexibility" has exerted a decisive influence on labor market policy making in the developed industrial economies in recent years. This paradigm rests on the central notion that competitive labor market forces will generally attain the most efficient match between labor supply and labor demand, and hence a lower rate of long-run structural or "equilibrium" unemployment. Government interventions aimed at enforcing particular labor market outcomes (such as minimum wages, unemployment insurance programs, collective bargaining structures, and other employee protections) tend to disrupt these competitive market forces, limit the "options" of labor market participants, and produce a less flexible, adaptive, and efficient labor market, marked in particular by higher rates of unemployment in the long run. The OECD *Jobs Study* (OECD 1994) provided the classic statement of this flexibility paradigm, and following its release member governments were entreated to adopt procompetitive policy reforms. Coincident with the rise of the flexibility paradigm was a widespread de-emphasis on the role of aggregate demand conditions in explaining unemployment and other negative labor market outcomes and a corresponding downgrading of the importance of macroeconomic policy as a means of reducing long-run unemployment.

As a result of the intellectual and policy dominance of this view—the OECD-IMF orthodoxy—most recent international comparisons of labor market structures and performance have tended to be conducted through a "flexibility lens." The typical depiction of Canada's labor market in an

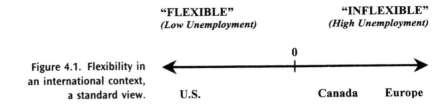

Figure 4.1. Flexibility in an international context, a standard view.

international context is to arrange countries on a one-dimensional scale of labor market flexibility (much like that shown in figure 4.1). The United States is considered to have a highly "flexible" labor market (and hence more efficient outcomes, including a lower rate of unemployment). Continental Europe is considered to have an "inflexible" labor market (and hence less efficient outcomes, including higher unemployment). Canada is typically placed somewhere between these two extremes. The emergence of an unemployment gap between Canada and the United States in the past two decades is often ascribed to Canada's labor market inflexibility. Various flexibility-enhancing policy measures, typically based on the U.S. model, are proposed to make Canada's labor market more efficient, thus reducing long-run unemployment.

The OECD itself has developed a long list of specific policy recommendations aimed at restructuring Canada's labor market along more flexible lines (OECD 1996). The OECD's annual country survey of the Canadian economy, for example, regularly reminds Canadian policy makers of the importance of labor market reforms; the most recent edition listed a dozen proposed flexibility-enhancing measures aimed at more fully attaining the goals of the *Jobs Study* (OECD 2001: 146–148). The OECD's proposals include heightened restrictions on unemployment insurance eligibility, more rigorous control of active labor market programming, and measures to reduce the extent to which educational credentials limit labor mobility within Canada. Since Canada's labor market policy making has been explicitly guided by the flexibility paradigm for much of the past decade, these recommendations receive close attention.

This chapter raises several questions about the standard view that Canada's relatively poor labor market performance is due to inflexible labor market structures, in the context of an empirical survey of comparative labor market outcomes in the 1990s. The first section suggests various different potential working definitions of the term "flexibility" and considers the differing patterns of observable behavior that might correspond to these respective conceptions. The second section then reviews key labor outcomes in the past decade, comparing Canada's experience to that of both the United States and a wide sample of other developed countries. This review confirms that by many measures (although not all), Canada's labor market performance in the 1990s was poor. The third section explores in more detail the extent to which Canada's labor market is indeed relatively "inflexible" in contrast to that of its southern neighbor. In a more common-sense, pragmatic understanding of the word, Canada's labor market does not at all seem "inflexible." If flexibility is interpreted in the concrete sense of being "able to change and to respond to change," Canada's labor market is indeed highly flexible—in fact, by many measures, more so than that of the United States.

The fourth section of the chapter argues that "flexibility" and "inflexibility" are not actually the appropriate terms with which to describe the unidimensional continuum considered in figure 4.1. What is more accurately being portrayed is a one-dimensional scale ranging from a "deregulated" labor market at one end (in which employment and distributional decisions are largely unconstrained by policy interventions and are instead subject to primary market determination) to a "regulated" labor market at the other end (in which explicit policy measures are taken to encourage or enforce employment and/or distributional outcomes more compatible with social preferences). A numerical index of labor market regulation for 17 OECD countries is constructed on the basis of seven different measures of labor market intervention. This index confirms the conventional perception that Canada's labor market is more regulated than that of the United States. In an international context, however, Canada's labor market is still relatively *unregulated*. Several European countries are located at the other extreme of this scale.

There is no consistent correlation, however, between degrees of labor market regulation and key measures of employment performance during the 1990s. Another economic factor that obviously influences employment performance is the relative vibrancy of aggregate demand conditions. The fifth section of the chapter thus reviews a range of indicators of the vibrancy of aggregate demand conditions for the same OECD countries. This review verifies that Canada experienced unusually weak demand conditions during the past decade, while the United States enjoyed relatively strong conditions (in large part because of a significantly more expansionary macroeconomic policy regime). Indeed, the demand-side differences between Canada and the United States are more pronounced than are the differences in the degree of labor market regulation. The strength of aggregate demand is positively and significantly correlated with employment performance in OECD countries during the 1990s. These results suggest a need for a two-dimensional model of labor market structures and performance, an example of which is presented in the final section of the chapter.

## 4.1 DEFINING "FLEXIBILITY"

In a common-sense understanding, "flexibility" refers to the ability to change and respond to change. Indeed, the 1994 OECD *Jobs Study* utilized a working definition something like this in introducing its agenda of policy reforms. The central goal of labor market policy, the OECD argued, should be "to improve the ability of economies and societies both to cope with, and benefit from, change, by enhancing the ability to adjust and adapt, and increasing the capacity to innovate and be creative" (OECD 1994: 43). The choice of terms is deliberately inoffensive: who could be opposed to "flexibility," in this understanding of the term?

Various failures to change and respond to change can be imagined, and hence an "inflexible" labor market could be seen to demonstrate various dysfunctional outcomes. Traditional competitive labor market analysis focuses on price and quantity adjustments in response to supply and demand changes. The problem of labor market inflexibility might then be conceived in simple "price" and "quantity" forms, as suggested by Kuhn (1997). Price inflexibility would be demonstrated by a failure of equilibrium wages to adjust to supply or demand changes.[1] Quantity inflexibility might refer to various regulatory or institutional measures that inhibit quick adjustments in the level of employment (compulsory layoff notice requirements, for example). Other, more complex forms of inflexibility are also possible. Inflexibility in the employment relationship might imply that the terms and forms of employment are unduly static, prohibiting needed flexibility and fluidity in, say, hours of work or the formal relationship between worker and employee (perhaps through prohibitions against flexible forms of employment such as contingent or contractual arrangements). A lack of mobility between economic sectors, or a lack of geographic mobility between regions, or even mobility by workers in and out of the labor force in response to changing market conditions might be indicative of other forms of labor market inflexibility.

Some dimensions of inflexibility might be complementary with others, while others might be substitutes. In a simplistic supply-and-demand partial equilibrium, for example, inflexibility in prices might be subsequently reflected in a perverse flexibility in employment levels—with labor demand unduly rising or falling in response to the imposition of some nonmarket-clearing wage level. In this instance, changes in employment levels are reflective of an *inability* to change on the part of wages, while flexibility in wages should theoretically allow for more "inflexibility" (i.e., stability) in employment levels.

In the parlance of labor and macroeconomists, however, "flexibility" has come to mean something quite different from the ability to change and respond to change. Within a competitive, neoclassical model of the functioning of labor markets, the term is largely synonymous with a labor market that is relatively more subject to market pressures in the determination of employment and earnings and relatively free from institutional or structural barriers that might interfere with or constrain competitive responses to various shocks or stimuli. The notion of flexibility advanced by advocates of more procompetitive labor market structures is not necessarily synonymous with the common-sense meaning of the term. The latter refers to a general ability to change; the former reflects a particular type of response to change in which some outcomes may not actually change at all. The resulting confusion probably plays a role in the policy debates that inevitably accompany the procompetitive policy reforms advocated by the OECD and others. In these debates, advocates of more competitive, deregulated labor markets are seen to be promoting the general goal of "flexibility," while opponents are correspondingly portrayed to be somehow in favor of "inflexibility."

This chapter surveys empirical evidence regarding the ability of Canada's labor market to change and to adapt to change, along several of the potential axes identified earlier. Some of these dimensions of change are seen as desirable by advocates of the OECD-IMF orthodoxy, while others are seen as perverse consequences of improper labor market functioning in other dimensions. What seems indisputable, however, is that Canada's labor market in the 1990s was a site of rapid and often painful change. Whatever may be wrong with Canada's labor market, it does not suffer from a lack of movement.

## 4.2 COMPARATIVE LABOR MARKET PERFORMANCE IN THE 1990S

Table 4.1 provides a summary of several key labor market indicators for Canada, the United States, Japan, the European Union, and the OECD as a whole, for the period between 1990 and 2000. Data are provided on the employment rate, the unemployment rate, labor force participation, the rate of job creation, and the rate of real wage growth. Canada was one of a handful of OECD countries in which the employment rate—employed workers as a share of the working-age population—declined over the decade as a whole. This is probably the best indicator of the relatively weak performance of Canada's labor market during that time. The unemployment rate averaged more than 9% over the decade, almost as high as average European unemployment during the same period (consistent with the dominant view that Canada suffers from a somewhat milder version of "Eurosclerosis"). Canada's unemployment rate declined later in the decade, however, as Canada's economic and labor market recoveries picked up steam. Labor force participation declined in Canada in the 1990s, in the wake of weak labor demand conditions. According to the final two labor market indicators, however, Canada performed better than the average OECD experience. The rate of job creation in the Canadian economy was higher than average in the OECD (matching U.S. job creation rates),[2] and the rate of real earnings growth (in the business sector) was higher than elsewhere in the OECD (including the United States).

Many policy discussions in Canada rely heavily on comparisons between Canada and the United States. Given the proximity of the United States, the importance of foreign trade and investment flows between the two countries, and the general importance of the United States in the global economy, this focus on bilateral comparisons is probably inevitable—although subsequent policy conclusions should certainly be tested against a wider sample. In the context of policy debates over labor

**Table 4.1. Key Labor Market Outcomes, 1990–2000 (%)**

| | Employment Rate | | Standardized Unemployment Rate | | Participation Rate | | Avg. Ann. Growth Employment | Avg. Ann. Growth Real Earnings |
|---|---|---|---|---|---|---|---|---|
| | Average | Change | Average | Change | Average | Change | | |
| | 1990–2000 | 1990–2000 | 1990–2000 | 1990–2000 | 1990–2000 | 1990–2000 | 1990–2000 | 1990–2000 |
| Canada | 59.4 | −0.3 | 9.3 | −1.3 | 65.5 | −1.2 | 1.3 | 1.1 |
| United States | 63.0 | +1.7 | 5.6 | −1.6 | 66.7 | +0.7 | 1.3 | 0.9 |
| Japan | 74.2 | +1.9 | 3.2 | +2.6 | 76.7 | +4.0 | 0.3 | 0.0 |
| European Union | 61.9 | +2.2 | 9.5 | +0.1 | 68.4 | +2.5 | 0.4 | 0.8 |
| OECD | 63.2 | +0.8 | 6.9[3] | +0.4 | 67.9 | +1.1 | 0.8 | n.a. |

Source: Author's calculations from *OECD Economic Outlook*; Statistics Canada, *Canadian Economic Observer.*
1. Compensation per employee, business sector only, deflated by growth in consumer prices.
2. Euro area only.
3. Commonly used definitions of unemployment.

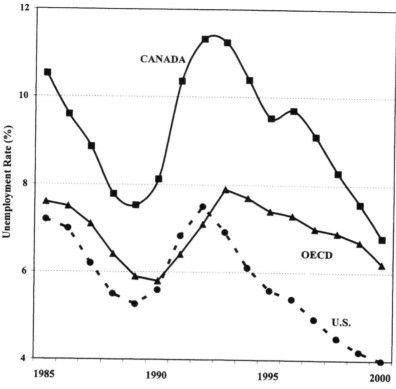

Figure 4.2. Unemployment rates, 1985–2000.

market flexibility, these comparisons to the United States take on a particular importance, since the United States is conventionally held to possess a prototypically flexible labor market. The relative deterioration of Canadian labor market performance vis-à-vis that of the United States would thus seem to provide prima facie support for the notion that more "flexible" labor market policies should be adopted in Canada.

There is no doubt that Canada's labor market performed more poorly than that of the United States throughout most of the 1990s. Canada's unemployment rate was significantly higher than that of the United States, and higher than the OECD average, throughout the 1980s and 1990s (see figure 4.2). The oft-discussed "unemployment gap" between the Canada and the United States first emerged during the early 1980s and widened to almost 5 percentage points in the early 1990s (Riddell and Sharpe 1998). Many commentators have suggested that this gap is largely due to structural differences in the labor markets of the two economies and have argued that Canada could reduce its unemployment rate by adopting U.S.-style labor market regulations and institutions.[3] It should be noted that close to 1 percentage point of this gap is attributable to differences in

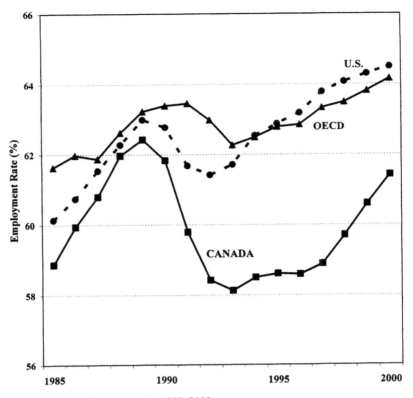

Figure 4.3. Employment rates, 1985–2000.

the methodology of labor force surveys in the two countries; the United States survey utilizes a stricter definition of labor force participation, and this reduces the apparent unemployment rate in the United States by up to 1 percentage point relative to the rate that would occur under Canadian definitions (Sunter 1998).

As indicated in figure 4.3, however, it was not until the 1990s that the unemployment rate gap between Canada and the United States (and the rest of the OECD, for that matter) was reflected in a corresponding *employment* rate gap. Canada's employment rate rose in step with that of the United States throughout the 1970s and 1980s, long after most of the supposedly "flexibility-inhibiting" policy changes (such as a major expansion of the unemployment insurance system in 1971) had been implemented. While some of these reforms may have affected variables such as labor force participation (hence impacting on the unemployment rate), they did not seem to have undermined Canada's relative employment performance. It was only in the 1990s that employment as a proportion of the working-age population fell below that of the United States, by a total of 4 percentage points by 1993, with a belated recovery later in the decade.

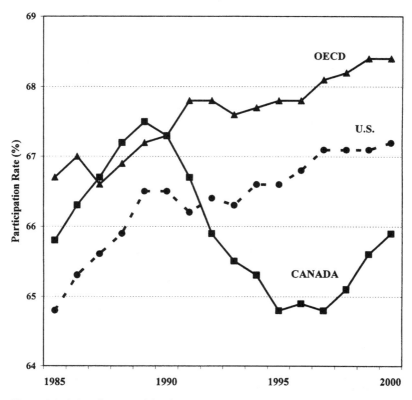

Figure 4.4. **Labor force participation rates.**

Several studies have since identified the decline in Canada's employment rate as the most important source of the relative decline in Canadian living standards, compared to those of the United States, during the 1990s.[4]

Canada's employment rate deteriorated relative to that of the United States by a far greater degree in the 1990s than is suggested by the data on unemployment rates in the two countries. This reflects a sharp decline in labor force participation in Canada, relative to the United States (see figure 4.4). The Canadian participation rate fell by 2.5 points between 1989 and 1995 and did not recover its prerecession peak during the entire decade. In contrast, the U.S. participation rate continued to increase throughout the 1990s, following only a modest setback in 1991. In the 1980s, Canada's participation rate averaged about one point higher than that of the United States, but since 1992 it has been significantly lower (at present by about 1.5 percentage points). The Canadian participation rate also seems to display a generally higher degree of volatility than the comparable rate in the United States; this is explored further later.

The decline in the Canadian employment rate in the 1990s occurred even as Canada was adopting labor market policy measures generally considered to be "procompetitive" (the most important being a major reduction in the generosity of unemployment insurance benefits). Again, this would not seem to support the notion that the differences in labor market outcomes between the two countries result primarily from structural or regulatory differences. Canada's employment performance kept pace with that of the United States throughout the 1970s and 1980s, even as its labor market regulations diverged in a more interventionist direction. Canada's relative employment performance then deteriorated just as important "flexibility-enhancing" reforms were being implemented.

On the other hand, it is clearly true that Canadian macroeconomic policies diverged significantly from those of the United States during the early and mid-1990s. During the early 1990s, Canada's central bank unilaterally pursued a far more anti-inflationary monetary policy than was followed by U.S. authorities. From 1990–1995, real short-term interest rates averaged more than 5% in Canada, compared to barely 1% in the United States. Later, Canadian governments adopted a uniquely severe stance of fiscal restraint, reducing government program spending by 8 percentage points of GDP between 1993 and 1999, compared to a corresponding decline of 3 points of GDP in the United States.

The negative consequences of contractionary macroeconomic policies for aggregate demand conditions (at least in the short run) are clearly relevant to the slower growth of output and employment that was experienced in Canada during most of the 1990s. One would think that these demand-side differences would be important in explaining Canada's relatively poor employment outcomes. Surprisingly, however, most labor policy discussion in Canada focused in the 1990s on the need for ongoing structural and institutional reforms to make the labor market more "flexible."

## 4.3 DIMENSIONS OF CHANGE

In fact, by a range of different indicators, Canada's labor market has proven itself to be extremely flexible, in the pragmatic sense proposed in the first section of this chapter—and in many aspects it has been even more flexible than that of the United States. The notion that Canadians have been protected or insulated from change by virtue of various regulations and protections, and that this insulation has itself become a source of labor market weakness, is not supported by a variety of data attesting to the rapid pace of change in Canada's labor market.

One indicator of "ability to change" might be the degree to which an economy can shift its labor resources from one industry to another in response to changing demand and technological conditions. Table 4.2 summarizes data regarding the volatility of sectoral employment in Canada and the United States from 1983 through 1997 for 35 industrial sectors at the 2-digit level. The volatility of sectoral employment might be measured with respect to absolute numbers of workers, or with respect to the

**Table 4.2. The Volatility of Sectoral Employment, Canada and the United States, 1983–1997 (35 Industries at 2-Digit Level)**

|  | Total Period | 1983–1989 | 1990–1997 |
|---|---|---|---|
| *Sectoral employment levels* | | | |
| Arithmetic mean, normalized standard deviation of employment[1] | | | |
| Canada | 10.40% | 7.25% | 6.73% |
| United States | 8.23% | 5.73% | 4.70% |
| Weighted average, normalized standard deviation of employment[1] | | | |
| Canada | 8.26% | 6.85% | 4.89% |
| United States | 9.31% | 6.20% | 5.19% |
| Industries in which volatility was greater in Canada (out of 35) | 25 | 25 | 26 |
| *Sectoral employment shares* | | | |
| Arithmetic mean, normalized standard deviation of employment shares[1] | | | |
| Canada | 9.95% | 5.27% | 5.74% |
| United States | 9.53% | 5.60% | 4.94% |
| Weighted average, normalized standard deviation of employment shares[1] | | | |
| Canada | 6.11% | 3.21% | 4.26% |
| United States | 6.26% | 3.38% | 3.43% |
| Industries in which volatility was greater in Canada (out of 35) | 19 | 14 | 19 |

Source: Author's calculations from *Statistics Canada*, Employment, Earnings, and Hours, and U.S. Department of Labor, Employment and Earnings.

1. Normalized standard deviation equals standard deviation as percentage of the sample mean (to eliminate units).

sectoral allocation of the total workforce. Hence, comparative data on both indicators are provided in table 4.2. It turns out that the Canadian economy is at least as "flexible" as that of the United States in shifting employment between different sectors. Table 4.2 presents normalized standard deviations of both the absolute levels of sector employment and the shares of sector employment in overall employment. In both cases, sectoral employment volatility is higher in Canada than in the United States in a majority of the 35 sectors considered during the period from 1983 through 1997. On an unweighted basis, the average volatility demonstrated in the 35 sectors is higher in Canada. On a weighted basis, average sectoral volatility is slightly lower in Canada (reflecting the fact that larger industries in the United States, such as business services and communications, have shown the greatest overall volatility). And, if anything, sectoral employment levels and shares have become more volatile in Canada relative to the United States in the 1990s; by most measures, the

Table 4.3. Regressions of Employment on GDP, Canada and the United States, 1976–1998

|  | Levels Regressions | First-Difference Regressions |
|---|---|---|
| *Canada* | | |
| Constant | 0.860 | −0.0013 |
|  | (3.726) | (−0.412) |
| Coefficient on GDP | 0.639 | 0.721 |
|  | (37.010) | (7.630) |
| Adj. $R^2$ | .984 | .732 |
| *United States* | | |
| Constant | 6.192 | 0.0016 |
|  | (61.020) | (0.645) |
| Coefficient on GDP | 0.628 | 0.583 |
|  | (53.411) | (8.224) |
| Adj. $R^2$ | .992 | .760 |

Source: Author's calculations from *Statistics Canada, Canadian Economic Observer*, United States Council of Economic Advisors, *Economic Report of the President*.
All regressions conducted using natural logs of the variables; t-statistics in parentheses; annual data.

volatility of sectoral employment increased in the 1990s in Canada but decreased in the United States.

Another feature of "flexibility" in the labor market might be the ease and speed with which employment decisions respond to changes in the broader economic environment. For example, it is often argued (in the "quantity" version of the flexibility paradigm) that overly generous employment security provisions inhibit the degree to which employers can respond to downturns in their product markets by reducing employment; hence, employers are reluctant to hire new workers even when they are needed, for fear that they will be prevented from downsizing excess workers during slower periods in the future. As a consequence, employment levels are relatively insensitive to fluctuations in demand (either upward or downward). One method of measuring the importance of this type of inflexibility is to econometrically evaluate the relationship between changes in demand conditions and changes in employment. Table 4.3 reports results from regressions of employment on GDP for the period from 1976 through 1998 for Canada and the United States, conducted in both levels and first-difference terms.[5] Variables are measured in natural log terms to ensure commensurability of coefficients between the two countries. In both types of regressions, the coefficient on GDP was higher for Canada than for the United States; in the first-difference regression, the coefficient was substantially higher for Canada than for the United States. This suggests that employment is more sensitive to demand conditions in Canada than in the UnitedStates, and hence employers are better able to adjust their hiring (and firing) decisions quickly in the wake of changing product market circumstances.

Table 4.4. Regressions of Participation on Employment, Canada and the United States, 1976–1998

|  | Levels Regressions[1] | First-Difference Regressions |
|---|---|---|
| *Canada* | | |
| Constant | −125.438 | 0.118 |
|  | (−2.350) | (1.687) |
| Coefficient on employment rate | 0.677 | 0.387 |
|  | (5.594) | (5.676) |
| Adj. $R^2$ | .689 | .598 |
| *United States* | | |
| Constant | −230.403 | 0.159 |
|  | (−4.655) | (3.406) |
| Coefficient on employment rate | 0.309 | 0.279 |
|  | (3.523) | (4.739) |
| Adj. $R^2$ | .947 | .505 |

Source: Author's calculations from *Statistics Canada, Canadian Economic Observer,* U.S. Council of Economic Advisors, *Economic Report of the President.* T-statistics in parentheses; annual data.
1. Levels regressions include a time trend.

A similar indication of flexibility in the labor market is the extent to which individual workers alter their fundamental decision to participate in the labor market on the basis of changing employment and macroeconomic circumstances. In other words, how elastic is labor supply to the general state of labor markets? It has been argued that overly generous social insurance programs perversely encourage "too much" labor force participation by encouraging individuals to maintain job searches in a particular region (or at least to *report* that they are maintaining job searches) when no realistic work opportunities are available. In this case, labor force participation is relatively insensitive to the general state of employment outcomes. Table 4.4 reports the results of regressions of labor force participation rates in Canada and the United States on the corresponding employment rate in each country, once again utilizing data from 1976 through 1998 and conducted in both levels and first-difference terms. A time trend is also included in the levels regression to reflect the long-run social and demographic influences on labor force participation (such as the increased formal work activity of women). Once again, the coefficients on the employment rate are substantially higher in both regressions for Canada than for the United States.

An alternative way of phrasing the same hypothesis would be to argue that the participation decisions of workers should respond to the *negative* prospects of unemployment, as well as or instead of to the *positive* lure of high employment rates. In this case, the participation rate (or changes in it) should be regressed on the unemployment rate (or changes in it). These regressions are reported in table 4.5. This time the results are mixed: the

Table 4.5. Regressions of Participation on unemployment, Canada and the U.S., 1976–1998

|  | Levels Regressions[1] | First-Difference Regressions |
|---|---|---|
| *Canada* | | |
| Constant | −146.765 | 0.163 |
|  | (−1.798) | (1.775) |
| Coefficient on unemployment rate | −0.631 | −0.850 |
|  | (−3.388) | (−10.238) |
| Adj. $R^2$ | .352 | .832 |
| *United States* | | |
| Constant | −339.608 | 0.214 |
|  | (−10.669) | (4.214) |
| Coefficient on unemployment rate | −0.724 | −0.786 |
|  | (−8.892) | (−13.655) |
| Adj. $R^2$ | .960 | .898 |

Source: Author's calculations from *Statistics Canada, Canadian Economic Observer*, U.S. Council of Economic Advisors, *Economic Report of the President*. T-statistics in parentheses; annual data.
  1. Levels regressions include a time trend.

coefficient on unemployment is higher for the United States in the levels regression but higher for Canada in the first-difference regression. Since the decline in the participation rate in Canada has probably weakened the extent to which the official unemployment rate accurately reflects the degree of labor market excess capacity (as the proportion of nonemployed adults who qualify as officially unemployed has fallen), it may be that the employment rate serves as the better indicator of labor market conditions for the purposes of participation decisions. At any rate, no case can be made on the basis of these findings that participation decisions in Canada are any *less* sensitive to broader economic conditions than is the case in the United States, and there is considerable evidence to suggest that they are *more* sensitive.[6]

Another dimension to labor market flexibility might be the extent to which employees are able to devise and implement alternative work arrangements to reflect uncertain circumstances in product markets or other factors that might inhibit the creation of traditional full-time, permanent positions. The OECD placed considerable emphasis on these dimensions of flexibility in its 1994 *Jobs Study*, advocating greater flexibility in working hours and support for self-employment and other forms of entrepreneurship. How does Canada fare in terms of this type of flexibility in work arrangements?

Part-time employment in Canada has grown substantially as a share of total employment over the last two decades (see table 4.6). Close to one in five Canadian workers is now employed on a part-time basis—and a considerable portion of those (about one-third, according to labor force surveys) would prefer to be working full-time. Since 1991, part-time

Table 4.6. Indicators of Flexibility in Employment Relationships, Canada
and the United States, 1980–2000 (%)

|  | 1980 | 1990 | 2000 | Change 1990–2000 |
|---|---|---|---|---|
| *Part-time employment share* | | | | |
| Canada | 14.4 | 17.0 | 18.1 | +1.1 |
| United States | 17.5 | 17.3 | 16.2 | −1.1 |
| *Self-employment share* | | | | |
| Canada | 13.2 | 14.3 | 16.2 | +1.9 |
| United States | 7.0 | 7.3 | 6.4 | −0.9 |
| *Voluntary quit rate[1]* | | | | |
| Canada | 1.22 | 1.29 | $0.89^2$ | −0.40 |
| United States | 0.83 | 0.83 | $0.56^2$ | −0.27 |

Source: Author's calculations from *Statistics Canada, Labour Force Historical Review* (Catalogue 71-004, CD-ROM), and U.S. Department of Labor, Bureau of Labor Statistics website.
  1. Voluntary unemployed quits as proportion of labor force.
  2. 1999 data.

employment has been more common in Canada than in the United States, where the incidence of part-time employment declined through most of the 1990s (likely because of tighter labor market circumstances there). The decline in the part-time employment share in Canada since 1997 (from 19.1% in 1997 to 18.1% in 2000) reinforces the suggestion that Canada's very slack labor markets were an important factor behind the earlier growth of part-time employment.

A similar degree of "flexibility" in Canada's labor market is also visible in comparative data on self-employment in the two economies. Self-employment in Canada has increased dramatically in the 1990s (table 4.6). Self-employment accounted for more than three-quarters of all net new jobs created in Canada between 1990 and 1997, and hence the incidence of self-employment (as a share of all employment) grew from an average of about 14% during the 1980s to more than 17% by 1997.[7] In contrast, self-employment is much less common in the U.S. economy and declined slightly during the 1990s.[8] Once again, it hardly seems that a lack of entrepreneurial creativity has held back Canada's labor market during the 1990s: Canadians have amply demonstrated their willingness and their ability to create work for themselves, even when paying jobs are hard to find. The relatively low earnings that are typical of the self-employed also attest to a high degree of wage flexibility on the part of these new entrepreneurs.[9]

There is one sense in which both the Canadian and the American labor markets have demonstrated a declining flexibility during the 1990s. Presumably, a flexible labor market is one in which *employees* also possess the ability to makes changes in their work activity, including the effective ability to leave jobs that are considered unappealing or inappropriate. The best measure of this type of flexibility would be a general quit rate: that is, the proportion of workers in any given year who voluntarily leave their jobs. These data are unavailable on a consistent time series basis for the two countries. A less appealing substitute measure for which data are available is the number of unemployed persons at any given point who voluntarily left their last job. This measure captures the degree to which workers who are not happy with their present work circumstance are effectively able to leave their job, even if it means enduring a spell of unemployment.

As indicated in the bottom panel of table 4.6, the number of unemployed quits as a proportion of the total labor force has declined significantly in both Canada and the United States. This likely reflects a generally heightened sense of economic insecurity on the part of workers in both countries, as well as (in Canada's case, anyway) the tightening of eligibility requirements for unemployment insurance (according to which individuals who quit their jobs were penalized beginning in 1990 and disqualified from benefits altogether beginning in 1993).[10] Despite the more stringent regulations regarding unemployment insurance eligibility, the incidence of unemployed job-quitters remains significantly higher in Canada than in the United States (which may suggest that Canadian workers still enjoy a greater "exit option" than American workers, even if that exit implies a spell of unemployment). In both countries, however, it seems that the effective ability of workers to voluntarily leave an initial job (especially if that departure implies a period of unemployment) has declined. This suggests a certain one-sidedness to the "flexibility" of modern labor markets: employers enjoy an enhanced ability to hire labor on flexible terms and conditions, but the effective ability of employees to exit undesired jobs seems to have declined.

A high degree of geographic labor mobility is another often-discussed characteristic of a flexible labor market. Discussions of this issue often point the blame at overly generous social insurance programs, which protect workers against the economic costs of unemployment and hence reduce their incentive to move elsewhere in search of better opportunities.[11] As table 4.7 indicates, however, it turns out that the residents of hard-hit regions of Canada have actually been more likely to move elsewhere in Canada than have residents of the poorest parts of the United States been likely to relocate within U.S. borders. Table 4.7 summarizes the net inward or outward migration from those Canadian provinces or U.S. states that demonstrate extreme outcomes (whether positive or negative) according to a range of different economic criteria: unemployment rates, personal incomes, or GDP per capita.[12]

By any of the preceding criteria, Newfoundland ranks as the least opportune province on labor market grounds: it has the highest unemployment, the lowest personal income, and the lowest GDP per capita of any Canadian province. Newfoundland experienced a net outward migration between 1990 and 1997 equal to 6.4% of its initial 1990 population.

Table 4.7. Indicators Geographic Labor Mobility in Canada and the United States, Net Domestic Migration, 1990–1997

| | Province | Canada Diff. from Cda. avg. 1990 | Net migration 1990–97 | State | U.S. Diff. from U.S. avg. 1990 | Net migration 1990–97 |
|---|---|---|---|---|---|---|
| *Unemployment* | | | | | | |
| Worst | Nfld. | +8.9 pts | −6.4% | W.Virg. | +2.8 pts | +0.6% |
| Best | Ont. | −1.8 pts | −0.4% | Nebraska | −3.4 pts | +0.3% |
| *Personal income[1]* | | | | | | |
| Worst | Nfld. | −25% | −6.4% | Missis. | −33% | +2.2% |
| Best | Ont. | +10% | −0.4% | N.H. | +36% | +1.2% |
| *GDP per capital* | | | | | | |
| Worst | Nfld. | −37% | −6.4% | W.Virg. | −31% | +0.6% |
| Best | Alta. | +16% | +2.1% | Conn. | +32% | −5.8% |
| *Largest flows* | | | | | | |
| Outward | Nfld. | — | −6.4% | N.Y. | — | −8.4% |
| Inward | B.C. | — | +5.9% | Nevada | — | +29.0% |

Source: Author's calculations from *Statistics Canada, Annual Demographic Statistics, Provincial Economic Accounts,* and *Canadian Economic Observer,* and the *U.S. Statistical Abstract.*
1. Average household income for the United States

In contrast, the worst-ranked U.S. states by these same criteria (West Virginia for the unemployment rate and GDP per capita, Mississippi for personal incomes) experienced seemingly perverse net *inward* migrations during the same period. High-ranked jurisdictions in both countries also demonstrated perverse migration responses; for example, high-ranked Ontario and Connecticut both experienced net outward migration.[13] The inward migration experienced into Alberta between 1990 and 1997 was greater than the inward migration to any top-ranked U.S. state.

Migration patterns clearly cannot be explained on the basis of simple economic differentials (such as unemployment or income levels) between regions. Some U.S. states experienced larger net migration flows than any Canadian province. For example, high-income New York State lost more of its population to outward migration between 1990 and 1997 than did impoverished Newfoundland; this mostly reflects the move of affluent families to out-of-state suburban areas. Meanwhile, fast-growing Nevada experienced a larger inflow of population than did Canada's fastest-growing province, British Columbia. These results are tinged by the fact that the average U.S. state represents a smaller segment of the overall national population than does the average Canadian province, and hence migration rates are not strictly comparable between the two countries (as discussed in note 11); on average, U.S. states experienced an absolute inward or outward migration equal to 4.7% of its starting population during the 1990–1997 period, versus 2.6% for the average Canadian province.

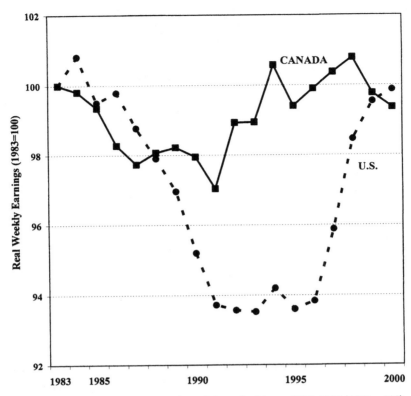

Figure 4.5. Real wage trends, Canada and the United States 1983–1998 (1983 = 100).

Nevertheless, at a minimum it seems safe to conclude that Canadians in general (and Newfoundlanders in particular) have demonstrated themselves at least as able and willing to relocate in response to economic circumstances (positive or negative) as Americans.

One final potential dimension of labor market flexibility in Canada and the United States is illustrated in figure 4.5, which portrays the evolution of real weekly earnings (deflated by changes in consumer prices) in the two countries since 1983. Real earnings declined in both countries during the 1980s and increased in both countries in the 1990s. The degree of volatility during both periods, however, was much higher in the United States; earnings there fell faster in the 1980s and increased faster in the 1990s (especially in the period since 1997, when the U.S. unemployment rate fell below 5%). On first glance, this might imply a greater degree of market responsiveness on the part of wages in the United States. It is misleading, however, to look only at cash earnings as a measure of labor market compensation; nonwage labor costs (including payroll taxes and benefits such as employer-provided health insurance) are an important and volatile component of overall labor costs.[14]

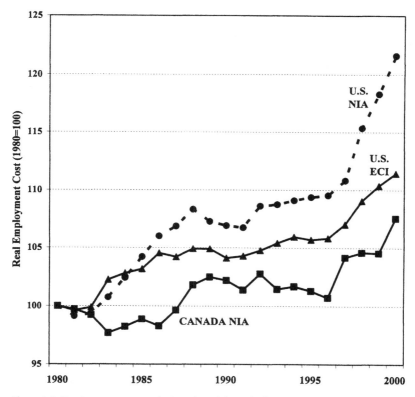

Figure 4.6. Employment cost trends, Canada and the United States, 1980–1999 (1980 = 100).

Therefore, figure 4.6 illustrates the trend since 1983 in the *total* employment cost index (labeled ECI, for private sector employers only) in the United States, after inflation. Total employment costs, in real terms, have increased slowly and steadily in the United States over the past two decades, showing little sensitivity to labor market conditions (although the apparent acceleration of employment costs since 1998 may reflect increasingly tight labor market conditions). Unfortunately, an equivalent index of total employment costs is not available for Canada. A rough equivalent can be constructed by calculating a measure of total labor income (from national income accounts data, including the cost of non-wage benefits but not counting payroll taxes) per employed worker, deflated to constant dollar terms. As indicated in figure 4.5, this measure (labeled NIA) rose in Canada in the late 1980s but remained largely stagnant during most of the 1990s. For consistency, figure 4.6 also illustrates the same NIA-derived measure for the United States; it increased more rapidly than the U.S. employment cost index.[15] If anything, these results may imply a higher degree of market responsiveness on the part of total labor compensation in Canada; employment costs grew when Canadian

Table 4.8. Regressions of Labor Income on Productivity and Unemployment, Canada and the United States, 1976–1998

|  | Levels Regressions | First-Difference Regressions |
|---|---|---|
| *Canada* | | |
| Constant | 2.959 | 0.0730 |
| Coefficient on | 0.149 | 0.813 |
| productivity | (2.675) | (3.062) |
| Coefficient on | −0.0715 | −0.0363 |
| unemployment | (3.110) | (1.889) |
| Adj. $R^2$ | .405 | .335 |
| *United States* | | |
| Constant | 2.583 | 0.0114 |
| Coefficient on | 0.129 | 1.120 |
| productivity | (2.105) | (3.939) |
| Coefficient on | −0.1200 | −0.0120 |
| unemployment | (4.124) | (0.806) |
| Adj. $R^2$ | .746 | .494 |

Source: Author's calculations from *Statistics Canada, Canadian Economic Observer*, U.S. Council of Economic Advisors, *Economic Report of the President*. All data stated in natural log terms; t-statistics in parentheses; annual data.

labor markets were tight in the late 1980s and late 1990s but were stagnant during the higher-unemployment period of the early and mid-1990s. In the United States, in contrast, employment costs (by these measures) tended to grow relatively monotonically.

To test the sensitivity of labor incomes to labor market conditions, a series of regressions was performed on the NIA-derived measures of real labor income for Canada and the United States. These regressions also include a measure of average real labor productivity,[16] to capture the extent to which higher incomes are reflecting productivity growth (as implied in the standard competitive model). Regressions were performed on both the levels of real labor compensation and their rates of annual change (both measured in natural log terms); the results, which are inconclusive, are summarized in table 4.8. In both sets of regressions, all coefficients take their expected signs and are generally significant (with the exception of the coefficient on unemployment in the first-difference regressions, which is significant only at the 10% level for Canada and not at all for the United States). In level terms, Canadian labor incomes are more sensitive to productivity growth than those in the United States, but the coefficient on the unemployment rate is smaller. In first-difference terms, the results are reversed; the coefficient on productivity is higher in the United States, while the coefficient on unemployment is higher in Canada. Both regressions fit the U.S. data better than the Canadian, perhaps indicating a greater influence of exogenous structural or institutional factors on labor incomes in Canada. The average standard deviation of the annual proportional change in this measure of real labor income is somewhat higher in the United States than in Canada (1.69 versus 1.38 over the 1976–1998 period), which may also indicate a higher level of flexibility in U.S. labor incomes. But no general case can be made on the basis of this evidence that U.S. labor incomes are consistently more sensitive to "market fundamentals" (productivity and excess supply) than are Canadian.

## 4.4 FLEXIBILITY, DEREGULATION, AND DISCIPLINE

The preceding data suggest quite strongly that Canada's labor market is not generally inflexible. Indeed, the degree of volatility in employment patterns, labor force participation, work arrangements, geographic mobility, and employment costs consistently matches or exceeds the corresponding patterns in the United States. Earnings may be slightly less flexible but are market-sensitive nonetheless. Far from being an insulated oasis of calm in a world of turmoil, Canada's labor market has reflected a fast pace of change, indeed. Canadian workers have responded to the difficult circumstances they face with new forms of flexibility: working in different industries, under different forms of employment contract, and in different parts of the country. All too often in the 1990s, Canadians simply withdrew from the world of work altogether. If "flexibility" is indeed interpreted as an ability to change and to adapt to change, it is hard to argue that Canada's labor market is inflexible or that its poor performance relative to the U.S. labor market in the 1990s reflects a shortage of flexibility.

Nevertheless, there is surely something to the one-dimensional labor market taxonomy that was illustrated in Figure 1—a taxonomy that places the United States on one end, continental Europe on the other, and Canada somewhere in between. This continuum may indeed illustrate some real pattern of structural variability in labor markets. It is just that this pattern has been misnamed with the deliberately inoffensive and seemingly neutral term "flexibility." What are the real differences that distinguish Canada's labor market from that of the United States, on one side, and from those of Europe on the other? The U.S. labor market does indeed stand out from those of other industrial economies, but not necessarily in terms of its ability to "adapt to change." Rather, there are other aspects to the functioning of the U.S. labor market that stand out as unique.

Consider the words of Alan Greenspan, chairman of the U.S. Federal Reserve Board, who described the labor market features that contributed to the success of the U.S. economy in the late 1990s as follows:

> Increases in hourly compensation . . . have continued to fall far short of what they would have been had historical relationships between compensation gains and the degree of labor market tightness held. . . . As I see it, heightened job insecurity explains a significant part of the restraint on

compensation and the consequent muted price inflation.... The continued reluctance of workers to leave their jobs to seek other employment as the labor market has tightened provides further evidence of such concern, as does the tendency toward longer labor union contracts.... The low level of work stoppages of recent years also attests to concern about job security.... The continued decline in the share of the private workforce in labor unions has likely made wages more responsive to market forces.... Owing in part to the subdued behavior of wages, profits and rates of return on capital have risen to high levels. (Greenspan 1997)

Some of the features highlighted by Greenspan reflect precisely a *lack* of flexibility in the labor market: a lack of response of compensation to tight labor markets, a reluctance of workers to leave their jobs, and the prevalence of long-term contracts that lock in employment arrangements for six or more years at a time. And so Greenspan's portrayal of the unique features of the U.S. model suggests that something other than flexibility is the key ingredient at work—or at least that "flexibility" is being interpreted once again from an unbalanced and one-sided perspective. It is, rather, a high degree of labor market *discipline* that seems to be the operative force. U.S. workers remain insecure despite a relatively low unemployment rate, and hence compensation gains—until the very end of the decade, anyway—were muted. This implies a consequent redistribution of income from labor to capital. In this environment, the monetary authority is willing to allow the unemployment rate to fall below previously acceptable levels, without fear of shrinking profit margins and/or accelerating inflation. Greenspan's story is more about *fear* than it is about flexibility—and hence this famous testimony has come to be known as Greenspan's "fear factor" hypothesis, in which he concisely described the importance of labor market discipline for his conduct of monetary policy.

Strictly speaking, the term "flexibility" need not imply any of these seemingly punitive features: a fear of economic deprivation, even in the context of a strong labor market, which leads workers to moderate their wage demands and limit their labor mobility. In applied practice, however, most proposals for flexibility-enhancing policy reforms have tended to promote something like this model of a more disciplined labor market: less social insurance and fewer income supports, available to fewer workers; reduced influence from unions and wage regulations on incomes; and a reduced degree of upward wage pressure corresponding to any given level of unemployment. With more reliance on private market forces as the dominant determinants of employment and compensation, this is also a highly *deregulated* form of labor market. In other words, the paradigm of labor market flexibility in practice can more appropriately be considered a model of labor market deregulation, in various forms.[17] Deregulation represents a shift away from attempts to deliberately regulate employment and compensation outcomes through policy interventions by governments or other nonmarket institutions and agencies. Since these interventions were typically motivated by a desire to increase wages, reduce poverty, and enhance the economic security of workers, this interventionist approach might also be labeled a "solidaristic" labor market strategy.

With the focus placed more appropriately on the varying intensity of labor market regulation, rather than on the revealed degree of flexibility (purely defined), a quantitative comparison of labor market structures and institutions in different OECD economies can be conducted as follows. Consider the following seven measures, each of which captures a dimension of efforts by governments or by nongovernmental institutions (such as trade unions) to deliberately regulate particular labor market outcomes (such as wages and income security). Unless noted, all variables are measured as of 1995 (mid-decade), for a sample of 17 OECD countries.[18] These include unemployment insurance coverage (as percentage of unemployed); trade union membership (as percentage of employed); public labor market program spending (as percentage of GDP); employee and employer payroll taxes (as percentage of average wages); an index of legislated protections against employee dismissal (measured as of the late 1990s and constructed and reported in OECD 1999); the incidence of poverty (percentage of population below OECD cutoff); and total government program spending (as percentage of GDP).

A labor market can be considered relatively deregulated, according to this approach, if unemployment insurance eligibility rules are relatively tight, if unions and collective bargaining are relatively less important in wage determination, if interventionist labor market programs are relatively modest, if payroll taxes are low, if protections against dismissal are weak, if antipoverty income supports are minimal, and if government program spending (which can be thought of as providing a form of "socialized" consumption that supplements the consumption possibilities generated through private incomes but that is not contingent on an individual's employment status) is low. In this type of labor market, therefore, the terms and conditions of employment are determined primarily through private contracts between employers and individual workers, and hence the incomes and economic prospects of workers depend primarily on what they are able to earn in the labor market (with relatively less supplementation from various forms of income supports or social consumption).

There are some ways in which a deregulated labor market might be "flexible" in the true sense of the word: for example, with less intrusive legislation governing issues such as employment security and notice of layoff, downsizing employers can clearly shed excess labor more quickly. But there are also aspects of a deregulated labor market that clearly *inhibit* flexibility in the common-sense understanding of the word. For example, in a system in which important health and pension benefits are provided largely or solely through employment contracts (rather than as a right of citizenship by the state), these programs are likely to be imperfectly portable (if at all), and this can constitute a significant barrier to workers'

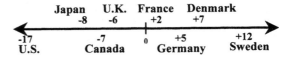

Figure 4.7. Regulation in
an international context,
selected scores,
7-component index.

mobility between employers. As in the vision of Alan Greenspan, therefore, deregulation and flexibility are not at all synonymous.

A numerical index of labor market regulation can be constructed as follows. Consistent data on each of these seven dimensions of the degree of labor market regulation are gathered for 17 OECD countries. Each data series is oriented so that a higher score reflects a higher degree of regulation. Each variable is normalized such that the unweighted mean score for the sample equals zero (and hence a positive score implies a relatively intense form of regulation and a negative score, a relatively lax one). Each variable is further normalized such that the standard deviation of each series is a constant.[19] Finally, an index of labor market regulation is calculated by averaging each country's scores over the seven indices considered.

Country-by-country scores in the seven component variables and on the overall constructed index of regulation are provided in table 4.9.[20] The positioning of selected countries according to this index is illustrated in figure 4.7. This index of regulation does indeed roughly correspond to the commonly expressed scale of "flexibility" that was portrayed simplistically in figure 4.1. The United States places far at one extreme of the scale, with what is by far the most deregulated (or "disciplined") labor market in the OECD. Several European countries (particularly the Scandinavian countries) rank at the other extreme, with tightly regulated (or "solidaristic") labor markets. The continental European countries demonstrate more moderate degrees of regulation. Canada scores somewhere between the United States and Europe—although by international standards, Canada's labor market is clearly relatively *deregulated*. In other words, while Canada's labor market is more regulated than that of the United States (i.e., is characterized by more generous social programs, stronger unions, and less poverty),[21] by the standards of the industrialized world as a whole Canada's labor market is nevertheless relatively free-wheeling.

## 4.5 REGULATION, DEMAND, AND EMPLOYMENT

The regulation index constructed in table 4.9 and depicted in figure 4.7 better accords with the international classification that implicitly underlies most presentations of the flexibility paradigm—a policy perspective that would more accurately be described as a "labor market deregulation

Table 4.9. Indices of Labor Market Regulation for Selected OECD Countries, 1995

| | UI coverage (% unempl'd)[1] | TU penetration (% employed) | Labor market programs (% GDP) | Payroll taxes (% average wages) | Dismissal protection (OECD index)[2] | Poverty (% pop'n below minimum) | Gov't program spending (% GDP) | Index of labor market regulation |
|---|---|---|---|---|---|---|---|---|
| Canada | 67 | 37 | 1.9 | 11 | 0.9 | 11.7 | 40.9 | -6.9 |
| OECD[3] | 89 | 40 | 2.9 | 23 | 1.9 | 9.3 | 37.5 | — |
| United States | 36 | 14 | 0.5 | 14 | 0.2 | 19.1 | 30.8 | -16.6 |
| Japan | 39 | 24 | 0.5 | 14 | 2.7 | 11.8 | 35.0 | -7.7 |
| Germany | 87 | 29 | 3.8 | 34 | 2.8 | 5.9 | 46.6 | 2.2 |
| France | 76 | 9 | 3.1 | 42 | 2.3 | 7.5 | 50.8 | 4.5 |
| Italy | na[4] | 44 | 2.0 | 39 | 2.8 | 6.5 | 41.8 | 3.7 |
| United Kingdom | 94 | 33 | 1.8 | 17 | 0.8 | 13.5 | 41.4 | -6.2 |
| Australia | 101 | 35 | 2.1 | 2 | 1.0 | 12.9 | 33.9 | -7.9 |
| Belgium | 138 | 52 | 4.2 | 36 | 1.5 | 5.5 | 45.1 | 6.4 |
| Denmark | 100 | 80 | 6.6 | 10 | 1.6 | 7.5 | 55.8 | 6.7 |
| Finland | 108 | 79 | 5.5 | 26 | 2.1 | 6.2 | 56.8 | 9.5 |
| Ireland | 149 | 49 | 4.3 | 16 | 1.6 | 11.1 | 33.8 | 0.4 |
| Netherlands | 125 | 26 | 4.8 | 37 | 3.1 | 6.7 | 46.4 | 7.4 |
| New Zealand | 127 | 24 | 1.9 | 0 | 1.7 | 9.2 | 37.2 | -4.5 |
| Norway | 94 | 58 | 2.1 | 18 | 2.4 | 6.6 | 48.3 | 2.6 |
| Spain | 40 | 19 | 2.8 | 29 | 2.6 | 10.4 | 40.2 | -2.9 |
| Sweden | 109 | 91 | 4.5 | 29 | 2.8 | 6.7 | 62.9 | 11.8 |

Source: Author's calculations from OECD Economic Outlook (column 7); OECD Employment Outlook (June 1999) (column 5); OECD Tax and Benefit Position of Workers (column 4), OECD Country Survey: Ireland (1997) (column 1); United Nations Development Program, Human Development Report (columns 2, 3, and 6).

1. Includes recipients of assistance and guaranteed income as well as unemployment insurance.
2. Index calculated for late 1990s.
3. Unweighted averages.
4. Data unavailable; regulation index calculated on basis of 5 components for Italy.

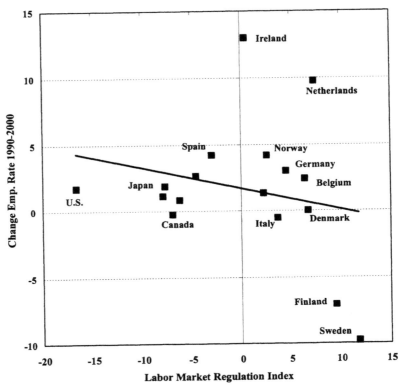

Figure 4.8. Labor market regulation and employment, selected OECD countries, 1990s.

paradigm." While this taxonomy seems to summarize international differences in the intensity of interventionist labor market regulations, it does not shed much light on international differences in labor market performance during the 1990s. There is no significant correlation between individual country scores on the regulation index and the change in their respective employment rates during the 1990s. As illustrated in figure 4.8, some countries with deregulated labor markets enjoyed relatively strong employment outcomes in the 1990s (including notably the United States), but so did several countries with relatively regulated labor markets (including Ireland, the Netherlands, and Norway).[22] Similarly, some countries with deregulated labor markets experienced declining employment rates in the 1990s (including Canada, Australia, and the United Kingdom), as did other countries with regulated labor markets (such as Italy and Germany). A regression of the change in employment rate on the index of labor market regulation for the 17 OECD countries considered produces a negative but statistically insignificant coefficient; if two outlier countries (Sweden and Finland) are excluded,[23] a regression of employment rate

Table 4.10. Aggregate Demand Indicators, 1990–2000

|  | Average real short-run interest rate (%) | Change gov't program spending (% GDP) | Change gov't revenue (% GDP) | Average output gap[1] (% GDP) | Avg. ann. growth real per capita GDP (%) |
|---|---|---|---|---|---|
| Canada | 4.5 | −6.1 | +1.0 | −1.5 | 1.7 |
| United States | 3.2 | −2.9 | +2.3 | −0.2 | 2.2 |
| Japan | 2.3 | +6.1 | −3.0 | +0.4 | 1.1 |
| European Union | 3.92 | −1.9 | +2.0 | −0.8 | 1.3 |
| OECD | n.a. | −0.7 | +1.7 | −0.4 | 1.7 |

Source: Author's calculations from OECD *Economic Outlook*, OECD *National Income Accounts*. Difference between actual output and potential as share of potential output.
1. Euro area only.

changes on labor market regulation produces a *positive* (but near-zero) coefficient.

The one-dimensional model of comparative labor market performance that informs the argument for deregulation needs to be supplemented, therefore, with additional information. In the Canadian context, it was suggested earlier that the uniquely difficult aggregate demand circumstances that were experienced during most of the 1990s might have been important in explaining the emergence of an "employment gap" between Canada and the United States—a gap that did not reveal itself until the 1990s (long after the interventionist labor market reforms of the 1970s). Perhaps a consideration of aggregate demand circumstances in various OECD countries would help to provide a better explanation of international differences in employment performance.

A variety of indicators of aggregate demand conditions are reported in table 4.10 for Canada, the United States, Japan, Europe, and the OECD as a whole. The table lists indicators of monetary policy (average short-term real interest rates) and fiscal policy (the change in all-government program spending as a share of GDP between 1990 and 2000 and the change in total government revenues as a share of GDP),[24] along with two general indicators of macroeconomic performance (the average gap between actual and potential output and the average annual growth in real per capita GDP). Table 4.10 reveals the uniquely negative aggregate demand conditions experienced by Canada in the 1990s. Canada's average output gap was significantly more negative than those for other OECD countries, and Canada's macroeconomic policy stance was significantly more contractionary than was experienced in the OECD as a whole. Of particular note, short-term real interest rates were especially high in Canada (especially earlier in the 1990s), and the decline in government program spending was severe.

Many continental European economies also experienced a period of sustained contractionary macroeconomic conditions during much of the

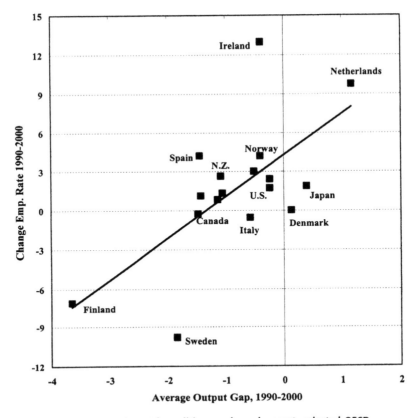

Figure 4.9. Aggregate demand conditions and employment, selected OECD countries, 1990s.

1990s. The transition to a common currency regime obviously impacted the macroeconomic environment faced by many of these countries, requiring tighter monetary and fiscal policy than would otherwise have been expected. As expected, the United States enjoyed relatively strong aggregate demand conditions during the 1990s. In particular, next to Japan, the United States experienced by far the most expansionary monetary policy regime in the whole OECD.

It turns out that the state of aggregate demand conditions explains far more of the international differences in employment performance during the 1990s than do cross-country differences in regulatory structures and institutions. As indicated in figure 4.9, there is a relatively strong positive relationship between the state of aggregate demand (symbolized here by the average output gap during the 1990–2000 period) and the change in a country's employment rate. A regression of the change in the employment rate on the average output gap for the same 17 countries considered earlier produces a highly significant positive coefficient—one that is not dependent on the inclusion of the two outlying countries (Sweden and Finland). The output gap alone explains 42% of the variation in employment rate performance, while differences in labor market regulation explain 5% (and without producing a significant coefficient on the regulation index). Aggregate demand obviously does not tell the whole story of an economy's employment performance—for example, the Netherlands and Germany experienced roughly equivalent macroeconomic conditions during the 1990s, but the Netherlands generated a large increase in the employment rate, while Germany experienced a decline—but it tells a lot. In particular, aggregate demand conditions seem considerably and consistently more important as an explanation of comparative labor market outcomes across countries in the 1990s than do cross-national differences in labor market institutions.

## 4.6 THINKING IN TWO DIMENSIONS

Canada experienced relatively negative labor market outcomes through most of the 1990s, even though it demonstrates a relatively deregulated labor market. Canada's macroeconomic circumstances during that decade, however, were uniquely poor. In terms of Canada-U.S. comparisons, aggregate demand conditions were far more different across the two countries in the 1990s than were regulatory structures. In an international context, Canada is relatively similar to the United States in labor market regulation (both countries have relatively deregulated labor markets), but it was strongly dissimilar in terms of macroeconomic conditions through most of the decade (U.S. conditions were expansionary, while Canada's were contractionary). At a bare minimum, then, this would suggest that an analysis of aggregate demand conditions should be incorporated into the core of international labor market comparisons—which in recent years have focused unidimensionally on comparative regulatory structures.

One possible conceptual model for considering these two sources of difference in international labor market performance is presented in table 4.11.[25] Countries can experience strong or weak aggregate demand

Table 4.11. Thinking in Two Dimensions, Regulation, Demand, and Labor Market Outcomes

| Intensity of Regulation<br>Intensity of Demand | Weaker<br>Regulation | Stronger<br>Regulation |
|---|---|---|
| Weaker demand | Poor employment growth, poor distributional outcomes (Canada?) | Poor employment growth, better distributional outcomes (Sweden?) |
| Stronger demand | Strong employment growth, poor distributional outcomes (U.S.?) | Strong employment growth, better distributional outcomes (Norway?) |

conditions in the context of a regulated or deregulated labor market. This generates a range of potential outcomes, as evidenced in the variety of labor market experiences that were visible across the OECD economies in the 1990s. Demand conditions are linked fairly predictably to employment outcomes. The intensity of labor market regulation, however, does not seem to be a reliable predictor of employment performance; the impact of varying degrees of labor market regulation may be visible instead in variables such as income distribution or the incidence of poverty. A relatively deregulated labor market tends to be marked by greater degrees of inequality and poverty in income distribution; this can occur within the context of relatively strong labor markets (such as the United States enjoyed through most of the decade) or relatively weak ones (such as those experienced in Canada). More aggressively regulated labor markets experience less extreme patterns of income distribution; once again, this can occur against a backdrop of stronger or weaker labor markets, with, say, Norway and Sweden providing polar cases of this range of possibilities in the 1990s.

There were not many countries that qualified for inclusion in the lower-right quadrant of table 4.11 (where strong demand conditions are combined with an interventionist regulatory stance) during the 1990s, but there are some: Norway, the Netherlands, and, to a lesser extent, Ireland, Denmark, and Austria. At any rate, the possibility of combining intense labor market regulation with strong demand conditions in order to produce the appealing combination of employment opportunity and social equality clearly cannot be ruled out of hand entirely. Given that many of the countries with relatively regulated labor markets experienced sluggish macroeconomic conditions through much of the decade largely because of a historic one-time event—the transition to a common European currency—this "best of both worlds" combination may prove to be more feasible in coming years. In many ways, meanwhile, Canada experienced the "worst of both worlds" during the 1990s: weak macroeconomic conditions combined with a movement away from interventionist labor and social policies. This combination produced both falling employment and rising inequality.

One central difficulty with the model sketched out in table 4.11 is that the two axes of the grid are clearly not mutually independent. The nature of labor market regulation has implications for macroeconomic functioning, through a range of different causal mechanisms. The direction of these effects is complex and indeterminate, however. There are ways in which labor market deregulation might strengthen aggregate demand conditions and hence generate employment, and there are channels through which it might weaken demand-side conditions. The net outcome is unclear. The case is commonly and implicitly made that since one large country with a deregulated labor market (namely the United States) enjoyed relatively strong demand conditions during the better part of one decade, there must be a positive and monotonic relationship between

Table 4.12. Deregulation and Demand, Interdependence and Indeterminacy

| Deregulation Initiative | Likely Effect | Impact on Demand and Employment |
| --- | --- | --- |
| Restrict union activity | Reduce wages | Increase private investment |
| Reduce minimum wages | | Increase export demand |
| Erode pay equity provisions | | Decrease private consumption |
| Reduce income support and unemployment insurance | Reduce incomes for nonemployed | Decrease private consumption |
| | Increase "incentive" to work; reduce wages | Increase private investment |
| | | Decrease private consumption |
| | Reduce labor force participation | Reduce unemployment rate |
| | | Decrease private consumption |
| | Lower payroll taxes | Increase private consumption |
| | | Decrease public consumption |
| | | Substitute labor for capital |
| Generally restrain wage pressures | "Permits" more monetary easing | Increase demand of all forms |

labor market deregulation and employment growth. A review of the broader international experience, however, reveals that this conclusion is clearly premature.

Some of the competing channels of causation that link the intensity of labor market regulation to the intensity of aggregate demand conditions are summarized in table 4.12.[26] One key outcome of labor market deregulation is likely to be the reduction of wage pressures (holding other factors, such as the level of unemployment or productivity growth, constant). Lower wages may stimulate more private investment spending and export demand (thanks to enhanced profitability and cost competitiveness, respectively), but they tend to reduce domestic consumption spending by workers. Scaling back the generosity of income support programs has a variety of effects. Consumption spending by those who relied on such programs declines. Many marginal workers may leave the labor force altogether; while this is "useful" in reducing the official unemployment rate, it probably contributes further to the decline in personal incomes and hence consumption. To the extent that generous income support programs exert a positive influence on wage levels, scaling them back reduces wage pressures (with the same indeterminate demand effects noted earlier). If savings from the reduction of income security programs are passed on in the form of tax reductions (such as lower premiums for unemployment insurance), then the personal spending of employed workers might increase, while other public programs (which may have been funded in part from payroll taxes, as is the case in many OECD countries) may be further cut back. Lower payroll taxes may encourage the substitution of labor for capital by private employers, thus creating some new jobs (although possibly with negative implications for productivity).

Perhaps the most powerful link between labor market regulation and aggregate demand conditions is one that operates through a policy response, rather than through an automatic market mechanism. If the central bank conducts monetary policy to deliberately restrain the growth of wages and other employment costs (on the assumption that these costs are the core driving force behind inflation), then monetary policy may shift to a more accommodating stance in the wake of labor market deregulation. The remarks of Alan Greenspan quoted earlier suggest that this has clearly occurred in the United States. To the extent that easy monetary policy was important to the U.S. expansion of the 1990s (and this extent seems considerable), and to the extent that monetary easing was "permitted" by the fact that deregulated U.S. labor markets showed little signs of upward wage pressure (at least until the end of the decade) even at very low unemployment rates, then labor market deregulation has clearly had powerful stimulative effects on demand and employment in the United States.

The policy channel linking monetary policy and labor market structures in the United States probably sheds more light on the apparent success of the U.S. economy during the 1990s than does the common claim that the U.S. labor market is more "flexible" and hence somehow more "efficient." U.S. monetary authorities were willing to maintain an easy policy stance as long as U.S. workers were sufficiently disciplined and wage growth was constrained, even as labor markets tightened. This is a rather different story, indeed, from the implicit assumption that a labor market free of government interference is one that attains a "better match" between supply and demand.[27] Meanwhile, the subsequent difficulties of the U.S. economy, in the wake of decline of stock market values beginning in 2000, indicate that even a free-wheeling, business-friendly structural environment provides no guarantee of sustained economic momentum and casts further doubt on the universal relevance of the U.S. model of labor market deregulation.

## 4.7 CONCLUSION

Canada's labor market performed badly in the 1990s, compared both to the set of industrialized countries and to its main comparator, the United States. This prompted numerous calls for structural reforms to labor markets, in hopes of making Canada's labor market more "flexible" and reducing long-run unemployment. Much evidence suggests, however, that Canada's labor market is not "inflexible" in the common sense of being able to change and to adapt to change. Indeed, according to many indicators, Canada's labor market has demonstrated a pace and extent of change that matches or exceeds that experienced in the United States. Where Canada differs from the United States in the sense implied by advocates of structural labor market reforms is not in its degree of "flexibility" so much as in its degree of *regulation*. Canada's labor

market is indeed more regulated than that of the United States, although by international standards Canada's labor market is relatively
deregulated.

There is no correlation, however, between the intensity of labor market
regulation and the employment performance of different countries during
the 1990s; aggregate demand conditions are a more powerful predictor
of employment performance than are comparative regulatory structures.
And Canada's relative labor market decline in the 1990s occurred precisely
during a time when far-reaching deregulatory policy initiatives were being
implemented, in line with the policy prescriptions of the OECD's *Jobs
Study*. It is hard to argue that these "flexibility-enhancing" initiatives have
made Canada's labor market more efficient or, indeed, flexible. Using a
two-dimensional framework for comparing labor market performance
across countries, in which both regulatory and macroeconomic factors are
taken into consideration, we can better understand the fact that labor
deregulation did not translate into improved labor market performance in
Canada (given the negative demand-side conditions that prevailed there
for most of the decade). Unfortunately, Canada's labor market experienced
the "worst of both worlds" during the 1990s: weak macroeconomic conditions and a movement away from interventionist labor and social policies. This combination produced both falling employment and rising
inequality.

*Acknowledgments* The author thanks David Howell, Tim Sargent, Andrew Sharpe,
and members of the Working Group on Labour Market Regulation and Deregulation for their helpful comments. An earlier version of this essay was published in
*Canadian Public Policy* 26 (Supp.), July 2000.

## Notes

1. Interestingly, and not coincidentally, advocates of proflexibility labor market
reforms are typically more concerned with the failure of wages to fall during times
of excess supply, than with the failure of wages to *rise* when demand conditions
are stronger. For example, Brodsky (1994) defines one characteristic of flexibility as
the ability to avoid wage increases that are greater than productivity increases; he
doesn't seem concerned with the possibility that wage increases might lag behind
productivity increases. This rather one-sided view of flexibility is not uncommon
in statements of the flexibility paradigm.

2. Of course, since Canada's population is growing 50% faster than that of the
OECD as a whole, Canada needs a higher-than-average rate of job creation simply
to maintain a given labor market supply-demand balance.

3. For representative presentations of this argument see Globe and Mail (1997)
and Cooper (1999).

4. See, for example, Tal (1999).

5. The levels regressions compare the natural log of employment to the
natural log of GDP; the first difference regressions compare changes in the two
variables.

6. The relative sensitivity of Canadian labor force participation is consistent with the findings of Elmeskov and Pichelman (1993).

7. Like part-time employment, self-employment has also declined in relative terms in Canada since 1997 as the ability of workers to find regular paid work in Canada's labor market has substantially improved.

8. Definitional issues once again complicate the comparison between Canada and the United States as illustrated in figure 4.6. Canadian statistics use a somewhat broader definition of self-employment (which includes incorporated working owners) than is the case in the United States, and this accounts for approximately one-third of the difference between the apparent self-employment rates in the two countries. See Manser and Picot (1998).

9. Almost 90% of the growth in self-employment in Canada during the 1990s consisted of self-employed individuals working on their own account (that is, with no employees). The average income of own-account self-employed in 1995 (*excluding* those with negative earnings) was just $22,900, roughly two-thirds the average earnings of paid employees. See Statistics Canada (1997): 10, 25.

10. In neither country can the decline in the proportion of unemployed job quitters be attributed to a decline in the duration of unemployment; if the average duration of unemployment were reduced, then a given incidence of voluntary job quitting would produce a lower average incidence of unemployed quits (simply because each individual who quit his or her job would not have to wait as long before starting another one). In the United States, although the duration of unemployment was no lower in 1999 than in 1976, the incidence of unemployed quits fell by almost half during the same time; in Canada, the duration of unemployment increased through most of the period covered.

11. See Coulombe (1997) for a recent version of this argument.

12. The data summarized in table 4.7 are not bilateral flows from the worst to the best jurisdiction in each instance; they indicate, rather, the total net outward flow (to all domestic destinations) from the worst jurisdiction, and the total net inward flow (again from all domestic sources) to the best. It should be noted that by virtue of the fact that Canada is divided into only 10 provincial jurisdictions, while the United States is divided into 50 states, for a given degree of *regional* mobility, statistics for Canada will reflect a lower level of *interprovincial* migration than comparable statistics will reveal for U.S. interstate migration, simply because a given relocation has a greater probability of crossing a jurisdictional boundary in the United States. For this reason, the data in table 4.7 may understate the true relative geographic mobility of Canadians.

13. Table 4.7 reports data on net interprovincial and interstate migration only. Including international immigration, Ontario experienced a net inward migration during the period.

14. Depending on design, payroll taxes in particular can demonstrate a perverse cyclical pattern; for example, Canada's unemployment insurance premiums rose steeply during the early 1990s to help fund the escalating recession-induced costs of the program.

15. This may be a result of the larger-than-average income gains enjoyed by U.S. managers and other professionals whose salaries are not considered in the calculation of the ECI.

16. The measure chosen is real GDP per employed worker; since the labor income measure is also stated in per-employee terms, this approach abstracts from the need to estimate hours worked. According to this measure, real productivity

has grown faster in the United States than in Canada during the time period covered, although this is largely the result of a growing gap between the two countries in average hours of work.

17. Some more careful presentations of the flexibility paradigm have tried to adopt more "neutral" characterizations of the term. See Brodsky (1994) on the evolution of competing definitions of labor market "flexibility." Standing (1997) denies that the flexibility paradigm reflects an agenda for deregulation, arguing instead that powerful mechanisms of market regulation serve to control labor market outcomes even after the retrenchment of activist public policy; this essay, however, adopts the view that greater reliance on private market forces is indeed equivalent to a process of deregulation, conventionally defined.

18. The labor market regulation index is constructed for 1995, which is approximately the midpoint of the period covered by the employment data portrayed in table 4.1; we assume that the impact of these labor market institutions on labor market functioning is felt in a gradual, long-term manner.

19. This second normalization (adjusting each series so that its standard deviation equals 10) is necessary to ensure that each variable carries equal weight in the calculation of the final index of regulation; otherwise, variables which demonstrated a greater degree of variability about the mean would be effectively weighted more heavily.

20. Buchele and Christiansen (1999) utilize a very different methodology, relying on factor analysis techniques to construct a similar index of labor market structures in OECD countries; it is interesting to note that the relative rankings produced by the two approaches are roughly similar, suggesting a certain robustness.

21. For all of these reasons, the Canadian labor market may consequently demonstrate less wage flexibility than that in the United States—which presumably was a large part of the motivation for these wage-regulating initiatives.

22. Figure 4.8 plots the index of labor market regulation against the change during the 1990s in the employment rate; a similar picture is attained if the unemployment rate is used instead of the employment rate.

23. Finland and Sweden both experienced severe exchange rate and interest rate shocks early in the period covered by this analysis, as a result of the breakdown of the European exchange rate mechanism; it seems imprudent to attach too much broader significance to the poor employment performance that followed these shocks, since that performance is at least somewhat unrelated to the highly regulated labor market structures of these two economies.

24. Changes in taxes and program spending are reported separately because of the possibility that a given change in each may have differing aggregate demand effects. Government debt service payments are not reported because of what are generally considered to be their weak demand-side effects.

25. Palley (1998) suggests a similar approach.

26. Any initial impacts of deregulation on employment, positive or negative, are likely to be amplified through subsequent macroeconomic repercussions. In other words, a policy initiative that initially increases (decreases) employment will produce further increases (decreases) in demand and hence employment as a result of the subsequent changes in consumer spending and other variables resulting from the initial effect.

27. Note also that the whole chain of causation takes as given a certain starting view on the part of monetary authorities, namely that growing wages in a tight

labor market inevitably cause inflation, which must be prevented through monetary intervention to reintroduce desired slack into labor markets. If central bankers possessed a different view regarding the causes and consequences of inflation, and if other mechanisms (such as forms of centralized wage bargaining) were in place to regulate the behavior of employment costs in a low-unemployment environment, then the positive relationship between deregulation and stimulative monetary policy would be broken.

## References

Brodsky, Melvin M. 1994. "Labor Market Flexibility: A Changing International Perspective." *Monthly Labor Review* 119(11) (November): 53–60.

Buchele, Robert, and Jens Christiansen. 1999. "Labor Relations and Productivity Growth in Advanced Capitalist Economies." *Review of Radical Political Economics* 31(1) (Winter): 87–110.

Cooper, Sherry S. 1999. "Vibrant U.S. Economy Points Way for Canada." *National Post*, January 17, p. C7.

Coulombe, Serge. 1997. "Regional Disparities in Canada: Characterization, Trends and Lessons for Economic Policy." Industry Canada, Ottawa. Working Paper No. 18, November.

Elmeskov, J., and K. Pichelman. 1993. "Unemployment and Labour Force Participation: Trends and Cycles." Working Paper No. 130. Paris: OECD Economics Department.

Globe and Mail. 1997. "A Frontal Assault on Unemployment." Five-part series of editorials, September 8–17, various issues.

Greenspan, Alan. 1997. Testimony before the Committee on the Budget, United States Senate, January 21.

Kuhn, Peter. 1997. "Canada and the 'OECD Hypothesis': Does Labour Market Inflexibility Explain Canada's High Level of Unemployment?" Working Paper No. 10, Canadian International Labour Network, McMaster University.

Manser, Marilyn E., and Garnett Picot. 1998. "The Role of Self-Employment in Job Creation in Canada and the United States." Mimeograph, Statistics Canada, November.

Organization for Economic Cooperation and Development (OECD). 1994. *OECD Jobs Study: Facts, Analysis, Strategies.* Paris: OECD.

———. 1996. "Implementing the OECD Jobs Strategy." *OECD Economic Surveys, 1995–96, Canada.* Paris: OECD.

———. 1999. "Employment Protection and Labour Market Performance." *OECD Employment Outlook* (June): 57.

———. 2001. "OECD Economic Surveys: Canada." Paris: OECD.

Palley, Thomas I. 1998. "Restoring Prosperity: Why the U.S. Model Is Not the Answer for the United State or Europe" *Journal of Post Keynesian Economics* 20(3) (Spring): 337–353.

Riddell, W. Craig, and Andrew Sharpe, eds. 1998. "The Canada-U.S. Employment Rate Gap: An Introduction and Overview." *Canadian Public Policy* 24, Supp. (February): 1–37.

Standing, Guy. 1997. "Globalization, Labour Flexibility and Insecurity: The Era of Market Regulation." *European Journal of Industrial Relations* 3(1): 7–37.

Stanford, Jim. 1995. "Bending Over Backwards: Is Canada's Labour Market Really Inflexible?" *Canadian Business Economics* 4(1) (Fall): 70–87.

Statistics Canada. 1997. "The Self-Employed" *Labour Force Update* (Autumn): 7–57.

Sunter, D. 1998. "Canada–U.S. Labour Market Comparison." *Canadian Economic Observer* (December): 3.1–3.18.

Tal, Benjamin. 1999. *Accounting for the Widening in the U.S.–Canada Income Gap.* Toronto: Canadian Imperial Bank of Commerce, June.

# 5

## Is the OECD Jobs Strategy behind U.S. and British Employment and Unemployment Success in the 1990s?

JOHN SCHMITT
JONATHAN WADSWORTH

### 5.1 INTRODUCTION

The most important theme of the Organization for Economic Cooperation and Development's (OECD) *Jobs Study* (1994a, 1994b), and of the substantial body of work that it subsequently inspired, was the need for labor market "flexibility."[1] In the *Jobs Study*, the OECD urged member countries to reform unemployment benefit systems so as to ensure that they did not "impinge" on the functioning of labor markets; to modify employment security provisions that "inhibit[ed]" employment expansion; to eliminate "impediments to, and restrictions on, the creation and expansion of enterprises"; to increase "flexibility" of working-time regulations; and, most important, to take action toward making "wage and labour costs more flexible by removing restrictions that prevent wages from reflecting local conditions and individual skill levels, in particular of younger workers" (OECD 1994a: 43). Like the OECD, the International Monetary Fund (IMF) has strongly promoted labor market deregulation as the cure for high unemployment (IMF 1999, 2003).

As part of the effort to sell the flexibility prescription, the OECD-IMF orthodoxy has implicitly, and sometimes explicitly, held up the United States and, to a lesser degree, its closest European counterpart, the United Kingdom, as models of labor market flexibility. Indeed, through most of the second half of the 1990s, both countries enjoyed low unemployment and high employment rates relative to most of the rest of the OECD, accompanied, it should be stressed, by the highest levels of income inequality and poverty seen in fifty years. In the standard account, U.S. and British flexibility made this employment performance possible. Key aspects of that flexibility included weak employment protection legislation; relatively low and declining union power; low levels of, and, in the case of the United States, short-lived, unemployment benefits; a low minimum wage floor; and extensive opportunities for employment at relatively low wages.

This chapter seeks to investigate the extent to which the OECD's particular logic of flexibility, which underpinned its influential *Job Study*, can actually explain the overall labor market performance of the United States and the United Kingdom during the past decade. We focus on a central implication of the OECD-IMF orthodoxy—that greater labor market flexibility should be associated with lower unemployment and higher employment of traditionally marginalized workers, including the less-skilled, particularly young workers, and those with lower levels of formal education. The reasoning behind the prediction is straightforward. Economic institutions such as the legal minimum wage, unemployment benefit programs, and labor unions create wage floors that raise the costs of employment, with particularly negative consequences for the demand for lower-productivity workers. Flexible systems, at least as defined by the OECD, by contrast, lower the relative costs of hiring less-skilled workers, pricing them back into jobs.

In what follows, we exploit two sources of variation in flexibility in order to measure the impact on employment and unemployment of marginalized workers over the 1990s. The first source of variation is strong institutional differences across OECD economies at the end of the 1990s, which yield large differences in "flexibility," at least as perceived by the OECD. Our approach here is to compare the "flexible" U.S. and British economies with those in other more "rigid" economies, especially France and Germany, two large economies that the OECD perceives to be particularly inflexible. To the extent that flexibility is important, the absolute, and especially the relative, employment opportunities for less-skilled workers should have been noticeably better in the United States and the United Kingdom than in other OECD economies in the same period. The second source of variation in flexibility is within the United Kingdom over time. During the 1980s, Britain implemented substantial labor market reforms, and the country found itself largely in a transitional state from more "rigid" institutions in the 1970s to the significantly more flexible arrangement that prevailed in the 1990s (see, among others, Blanchflower and Freeman, 1994; Gregg and Wadsworth, 2000; Schmitt, 1995; and Dickens, Gregg, and Wadsworth, 2000). To the extent that "flexibility" is important to Britain's recent economic performance, the labor market experience of the less skilled should show improvement between the 1980s and the 1990s.[2]

To preview our results, our principal findings challenge this key implication of the orthodox view. The international data for the end of the 1990s, as well as the data for Britain in the 1980s and 1990s, consistently demonstrate that marginal workers in the "flexible" United States and United Kingdom fare no better, and frequently far worse, than their counterparts in most of the rest of the OECD. None of the evidence we present can definitively reject the flexibility hypothesis, since other factors[3] could also be at play, and our ability to control for them is limited by the nature of the data we present. Nevertheless, the systematic nature of our results, over a wide range of types of workers, across all the major economies of the OECD, raises serious questions about the usefulness of OECD-IMF notions of flexibility as a basis for economic policy. At a minimum, the data suggest that "flexibility" is neither a necessary nor a sufficient condition for improving the labor market opportunities for marginal workers and that different economic systems as practiced in other countries seem perfectly capable of producing the same, if not better, labor market outcomes.[4]

The rest of the chapter is organized as follows. The next section briefly reviews the basic institutions of the U.S. and British labor markets and relates this basic structure to the OECD's specific recommendations for the two countries. The third section implements our first simple test of the importance of flexibility for overall performance, by comparing the experience of less-skilled workers in the United States and the United Kingdom with similar workers in the rest of the OECD. The fourth section compares the economic circumstances of less-skilled workers in the flexible United Kingdom of the 1990s with those that faced less-skilled workers in the more rigid Britain of the 1980s. The final section concludes with a discussion of the implications of our findings for future labor market policy in the OECD countries.

## 5.2 THE UNITED STATES AND THE UNITED KINGDOM AS OECD IDEALS

By the second half of the 1990s, the United States and the United Kingdom stood as nearly ideal examples of the OECD's version of labor market flexibility.[5] The United States, in particular, appeared to embody almost all of the organization's criteria for flexibility. In the original *Jobs Study*, for example, the OECD offered seven recommendations for policy changes in the United States, the fewest number of recommendations directed at any of the 25 countries studied (OECD 1999: 182–183).[6] Moreover, an examination of the OECD's particular recommendations suggests that the organization's principal concerns in the United States were not, as was overwhelmingly the case elsewhere, with reducing the role of the government in the economy. The OECD instead argued for changes to the U.S. educational system (three of the recommendations); the *expansion* of the Earned Income Tax Credit (EITC); and the *expansion* of eligibility for unemployment insurance. Only two of the recommendations reflected worries about institutional rigidities: the OECD's support for "welfare reform," which was under debate at that time in the United States, and a recommendation to reform social assistance programs for the disabled in order to reduce work disincentives.[7] On balance, the OECD believed that in the United States, "policy settings appear to be generally effective at creating a dynamic and flexible economy" (OECD 1996d: 74). The OECD's lack of concern about flexibility in the United States was such that by the time the group issued a second set of recommendations to the United States in 1999, full implementation of the reforms would, in practice, most likely have led to more, not less, government intervention in the U.S. economy. In addition to repeating earlier unimplemented recommendations, the 1999 recommendations urged the United States to increase access to training, child care, and health insurance for the poor.

By the end of the 1990s, the OECD also had a favorable opinion of the British economy, largely in response to the successful implementation from the early 1980s on of broad measures to increase labor market flexibility. According to the OECD (1996c): "By the mid-1990s, most of the priority areas for reform had been addressed" (81), and "[w]ithin this broad orientation, significant reforms ha[d] been implemented to improve the efficiency of markets, as well as to enhance the skill, knowledge base and innovative capacity of the economy" (81). The *Jobs Study* made only 10 recommendations with respect to the British economy, the third lowest number of recommendations after the United States and Australia (9) (OECD 1999a: 182–183). The recommendations focused on improving the "labor force skills and competences" of the British workforce, a suggestion that was largely ignored, with the British government's emphasis instead placed on improving the skills of the future workforce by targeting education in schools; increasing the efficiency of Active Labor Market Policies (ALMPs), which became the main focus of labor market policy under the Labor government elected in 1997; and reforming the unemployment insurance and related benefit system, which the OECD recognized, in any event, was already "basically sound." In short, by the end of the 1990s, the British economy appeared to be substantially in line with the OECD's prescription for flexibility.[8]

Figures 5.1 and 5.2 show that by the year 2000, the United States and the United Kingdom had indeed among the lowest levels of unemployment and the highest levels of employment in the OECD.[9] Four countries with significant interventionist traditions, however, had lower unemployment rates than the United States (4.0) in 2000, namely the Netherlands (2.8%), Switzerland (3.0%), Norway (3.5%), and Austria (3.7%). The United Kingdom (5.5%), along with Ireland (4.2%), Portugal (4.2%), Denmark (4.2%), and Japan (4.7%), did not trail far behind. In the same year, almost three-fourths (74.1%) of the working-age population of the United States was employed. Only Switzerland (79.6%), Norway (77.8%), Denmark (76.4%), and Sweden (74.2%) had higher rates (see figure 5.2). In the United Kingdom, 72.4% of the working-age population was at work, just behind the Netherlands (72.9%). Remarkably, especially after the British experience of the early 1980s and early 1990s, both the United States and the United Kingdom managed to achieve low unemployment and high employment levels without igniting inflation (see table 5.1).[10] Again, the absence of noticeable inflationary pressure was also a feature of the other

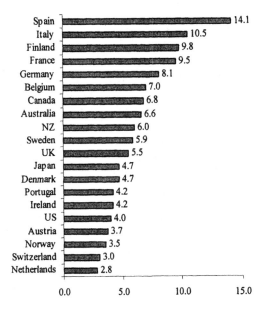

Figure 5.1. Standardized unemployment rate, 2000 (%). Source: OECD, *Employment Outlook* (June 2001), table A. Figure for Switzerland refers to 1999.

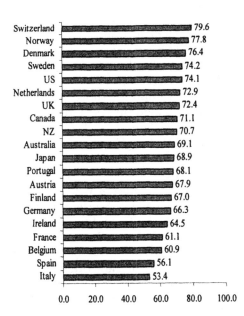

Figure 5.2. Employment-to-population rate, 2000 (%). Source: OECD, *Employment Outlook* (June 2001), table B.

Table 5.1. Macroeconomic Performance, 1990s

|  | United States | United Kingdom |
|---|---|---|
| Business cycle (year) |  |  |
| Peak, early 1990s | 1989 | 1990 |
| Trough, 1990s | 1992 | 1993 |
| Peak, late 1990s | 2000 | 2000 |
| Annual growth real GDP (%) |  |  |
| Peak to peak | 3.1 | 2.2 |
| Peak to peak, per capita | 2.1 | 1.9 |
| Unemployment rate (%) |  |  |
| Low, early peak | 5.3 | 6.9 |
| High, trough | 7.5 | 10.6 |
| Low, late peak | 4.0 | 5.3 |
| Average, peak to peak | 5.6 | 7.9 |
| Employment-to-population rate (%) |  |  |
| Low, early peak | 72.5 | 72.5 |
| High, trough | 71.0 | 68.4 |
| Low, late peak | 74.1 | 72.4 |
| Annual inflation rate (%) |  |  |
| Low, early peak | 4.8 | 10.4 |
| High, trough | 3.0 | 1.3 |
| Low, late peak | 3.4 | 3.1 |
| Average, peak to peak | 3.2 | 3.6 |

Sources and notes:
Business cycles defined by high and low annual unemployment rates.
GDP: United States billions of chained 1996 dollars; Bureau of Economic Analysis, http://www.bea.doc.gov, NIPA, table 1.10, accessed August 21, 2001.
Population: United States: ERP (February 2001), table B-34, p. 315.
Unemployment: United States: Bureau of Labor Statistics (BLS), http://stats.bls.gov/webapps/legacy/cpsatab1.htm, series
LFU21000000, accessed April 30, 2001.
Employment-to-population: Authors' analysis of U.S. CPS and U.K. LFS data.
Excluding students in the United Kingdom: 76.9 in 1990; 70.7 in 1993; and 74.7 in 2000.
Ages 16–64 only.
Inflation: change in the average year-on-year consumer price index.
U.S.: BLS, ftp://ftp.bls.gov/pub/special.requests/cpi/cpiai.txt, accessed April 30, 2001. Inflation peaked in 1990 (5.4%); troughed in 1994 (2.6%) and 1998 (1.6%).

economies with a better employment and unemployment records than either Britain or the United States in 2000.

The labor market data summarized in table 5.2 illustrate the high level of OECD-style flexibility in the United States and the United Kingdom at the end of the 1990s. In 2000, by European standards, unionization rates were low in both countries (13.9% in the United States, 26.8% in the United Kingdom).[11] The minimum wage was only about half of the national median wage (43% in the United States, 51% in the United Kingdom). Average unemployment benefits were meager (about 38% of

**Table 5.2. Labor Market Flexibility in the United States and the United Kingdom**

| | United States | | | United Kingdom | | |
|---|---|---|---|---|---|---|
| | c. 1980 | c. 1990 | c. 2000 | c. 1980 | c. 1990 | c. 2000 |
| Unionization rate (%)[1] | 24.1 | 16.4 | 13.9 | 49.0 | 35.3 | 26.8 |
| National minimum wage[2] | | | | | | |
| As share median hourly earnings (%) | 54.9 | 38.8 | 43.2 | none | none | 51.0 |
| Unemployment insurance[3] | | | | | | |
| Duration (months) | ~6 | ~6 | ~6 | 12/indef | 12/indef | 6/indef |
| As share median weekly earnings (%) | 37.4 | 38.0 | 38.1 | 28 | 16 | 50 |
| Share unemployed receiving (%) | 42.2 | 33.8 | 38.0 | 65 | 54 | 41 |
| Employment protection[4] | | | | | | |
| Index | — | 0.2 | 0.2 | — | 0.8 | 0.8 |
| Rank (from least to most strict) | — | 1/20 | 1/27 | — | 2/20 | 2/27 |
| Real wage flexibility[2] (1980 = 100) | | | | | | |
| 10th percentile | 100.0 | 84.0 | 91.5 | 100.0 | 94.2 | 105.3 |
| 50th percentile | 100.0 | 97.6 | 99.6 | 100.0 | 116.3 | 126.1 |
| 90th percentile | 100.0 | 104.5 | 114.1 | 100.0 | 132.1 | 145.7 |
| Relative wage flexibility | | | | | | |
| 90th/10th percentile | 3.49 | 4.35 | 4.35 | 3.44 | 4.02 | 3.80 |
| 50th/10th percentile | 1.78 | 2.07 | 1.94 | 1.82 | 1.97 | 1.91 |
| 90th/50th percentile | 1.96 | 2.10 | 2.24 | 1.89 | 2.04 | 1.98 |

Sources:
*Unionization rates*: United States: Economic Policy Institute, http://www.epinet.org/datazone/dznational.html, accessed September 29, 2001. United Kingdom: David Metcalf; British Unions in State of Working Britain Update, CEP, LSE, November 2001.

*Minimum wage*: United States: values of the minimum wage and median hourly and earnings from EPI, http://www.epinet.org/datazone/dznational.html, accessed September 29, 2001; updated using Jared Bernstein, *Quarterly Wage and Employment Series, 2000:4*, vol. 2. no. 2, March 2001, table. 3.
United Kingdom: Authors' calculations from LFS.

*Unemployment insurance*: United States: Data on "average weekly check" from the Economic Report of the President, February 2001, table B-45, p. 327; data on corresponding usual weekly earnings of full-time wage and salary workers from EPI, http://www.epinet.org/datazone/dznational.html, accessed September 29, 2001.

United Kingdom: unemployment insurance figures first; means tested unemployment assistance second
Replacement rates taken from OECD; Benefit Systems and Work Incentives; http://www1.oecd.org/els/pdfs/SOCDOCA031.pdf; OECD, Employment Outlook, 1993; and percentage of claimaints from authors' own calculations using LFS of share of ILO unemployed claiming benefit.

*Employment protection legislation*: OECD, *Employment Outlook*, June 1999, table 2.2, p. 57.
*Wage flexibility*: United States: as minimum wage.
United Kingdom: General Household Survey, 1980–1998, authors' calculations
1. Unionization rates for the United States refer to workers who are either members of or represented by a union at their place of employment; data refer to 1979, 1989, and 1999.
2. Minimum wage and wage flexibility data for the United States refer to 1979, 1989, and 2000. Wage flexibility data for the United Kingdom refer to 1980, 1990 and 1998. In the 1970s and 1980s, the United Kingdom had a system of wages councils that set minimum wages for some industries and occupations, but no national minimum wage. Wages councils were abolished in 1993; a national minimum wage went into effect in 1997.
3. U.S. unemployment insurance figures refer to "average weekly check" as a share of usual weekly earnings of full-time wage and salary workers. Data refer to 1979, 1989, and the first 10 months of 2000.
4. OECD employment protection legislation data refer to the late 1980s and the late 1990s.

medianweekly earnings in the United States and about 50% in the United Kingdom), relatively hard to come by (only 38% of the ILO-unemployed in the United States and 41% of the ILO-unemployed in the United Kingdom received benefits), and, in the United States, short-lived.[12] Employed workers also had the lowest (United States) and next-to-lowest (United Kingdom) levels of formal employment protection in the OECD. These institutional arrangements contributed to what were in 2000 among the highest levels of wage dispersion in the OECD (see the last three rows of table 5.1).

While the trends are not completely consistent, the data in table 5.2 also show a general rise over the 1980–2000 period in these measures of flexibility in the United Kingdom. Britain did introduce a national minimum wage in 1997—despite OECD objections—but the policy change conformed with the OECD's recommendation that, if implemented, the new minimum be set at a "prudent" level and include a separate and lower youth rate (OECD 2000: 117–119). In 1983, the government also eliminated earnings-related unemployment insurance payments, which was followed by a successive tightening of eligibility rules and restrictions on means-tested payments. At the same time, the share of the unemployed who received unemployment benefit fell significantly, from 65% in 1980 to 41% in 2000. The period of eligibility for the insurance component of unemployment benefit also dropped from 12 to 6 months. The biggest increase in "flexibility" was undoubtedly related to the sharp drop in unionization, from just under half (49%) of the British workforce in 1980 to just over one-fourth (26.8%) in 2000.[13] Real wage growth across the wage distribution provides a simple way for evaluating the impact of these and other moves toward flexibility. Between 1980 and 2000, real wages at the 10th percentile rose about 5% in Britain; over the same period, real wages at the 90th percentile increased about 46%.

## 5.3 TESTING THE STRATEGY: THE UNITED STATES AND THE UNITED KINGDOM VERSUS THE REST OF THE OECD

To the extent that flexibility lies behind low unemployment and high employment rates in the United States and the United Kingdom, the international data should show consistently better employment opportunities for the less skilled in the United States and the United Kingdom.[14] To the extent that we don't observe such a pattern, the data may be suggesting that the reason for the relatively strong aggregate performance of the United States and the United Kingdom in the 1990s was not, in fact, related to flexibility.

### 5.3.1 Youth

We begin by comparing the prospects of young workers in the United States and the United Kingdom with those of young people in the rest of the OECD. Figure 5.3 shows the unemployment rate for 16- to 24-year-olds

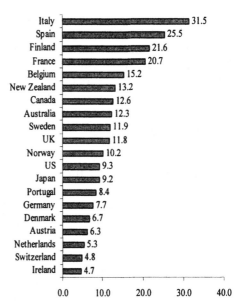

**Figure 5.3. Youth unemployment rate, 2000 (%). Source: OECD, *Employment Outlook* (June 2001), table C. Ages 15–24 except Norway, Spain, Sweden, the United Kingdom, and the United States, which refer to 16–24.**

in 2000. Despite the relative flexibility of the U.S. and British economies,[15] the youth unemployment rate in the two countries was solidly in the middle of the range for the OECD. Ireland (4.7%), Switzerland (4.8%), the Netherlands (5.3%), Austria (6.3%), Denmark (6.7%), Germany (7.7%), Portugal (8.4%), and Japan (9.2%) all had lower youth unemployment rates than did the United States (9.3%); these same countries and Norway (10.2%) had lower rates than did the United Kingdom (11.8%). And Sweden (11.9%), not generally known for its OECD-style flexibility, had a youth unemployment rate that was essentially identical to that of the United Kingdom. The middling youth unemployment performance in the United States and the United Kingdom seems especially odd given the two countries' relatively low rate of overall unemployment.[16]

Comparisons of absolute unemployment rates, however, may not capture the main thrust of the OECD's argument: that at any given level of unemployment, flexibility should reduce the *relative* unemployment rate of the less skilled by allowing them to price themselves into relatively low-paying jobs. Figure 5.4 examines data on the ratio of unemployment rates for younger and older workers. By this measure, the United States actually has one of the worst relative unemployment rates in the OECD; the United Kingdom also fares poorly. Greater flexibility in the United States and the United Kingdom appear to be associated with *higher*, not lower, relative unemployment rates for young workers.

Glyn and Salverda (2000) have criticized the use of the ratio of unemployment rates across skill groups as a method of measuring the relative prospects that face different skill groups in different countries. They argue

Figure 5.4. Ratio of youth to prime-age unemployment rate, 2000. Source: Authors' analysis of OECD, *Employment Outlook* (June 2001), table C. Ratio of unemployment rates for ages 15–24 (except Norway, Spain, Sweden, the United Kingdom, and the United States, which refer to 16–24) to 25–54.

that the *difference* in unemployment rates between less-skilled and more-skilled workers better captures the relative probabilities of less-skilled workers being unemployed.[17] Figure 5.5 presents this alternative measure of the youth employment gap for the same countries and years presented in figure 5.4. By this alternative measure, the United States does substantially better than it did using the ratio of unemployment rates, but the U.S. economy is still only in the middle of the distribution. The relative position of the United Kingdom is about the same in both measures—closer to the bottom of the performance chart than it is to the top.

Until now, we have compared youth unemployment rates across countries at the same point in time (2000). Institutional flexibility, however, may benefit less-skilled workers primarily by allowing relative wage adjustments to economic shocks over time.[18] Figure 5.6, therefore, compares the *change* in relative youth unemployment rates (measured as the ratio of youth to prime-age unemployment) between 1990 and 2000, years that correspond, approximately, to the peaks of the economic cycles in the United States and the United Kingdom. A positive change indicates that the gap in relative unemployment rates widened. According to these data, the relative youth unemployment rate rose in the United Kingdom (up 54%) and in the United States (up 23%), suggesting that the flexibility in those countries did not prevent a relative deterioration for youth in the 1990s. The rise in the relative youth unemployment rate in the United Kingdom, in fact, was the second largest in the OECD in the 1990s. By this same measure, relative youth unemployment rates actually improved in several "rigid" economies, including Finland and Sweden.

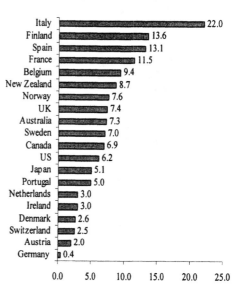

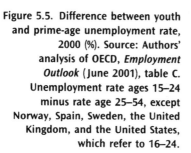

Figure 5.5. Difference between youth and prime-age unemployment rate, 2000 (%). Source: Authors' analysis of OECD, *Employment Outlook* (June 2001), table C. Unemployment rate ages 15–24 minus rate age 25–54, except Norway, Spain, Sweden, the United Kingdom, and the United States, which refer to 16–24.

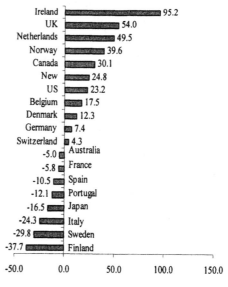

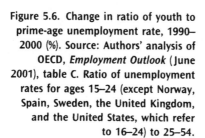

Figure 5.6. Change in ratio of youth to prime-age unemployment rate, 1990–2000 (%). Source: Authors' analysis of OECD, *Employment Outlook* (June 2001), table C. Ratio of unemployment rates for ages 15–24 (except Norway, Spain, Sweden, the United Kingdom, and the United States, which refer to 16–24) to 25–54.

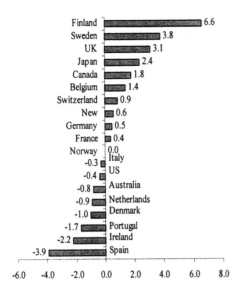

Figure 5.7. Change in prime-age minus youth unemployment rate, 1990–2000 (%). Source: Authors' analysis of OECD, *Employment Outlook* (June 2001), table C. Ratio of unemployment rates for ages 15–24 (except Norway, Spain, Sweden, the United Kingdom, and the United States, which refer to 16–24) to 25–54.

As mentioned earlier, however, the ratio of unemployment rates may not be the best way to measure the relative youth unemployment rate. Figure 5.7, therefore, examines changes in the relative youth unemployment rate by comparing changes between 1990 and 2000 in the difference between youth and prime-age unemployment rates. As in figure 5.6, a positive change indicates that the gap in unemployment between younger and older workers widened. This second measure confirms the significant relative deterioration for young workers in Britain, with the unemployment gap rising 3.1 percentage points over the 1990s, the third worst deterioration after Finland and Sweden.[19] At the same time, the new measure suggests that the conditions facing younger workers in the United States improved slightly over the 1990s, as the unemployment gap between younger and older workers fell about 0.4 percentage points. Nevertheless, six other OECD countries saw relative improvements that were larger than that of the United States, and the deterioration in Germany and France was fairly small (0.4 to 0.5 percentage points).

Since young workers who can't find work may leave the labor force altogether and therefore not be recorded as unemployed, an analysis that focuses exclusively on unemployment may miss important aspects of labor market flexibility. Figures 5.8–5.10, therefore, repeat the preceding analysis using employment-to-population rates, rather than unemployment rates. In general, the switch to employment rates shows the United States and United Kingdom in a better light, but the outcome of this new analysis does not square well with the OECD's flexibility thesis, either.

Figure 5.8 reports youth employment-to-population rates for the OECD countries. The United States and the United Kingdom are both near the

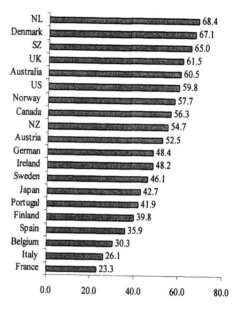

Figure 5.8. Youth employment rate, 2000 (%). Source: OECD, *Employment Outlook* (June 2001), table C. Ages 15–24 except Norway, Spain, Sweden, the United Kingdom, and the United States, which refer to 16–24.

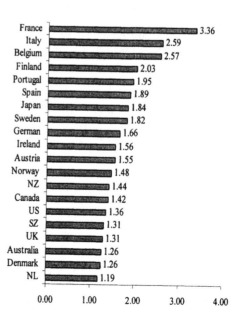

Figure 5.9. Ratio of prime-age to youth employment rate, 2000. Source: Authors' analysis of OECD, *Employment Outlook* (June 2001), table C. Ratio of employment rate for ages 25–54 to age 15–24 except Norway, Spain, Sweden, the United Kingdom, and the United States, which refer to 16–24.

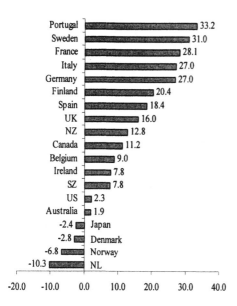

Figure 5.10. Change in ratio of prime-age to youth employment rate, 1990–2000 (%). Source: Authors' analysis of OECD, *Employment Outlook* (June 2001), table C. Ratio of employment rates for ages 25–54 to 15–24 (except Norway, Spain, Sweden, the United Kingdom, and the United States, which refer to 16–24).

top of the OECD, while three relatively "inflexible" economies—Belgium, Italy, and France—had the lowest rates. At the same time, several countries with very different degrees of flexibility (the Netherlands, Denmark, Switzerland, Australia, and Norway) did as well or better than did the United States and the United Kingdom. The data on relative employment rates in figure 5.9 (the ratio of older to younger employment rates) tell a similar story.[20] In both graphs, the United States and the United Kingdom appear to have among the smallest youth employment gaps, but a number of countries do as well or better than the United States and the United Kingdom.

The data on changes in the youth employment gap over time (in figure 5.10) provide even less support for the flexibility hypothesis. The United States did see only a slight increase the youth employment gap over the 1990s, compared to much larger increases in most of the OECD. The United Kingdom, however, experienced a relatively steep rise in the youth employment gap.[21] Over the same period, the youth employment gap actually fell in four OECD countries (Japan, Denmark, the Netherlands, and Norway).[22]

### 5.3.2 Less-Educated Workers

A second group of less-skilled workers that should have benefited from U.S.- and U.K.-style flexibility includes less-educated workers. In this subsection of the chapter, we repeat the preceding comparison of international unemployment and employment rates, this time focusing on adult (25–64 year old) workers with less than a completed secondary education. As

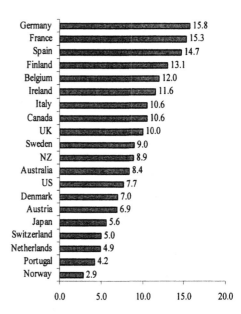

Figure 5.11. Less-educated unemployment rate, 1999 (%). Source: OECD, *Employment Outlook* (June 2001), table D. Less-than-upper-secondary education, ages 25–64.

with younger workers, we show that flexibility appears to have done little to improve the circumstances of these older, less-educated workers.

Figure 5.11 shows the unemployment rate of less-educated workers in the main OECD countries in 1999. Despite their high degrees of flexibility, the United States and the United Kingdom managed to produce unemployment rates for the less educated that were only in the middle of the OECD distribution. Seven OECD countries had lower unemployment rates for less-educated adults than the United States; 10 OECD countries (excluding the United States) had lower rates than the United Kingdom. The United States and the United Kingdom also had among the highest gaps in the unemployment rates between more- and less-educated adult workers (see figures 5.12 and 5.13).[23]

Figures 5.14 and 5.15 display the corresponding results for employment rates for the less educated. Once again, the employment rate for less-educated workers in the United States is in the middle of the rankings for the OECD. The United Kingdom, however, is now closer to the bottom (see figure 5.14). With respect to relative employment rates, the United States falls in the middle of the performance range for the OECD, while the United Kingdom shows the fourth highest gap in the OECD, measured using the employment ratio (figure 5.15).[24]

Erdem and Glyn (2001) and Glyn and Salverda (2000) have argued that comparisons of economic outcomes by educational attainment may be misleading because different countries (or national regions or historical time periods) may have very different shares of their population in various fixed educational categories. In 1994, for example, about 65% of

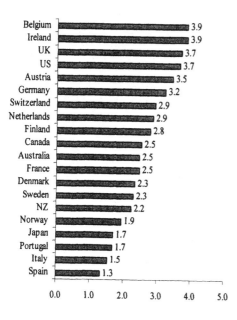

Figure 5.12. Ratio of least to most educated unemployment rate, 1999. Source: Authors' analysis of OECD, *Employment Outlook* (June 2001), table D. Ratio of unemployment rates for less-than-upper-secondary to tertiary education, ages 25–64.

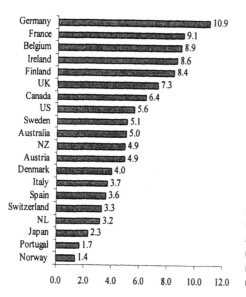

Figure 5.13. Difference between least and most educated unemployment rate, 1999 (%). Source: Authors' analysis of OECD, *Employment Outlook* (June 2001), table C. Unemployment rate for less-than-upper-secondary minus tertiary, ages 25–64.

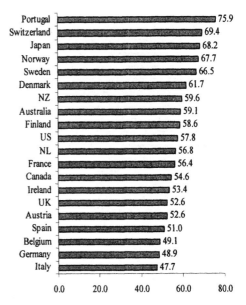

Figure 5.14. Less-educated
employment rate, 1999 (%).
Source: OECD, *Employment Outlook*
(June 2001), table D. Less-than-upper-
secondary education, ages 25–64.

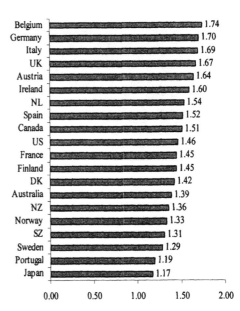

Figure 5.15. Ratio of most to least
educated employment rate, 1999.
Source: Authors' analysis of OECD,
*Employment Outlook* (June 2001),
table D. Ratio of employment rates
for tertiary education to less-than-
upper-secondary, ages 25–64.

the male labor force ages 25–64 in Italy had only a lower secondary education, compared to about 15% in the United States (Glyn and Salverda 2000: 37). These differences may distort the meaning of the absolute and relative unemployment rate comparisons in figures 5.11–5.15. These same authors propose calculating employment rates for each fourth of each country's educational distribution and comparing these across countries and over time.

Figures 5.16–5.18 summarize their main findings for men in the bottom education quartile (Q1 in Glyn's terminology). In absolute terms, the least-educated fourth of the population in the United States did well, trailing only Japan, Switzerland, and Portugal (see figure 5.16). The least educated in the United Kingdom, however, managed only a middling performance. Despite their economies' greater flexibility, the relative employment rates for the bottom quartile in the United States and in the United Kingdom were worse than the absolute results (see figure 5.17, where Q4 refers to the top education quartile). In relative terms, the least-educated workers were better off in Germany, Sweden, Switzerland, Japan, and Portugal than they were in the United States. The United Kingdom actually had the fifth worst relative employment rate measured using the Q4-Q1 gap.

Nor did greater flexibility appear to be particularly helpful in reducing growth in the relative employment gap over time. Between the early 1980s and the mid-1990s, the Q4-Q1 employment gap rose in almost every OECD country for which data are available (see figure 5.18). The growth was small in the United States (up 1.4 percentage points), but large in the United Kingdom (up 13.2 percentage points), which was second only to

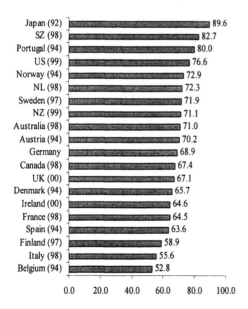

Figure 5.16. Employment rates, men bottom education quartiles, 1990s (%). Source: Glyn (2001), table 2; Glyn and Salverda (2000), table 2.2. Ages 25–64.

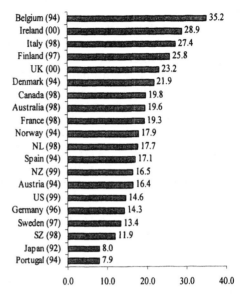

Figure 5.17. Difference in employment rates, Q4-Q1, 1990s (%). Source: Glyn (2001), table 2; Glyn and Salverda (2000), table 2.2. Ages 25–64. Q4 is most educated quartile; Q1, least.

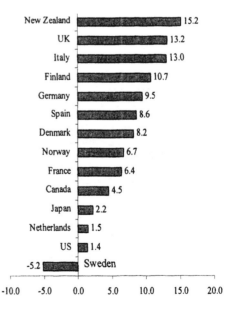

Figure 5.18. Change in Q4-Q1 employment rate difference, 1981–1994 (%). Source: Glyn and Salverda (2000), table 2.2. Germany, 1980–95; Italy, 1980–94; Finland, 1982–94; Japan, 1979–92; Sweden, 1981–94. Ages 25–64.

New Zealand. Sweden, generally cited as one of the most rigid of the OECD economies, was the only country where the Q4-Q1 educational employment gap narrowed over the period (down 5.2 percentage points).

As was the case with the data for younger workers, the data for older, less-educated workers seem to provide little support for the flexibility thesis. If anything, the unemployment and employment data for less-educated workers suggest that flexibility may be associated with *worse*, not better, labor market outcomes for these less-skilled workers.

### 5.3.3 Regions

The flexibility thesis emphasizes the benefits of flexibility for less-skilled workers, who would otherwise be "priced out" of work by rigid institutions. The preceding discussion of younger workers and less-educated workers follows the lines of this skill argument closely. A slight variation on the flexibility argument concerns the positive impact of flexibility on the regional dispersion of unemployment. All else constant, flexible economies should be better positioned to adjust to regional economic shocks and should therefore have more uniform unemployment rates across national regions.

Figure 5.19 shows the coefficient of variation of regional unemployment, one measure of the regional dispersion of unemployment, for various OECD economies in the mid- to late 1990s. The biggest problem with such comparisons is that the number, size, and economic meaning of regions vary widely across the OECD. Moreover, the measured degree of dispersion is sensitive to the number of regions entering into each national

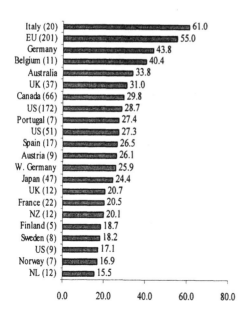

Figure 5.19. Coefficient of variation of regional unemployment rate, 1997 (%). Source: OECD, *Employment Outlook* (June 2000), table 2.1, and Mishel et al. (1999), table 7.6. Australia, 1999; Ireland and New Zealand, 1996; United States (172 and 51), 1996; Japan, 1995.

calculation (generally speaking, more regions mean higher degrees of dispersion). With these caveats in mind, the data in figure 5.19 show no clear pattern. The U.S. data, analyzed using three different regional breakdowns (9, 51, and 172 regions) and the U.K. data, analyzed using two regional breakdowns (12 and 37), are distributed across almost the full range of coefficients of variation in the OECD. The data, however, certainly show no tendency in the United States or in the United Kingdom toward substantially narrower dispersion in regional unemployment rates.

### 5.3.4 Long-Term Unemployed

If the OECD-IMF flexibility thesis is correct, another group that should be well situated to take advantage of flexibility are the long-term unemployed. In labor markets with rigid relative wages and employment legislation, employers may be reluctant to hire long-term unemployed workers either because employers believe that the long-term unemployed are inherently less capable than other workers or because employers fear that workers' skills may have eroded over the course of a long spell of unemployment. By the logic of the orthodox view, flexibility should help to place the long-term unemployed back in work as well as reduce inflows into long-term unemployment. If this were the case, we would expect to see much lower long-term unemployment rates in the United States and the United Kingdom than we do in more rigid economies.[25]

The data in figure 5.20 on long-term unemployment shares (the long-term unemployed as a share of all unemployed) for the OECD countries in 2000 do provide some support for the potential benefits of flexibility in

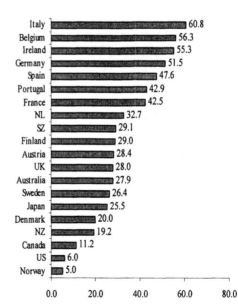

Figure 5.20. Long-term unemployment, 2000 (% of all unemployed). Source: OECD, *Employment Outlook* (June 2001), table G. Share of all unemployed for 12 months or more. Figure for Ireland is from 1999.

this case. The United States had the second lowest long-term unemployment share (6.0%). The United Kingdom is in the middle of the table but had a long-term unemployment share (28.0%) that was well below that of some of the larger, higher-unemployment European economies such as Italy (60.8%), Germany (51.5%), Spain (47.6%), and France (42.5%). That said, a number of OECD economies do as well or better than the United Kingdom, including Austria (28.4%), Sweden (26.4%), Denmark (20.0%), and Norway (5.0%).

The low long-term unemployment rate in the United States is consistent with the view that greater flexibility can combat long-term unemployment. Nevertheless, that the United Kingdom does only moderately well and that other, less flexible economies have also fared reasonably well in lowering long-term unemployment suggest, at the very least, that other, less flexible institutional arrangements can also achieve the same ends.

One possible objection to the tests summarized in figures 5.3–5.20 is that smaller OECD economies are not the best test of the OECD-IMF orthodoxy. Table 5.3, therefore, focuses attention on just the United States, the United Kingdom, and two large economies, France and Germany, both of which are deemed to be inflexible by the OECD and others. The rows of the table correspond to each of the tests presented in the figures.[26] The columns show the rank order for each test for the subset of the four large OECD economies. For ease of reference, the actual value of each statistic for each country appears in parentheses after the country abbreviation.

The OECD-IMF orthodoxy would predict that, for each test, the highly flexible United States should receive a rank of one; the flexible United Kingdom, a rank of two; and rigid France and Germany, ranks of either three or four. In fact, this ordering occurs in only 4 of the 17 tests summarized in table 5.3. A less stringent ordering—the United States and the United Kingdom at one or two and France and Germany at three or four—occurs in only 6 of the 17 tests. The United States has a modal rank of one but scores last in 3 of the 17 tests (and last in 3 of the 12 tests that involve only relative comparisons, which are more in line with the reasoning of the flexibility thesis). Perhaps the most striking feature of the table, though, is how similar the United Kingdom's performance is to those of France and Germany. The United Kingdom finished third or fourth in 11 of the tests, with France and Germany finishing third or fourth 10 times each. The United Kingdom ranked first in two tests, while France ranked first three times, and Germany, four times. The flexibility thesis does fare better when the smaller OECD economies are excluded from the analysis, primarily because several smaller, more rigid economies no longer outperform the United States. Greater OECD-style flexibility in the United Kingdom, however, does not appear to have produced better relative outcomes for marginalized workers there than France and Germany achieved with their apparently more rigid labor markets.

In sum, the international data for 1990–2000 give little support to the view that greater flexibility in the United States and the United Kingdom

**Table 5.3. Summary of Results for France, Germany, United Kingdom, and the United States, 2000**

|  | Rank | | | |
|---|---|---|---|---|
|  | Best | 2nd | 3rd | Worst |
| *(a) Youth* | | | | |
| Unemployment | | | | |
|     Rate (Figure 3) | GE (7.7) | U.S. (9.3) | U.K. (11.8) | FR (20.7) |
|     Ratio (4) | GE (1.1) | FR (2.3) | U.K. (2.7) | U.S. (9.3) |
|     Difference (5) | GE (0.4) | U.S. (6.2) | U.K. (7.4) | FR (11.5) |
|     Change 1990–2000 ratio (%) (6) | FR (−5.8) | GE (7.4) | U.K. (23.2) | U.S. (54.0) |
|     Change 1990–2000 difference (7) | U.S. (−0.4) | FR (0.4) | GE (0.5) | U.K. (3.1) |
| Employment | | | | |
|     Rate (8) | U.K. (61.5) | U.S. (59.8) | GE (48.4) | FR (23.3) |
|     Ratio (9) | U.K. (1.31) | U.S. (1.36) | GE (1.66) | FR (3.36) |
|     Change ratio (%) (10) | U.S. (2.3) | U.K. (16.0) | GE (27.0) | FR (28.1) |
| *(b) Least educated* | | | | |
| Unemployment | | | | |
|     Rate (11) | U.S. (7.7) | U.K. (10.0) | FR (15.3) | GE (15.8) |
|     Ratio (12) | FR (2.5) | GE (3.2) | U.K. (3.7) | U.S. (3.7) |
|     Difference (13) | U.S. (5.6) | U.K. (7.3) | FR (9.1) | GE (10.9) |
| Employment | | | | |
|     Rate (14) | U.S. (57.8) | FR (56.4) | U.K. (52.6) | GE (48.9) |
|     Ratio (15) | FR (1.45) | U.S. (1.46) | U.K. (1.67) | GE (1.70) |
| *(c) Bottom quartile of education* | | | | |
| Employment | | | | |
|     Rate (16) | U.S. (76.6) | GE (68.9) | U.K. (67.1) | FR (64.5) |
|     Difference (17) | GE (14.3) | U.S. (14.6) | FR (19.3) | U.K. (23.2) |
|     Change 1990–2000 difference (18) | U.S. (1.4) | FR (6.4) | GE (9.5) | FR (13.2) |
| *(d) Duration* | | | | |
| Unemployment (20) | U.S. (6.0) | U.K. (28.0) | FR (42.5) | GE (51.5) |
| *Distribution of rankings* | | | | |
| United States | 8 | 6 | 0 | 3 |
| United Kingdom | 2 | 4 | 8 | 3 |
| Germany | 4 | 3 | 5 | 5 |
| France | 3 | 4 | 4 | 6 |

Excludes tests based on regional unemployment rates (figure 5.19) because of differences in number and sizes of regions across countries. In 24% of tests, rankings are (1) for the United States, (2) for the United Kingdom, and (3) or (4) for France or Germany; in 35% of tests rankings are (1) or (2) for the United States or United Kingdom and (3) or (4) for France or Germany.

benefited less skilled or otherwise disadvantaged workers in those economies. Despite low aggregate unemployment rates in the United States and the United Kingdom at the end of the 1990s, unemployment rates for youth and for the less educated in the two countries were only in the middle of the range for the OECD, while relative unemployment rates (measured by the ratio of youth to older unemployment rates) were often worse, sometimes far worse, than the average for the OECD. Flexibility also failed to prevent deterioration in the relative position of younger and less-educated workers over the 1990s. Employment and unemployment gaps for younger and less-educated workers actually expanded by most measures in both countries during the 1990s, especially in the United Kingdom. Flexibility also appeared to have had little impact on the regional dispersion of unemployment rates, though arguably they may have made a more positive contribution to the lower long-term unemployment rate in the United States.

## 5.4 TESTING THE STRATEGY: THE UNITED KINGDOM IN THE 1990S VERSUS THE 1980S

This section turns to the second source of variation in "flexibility": the substantial changes in the institutional structure that took place between the 1980s and 1990s in the United Kingdom.[27] The logic and the structure generally follow the preceding section. We compare the labor market outcomes in the 1980s to those of the 1990s for younger workers, less-educated workers, British regions, and the long-term unemployed. If the flexibility thesis is correct, we would expect to see lower absolute and relative unemployment rates for younger and less-educated workers in the 1990s than in the 1980s. We would also expect to see less regional dispersion in unemployment rates and lower rates of long-term unemployment in the 1980s than in the 1990s.

### 5.4.1 Youth

Table 5.4 displays unemployment, employment, and not-in-the-labor-force rates by age and gender for U.S. and British workers for various years since the end of the 1980s. For each country, the first year is the peak of the 1980s business cycle (measured as the local low point for unemployment); the second year is the trough in the 1990s cycle; and the final year is the most recent business cycle peak. For the present analysis, the most important feature of the data is that, among 18- to 24-year-olds, the unemployment rate at the end of the 1990s business cycle (10.4%) was essentially identical to the rate achieved at the end of the 1980s cycle (10.3%) (see panel (a)). If we exclude students from the analysis, the youth unemployment rate was actually slightly higher in 2000 (10.8%) than it was in 1990 (10.4%). Moreover, the youth unemployment rate, relative to that for older workers, was considerably worse in 2000 than it had been in 1990. In 1990, the difference between the unemployment rates of 18- to 24-year-olds (excluding students) and 25- to 54-year-olds was 4.3 percentage points; by 2000, the gap had grown to 6.4 percentage points.

A similar story holds for youth employment rates. Excluding students from the analysis, the share of employed 18- to 24-year-olds fell from 79.4% in 1990 to 76.1% in 2000 (see panel (b)). Over the same time period,

**Table 5.4. Employment-to-Population and Unemployment Rates, by Age and Gender, 1990s**

|  | United States | | | United Kingdom | | |
|---|---|---|---|---|---|---|
|  | 1989 | 1992 | 2000 | 1990 | 1993 | 2000 |
| *(a) Unemployed* | | | | | | |
| All, 18–24 | 9.1 | 11.8 | 8.2 | 10.3 | 17.5 | 10.4 |
| Excluding students | — | — | — | 10.4 | 18.1 | 10.8 |
| All, 25–54 | 3.6 | 5.4 | 3.1 | 6.1 | 8.8 | 4.4 |
| All, 55–64 | 2.5 | 4.0 | 2.4 | 7.8 | 11.0 | 4.7 |
| Men, 18–24 | 9.2 | 12.7 | 8.4 | 11.3 | 21.2 | 11.8 |
| Excluding students | — | — | — | 11.4 | 21.8 | 12.2 |
| Men, 25–54 | 3.3 | 5.4 | 2.9 | 6.0 | 10.5 | 4.8 |
| Men, 55–64 | 2.7 | 4.5 | 2.2 | 8.8 | 13.1 | 5.6 |
| Women, 18–24 | 9.0 | 10.9 | 8.0 | 9.1 | 12.9 | 8.6 |
| Excluding students | — | — | — | 9.2 | 13.3 | 8.9 |
| Women, 25–54 | 3.9 | 5.4 | 3.3 | 6.3 | 6.6 | 4.0 |
| Women, 55–64 | 2.3 | 3.4 | 2.5 | 5.4 | 6.1 | 3.1 |
| *(b) Employed* | | | | | | |
| All, 18–24 | 67.6 | 63.8 | 67.4 | 74.2 | 62.8 | 66.2 |
| Excluding students | — | — | — | 79.4 | 70.4 | 76.1 |
| All, 25–54 | 79.9 | 78.4 | 81.5 | 79.1 | 76.0 | 80.1 |
| All, 55–64 | 53.7 | 53.5 | 57.6 | 58.7 | 53.9 | 58.1 |
| Men, 18–24 | 72.5 | 67.8 | 70.7 | 78.9 | 64.6 | 69.6 |
| Excluding students | — | — | — | 85.1 | 73.1 | 81.2 |
| Men, 25–54 | 89.9 | 86.9 | 89.0 | 89.5 | 83.5 | 87.4 |
| Men, 55–64 | 64.8 | 63.1 | 65.7 | 62.3 | 55.7 | 59.6 |
| Women, 18–24 | 62.9 | 60.0 | 64.2 | 69.2 | 61.0 | 62.6 |
| Excluding students | — | — | — | 73.4 | 67.6 | 70.7 |
| Women, 25–54 | 70.4 | 70.3 | 74.3 | 68.6 | 68.4 | 72.7 |
| Women, 55–64 | 43.9 | 44.8 | 50.3 | 51.8 | 50.5 | 55.4 |
| *(c) Not in labor force* | | | | | | |
| All, 18–24 | 23.3 | 24.4 | 24.4 | 15.5 | 19.7 | 23.4 |
| Excluding students | — | — | — | 10.2 | 11.5 | 13.1 |
| All, 25–54 | 16.5 | 16.2 | 15.4 | 14.8 | 15.2 | 15.5 |
| All, 55–64 | 43.8 | 42.5 | 40.0 | 33.5 | 35.1 | 37.2 |
| Men, 18–24 | 18.3 | 19.5 | 20.9 | 9.8 | 14.2 | 18.6 |
| Excluding students | — | — | — | 3.5 | 5.1 | 6.6 |
| Men 25–64 | 6.8 | 7.7 | 8.1 | 4.5 | 6.0 | 7.8 |
| Men, 55–64 | 32.5 | 32.4 | 32.1 | 28.9 | 31.2 | 34.8 |
| Women, 18–24 | 28.1 | 29.1 | 27.8 | 21.7 | 26.1 | 28.8 |
| Excluding students | — | — | — | 17.4 | 19.1 | 20.4 |
| Women, 25–54 | 25.7 | 24.3 | 22.4 | 25.1 | 25.0 | 23.3 |
| Women, 55–64 | 53.8 | 51.8 | 47.2 | 42.8 | 43.4 | 41.5 |

Analysis of U.S. CPS and U.K. LFS data.

the share of 25- to 54-year-olds in work rose a full percentage point, from 79.1% to 80.1%.

Contrary to the basic prediction of the flexibility thesis, the greater degree of labor market flexibility in Britain in the 1990s, at least as perceived by the OECD, appears to be associated with deterioration in both the absolute and the relative unemployment and employment rates of younger workers.

### 5.4.2 Less-Educated Workers

Table 5.5 presents comparable unemployment, employment, and not-in-the-labor-force data for less-educated workers ages 25–64. As with youth, the data for less-educated workers show both absolute and relative deterioration in the United Kingdom between 1990 and 2000. The unemployment rate of those with no formal qualifications increased from 10.1% to 11.1% over the period 1990–2000. Meanwhile, the unemployment rate for those with a university degree or more fell from 2.7% to 2.3% (see panel (a)).[28] Between 1990 and 2000, the employment rate for the

Table 5.5. Employment-to-Population, Unemployment, and Inactivity Rates, by Education Level, 1990s

| | United States | | | United Kingdom | | |
|---|---|---|---|---|---|---|
| | 1989 | 1992 | 2000 | 1990 | 1993 | 2000 |
| **(a) Unemployed** | | | | | | |
| Lowest level of education | 6.6 | 10.0 | 6.5 | 10.1 | 13.6 | 11.1 |
| Lower second | 3.6 | 5.7 | 3.5 | 6.0 | 9.2 | 6.6 |
| Upper secondary | 2.9 | 4.9 | 2.7 | 4.7 | 7.5 | 4.5 |
| University or more | 2.0 | 2.8 | 1.6 | 2.7 | 4.4 | 2.3 |
| Ratio university to lowest | 3.33 | 3.55 | 3.97 | 3.74 | 3.09 | 4.83 |
| Difference university–lowest | −7.8 | −11.2 | −8.0 | −7.4 | −9.2 | −8.8 |
| **(b) Employed** | | | | | | |
| Lowest level of education | 56.8 | 53.3 | 59.0 | 63.3 | 57.8 | 50.4 |
| Lower secondary | 74.3 | 72.8 | 75.1 | 76.8 | 73.6 | 73.2 |
| Upper secondary | 80.4 | 78.9 | 80.8 | 84.2 | 79.5 | 79.8 |
| University or more | 86.5 | 85.9 | 85.5 | 89.3 | 86.8 | 88.2 |
| Ratio university to lowest | 1.65 | 1.80 | 1.64 | 1.41 | 1.50 | 1.75 |
| Difference university–lowest | 29.8 | 32.6 | 26.5 | 26.0 | 29.0 | 37.8 |
| **(c) Not in the labor force** | | | | | | |
| Lowest level of education | 39.2 | 40.7 | 36.9 | 29.6 | 33.1 | 43.3 |
| Lower secondary | 22.9 | 22.8 | 22.2 | 18.3 | 19.0 | 21.6 |
| Upper secondary | 17.1 | 17.1 | 17.0 | 11.7 | 14.1 | 16.4 |
| University or more | 11.7 | 11.6 | 13.1 | 8.3 | 9.2 | 9.7 |
| Ratio university to lowest | 3.56 | 3.79 | 3.22 | 3.6 | 3.6 | 4.5 |
| Difference university–lowest | −7.8 | −11.2 | −8.0 | −21.3 | −23.9 | −33.6 |

Analysis of U.S. CPS and U.K. LFS data. Population ages 25–64.

least-educated group fell sharply, from 63.3% to 50.4%, much more than the 1.1 percentage point decline over the same period for workers with a university degree (see panel (b)). Again, the data run counter to the prediction of the flexibility thesis. Greater flexibility was associated in the United Kingdom at the end of the 1990s with worse, not better, labor market outcomes for less-educated workers.

### 5.4.3 Regions

In its 1996 *Economic Survey* of the British economy, the OECD commented that "One manifestation of the more flexible labour market [in the United Kingdom] has been a marked narrowing in the dispersion of unemployment rates across regions compared with the 1980s" (OECD 1996e: 86).

The data in table 5.6, however, raise questions about the magnitude of the reduction in regional dispersion. The table presents unemployment, employment, and not-in-the-labor-force rates for 51 U.S. states and 19 British

Table 5.6. Employment and Unemployment Rates, Regional Variation, 1990s

|  | United States | | | United Kingdom | | |
|---|---|---|---|---|---|---|
|  | 1989 | 1992 | 2000 | 1990 | 1993 | 2000 |
| *(a) Unemployed* | | | | | | |
| Lowest regional rate | 2.5 | 2.7 | 2.1 | 4.7 | 8.2 | 3.4 |
| 20th percentile rate | 3.5 | 4.4 | 3.2 | 4.9 | 8.7 | 4.3 |
| 80th percentile rate | 5.8 | 7.1 | 4.8 | 9.3 | 13.3 | 8.0 |
| Highest regional rate | 7.7 | 10.0 | 6.9 | 13.5 | 16.2 | 10.8 |
| 80th–20th | 2.3 | 2.7 | 1.6 | 4.4 | 4.6 | 3.7 |
| High–low | 5.2 | 7.3 | 4.8 | 8.8 | 8.0 | 7.4 |
| Coefficient of variation | 0.276 | 0.252 | 0.273 | 0.319 | 0.224 | 0.312 |
| *(b) Employed* | | | | | | |
| Lowest regional rate | 58.4 | 47.7 | 54.0 | 64.1 | 60.3 | 64.5 |
| 20th percentile rate | 69.4 | 58.1 | 62.0 | 67.5 | 63.2 | 65.6 |
| 80th percentile rate | 77.3 | 65.6 | 68.7 | 77.4 | 72.7 | 76.6 |
| Highest regional rate | 78.8 | 68.0 | 72.0 | 80.5 | 75.0 | 79.7 |
| 80th–20th | 7.9 | 7.5 | 6.7 | 9.9 | 9.5 | 11.0 |
| High–low | 20.4 | 20.3 | 18.0 | 16.4 | 14.7 | 15.2 |
| Coefficient of variation | 0.065 | 0.067 | 0.059 | 0.073 | 0.071 | 0.069 |
| *(c) Not in labor force* | | | | | | |
| Lowest regional rate | 18.0 | 16.7 | 14.3 | 15.2 | 18.0 | 17.5 |
| 20th percentile rate | 19.7 | 20.5 | 19.1 | 17.1 | 19.8 | 19.2 |
| 80th percentile rate | 26.4 | 25.7 | 24.9 | 24.3 | 26.9 | 26.2 |
| Highest regional rate | 37.0 | 35.5 | 31.5 | 26.6 | 29.6 | 30.5 |
| 80th–20th | 6.7 | 5.2 | 5.8 | 7.2 | 7.1 | 7.0 |
| High–low | 19.0 | 18.8 | 17.2 | 11.4 | 11.6 | 13.0 |
| Coefficient of variation | 0.163 | 0.162 | 0.163 | 0.169 | 0.159 | 0.171 |

Analysis of U.S. CPS and U.K. LFS.

regions for key years since the end of the 1990s. The data show only small declines between 1990 and 2000 in the United Kingdom in the coefficient of variation of regional unemployment (from 0.319 to 0.312) and regional employment (from 0.073 to 0.069). The coefficient of variation in inactivity rates even rises, albeit marginally, over the same period. Greater flexibility appears to have made little contribution to the reduction in the dispersion of unemployment across comparable points in the last two business cycles. [29]

### 5.4.4 Long-Term Unemployment

The international data on long-term-unemployment shares in figure 5.20 demonstrated that, in 2000, the United Kingdom had a better than average record in the OECD with respect to long-term unemployment (defined as out of work for 12 months or more). The data in table 5.7, however, show no improvement in the long-term unemployment rate between the two cyclical peaks of 1990 (47.5%) and 2000 (49.2%) (where the definition of long-term unemployed are those out of work for six months or more). In fact, the greater flexibility at the end of the 1990s appears to have been associated with a slightly higher long-term unemployment rate than was the case at the end of the less-flexible 1980s.

### 5.4.5 Summary Regressions

The data for youth, the less educated, British regions, and the long-term unemployed display a consistent pattern. Contrary to the central argument of the flexibility thesis, the absolute and relative circumstances of less-skilled and more marginal workers were generally worse at the end of the 1990s than they were at the end of the 1980s. The only exception is a slight reduction in the inequality of regional employment and unemployment rates. Table 5.8 uses a simple regression analysis framework to test more formally for evidence of structural benefits of OECD-style flexibility in the 1990s. Our intention is to try to summarize whether the labor market performance of the disadvantaged groups that we have identified moved more in line with aggregate labor market performance in the

Table 5.7. Unemployment Duration, 1990s (Percentage of All Unemployed)

|  | United States | | | United Kingdom | | |
|---|---|---|---|---|---|---|
|  | 1989 | 1992 | 2000 | 1990 | 1993 | 2000 |
| Less than 5 weeks | 48.6 | 35.1 | 45.0 | 18.3 | 6.8 | 17.4 |
| 5 weeks to 6 months | 41.5 | 44.6 | 43.6 | 34.2 | 27.3 | 33.4 |
| 6 months or more | 9.9 | 20.3 | 11.4 | 47.5 | 65.9 | 49.2 |

Source: U.S. BLS, http://stats.bls.gov/webapps/legacy/cpsatab6.htm, series LFU2430000310000 and LFU2430000060000, extracted May 4, 2001; and analysis of U.K. LFS data.

Table 5.8: Responsiveness of Various Groups' Circumstances to Changes in Employment, Unemployment, and GDP in the 1980s and 1990s

| | United States Change | | United Kingdom Change | |
|---|---|---|---|---|
| | 1980s | 1990s | 1980s | 1990s |
| *(a) Impact of 1 percentage point change of total unemployment rate on:* | | | | |
| Least-educated unem. rate | 1.55** | 0.27** | 0.98** | 0.17** |
| | (0.11) | (0.06) | (0.10) | (0.05) |
| Youth unem. rate | 1.46** | 0.10** | 1.53** | 0.12** |
| | (0.04) | (0.02) | (0.14) | (0.07) |
| Male, 55–64, unem. rate | 0.69** | 0.11 | 0.95** | 0.19** |
| | (0.07) | (0.04) | (0.11) | (0.05) |
| Coefficient of variation, | −0.85 | −0.82** | −1.35** | −0.81** |
| regional unemployment | (0.51) | (0.29) | (0.27) | (0.13) |
| Log real mean wage | −0.47# | −1.12** | −0.36 | −0.89 |
| | (0.27) | (0.15) | (2.10) | (0.92) |
| Real median wage | −0.68* | −0.66** | −0.49 | −0.47 |
| | (0.31) | (0.18) | (1.68) | (0.69) |
| Real 90th percentile wage | −1.74** | 0.07 | −0.04 | −1.16 |
| | (0.46) | (0.27) | (2.55) | (1.09) |
| Real 10th percentile wage | −0.31 | −1.02* | −0.74 | 0.06 |
| | (0.82) | (0.47) | (1.28) | (0.54) |
| *(b) Impact of 1 percentage point change in total employment rate on:* | | | | |
| Least-educated emp. rate | 0.66** | −0.04 | 0.48 | −0.10** |
| | (0.23) | (0.02) | (0.42) | (0.02) |
| Youth emp. rate | 0.95** | −0.05** | 1.93** | −0.12** |
| | (0.13) | (0.009) | (0.33) | (0.02) |
| Male, 55–64, emp. rate | −0.09 | −0.02 | 1.53** | −0.13** |
| | (0.27) | (0.02) | (0.50) | (0.03) |
| Coefficient of variation, | 0.02 | −0.007 | −0.54 | 0.04 |
| regional employment | (0.07) | (0.005) | (0.51) | (0.03) |
| *(c) Impact of 1 percentage point change in GDP growth on:* | | | | |
| Least-educated unem.rate | −0.04 | −0.51* | 0.26 | −0.08 |
| | (0.23) | (0.24) | (0.34) | (0.33) |
| Youth unem. rate | −0.18 | −0.63** | 0.29 | −0.35 |
| | (0.20) | (0.20) | (0.44) | (0.49) |
| Male, 55–64, unem. rate | 0.05 | −0.26* | 0.11 | −0.14 |
| | (0.11) | (0.11) | (0.29) | (0.33) |
| Coefficient of variation, | 1.08** | −0.76* | 0.80 | −1.15# |
| regional unemployment | (0.31) | (0.31) | (0.56) | (0.62) |
| Least-educated emp. rate | 0.12 | 0.08 | 0.30 | −2.23** |
| | (0.22) | (0.22) | (0.45) | (0.44) |
| Youth emp. rate | 0.31# | 0.18 | 0.03 | −1.77* |
| | (0.18) | (0.18) | (0.57) | (0.64) |
| Male, 55–64, emp. rate | −0.11 | −0.26 | −0.32 | −1.61* |
| | (0.23) | (0.24) | (0.70) | (0.78) |

(Continued)

Table 5.8. (*Continued*)

| | United States Change | | United Kingdom Change | |
|---|---|---|---|---|
| | 1980s | 1990s | 1980s | 1990s |
| Coefficient of variation, regional employment | 0.10# (0.05) | −0.13* (0.05) | 0.07 (0.57) | 0.59 (0.63) |

Source: Authors' analysis of U.S. CPS, U.K. LFS, and other data presented in earlier figures and tables.
Coefficients from an OLS regression where the variable in each row is the dependent variable and the independent variables are a constant, and the variable in each section heading (the overall unemployment rate in (a); the overall employment rate in (b); and the percentage-point growth in real GDP in (c)) alone and interacted with a time dummy for the decade of the 1990s.
U.S. data for 1979–2000; U.K. data for 1979–1999.
Standard errors in parentheses.
** indicates statistical significance at the 1% level.
* indicates statistical significance at the 5% level.
# indicates statistical significance at the 10% level.
All variables, except wages, are expressed as shares.

1990s than it did in the 1980s. Table 5.8 shows the results from a series of simple regressions of annual time-series data:

$$y_t = \alpha + \beta_1 x_t + \beta_2 x_t * 1990S_t + \varepsilon_t$$

where $y_t$ is the economic outcome variable listed in each new row of the table in year t (the least-educated unemployment rate, for example); $x_t$ is the aggregate economic variable listed at the beginning of each panel of the table (the overall unemployment rate in panel (a), the overall employment rate in panel (b), and GDP growth in panel (c)); and $1990S_t$ is a binary variable that takes the value of one for the years 1989–2000 in the case of the United States and 1990–2000 in the case of the United Kingdom.[30] The regression estimates of $\beta_1$ summarize the apparent effect in the 1980s of changes in aggregate unemployment, employment, and GDP growth on the unemployment, employment, and wage rates of various subgroups of interest. Estimates of $\beta_2$ capture any differential effect in these macroeconomic relationships in the 1990s, relative to the 1980s.[31]

Given that the United States had roughly similar degrees of flexibility in the 1980s and 1990s, by the orthodox OECD-IMF logic we would expect little difference in the effect of macroeconomic changes on the outcomes of marginalized groups. If anything, the United States may have been somewhat less flexible at the end of the 1990s than it was at the end of the 1980s because of increases in the federal minimum wage (1990, 1991, 1996, and 1997), the Family and Medical Leave Act (1993), the Americans with Disabilities Act (1990), and a mild resurgence in union power, if not union membership. In the context of the regressions in table 5.8, we would probably expect either small and statistically insignificant effects in the

1990s relative to the 1980s (the $\beta_2$ coefficient) or small, statistically significant changes in the direction of less responsiveness, if we believe that the combination of institutional changes over the 1990s had an important impact on the U.S. labor market.

Given that by the end of the 1990s, the United Kingdom had consolidated many of the reforms initiated in the 1980s and enacted additional reforms throughout the 1990s, the flexibility hypothesis would predict, all else constant, that the unemployment and employment outcomes of marginal groups would be more responsive to aggregate economic developments in the 1990s than they were in the 1980s. With respect to the regressions in table 5.8, we would expect the $\beta_2$ coefficient to be large, statistically significant, and in the direction of greater sensitivity of marginal outcomes to aggregate changes.[32]

Turning first to the impact of changes in the aggregate unemployment rate (panel (a)), both countries show small increases in the 1990s in the responsiveness to the overall unemployment rate of the unemployment rates for workers with the lowest education levels, youths ages 18–24, and males ages 55–64. In proportional terms, the rise in responsiveness is nearly identical across the two countries. For those with the lowest levels of formal education, responsiveness to the aggregate unemployment rate rose about 17% in both the United States and the United Kingdom; [33] for youths, responsiveness increased about 7% in the United States and 8% in the United Kingdom and for older men, about 16% in the United States and 20% in the United Kingdom.

With respect to the United States, the OECD-IMF reasoning offers no explanation for the increase in the "efficiency" of the labor market in the in 1990s.[34] The greater responsiveness of marginal unemployment outcomes to aggregate unemployment in the United Kingdom, however, is, at first glance, consistent with the flexibility hypothesis. Two factors suggest caution here. First, even at face value, the payoff to the large-scale restructuring of the British economy appears to be modest. According to the results in table 5.8, improvements between the 1980s and the 1990s in the apparent efficiency of the British labor market reduced the youth unemployment rate by about 0.2 percentage points relative to what it would have been with the 1980s structures in place (a 0.016-point decline in the aggregate unemployment rate between 1990 and 2000 times the 0.12 additional effect for the 1990s). Second, and more important, as we shall see again, all of the decline in unemployment reflects *shifts out of the labor force*, not shifts into employment.

Panel (b) examines the shifting impact of changes in the overall employment rate on the employment rates of less-skilled and marginal workers. In general, the U.S. results are consistent with the implied prediction of the OECD-IMF model: the data show no sign that the employment rates of marginal workers were more responsive to overall employment changes in the 1990s than they were in the 1980s.[35] The results for the United Kingdom, however, generally contradict the OECD-IMF thesis. Employment of marginal groups was less responsive to aggregate employment rates in the 1990s than it was in the 1980s. The economic magnitude is small, but the results are statistically significant. The statistically significant declines in the unemployment rates of marginal workers observed in the regressions in panel (a), therefore, were not associated with corresponding increases in employment for these groups. This outcome suggests (and we will corroborate this with aggregate data) that the declines in unemployment reflected workers leaving the labor force rather than finding jobs.

Panel (c) reports on the labor market impact of GDP growth. In the United States in the 1990s, GDP growth had a large effect on the unemployment rates of marginalized workers, a relationship that did not hold in the 1980s. The United Kingdom, however, showed no structural change in the impact of GDP growth on the unemployment rate of marginalized workers, except for a marginally significant impact on the coefficient of variation of regional unemployment in the 1990s. Contrary to the OECD-IMF orthodoxy, the U.K. data show a *reduction* during the 1990s in the responsiveness of employment rates for marginal workers to changes in aggregate employment.

Given the absence of any major movement toward greater flexibility in the U.S. labor market in the 1990s, the frequently observed improvements in labor market outcomes for disadvantaged groups in the United States suggest that factors other than "flexibility" were also at play. (Sustained low unemployment for the first time since the 1960s presents itself as one plausible alternative explanation.) Given that the U.K. labor market was substantially closer to the OECD ideal in 1990s than it was in the 1980s, the decidedly mixed results for the United Kingdom in the 1990s provide little support for the flexibility thesis.

### 5.4.6 Flow analysis for the United Kingdom

The fundamental logic of the OECD-IMF orthodoxy is that labor market flexibility allows less-skilled workers to price themselves into jobs. The preceding analysis of the deteriorating absolute and relative position of marginal workers in the United Kingdom in the 1990s runs counter to the basic message of the *Jobs Study*. As the regressions in table 5.8 hint, the driving force behind falling unemployment rates in the 1990s in Britain was not that less-skilled workers were priced into jobs but rather that they were shifted out of the labor force altogether. Table 5.9 illustrates this important phenomenon at the aggregate level. The table reports transition rates across various labor market states for the years 1989–1990, 1992–1993, and 1999–2000. The rows in each panel give the labor market state in the first of each pair of years; the columns give the labor market state in the second year of each pair.

According to the data in table 5.9, of those unemployed in the United Kingdom in 1989, 38.4% were working and 26.1% had left the labor force in 1990. By the end of the 1990s business cycle, however, of

Table 5.9. Year-to-Year Changes in Labor Market Status, United Kingdom

| (a) 1989–1990 | Employed 1990 | Unemployed 1990 | Inactive 1990 |
|---|---|---|---|
| Employed 1989 | 91.5 | 2.4 | 6.0 |
| Unemployed 1989 | 38.4 | 35.5 | 26.1 |
| Inactive 1989 | 9.9 | 3.4 | 86.7 |
| (b) 1992–1993 | Employed 1993 | Unemployed 1993 | Inactive 1993 |
| Employed 1992 | 91.5 | 3.1 | 5.3 |
| Unemployed 1992 | 34.7 | 47.6 | 17.8 |
| Inactive 1992 | 11.0 | 5.3 | 83.6 |
| (c) 1999–2000 | Employed 2000 | Unemployed 2000 | Inactive 2000 |
| Employed 1999 | 91.5 | 2.1 | 6.5 |
| Unemployed 1999 | 35.6 | 33.5 | 31.0 |
| Inactive 1999 | 10.1 | 3.0 | 87.0 |
| (d) Change 1989–1990 to 1999–2000 | Employed Year 2 | Unemployed Year 2 | Inactive Year 2 |
| Employed year 1 | 0.0 | −0.3 | 0.5 |
| Unemployed year 1 | −2.8 | −2.0 | 4.9 |
| Inactive year 1 | 0.2 | −0.4 | 0.3 |

Source: Analysis of U.K. LFS.

those unemployed in 1999, only 35.6% were working in 2000, while 31.0% had left the labor force. These transition data underscore a central feature of the British economy in the 1990s. Since the aggregate employment-to-population rate was almost identical in 1990 (72.5%) and 2000 (72.4%), all of the 1.6 percentage point net decline in the unemployment rate over the period reflected workers' decisions to leave the labor market.

## 5.5 SOME COMMENTS AND CONCLUSIONS

Taken together, the international data for the late 1990s and the national data for the United Kingdom in the 1980s and 1990s provide remarkably little support for the orthodox faith in the benefits of OECD-style labor market flexibility. Despite the high praise of the OECD for the flexible U.S. and British economies, younger workers and less-educated workers had no better employment or unemployment outcomes in absolute or relative terms in those economies at the end of the 1990s than did similar workers in other, far less flexible economies. In fact, in relative terms, the prospects facing these marginal groups were often substantially worse in the United States and especially the United Kingdom. The international evidence on regional unemployment and long-term unemployment rates is only slightly more encouraging. When we focus more specifically on the United Kingdom, the serious restructuring of the country's labor market since the early 1980s appears to have produced no noticeable improvement in the labor market prospects that faced less-skilled workers the 1990s relative to the 1980s. In fact, despite improvements in overall unemployment, the British data for less-skilled workers show consistent deterioration between 1990 and 2000. That, in a statistical sense, rising nonparticipation accounts for all of the improvement in aggregate unemployment appears to contradict directly the free market logic behind much of the OECD's *Jobs Study*.

Data for the OECD countries, then, appear strongly at odds with the microeconomic model that has guided the OECD's recommendations to member countries and that has informed much government thinking on international differences in unemployment. If OECD-style flexibility was not behind the relatively low unemployment and relatively high employment rates in the United States and the United Kingdom in the second half of the1990s, then what was? A complete answer to that question is beyond the scope of this chapter, but the microeconomic evidence presented here points firmly in the direction of macroeconomic phenomena. As Nickell and Bell (1995) and others have observed, if unemployment rates across skill groups are relatively compressed in many high-unemployment countries, then unemployment is too high for *all skill groups*, suggesting that the problem may lie with aggregate rather than relative demand.

Much circumstantial evidence supports the centrality of macroeconomics in the success of both economies in the 1990s.[36] U.S. and U.K. policy makers allowed the economy to operate for most of the second half of the 1990s at unemployment rates that were, even through the end of the decade, below consensus estimates of the nonaccelerating inflation rate of unemployment (NAIRU). Interest rate policy was consistently much more lax in the United States in the 1990s than it was in continental Europe. An enormous stock market bubble certainly translated into a substantial boost to U.S. GDP, even assuming very modest wealth effects (see, for example, Poterba 2000 or Baker 2000). A simultaneous boom in the real estate market, combined with a highly developed and flexible market for housing equity loans, undoubtedly fueled further growth in household consumption.

In the United Kingdom, the recession of the early 1990s was deeper than it was in the United States, but the depth of the recession probably influenced the Major government's decision to withdraw from the European Exchange Rate Mechanism in 1992, setting the stage for a significant devaluation and a period of resumed growth. Britain's own financial and real estate booms (especially in the southeast), as well as strong growth in the country's main trading partners (see Baker and Schmitt 1999), provided sufficient macroeconomic stimulus to push annual GDP growth above the 2% rate, the level that seems to be needed to promote job growth, for seven consecutive years. At the same time, at least part of Britain's "success" in lowering unemployment may be tied to two decades of rising pressure on the economic circumstances of the unemployed. For some, this pressure hastened the transition from unemployment to work. For many others, however, the declining generosity of unemployment benefits, administrative tightening of access to benefits, and the lack of suitable employment opportunities led to labor force withdrawal (see Schmitt and Wadsworth 2000).

Our analysis has important implications for policy. As has been well documented elsewhere, including other chapters in this volume, policies consistent with OECD *Jobs Study* recommendations have contributed to rising economic inequality in the countries that have implemented them. This should not be particularly controversial, since the stated goal of these policies has been precisely to raise inequality in order to price less-skilled workers back into a labor market where technology and trade have lowered the monetary value of the work they perform. The empirical evidence presented here, however, demonstrates that such inequality is no guarantee of improved opportunities for less-skilled workers. As the data for the United States and the United Kingdom show, OECD-style flexibility is not a sufficient condition for improving the circumstances facing less-skilled workers. And as the data for many other countries show—especially Austria, Denmark, the Netherlands, and Sweden—OECD-style flexibility is not a necessary condition for good employment performance.

*Acknowledgments* This chapter was originally prepared for a conference titled "Liberalization and Employment Performance in the OECD," held at CEPA, New School University, May 18–19, 2001. It was revised in June 2003. We thank David Howell, Andrew Glyn, Richard Freeman, and participants at the conference for their many helpful comments.

### Notes

1. By the OECD, see, for example, *OECD Jobs Study: Facts, Analysis, Strategies* (1994); *OECD Jobs Study: Evidence and Explanations* (1994); *OECD Jobs Study: Implementing the Strategy* (1995); *OECD Jobs Study: Enhancing the Effectiveness of Active Labour Market Policies* (1996); *OECD Jobs Study: Pushing Ahead with the Strategy* (1996); and, more recently, special sections of country-specific OECD Economic Surveys.

2. A separate approach to the issues addressed here focuses on international differences in the distribution of workers' skills. International differences in earnings inequalities may reflect differences in the distribution of economically productive skills, rather than different institutional arrangements (Nickell and Layard 1999). If this is an important factor, a compressed wage distribution may have little impact on employment or unemployment rates in country that also has a compressed skill distribution. Devroye and Freeman (2001), however, conclude that "differences in skill dispersion across countries explain only a modest portion of differences in the dispersion of earnings across countries." Freeman and Schettkat (2000) reach a similar conclusion in a detailed comparison of U.S. and German data. For a more complete and critical discussion of the "skills dispersion" view, see Howell and Huebler (chapter 2).

3. For a helpful discussion of these other factors and broader questions of causality, see Erdem and Glyn (2001).

4. Our approach shares Freeman's (2000) concern that tests of competing economic "models" should factor in "various dimensions of aggregate economic performance" (S190) and evaluate results over "at least a decade or so" (S191). Many of our simple tests rely on Freeman's logic that if one particular set of institutional arrangements dominates others, then "copying this or that feature of the single peak economy" (such as increasing specific kinds of flexibility, in our case) "ought to raise social outcomes" and that "large scale movements toward [the single peak economy] ought to be relatively costless" (S191).

5. For a summary of recommendations, see the OECD Jobs Study (OECD 1994a). For more detailed information, see OECD 1996a–e, 1999a–b, and 2000.

6. Germany had the highest number of specific recommendations (40). Other advanced OECD countries with 20 or more recommendations included Austria (33), Belgium (26), France (28), Italy (21), Finland (31), the Netherlands (27), Portugal (23), Spain (34), Sweden (24), and Norway (28).

7. Of these recommendations, the United States did implement a version of "welfare reform" and did expand the EITC. The United States, however, took no action on the proposed educational reforms; did not reform assistance programs for the disabled; and did not expand eligibility for the unemployment insurance system.

8. Arguably, the movement toward more flexible labor markets ended, or may have even been reversed slightly, with the election of the Labour government in 1997 and its subsequent reforms. The scale and timing of these changes, however, are unlikely to have a significant effect on our tests comparing the United Kingdom in the 1990s and in the 1980s.

9. Of course, all countries in figures 5.1 and 5.2 are not at the same point in the economic cycle, but we don't believe that controlling for this would significantly change the conclusions we draw from these and similar figures and tables that appear later in this chapter.

10. Note, too, that none of the other countries with low unemployment rates at the end of the 1990s suffered significant rates of inflation, either.

11. Coverage is more important for wage determination, but this too had fallen, to around 30% in the United Kingdom by 2000. Membership and coverage rates in the United States are fairly close to one another.

12. The figures here for replacement ratios are averages; replacement ratios vary considerably by household circumstances. Our estimate of the share of ILO-unemployed may slightly underestimate the actual share of ILO-unemployed receiving benefit, since some recipients of unemployment benefits are actually inactive by the ILO definition.

13. Employment protection did not change between 1990 and 2000 (no comparable data are available for 1980). The United Kingdom's index and rank, however, remained extremely low.

14. Our analysis relies almost entirely on aggregate data for the OECD countries prepared and published by the OECD. Several papers have used microdata for smaller subsets of OECD countries to examine closely related issues, arriving at broadly similar conclusions to the ones here. See, for example, Krueger and Pischke (1997) and Card, Kramarz, and Lemieux (1999). Other papers that use aggregate cross-country data and arrive at similar conclusions include Nickel and Bell (1995), Glyn and Salverda (2000) and Howell and Huebler (chapter 2).

15. In Britain, the introduction of the New Deal, which provided compulsory job or education placements for youths unemployed for more than six months, should have enhanced any positive effects of flexibility.

16. One complication here is that international differences in school attendance rates can have a significant impact on conventionally measured unemployment and employment rates. In the mid-1990s, just over 10% of U.S. males and almost 20% of U.S. females in the 16- to 24-year-old age range were neither attending school nor at work; about 19% of British males and about 24% of British females were in the same situation. These nonparticipation rates for U.S. females and for British males and females were among the highest in the OECD; the U.S. male rate was in the middle range for the OECD (see OECD 1999b: figure 3.5). If the same relative positions held in 2000, an international analysis of relative unemployment rates that took nonparticipation rates into account would, in general, reinforce the conclusions drawn here using conventionally measured unemployment rates.

17. For a complete discussion of their position, see Glyn and Salverda (2000) and Glyn (2001).

18. Moreover, as Freeman (2000) argues, if the U.S. model represents a unique set of institutional arrangements associated with the best all-around performance among advanced capitalist economies, movements over time toward institutional arrangements similar to the those in the United States should be associated with improvements in performance indicators.

19. A comparison of the results in figures 5.6 and 5.7 for Finland and Sweden suggest caution in interpreting changes in relative measures. Using changes in the ratio, as in figure 5.6, Finland and Sweden show the largest improvements in relative unemployment rates; using changes in differences, as in figure 5.7, Finland and Sweden show the biggest deterioration in relative unemployment rates. A look at the underlying unemployment rates gives a clearer picture of what happened. In Sweden, in 1990, the unemployment rate for 15- to 24-year-olds was 4.5%; the rate for 25- to 54-year-olds was 1.3%; in 2000, the 15- to 24-year-old rate was 11.9%; the 25- to 54-year-old rate, 4.9%. Between 1990 and 2000, the unemployment rate for both young and old deteriorated sharply. The unemployment rate for 15- to 24-year-olds more than doubled; the rate for 25- to 54-year-olds, however, more than tripled. As a result, the relative unemployment rate actually improved, even as the absolute situation of both young and old workers deteriorated. In percentage point terms, the rise in unemployment between 1990 and 2000 was larger for young workers (up 7.4 percentage points) than it was for older workers (up 3.6 percentage points). By this measure, the relative circumstances facing younger workers clearly deteriorated.

20. A graph of younger minus older employment rates (not shown) yields similar results.

21. The poor relative performance of the United Kingdom is even sharper if the youth employment gap is measured using the change in the employment gap measured in percentage-point terms (not shown).

22. Two features of the OECD youth employment data caution further against drawing strong conclusions from the preceding figures. First, the OECD data for the United States and the United Kingdom (as well as the data for Norway, Spain, and Sweden) cover youths ages 16–24, while the data for the rest of the sample cover youth ages 15–24. Given that the share of 15-year-olds at work is very low across all the advanced OECD economies, this slight difference in the sample population biases upward the employment rates in the United States and the United Kingdom (as well as in Norway, Spain, and Sweden) relative to the rest of the sample. The magnitude of this bias is potentially large. Our own analysis of the

U.S. Current Population Survey, for example, shows that, in 2000, the employment rate for 15- to 24-year-olds was 5.5 percentage points lower than the rate for 16- to 24-year-olds.

A second problem with the OECD youth employment data is, as mentioned earlier, that they don't take into account international differences in school attendance. Countries where young people are attending school (presumably a good thing) appear to have a low youth employment rate (interpreted here as a bad thing). Ideally, the employment data in these figures should show employment rates excluding those involved in full-time schooling. Such data, however, are not available on an internationally comparable basis for the period of interest here. OECD data for the mid-1990s on the share of 16- to 24-year-olds who were neither attending school nor employed (referred to earlier) suggest that the apparently weak employment performance in some countries may simply reflect high rates of school attendance. (OECD 1999a: figure 3.5). According to these data (which do not cover all the countries in figure 5.8), several countries that had a lower youth employment rate than the United States and the United Kingdom in figure 5.8 actually had higher combined employment and schooling rates. Germany, Portugal, the Netherlands, Austria, and Denmark all had a higher share of male youth in school or at work than did the United States; Australia, Belgium, France, Canada, Finland, Ireland, Portugal, Germany, Denmark, the Netherlands, and Austria all had higher shares of female youth in school or in work than did the United States. Failure to take schooling into account has a particularly large effect on the United Kingdom. Britain, which had one of the highest youth employment rates in figure 5.8, had the OECD's second lowest rate of young males in work or in school and the third lowest rate for females. The significant deterioration in the apparent performance of the youth labor market in the United States and especially the United Kingdom once schooling patterns are factored in is consistent with the OECD's long-term concerns about the education and training systems in both countries.

One final point: both of these data issues affect interpretation of the data across countries in the same year. To the extent that these factors are constant over time (true of the age range difference, but probably less true for schooling rates), these factors should not adversely affect conclusions related to the change in the youth employment gap in figures 5.11 and 5.12.

23. Unfortunately, no comparable data on unemployment and employment rates by education exist for the late 1980s or early 1990s, so we cannot examine changes in these gaps over time.

24. Britain has the second highest gap measured using employment rate differences (not shown).

25. Since 1986, successive governments have adopted an increasingly interventionist stance with respect to the long-term unemployed in the United Kingdom, culminating in the introduction in 1988 of the New Deal job placement schemes for long-term unemployed youth (those unemployed six months or longer) and adults (unemployed two years or longer).

26. Except figure 5.19, where the differences in the number and the size of regions across countries make it difficult to formulate a clear test.

27. For other analyses of the British labor market in the 1990s, see, among others, Gregg and Wadsworth (2000); Dickens, Gregg, and Wadsworth (2000); and Nickell (2001).

28. The size of the group with no qualifications fell from around 30% at the beginning of the decade to about 15% at the end of the decade; meanwhile,

the share with degrees grew from about 10% to about 15%. Given these supply changes, the outcomes we observe seem even more remarkable.

29. Erdem and Glyn (2001) demonstrate that these aggregate results also hold for less-educated workers across regions in the United States, the United Kingdom, France, and western Germany. Their table 3 shows that, in 1996, the standard deviation of employment rates across regions was not especially low for the United Kingdom or the United States relative to France or western Germany. Moreover, the standard deviation of employment rates for the least educated quarter of the population was distinctly higher in the United Kingdom than it was in the other three countries (and no lower in the United States than it was in France or Germany).

30. Note that, if the flexibility thesis holds, by including the peak year from the 1980s business cycle in the 1990s binary variable, we bias our results in favor of finding positive structural shifts in the 1990s.

31. The full effect in the 1990s is the sum of the 1980s coefficient (in column 1) and the interaction term for the 1990s (in column 2).

32. Evidence of a differential positive response to unemployment in the 1990s, could, of course, indicate more cyclical sensitivity in the downswing or the upswing or both. Our data, however, are not rich enough to be able to distinguish between these two effects.

33. To calculate the increase in responsiveness between the 1990s and the 1980s, we divide the 1990s interaction coefficient (0.27 for the United States) by the baseline coefficient for the 1990s (1.55). For the United Kingdom, the corresponding calculation is 0.17/0.98.

34. By "efficiency" here, we are referring only to the generally greater responsiveness in the 1990s of marginalized workers' employment circumstances to general economic circumstances.

35. The youth employment rate appears to have been statistically significantly less responsive to changes in overall employment in the 1990s than it was in the 1980s.

36. For critical analyses of macroeconomic policy in the United States in the 1990s, see Godley (2000), Godley and Izurieta (2001), Baker (2001), and Weller (2001).

## References

Baker, Dean. 2000. "Double Bubble: The Over-Valuation of the Stock Market and the Dollar." Washington, D.C.: Center for Economic and Policy Research.

———. 2001. "The New Economy Goes Bust: What the Record Shows." CEPR Briefing Paper. Washington, D.C.: Center for Economic and Policy Research.

Baker, Dean, and John Schmitt. 1999. "Die makroökonomischen Wurzeln der hohen Arbeitslosigkeit in Europa—Der Einfluß des Wachstums im Ausland." WSI Mitteilungen (December): 839–850.

Blanchflower, David G., and Richard B. Freeman. 1994. "Did the Thatcher Reforms Change British Labour Market Performances?" In The U.K. Labour Market: Comparative Aspects and Institutional Developments, edited by Ray Barrell. Cambridge: Cambridge University Press.

Card, David, Francis Kramarz, and Thomas Lemieux. 1999. "Changes in the Relative Structure of Wages and Employment: A Comparison of the United States, Canada, and France." Canadian Journal of Economics 32(4): 843–877.

Devroye, Dan, and Richard Freeman. 2001. "Does Inequality in Skills Explain Inequality in Earnings Across Advanced Countries?" National Bureau of Economic Research Working Paper No. 8140.

Dickens, Richard, Paul Gregg, and Jonathan Wadsworth. 2000. "New Labour and the Labour Market." CMPO Working Paper No. 00/19, University of Bristol.

Erdem, Esra, and Andrew Glyn. 2001. "Job Deficits in U.K. Regions." *Oxford Bulletin of Economics and Statistics* 63 (Special Edition): 1–16.

Freeman, Richard. 2000. "The U.S. Economic Model at Y2K: Lodestar for Advanced Capitalism?" *Canadian Public Policy—Analyse de Politiques* 26 (Supp./ Numéro spécial 1).

Freeman, Richard, and Ronald Schettkat. 2000. "Skill Compression, Wage Differentials and Employment: Germany versus the United States." National Bureau of Economic Research Working Paper No. 7610.

Glyn, Andrew. 2001. "Employment Inequalities and the Unskilled in the North." Unpublished manuscript, Oxford University, September.

Glyn, Andrew, and Wiemer Salverda. 2000. "Employment Inequalities." In *Labour Market Inequalities: Problems and Policies of Low-Wage Employment in International Perspective*, edited by M. Gregory, W. Salverda, and S. Bazen. Oxford: Oxford University Press.

Godley, Wynne. 2000. "Seven Unsustainable Processes: Medium-Term Prospects and Policies for the United States and the World." Special Report, Levy Economics Institute of Bard College.

Godley, Wynne, and Alex Izurieta. 2001. "The Developing U.S. Recession and Guidelines for Policy." Strategic Analysis, Levy Economics Institute of Bard College.

Gregg, Paul, and Jonathan Wadsworth, eds. 2000. *The State of Working Britain*. Manchester: Manchester University Press.

Krueger, Alan B. and Jörn-Steffen Pischke. 1997. "Observations and Conjectures on the U.S. Employment Miracle." Industrial Relations Section Working Paper No. 390, Princeton University.

Nickell, Stephen. 2001. "Has U.K. Labour Market Performance Changed?" Speech before the Society of Business Economists, London, May 16.

Nickell, Stephen, and Brian Bell. 1995. "The Collapse in Demand for the Unskilled and Unemployment across the OECD." *Oxford Review of Economic Policy* 11(1): 40–62.

Nickell, Stephen, and Richard Layard. 1999. "Labor Market Institutions and Economic Performance." In *Handbook of Labor Economics*, vol. 3, edited by Orley Ashenfelter and David Card. Amsterdam: Elsevier Science B.V. pp. 3029–3084.

Organization for Economic Cooperation and Development. 1994a. *OECD Jobs Study: Facts, Analysis, Strategies*. Paris: OECD.

———. 1994b. *OECD Jobs Study: Evidence and Explanations*. Paris: OECD.

———. 1995. *OECD Jobs Study: Implementing the Strategy*. Paris: OECD.

———. 1996a. *OECD Jobs Study: Enhancing the Effectiveness of Active Labour Market Policies*. Paris: OECD.

———. 1996b. *OECD Jobs Study: Pushing Ahead with the Strategy*. Paris: OECD.

———. 1996c. *Economic Survey: United Kingdom*. Paris: OECD.

———. 1996d. *OECD Economic Surveys: United States*. Paris: OECD.

———. 1996e. *OECD Economic Surveys: United Kingdom*. Paris: OECD.

———. 1999a. *Implementing the OECD Jobs Study: Assessing Performance and Policy*. Paris: OECD.

————. 1999b. *OECD Economic Surveys: United States*. Paris: OECD.

————. 2000. *OECD Economic Surveys: United Kingdom*. Paris: OECD.

Poterba, James M. 2000. "Stock Market Wealth and Consumption." *Journal of Economic Perspectives* 14(2): 99–118.

Schmitt, John. 1995. "The Changing Structure of Male Earnings in Britain, 1974–1988." In *Differences and Changes in Wage Structures*, edited by Richard B. Freeman and Lawrence F. Katz. Chicago: University of Chicago Press.

Schmitt, John, and Jonathan Wadsworth. 2000. "You Won't Feel the Benefit: Changing Unemployment Benefit Entitlement and Unemployment Outflows in Britain." Unpublished manuscript, Centre for Economic Performance, London School of Economics.

Weller, Christian. 2001. "Lessons from the 1990s: Long-term Growth Prospects for the United States." *New Economy* 9(1): 57–61.

# 6

## Labor Market Success and Labor Market Reform: Lessons from Ireland and New Zealand

ANDREW GLYN

The labor market experience of Ireland in the 1990s was entirely exceptional. Employment grew at 3.9% per year. Although the working population grew rapidly (boosted at the end of the period by returning emigrants), the employed share of the working age population (the employment rate) still rose by more than 10%. This was the sharpest increase among OECD countries, which on average recorded little change. Irish unemployment, which had been the second highest in the OECD as late as 1993 (15.6%), had fallen to 4.2% in 2000, among the very lowest in OECD (see figure 6.1).[1]

New Zealand's employment performance in the 1990s was less spectacular. Employment grew at 1.8% per year, and this pushed the employment rate up by 3%. Unemployment fell over the 1990s by around one-quarter to reach 6.1%, somewhat below the OECD average.

What can be learned from comparing these two small countries? The remarkable turnaround in the Irish economy occurred under a series of national wage agreements, apparently flying in the face of the general move to labor market deregulation. By contrast, the mediocre performance in New Zealand followed perhaps the most thoroughgoing deregulation of the labor market of any OECD country. Yet, according to the OECD, structural unemployment, which abstracts from temporary cyclical factors (also known as the NAIRU), fell only by about 1.5% in the 1990s in New Zealand, while the fall in the Irish NAIRU was put at 7.5% points,[2] much the biggest decline of any country.

The contrasting experiences of these two small countries appears to challenge the orthodox free market view that labor market deregulation is

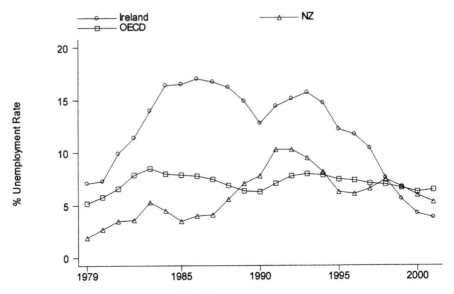

Figure 6.1. Unemployment rates 1979–2001.

essential for good employment performance. In order to evaluate this
impression, we proceed by looking in some detail at the recent employment outcomes and the evolution of labor market institutions in the two
countries and provide a summary account of the surrounding macroeconomic circumstances and policies. While comparison of two countries
can never provide conclusive proof of such general propositions as those
concerning the efficacy of labor market deregulation, it can certainly
contribute to the rebuttal of simplistic positions.

## 6.1 IRELAND

### 6.1.1 Labor Market Outcomes

The reversal in Irish economic fortunes dates back to the program of fiscal
consolidation and wage restraint implemented in 1987 (see O'Reardon
1999 for an extensive analysis), although the sustained period of spectacular growth began only in 1994. Over the 1990s as a whole, per capita
GDP grew at 5.7% per year (fastest among the OECD countries), and the
basis for this remarkable record has been very fully analyzed by the
OECD (1999a). It emphasizes the facilitating role of the plentiful supply of
labor (unemployed, underemployed in agriculture, and returned migrants
from the United Kingdom), improved educational levels, and the receipt
of structural funds from the EU, which improved the infrastructure.
Capital stock growth averaged 2%–3% per year from the mid-1980s before accelerating to 6% per year during the second half of the 1990s. TFP

growth rose from 3% per year in the early 1970s to nearly 4% per year during the 1990s (OECD 2001).

The factor that the OECD most emphasized in explaining the rapid growth of employment in Ireland was the country's success in attracting foreign investment, which underpinned capital accumulation and productivity growth in manufacturing. By 1996, the FDI stock was contributing one-quarter of GDP, one-half of manufacturing employment, and more than 80% of industrial exports. Among the factors helping to explain the FDI boom were the supplies of skilled and unskilled labor "at reasonable cost" (OECD 1999a: 53), reflecting Ireland's initially relative low level of development. However, while the fiscal consolidation of the late 1980s is mentioned as a permissive factor that boosted confidence, labor market reforms (or deregulation) do not figure in the OECD's explanation of FDI inflows. The OECD did give some rather grudging credit to the incomes policy, which represented a move away from deregulation. As analysed further later in this chapter, the succession of centralized wage agreements helped to preserve and even improve Ireland's relatively favorable cost position.

The expansion of employment in Ireland took place from a very poor starting point. In 1990, the employment rate in Ireland was 52.3%, with only Spain having a lower rate. Just over one-third of women were in paid employment in 1990, and the subsequent boom brought a much sharper rise in female employment (in absolute terms, the employment rate rose more than twice as fast for women, by nearly 15 percentage points). The differential between men's and women's employment rates (22%) was still the fifth highest among OECD countries in 1999, but only 3 percentage points above the EU average. Though far from eliminated, this major source of employment inequality in Ireland has at least been eroded in the boom.

Lack of work has been spread relatively uniformly across age groups in Ireland. The excess of unemployment for 15- to 24-year-olds over that for 25- to 54-year-olds was never very high, and it has shrunk even further during the boom. Although those over 55 are nearly 30% less likely to be employed in Ireland than those under 55, the differential is not unusually high by international standards; it grew somewhat over the 1990s (probably part because of the decline in agriculture).

Long-term unemployment fell rapidly once unemployment declined in the second half of the 1990s; those out of work for more than 12 months fell from two-thirds to around two-fifths of the unemployed. However, some part of this fall may represent the recruitment of the long-term unemployed into various labor market schemes, rather than their movement into jobs (O'Connell 2000). Part-time working is less prevalent in Ireland than in the EU as a whole, and a small (13%) and declining proportion of part-timers say they would prefer a full-time or additional part-time work. The proportion of employment represented by temporary contracts was 7.4% in 1997 (three-quarters of the EU average).

**Table 6.1. Labor Market Outcomes Compared**

| | Ireland | | New Zealand | |
|---|---|---|---|---|
| | 1990 | 1999 | 1990 | 1999 |
| Unemployment Rate | 13.2 | 5.8 | 7.8 | 6.9 |
| Employment Rate | 52.3 | 62.5 | 67.3 | 70.0 |
| Long-term Unemployment (% of total) | 64 | 43 | 21 | 21 |
| Employment Gaps[1] | | | | |
| Women/men | 31% | 22% (5/21) | 18% | 14% (= 12/21) |
| Young Workers/prime | 5% | 3% (18/21) | 8% | 8% (9/21) |
| Older Workers/prime | 22% | 29% (15/21) | 35% | 20% (18/21) |
| Least Qualified/most qualified | 34% | 38% (2/20) | 22% | 23% (7/20) |
| | 1987 | 1997 | 1984 | 1997 |
| Wage Inequality: d9:d1[2] | 3.71 | 3.96 | 2.83 | 3.41 |

1. Women: Excess of nonemployment (unemployment to plus inactivity) compared to men. Young workers: excess of unemployment rates for 15- to 24-year-olds compared to ages 25–54. Older workers: excess of nonemployment rates for ages 55–64 compared to 25–54. Least qualified: excess of nonemployment rate for bottom educational quartile compared to top educational quartiles.
  Bracketed figures show rankings (e.g., 5/21 means fifth highest among 21 OECD countries, i.e., *fifth most unequal*).
  2. Ratio of weekly earnings of full-time workers at 9$^{th}$ and 1$^{st}$ decile.
  Source: OECD (2000b) and author's calculations from labor force statistics for less qualified; OECD *Structure of Earnings* database (2001).

The most intractable employment problem concerns the least qualified; in 1994, only Belgium had a greater differential between employment rates for the most and for the least educated.[3] In 2000, 38% fewer of those in the bottom quarter of the educational distribution had jobs in Ireland compared to those in the most-educated quarter. It might be expected that the expansion of employment would have benefited the least qualified disproportionately, as better-qualified groups moved up the jobs ladder, opening up employment opportunities below them. In fact, the story is quite complicated. Until 1997, as table 6.2 reports in more detail, employment rate differentials actually rose in Ireland. The employment rate for the least-educated men fell, and the employment rate for less-educated women rose much less than that for the best educated. For both men and women, the employment disadvantage of the least qualified increased during the first part of the boom. The problem was not confined to the oldest age groups, likely to face the greatest problems of adapting to the rapidly changing economy. For example, while 91.5% of the best-educated quarter of men ages 25–34 had jobs in 1997, only 67.5% of the least-educated quarter in that age group were at work.

After 1997, the situation appears to have changed. The employment rate for the least-educated men grew noticeably, and the differential in employment rates declined; for women, employment at the bottom

Table 6.2. Ireland: Employment and Wages of the Least Qualified

| | Employment Rate, Men | | Employment Rate, Women | | Real-Wage Workers | | Wage differential | |
|---|---|---|---|---|---|---|---|---|
| | level Q1[1] | Q4-Q1 | level Q1 | Q4-Q1 | at 1st decile | d5/d1[2] hourly | d9/d5[3] all | d5/d1[2] FT Men > 21 |
| 1987–88 | 64.0 | 26.0 | 15.1 | 40.7 | 100.0 | 2.13 | 1.96 | 1.59 |
| 1994 | 58.5 | 30.4 | 18.1 | 49.7 | 113.2 | 2.13 | 2.24 | 1.82 |
| 1997 | 57.5 | 32.8 | 22.8 | 50.2 | 120.4 | 2.08 | 2.33 | 1.75 |
| 1998 | 60.1 | 31.2 | 26.2 | 47.8 | | | | 1.61 |
| 1999 | 62.5 | 29.6 | 28.0 | 48.8 | | | | |
| 2000 | 64.6 | 28.9 | 30.2 | 48.5 | | | | |

1. Q1 refers to bottom educational quartile, Q4 to top quartile.
2. d5/d1 is ratio of wages at median to bottom decile.
3. d9/d5 is ratio of wages at top decile to median.
Source: Employment rates author's calculations from Labor Force and Household Surveys; wage differentials-Barrett et al. (2000), tables 7.1 and 7.4, and Brian Nolan real wages from d5/d1 and hourly manufacturing real wages.

continued to grow quite strongly, and the disadvantage as compared to the most qualified stopped rising.[4]

Conventional wisdom would expect wide differences in employment rates across educational groups where the wage distribution was compressed (see Glyn 2000 and chapters 2 and 5). Is this the explanation for the lack of work for the least qualified in Ireland? On the contrary, cross-country data for pay dispersion suggests that only Canada and the United States have wider wage differentials than Ireland between the top and the bottom deciles or between the bottom decile and the median (Barrett et al. 2000 and OECD Earnings Database).[5]

The pattern of wage differentials over the period of Irish expansion is intriguing. Dispersion rose rapidly between 1987 and 1994. International comparisons suggest that the increase in dispersion in Ireland was faster than the rate for any other OECD country over these years. However, table 6.2 shows that there was no marked decline in the relative wages of the bottom compared to the middle (a decline for men was offset by the improved position of low-paid women workers). So all the action over wage inequality took place in the top half of the distribution, reflecting a widening of education differentials as employment boomed. Between 1994 and 1997, when employment was growing very rapidly, pay dispersion at the bottom seems to have declined slightly. The provisional data for men in 1998 show a steep decline in differentials at the bottom, which is consistent with the substantial rise in employment of the least-qualified men, noted earlier.[6] The implication is that over the decade after 1987, real wages at the bottom of the distribution grew a little faster than the average wage, probably close to 2% per year.

The boom was clearly associated with greater pay inequality in the top half of the distribution. Up to 1997, the labor market position of those at the bottom declined relatively in terms of employment (absolutely as well for men) but held more or less steady in terms of pay compared to the middle. Half the fall in Irish unemployment happened after 1997, and it appears that the employment rate of those at the bottom of the labor market has improved quite noticeably since then, coinciding with some relative improvement in their pay, as well. So the boom finally had a quite marked effect on the labor market position of those at the bottom of the distribution. The idea that eventually a sustained rise in employment will spread to the least qualified seems to be supported by the Irish experience.

### 6.1.2 Labor Market Institutions

Both trade union membership in Ireland and coverage of collective agreements has been quite high by OECD standards and has shown no noticeable change over the past two decades. A centralized system of wage negotiation broke down in the early 1980s and was restored only in 1987 (see discussion). Ireland has spent quite heavily on Active Labor Market Policies (including on public employment services, on training, and on direct job creation) There was no minimum wage in Ireland until 2000, although there was some centralized setting of minimum rates in low-paid industries. Finally, although Ireland prides itself on its educational level, the dispersion of educational outcomes as measured by literacy scores is typical of the Anglo-Saxon countries, considerably higher than on continental Europe (see Blau and Kahn 2001; chapter 2).

The two most important labor market institutions typically blamed for high unemployment are the unemployment benefit system and employment protection legislation. The OECD's 1997 report on Ireland contains a chapter called "Implementing the OECD Jobs Study." It admitted that the Irish replacement rate was "not especially high" compared to other OECD countries (see table 6.3) but reported that "entitlements are notable for their indefinite duration at a fixed level" which is "likely to have increased long-term unemployment" (82–83). The results of an econometric study were reported, suggesting that the rise in replacement rates in the early 1980s was responsible for as much as half the 10 percentage point rise in structural unemployment.

But by 2001, unemployment had fallen dramatically. The OECD noted that "not only has the level of long-term unemployment declined with growth but also by more than total unemployment" (64). Were declining replacement rates responsible for this turnaround? It is true that, with the rapid growth of real earnings in the 1990s, replacement rates had declined slightly, especially for single people (OECD 1999: figure 6). But it is quite implausible that these marginal declines have played a significant role in the employment recovery. Eligibility criteria were tightened somewhat in the late 1990s, but this occurred after labor force survey measures of unemployment had declined sharply and was part of an antifraud drive

Table 6.3. Labor Market Institutions and Policies

| | Ireland c. 1990 | Ireland c. 1999 | New Zealand c. 1990 | New Zealand c. 1999 |
|---|---|---|---|---|
| 1. Trade union density | 57 | 54 1994 OECD | 45 (7/19) | 20 (16/19) |
| 2. Bargaining coverage | | High (SN) | 67 (15/19) | 31 (1994) (17/19) |
| 3. Coordination of bargaining | High from 1987 | High | (= 19/19) | (= 19/19) |
| 4. Minimum wage (% hourly manufacturing pay) | None | None until 2000 | Sharp fall 1978–82 (20%) reversed in mid-1980s; steady fall of about 10% in early 1990s reversed in 1996. | 53% (5/10) |
| 5. Employment protection Legislation strictness | 15/19 | 17/21 | | 19/21 |
| 6. Replacement ratios (Net, average of household type) | Little change over 1980s and first half of 1990s | 37% (14/18) | Little change over 1980s and early 1990s, then "substantial" reductions and tightened eligibility (OECD 2000, p. 126) | 34% (15/18) |
| 7. Benefit duration, 1989–94 | Indefinite | | Indefinite | |
| 8. Literacy skills: excess of median over first decile (men) | | 88% (4/9) | | 80% (5/9) |
| 9. Active labor market policies, % GDP | | 1.7 (96) (4/20) | | 0.6 (98) (12/20) |

Rows 1–3: OECD (1997), table 3.3.
Row 4: OECD (1998), table 2.3.
Row 5: OECD (1999b), table 2.5.
Row 6: OECD (1997), table 29.
Row 7: Nickell and Layard (1999), table 6.
Row 8: Blau and Kahn (2000), table 1.
Row 9: OECD (1991), table H.

(people were seen as both having work and claiming benefits, rather than not having work because of the availability of benefits). Those unemployed for more than nine months were obliged to be involved with the public employment service, and this has probably helped to pull down the number of long-term unemployed. But the major factor has surely been the overall rise in labor demand, which, as was equally true in the United Kingdom in the employment booms of the later 1980s and 1990s, dragged down long-term unemployment. The precipitate fall in total and long-term unemployment during the 1990s, without major reform of the benefit system, makes wholly implausible the OECD's earlier claim that the benefit system was a major factor behind the extreme levels of joblessness in Ireland.

Irish employment protection legislation has been consistently very weak; the OECD's recent ranking puts Ireland near the bottom of the regulation league, with only the United States, Canada, and the United Kingdom below. Temporary employment is regulated particularly lightly, and collective dismissals are easier in Ireland than in any other European country (OECD 1999b: table 2.5). Most important, there were no significant declines in the strictness of employment protection since the period of high unemployment in the late 1980s in any of the 18 indicators of the degree of the regulation of permanent temporary employment assembled by the OECD (1999b: tables 2.2 and 2.3). Since employment protection was already comparatively light, it can hardly have played a significant role in the high unemployment in Ireland, nor did labor market reform in this sphere play any role in its subsequent fall.

Ireland certainly does not conform to a North European pattern of tight labor market regulation and high benefits. However, this was as true in the period of high unemployment as for the period of sharp labor market improvement. The one significant shift in the labor market institutions and policies in the 1980s that could have made an important contribution to the employment "miracle" of the 1990s was the recentralization of the wage bargaining system and the succession of social pacts.

### 6.1.3 Wage Bargaining

While inflationary pressure did increase at the end of the 1990s, the continuation of the boom was not seriously jeopardized. How important was the centralized system of wage negotiations in facilitating the remarkable macroeconomic expansion and in enabling those at the bottom of the labor market to improve their absolute and, eventually, even their relative position in terms of pay and jobs?

There can be little doubt that the increase in cost competitiveness in Ireland since 1997 has been integral to the boom and improvement in employment (OECD 1999a). Between 1985 and 1999, hourly compensation for production workers in manufacturing grew by 81% in Ireland, virtually the same rate of increase as in Germany (76%) and slower than that in the United Kingdom (111%). With a relatively stable effective exchange rate after 1990, Ireland had a modest advantage in terms of the trend of dollar wage costs per hour, and a considerable one against the United Kingdom after the appreciation of sterling at the end of the 1990s. But the decisive advantage came from the very rapid rise in manufacturing productivity in Ireland, which brought an enormously favorable trend in costs per unit of output. These were halved against the OECD as a whole between 1986 and 1998, with an even greater advantage against the United Kingdom; between 1998 (the last year on the chart) and 2000, Irish RULC declined by a further 14%. The result has been a doubling of Ireland's share of export markets. In a country with exports at around 60% of GDP in 1990, the impact on the growth of demand has been huge. In recent years, exports have reached nearly 90% of GDP.

A central element in this pattern has been the growth of labor productivity, boosted by the inward FDI in particular. But the competitive benefits would have been limited had wages risen sharply, which makes pay bargaining a central element in the story. Since 1986, wages have been coordinated through a series of "Social Partnership" agreements involving the trade unions and employers (at first reluctantly), a return to centralized coordination, which had been abandoned some years earlier.[7] There have been five of these three-year agreements, and their titles convey the shift of emphasis from coping with a crisis of exploding public debt in 1987 through to sharing out the fruits of the boom more recently:

Program for National Recovery (1987–1990)
Program for Economic and Social Progress (1991–1993)
Program for Competitiveness and Work (1994–1996)
Partnership 2000 for Inclusion, Employment and Competitiveness (1997–2000)
Program for Prosperity and Fairness (2000–2002)

At the core of these agreements has been acceptance by the trade unions of relatively modest increases in money wages. For example, the Program for National Recovery (PNR) provided for money wage increases not exceeding 2.5%, with a flat rate minimum increase to help the low paid, and brought, according to the OECD, "general adherence" in the context of an improved industrial relations climate (1991: 15). The norms for money wage increases continued in the range of 2%–3% per year (raised to about 5% per year in the latest agreement). In the second agreement, there was a substantial addition for local bargaining, but this was subsequently opposed by the employers on the grounds that it would bring two-tier bargaining and presumably bigger pay increases (Hardiman 2000). Minimum absolute increases designed to improve the position of the low paid were featured until 1996. And, as noted earlier, a national minimum wage was introduced in 2000.

In return, the government agreed to reduce the tax burden on workers, allowing take-home pay to rise faster than otherwise; in the PNR, income taxes were to be cut by around 8%, with a bias toward the low paid. In the context of fiscal consolidation (the deficit was 10% of GDP in 1986), there was stress on maintaining essential public services and the real value of benefits (see O'Reardon 1999). The fourth round (covering the late 1990s) focused on social exclusion and an antipoverty program, with representatives of the unemployed included in the negotiations. However, the pattern of tax reductions shows little consistent commitment to progressive changes. For example, although the 1999 budget included tax changes designed to help the least well off , after trade union threats to withdraw from the social partnership arrangements, the 2000 budget again favored the best off. A comprehensive analysis of budgetary changes (Callan and Nolan 2000) showed that the top deciles consistently gained proportionately more from budget changes (mainly tax cuts) than did the middle deciles of the distribution and that the bottom deciles (whose incomes derive mainlyfrom state benefits) gained only relative to the middle deciles in the years before 1994. Overall, therefore, the tendency toward increased inequality in the top half of the income distribution deriving from greater wage inequality has been reinforced, rather than tempered, by tax changes.

The OECD has been characteristically grudging in its evaluation of the impact of the wage agreements. In 1988, it reckoned that most of the slowdown in wage increases reflected the rise in unemployment and a decline in energy costs. In 1995 (33), it presented the centralized agreements as attempting to overcome labor market inflexibilities that would otherwise have pushed up inflation as unemployment fell and complained that the agreements had boosted the pay of public-sector workers and introduced "some rigidity in relative wage structures" in the context of shrinking demand for unskilled labor. The chapter "Implementing the Jobs Strategy" in the OECD's 1997 survey of Ireland admitted that "The central wage agreements have helped to reduce industrial unrest; the number of days lost to labor disputes was the lowest since 1923. Moreover they may have had a positive effect in moderating pay settlements during a period of rapid growth" (91). The OECD suggested that the tax cuts did bring restraint to wage increases. In 1999, it noted that "Despite much stronger economic performance than assumed in the agreement ... 88.8 per cent [of private pay settlements in the first 18 months of Partnership 2000] followed the terms of the agreement" (1999a: 92). By the middle of 2000, wages were rising well above the norm, especially in construction and retail, which are insulated from international competition. Pressure from public-sector workers led to additional increases for them as well. This recent episode illustrates the strain on centralized norms when demand for labor grows very intense.

Some local observers have remained skeptical throughout. Fitzgerald (1999) concluded that the impact of the partnership approach to wage bargaining has been "less significant than many observers assume," since it just validated "the results which labor market forces made inevitable" while helping to bring about a "more orderly labor market" (94). The OECD's *Survey* in 2001 also reported no evidence of a significant effect on wages over the period of the centralized agreements.

Really there are two separate questions. First, did the centralized wage agreements play a key role in the disinflation of the late 1980s (earnings increases were 7% in 1986 and ranged from 4.5% to 6% over the next seven years)? Here, the story that market forces, ledby the high unemployment–dominated wage outcomes, reinforced by the U.K. recession in the early

1990s, probably has some force. However, the second question concerns the role of the agreements in the continued moderation of wage increases and the relative absence of industrial conflict in the extraordinary boom in employment of the late 1990s. Of course, such a pattern is not unique: the employment expansion in the United Kingdom brought lower inflation than was widely anticipated. But the fall in the U.K. NAIRU, as estimated by OECD, was only one-fifth of the estimated fall in Ireland, and Ireland did not experience the other institutional changes to which the fall in the U.K. NAIRU is often attributed—the decline in replacement rates and the legislative weakening of trade unions. The rapid growth of labor productivity (3.2% trend growth in 1990–1998, according to OECD) was not translated into rapid growth of real wages. The growth of real hourly wages in manufacturing was only 1.1% over the period 1990–1999.[8] Thus, the explanation for moderation in money wage claims was not rapid growth in real wages. On the contrary, the bargaining really was extremely restrained in real as well as in nominal terms.

The other side of this coin was a very sharp rise in profitability. The gross-profit share in industry, transport, and communication rose from 45.1% in 1987 to 57.7% in 1995, by far the highest in any European economy (OECD 1999c: 83). Unfortunately, the series does not continue beyond 1995, but we do know that the share of operating surplus in GDP (a broader measure) rose by a further quarter between 1995 and 1999 (Walton 2000).

The rise in profitability, at the same time that wages were restrained, coincided with little industrial conflict. Days lost in strikes averaged 104 per thousand employees over the period 1989–1998, less than one-quarter the level in the period 1980–1986 (Davies 2000). The decline was not as big as in the United Kingdom but still represented a striking fall in the context of such a buoyant labor market.

At the very least, the wage agreements must have played a role in the prolonged combination of wage moderation, sharply falling unemployment, rising profitability, and industrial peace. The conclusion from a recent study from the New York Federal Reserve Bank (Tille and Yi 2001) that the wage moderation was more important for the stabilization period 1987–1993 than during the subsequent employment boom is very far from obvious. The OECD, it may be noted, offers absolutely no explanation whatsoever for the huge decline in its estimate of the NAIRU in Ireland. The interpretation offered here is supported by much of the detailed evidence in the recently published and comprehensive study by Honahan and Walsh (2002).

## 6.2 NEW ZEALAND

In contrast to Ireland's boom, New Zealand's growth performance in the 1990s has been poor. GDP rose by a respectable 2.4% per year over the period 1990–1999, but with a rapid growth of population, GDP per capita grew at only 1% per year, about half the OECD average. Both per capita GDP and total factor productivity growth were about 1% per year slower than in Australia, an obvious country for comparison. The trend growth of labor productivity in New Zealand was only 0.4% per year, matched only by Switzerland in the OECD in terms of the feebleness of growth (OECD 2000a).

This poor productivity performance in the 1990s appears to decisively refute the view that the economic reforms in New Zealand were bringing about a major improvement in efficiency, a view that has been promoted at length by a group of private-sector and academic economists in one of the very few country studies ever published in the pages of the *Journal of Economic Literature* (Evans et al. 1996). Quiggin (2001: 104–105) has pointed to the hollowness of this attempt: "it is difficult to avoid the conclusion that the statistical evidence presented by Evans et al. was selected on the basis that it was the only available measure that gave any support to their highly favourable account of the reforms." A subsequent detailed analysis of economic growth by the New Zealand Treasury had to acknowledge the very poor record of the 1990s and could only offer the feeble suggestion that more time was required: "growth has probably been limited up to the present by transitional factors inherent in the reform process itself. Adjustment may be costly, slow and have benefits, which though cumulatively large, may be slow to appear and not fully measured" (Galt 2000: 56). The OECD's *Survey* for 2002 noted the "far from impressive" growth figures, commenting that "These reforms have had a profound effect on macroeconomic stability and the overall efficiency of the economic system, but it has taken some time for the effects to show up in the productivity statistics" (74). How a "profound effect ... on the overall efficiency of then economic system" could *not* "show up in the productivity statistics" is never explained.

New Zealand embarked on its wide-ranging series of "reforms," first under the Labor government in 1983, including deregulating the financial system plus abandoning the fixed exchange rate, shifting from import quotas to tariffs and from direct to indirect taxes, privatizing and deregulating product markets, and granting the Central Bank the statutory duty to achieve stability in the general level of prices. When the right-wing National Party gained power in 1990, it moved to similarly radical measures in the labor market, in which, until then, wage bargaining had been "multitiered," with national awards, collective agreements at the enterprise level, a national minimum wage, and "general wage adjustments made by the government or by the arbitration court" involving varying degrees of government intervention. The 1991 Employment Contracts Act (ECA) was aimed at "making employment contracts similar to those in all other areas of activity with the aim of encouraging decentralised bargaining" (OECD 1996: 55). Bargaining over an employment contract could be collective or with an individual, and strikes were legal only after the expiration of a contract and could not be used to force other employers to join a contract (secondary strikes). An Employment Court and Tribunal was available to enforce or set aside the contracts.

The OECD (1996: 54) noted that "the form of bargaining arrangement ... is most like that prevailing in North America where recognition of bargaining representatives needs to be established at the beginning of each bargaining round" but that there were a number of differences, all in the direction of less regulation:

- No statutory requirement to "bargain in good faith," with agreements requiring workers to belong to a union or that give preference to union workers explicitly prohibited
- No statutory job protection obligations in the form of a minimum notice period or severance pay

The impact on trade unions was traumatic. Union density and the coverage of collective bargaining both halved, the biggest fall in any OECD country (see table 6.1). Days occupied in strikes fell from 350 per thousand employees over 1980–1984 to 77 in the 1990s, which was a decline similar in proportion to that in Ireland. In the two years following the Act, only 60% of settlements were within 1% of the modal settlement (itself zero), compared to 90% in the early 1980s, and the most unionized sectors experienced both the biggest declines in unionization and well-below-average wage increases. One-third of business reported that the most important factor in improving productivity was the ECA, while another survey reported that 59% of businesses believed that it had led to more flexible work practices and 38% to fewer demarcation disputes, and 44% believed that it had made pay more performance based (Evans et al. 1996).

The labor market reform in New Zealand was described by the OECD (1996: 46) as "substantial and probably greater than in any other OECD country over the same period." As well as the legal changes already noted, the OECD reported "major cuts and a tightening in the eligibility for unemployment related benefits" (46), and by the mid-1990s the replacement ratio was well below the OECD average. Employment protection was reckoned as the third lowest in the OECD, and the lowest of all in relation to collective dismissals (OECD 1999b: table 2.5) Not surprisingly, the OECD's chapter "Implementing the Jobs Study" noted that "there is probably less need to take action on many of these fronts [including measures to increase labor market flexibility] than is the case in most other OECD countries" (OECD 1996: 61). Its synopsis of recommendations for New Zealand focused on labor force skills, was silent on employment protection, and suggested only that New Zealand "continue(s) to review the current tax/benefit system to reduce work disincentives" and "monitor the effects of the minimum wage" (62–63).

The radical weakening of trade unions, together with cuts in benefits in the context of extremely weak employment protection, should have been precisely the package to radically reduce the NAIRU. Measuring the macroeconomic effect of the labor market reforms on the NAIRU defeated even the OECD, which was unable to detect "any stable empirical relationships for average wages, even in the pre-reform period" (1998: 57). In subsequent work (OECD 2002b) it estimated a 1.5% decline in the NAIRU; this was far from impressive, since it left the NAIRU 4 percentage points higher than the estimated level for the early 1980s, prior to the implementation of any of the reforms to the labor market or in other fields.

The return of a Labor government brought the 2000 Employment Relations Act, which included some moves back from the extremes of deregulation toward what was more typical in OECD countries—it required good-faith bargaining, in general prohibited the replacement of striking workers, legalized strikes in support of multiemployer bargains, and stipulated that only unions could negotiate collective agreements. The OECD reckoned that labor market flexibility would be reduced, union membership might increase by around one-half, and wage pressure might grow, but it concluded that "a return to the highly centralised (and distortionary) system that prevailed prior to the ECA is unlikely" (OECD 2000c: 78).[9]

It is at the bottom of the labor market that the biggest effects of the labor market deregulation might be anticipated. In particular, a substantial increase in wage inequality combined with rapid expansion of employment of the least qualified in response would presumably be the desired outcome. The data for employment of the least qualified and for wage dispersion tell a rather surprising story, however.

While there was a rapid increase in wage dispersion at the top of distribution, concentrated in the 1990s after the ECA was enacted, wage dispersion at the bottom (d5/d1) increased only moderately (table 6.4). The minimum wage, not ungenerous by international standards (see table 6.3), may have played a role, but it was declining in relative value throughout the 1990s. Substantial reductions in the level of, and tightened eligibility for, unemployment benefits should have worked in the same direction of encouraging wage dispersion at the bottom end. So the rather

Table 6.4. New Zealand: Employment and Wages of the Least Qualified

| | Employment Rate, Men | | Employment Rate, Women | | | Wage Differential Men and Women | |
|---|---|---|---|---|---|---|---|
| | level Q1 | Q4-Q1 | level Q1 | Q4-Q1 | Real-Wage d1 Workers | d5/d1 | d9/d1 |
| 1984 | | | | | 100 | 1.70 | 1.70 |
| 1991 | 71.2 | 16.7 | 48.5 | 22.0 | 97.1 | 1.75 | 1.74 |
| 1997 | 71.9 | 16.7 | 49.1 | 27.3 | 98.4 | 1.79 | 1.91 |
| 1999 | 71.1 | 16.5 | 49.1 | 25.7 | | | |

Sources: Employment rates are author's calculations from Labor Force Survey; wage dispersion from OECD *Structure of Earnings Database* (2001).

modest increase is quite surprising. Part of the explanation may be that the wage dispersion figures apply to full-time workers only. Part-time workers make up 23% of total employment in New Zealand and contributed three-quarters of the rise in jobs in the 1990s; since the hourly earnings of part-time workers are typically below the average, the rise in wage dispersion in the economy as a whole may be underestimated.

The data for employment rates (table 6.4) show little change at the bottom end of the labor market for men. As employment expanded from the recession of the early 1990s, employment of the less qualified rose as well, but the differential (moderate by international standards before the reforms) was hardly affected. Less-educated women missed out on the expansion of job opportunities for women generally, so that their employment disadvantage rose somewhat.

Despite the feeble growth of productivity, the extremely slow pace of real wage increases (0.8% per year between 1990 and 1999)[10] brought a strong rise in profitability. Between 1983, when the reforms began, and 1994, the gross-profit share in industry transport and communication rose from 42.8% to 51.3%.

New Zealand is famous (notorious) for the form of its central bank independence and for the singlemindedness of its monetary policy. Inflation (GDP deflator) over the years 1989–1999 was 1.5% per year, the lowest in the OECD except for Japan's. In the mid-1990s, New Zealand suffered a severe currency overvaluation (relative unit labor costs rising by well over one-third between 1992 and 1997). This contrasts with the growing undervaluation of the Irish currency as the 1990s progressed. Growth rates and employment improved at the end of the 1990s, when the effective exchange rate began a long downward slide. The fundamental point is that even an exceptionally deregulated labor market, such as New Zealand, is far from immune to the macroeconomic pressures generated by extremely tight monetary policy.

## 6.3 CONCLUSIONS

When we attempt to draw lessons from the experience of Ireland and New Zealand, we must recognize their small size: each country's employment, around 1.5 million, is less than that of half the U.S. states and of more than half the German Lander and U.K. regions. The astonishing increase in Irish export competitiveness, for example, would have been very difficult to sustain for a larger economy. The succession of centralized pay agreements is the only change in the labor market institutions and policies that contributed in a substantial way to Ireland's employment success. Although Ireland does not have a highly regulated labor market, this was equally true in the period of very high unemployment. Deregulation played no significant role in the employment boom of the 1990s, which brought Ireland's NAIRU down more than that of any other

OECD country and which eventually brought benefits to even the most disadvantaged sections of the labor market.

New Zealand implemented the orthodox prescriptions for labor market deregulation most faithfully. Macroeconomic performance was weak, constrained no doubt through much of the 1990s by the obsessively tight macroeconomic policy. The discernible impact of deregulation in labor market outcomes was small. Employment performance was moderate. Wage inequality at the bottom of the distribution rose less than expected. Rapid expansion of employment, especially for the less qualified, did not materialize. The fall in the NAIRU as computed by OECD was small, and by the turn of the century the NAIRU was estimated to be higher than it had been in 1980, before the deregulatory onslaught. One familiar response to the lack of success for deregulation is to claim special factors (small size and geographical isolation tend to feature strongly in this case) and to demand more of the same medicine. An analysis by the New Zealand Treasury devoted to lessons from the Irish experience concluded that, "While Ireland has not undertaken microeconomic reform to the extent that New Zealand has our position in the world may mean we have to address rigidities faster & more rigorously to remain in the game" (Box 1998: 8).

Labor market behavior is of central importance in macroeconomic outcomes. The problem of combining low inflation with sustained high levels of employment has been a key question in the OECD countries for at least 40 years. Wage moderation achieved by coordinated and centralized bargaining is still wage moderation. It may bring rapid increases in profits, as the Irish case shows, and is subject to all kinds of strains and tensions. But, in the context of social pacts with explicit redistributive goals, it is a form of social regulation that, the case of Ireland, among others, suggests, was at least consistent with remarkable employment performance. The very specific circumstances in Ireland (its very small size and degree of openness, its attraction for export-oriented FDI) were also essential in generating the macroeconomic conditions for rapid growth and falling unemployment. It is only when wage moderation provokes a very strong response from business investment that demand takes care of itself (Marglin and Bhadhuri [1991], Bowles and Boyer [1998]), leading to rapid increases in employment.

These case studies do not pretend to show that the "employment miracle" in Ireland would have occurred in just the same way even if Ireland had been at the top of the OECD league tables in terms of employment protection and unemployment benefit replacement ratios or that labor market deregulation in New Zealand had no impact at all on employment outcomes. Measures designed to preserve workers' security at work or their incomes when out of work may obviously have some contradictory effects on employment outcomes, and these have to be set against their manifest benefits for the large numbers of people covered by them.

However, the labor market experience described in this chapter does demonstrate conclusively that the comparative employment performance of these two countries in the 1990s has not been dominated by the degree to which they have followed the OECD's prescription of labor market deregulation. Ireland's rapid rise in employment cannot be attributed to measures to deregulate the labor market. New Zealand's radical deregulation did not bring sharp employment gains, despite the fact that it also followed an extremely orthodox macroeconomic policy, fully in the spirit of the OECD's *Job Study* injunction to strive for macroeconomic stability. It is clear, then, that extensive labor market deregulation is neither a necessary nor a sufficient condition for a radical improvement in employment. This is hardly a startling conclusion, but it is important precisely because of the sweeping way in which labor market deregulation is frequently advocated.

*Acknowledgments* This chapter was originally prepared for the Conference on Liberalization and Employment Performance in the OECD, organized by CEPA, New School University, and held in New York on May 18–19, 2001. I am most grateful to Sandy Charlton, Colm O'Reardon, and Brian Nolan for their advice and to David Howell, an anonymous reviewer, and conference participants for their comments.

## Notes

1. In this chapter, the many comparisons with other OECD countries are confined to the "old OECD," for which data are available. That is, they exclude Korea, Mexico, Turkey, and the transition economies, together with Iceland and Luxembourg, which are omitted on grounds of size.

2. The latest OECD estimates show the Irish NAIRU declining from 14.2% in 1990–1992 to 5.7% in 2002, while in New Zealand the fall was from 7% to 5.4% (OECD 2002b: Annex table 23).

3. This was the case for both men and women in 1994 (see Glyn and Salverda 2000: table 2.2).

4. The survey method changed between 1997 and 1998, which may account for some of the change between those two years. With the exception of the fall in Q4-Q1 for women, however, the changes do not look out of line with what happened in 1999 and 2000, and the Statistical Office is of the opinion that the impact was relatively slight.

5. The OECD warns of the difficulties of comparing these series across countries, but it seems unlikely that the broad conclusion of large pay differentials in Ireland is misleading.

6. Personal communication from Brian Nolan, who also notes that the relatively muted response of employers to the introduction of a national minimum wage, set at what had been regarded as rather a high level in relation to average earnings, is also indicative of the strong demand for labor at the bottom end of the distribution.

7. For background to, and analysis of, this process see Hardiman (2000) and O'Donnell and O'Reardon (1997, 2000).

8. Hourly compensation from BLS, deflated by private consumption deflator. If this series is deflated by consumer prices, the growth rate is 1.8% pa; if the (rather erratic) OECD series for average compensation in the business sector is deflated by the implicit consumer deflator, the growth rate is 0.6% pa.

9. The OECD's latest estimates can detect no rise in the NAIRU after 2000, despite the shift the shift to multiemployer contracts and industrywide bargaining, which the 2002 OECD *Survey of New Zealand* (OECD 2002a) describes as "arguably the least satisfactory wage-setting arrangement to encourage high employment" (83). The OECD warns that, although this has had little impact on wages so far, "the risk remains of a shift towards more centralised bargaining" (106), never contemplating the possible advantages of much more centralized and coordinated bargaining suggested by the cases of Ireland and the Netherlands, among others!

10. BLS hourly compensation in manufacturing deflated by the implicit consumption deflator.

## References

Barrett, A., J. Fitzgerald, and B. Nolan. 2000. "Earnings Inequality, Returns to Education and Low Pay." In *Bust to Boom: The Irish Experience of Growth and Inequality*, edited by B. Nolan, P. O'Connell, and C. Whelan. Dublin: Institute of Public Administration.

Blau, F., and L. Kahn. 2001. "Do Cognitive Test Scores Explain Higher U.S. Wage Inequality?" Cornell University, National Bureau of Economic Research, working paper #8210.

Bowles, S., and R. Boyer. 1998. "Wages, Aggregate Demand, and Employment in an Open Economy: An Empirical Investigation." In *Macroeconomic Policy after the Conservative Era*, edited by G. Epstein and H. Gintis. Cambridge: Cambridge University Press.

Box, S. 1998. "The Irish Economy: Lessons for New Zealand." New Zealand Treasury: Treasury Paper No. 1.

Callan, T., and B. Nolan. 2000. "Taxation and Social Welfare." In *Bust to Boom: The Irish Experience of Growth and Inequality*, edited by B. Nolan, P. O'Connell, and C. Whelan. Dublin: Institute of Public Administration.

Davies, J. 2000. "International Comparisons of Labor Disputes in 1998." *Labor Market Trends* 108 (April): 147–153.

Evans, L., A. Grimes, B. Wilkinson, and D. Teece. 1996. "Economic Reform in New Zealand 1984–95: The Pursuit of Efficiency." *Journal of Economic Literature* 34(4): 1856–1902.

Fitzgerald, J. 1999. "Wage Formation in the Irish Labor Market." In *Understanding Ireland's Economic Growth*, edited by F. Barry. Basingstoke: Macmillan.

Galt, David. 2000. "New Zealand's Economic Growth." New Zealand Treasury: Treasury Paper No. 9.

Glyn, A. 2000. "Unemployment and Inequality." In *Macroeconomics*, 2nd ed., edited by T. Jenkinson. Oxord: Oxford University Press.

Glyn, A., and W. Salverda. 2000. "Employment Inequalities." In *Labor Market Inequalities: Problems and Policies of Low-Wage Employment in International Perspective*, edited by M. Gregory, W. Salverda, and S. Bazen. Oxford: Oxford University Press.

Hardiman, N. 2000. "Social Partnership, Wage Bargaining and Growth." In *Bust to Boom: The Irish Experience of Growth and Inequality*, edited by B. Nolan, P. O'Connell, and C. Whelan. Dublin: IPA.

Honahan, P., and B. Walsh. 2002. "Catching Up with the Leaders: The Irish Hare." *Brookings Papers on Economic Activity* 1: 1–57.

Marglin, S., and A. Bhadhuri. 1991. "Profit Squeeze and Keynesian Theory." In *The Golden Age of Capitalism*, edited by S. Marglin and J. Schor. Oxford: Oxford University Press

Nickell, S., and R. Layard. 1999. "Labor Market Institutions and Economic Preface." In *Handbook of Labor Economics*, edited by O. Ashenfelter and D. Card. North Holland.

O'Connell, P. 2000. "The Dynamics of the Irish Labor Market in Comparative Perspective." In *Bust to Boom: The Irish Experience of Growth and Inequality*, edited by B. Nolan, P. O'Connell, and C. Whelan. Dublin: IPA.

O'Donnell, R., and C. O'Reardon. 1997. "Ireland's Experiment in Social Partnership 1987–96." In *Social Pacts in Europe*, edited by G. Fajertag and P. Fochet. Brussels: European Trade Union Institute.

———. 2000. "Social Pacts in Irelands Economic Transformation." In *Social Pacts in Europe—New Dynamics*, edited by G. Fajertag and P. Fochet. Brussels: European Trade Union Institute

O'Reardon, C. 1999. "The Political Economy of Inequality: Ireland in a Comparative Perspective." Ph.D. diss., Oxford University.

Organization for Economic Cooperation and Development (OECD). 1991. *Economic Survey of Ireland*. Paris: OECD.

———. 1995. *Economic Survey of Ireland*. Paris: OECD.

———. 1996. *Economic Survey of New Zealand*. Paris: OECD.

———. 1997. *Economic Survey of Ireland*. Paris: OECD.

———. 1998. *Economic Outlook* (July). Paris: OECD.

———. 1999a. *Economic Survey of Ireland*. Paris: OECD.

———. 1999b. *Employment Outlook*. Paris: OECD.

———. 1999c. *Historical Statistics 1960–97*. Paris: OECD.

———. 2000a. *Economic Outlook* (July). Paris: OECD.

———. 2000b. *Employment Outlook*. Paris: OECD.

———. 2000c. *Economic Survey of New Zealand*. Paris: OECD.

———. 2001. *Economic Survey of Ireland*. Paris: OECD.

———. 2002a. *Economic Survey of New Zealand*. Paris: OECD.

———. 2002b. *Economic Outlook* (June). Paris: OECD.

Quiggin, J. 2001. "Social Democracy and Market Reform in Australia and New Zealand." In *Social Democracy in Neoliberal Times*, edited by A. Glyn. Oxford: Oxford University Press.

Tille, C., and K-M. Yi. 2001. "Curbing Unemployment in Europe: Are There Lessons from Ireland and the Netherlands?" *Current Issues in Economics and Finance* 7(5) (May): 1–6.

Walton, R. 2000. "International Comparisons of Company Profitability." *Economic Trends* 565: 33–46.

# 7

## Employment Performance and Labor Market Institutions: The Case of Spain

RAFAEL MUÑOZ DE BUSTILLO LLORENTE

### 7.1 INTRODUCTION

Since the early 1980s, Spain's unemployment rate has been much higher than that of any other member country of the Organization for Economic Cooperation and Development (OECD). For the OECD-IMF orthodoxy, which finds the source of high European unemployment in the rigidities imposed by labor market institutions, this would seem to be a puzzling result, since Spain has followed a policy of deregulation and reduction of real labor costs since the mid-1980s. It should be noted that Spain's labor costs were already among the lowest in the European Union and that the construction and consolidation of the welfare state in Spain started much later than in the rest of Western Europe and has not yet reached the same level of development as that of other European countries.[1] So Spain does not have, at least at first glance, many of the institutional features that predict persistent high unemployment according to the orthodox view. Furthermore, from the beginning of the economic recovery of the mid-1990s, employment in Spain has shown a higher rate of growth than in the rest of Europe, with an extraordinary 9 percentage point reduction in the unemployment rate from 1996 to 2001 (OECD 2002, Statistical Annex Table A).

The orthodox interpretation of the causes of unemployment in Europe focuses on the inadequacy of its labor market institutions when confronted with the exogenous shocks of the 1970s (IMF 1999). According to the OECD, this is precisely the problem for Spain: "An unfortunate combination of rigid corporatist structures, an increasingly generous welfare system, and a wage bargaining system that takes insufficient account of local labor market conditions . . . has made for a particularly inflexible labor market"

(OECD 1996: 61). In a more recent report, the OECD adds that "In assessing Spain's poor labor market performance up to the mid-1990s, it is clear that strict employment protection legislation and its interaction with other labor market policies has been a central element" (OECD 2000a: 54).

The purpose of this chapter is to explore the sources of Spain's extremely high unemployment throughout the 1980s and 1990s and the impressive employment recovery in recent years and, more specifically, to consider the role played by the policies implemented by the Spanish government in the framework of the "ten commandments" of the OECD *Jobs Study* (see table 1.1) and the EU employment strategy. The first part of the chapter (sections 7.1 and 7.2) provides a short account of the history of unemployment in Spain, including the different interpretations of the coexistence of social peace and massive unemployment. With this background, the second part is devoted to the analysis of the different policy measures taken to address the problem of unemployment, seeking to evaluate their real impact on the labor market. This analysis includes a detailed account of the pattern of employment creation and the characteristics of the jobs generated since the recovery of the economy in 1994. Special attention is paid to the specific features of the Spanish labor market (e.g., flexibility for dismissal and redundancy, the generosity of the unemployment compensation system, and the loosely coordinated system of wage bargaining) considered by the OECD-IMF orthodoxy to be the major sources of the high unemployment problem in Spain. The final section presents a summary of the major conclusions of the chapter.

## 7.2 OVERVIEW OF THE EVOLUTION AND CHARACTERISTICS OF SPANISH UNEMPLOYMENT

In order to better understand the problem of unemployment in Spain, it is useful to review its roots and its historical evolution, because, as we will see, due to specific features of its history, in the last quarter of the twentieth century Spain experienced specific shocks different from those suffered by the rest of the OECD. Spain managed to keep its unemployment rate at a very low level (under 3%) through the 1960s and the early 1970s. From 1975, Spain experienced huge increases in unemployment, which reached 21% in 1985–1986. The recovery of the Spanish economy in the late 1980s, with growth rates above 5% in 1987 and 1988, meant that the unemployment rate decreased to 16% in 1991, only to increase again afterward, at a very fast rate, as a result of the economic recession of 1992–1993, reaching an all-time high of 24% in 1994.

In order to understand the gargantuan increase of unemployment from 1977 to 1987, it is important to consider the following facts:

1. Spain had a very late and fast transition from an agriculture-based economy to an industrial and services-based economy. Thus, when the rest of the European economies had already absorbed

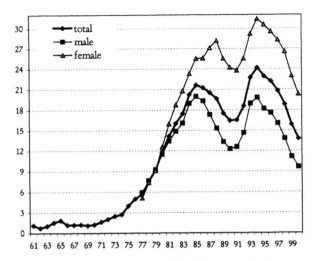

Figure 7.1. Unemployment rate (%), Spain, 1961–2000. Source: Author's analysis of *Encuesta de población* activa (Labor Force Survey) data.

the surplus labor of the agricultural sector, Spain was still in the process of absorbing it.[2] As we can see in table 7.1, Spain, at the beginning of the 1980s was still, at least from a comparative perspective, a fairly agricultural country. Since then, the share of agricultural employment in total employment in Spain has dropped 11 percentage points—8 points from 1980 to 1991 and 3 more from 1991 to 1999—an equivalent of 1.3 million jobs altogether (around 10% of total employment in 1999).

2. Emigration, first to central and South America in the first part of the twentieth century and later to western and central Europe (e.g., Germany, France, Switzerland, the Benelux countries), was always an escape hatch for Spanish surplus labor. The economic crises of the 1970s not only meant the elimination of this source of

Table 7.1. Share of Agricultural Employment in Total Employment, United States, European Union, and Spain

|                       | 1960 | 1980 | 1991 | 1999 |
|-----------------------|------|------|------|------|
| United States         | 8.3  | 3.4  | 2.8  | 2.5  |
| European Union (12)   | 22.6 | 9.4  | 6.4  | 4.5[1] |
| Spain                 | 38.7 | 17.9 | 9.9  | 6.9  |

1. EU 15.
  Source: Eurostat and Cronos database, U.S. Bureau of Labor Statistics, *Employment and Earnings*, and Instituto Nacional de Estadística, *Encuesta de población activa*.

unemployment reduction but started a process of homecoming by many of the Spanish workers resident abroad,[3] thus increasing the pool of labor in the face of shrinking labor demand. From 1960 to 1973, more than 1 million Spaniards emigrated to other European countries. In 1970, there were around 2.5 million Spaniards living abroad. A quarter of a century later, the figure was 1.4 million. Beginning in 1974, the inflow of former emigrants was higher than the outflow of new emigrants. From 1970 to 1973, there was a net outflow of emigrants of more than 25,000 per year, whereas from 1974 to 1979 there was a net inflow of 250,000. This process of "homecoming" still goes on to this day (in 2000 the net in flow was 43,000).[4]

3. Although, from a comparative point of view, the average Spanish labor force participation rate is very low and has remained at roughly the same level since 1964, from 1985 on there has been a significant increase in the female labor force participation rate, rising from 27% in 1985 to 39.7% in 1998. In fact, from 1985 to 1998, the number of women of working age increased by 2.2 million, while during those years the female labor force increased by 2.7 million, or 123% (the equivalent increase among men was less than 25%). Thus, while in 1985 the ratio of men to women in the labor force was 2.4:1, in 2000 it was 1.5:1.

4. In a period of 10 years, starting in 1975, the year of the death of Francisco Franco, and ending in 1986, the year Spain became the twelfth member of the EU, Spain went through huge institutional changes. These included the liberalization of the economy, the building of a modern state (with public expenditure as a percentage of the GDP going from 26% to 47%), the democratization of its political system (with a new constitution in 1978), and the opening of the economy (with exports and imports as a percentage of the GDP climbing from 30% in 1975 to 56% in 1999). Just as happened with the short-lived Second Republic, which lasted from 1931 to 1939, this second attempt to develop democratic institutions and modernize the country coincided with a worldwide recession, making things more difficult from an economic and social point of view.

A detailed account of all of these changes is beyond the scope of this essay. Nevertheless, it is important to stress the scale of the changes. For example, the change in the underlying growth model for the economy produced, among other things, a huge restructuring of the industrial sector, characterized by substantial downsizing of employment in many manufacturing firms. Furthermore, Spain faced the challenge of the modernization of its economy armed with very-low-quality institutions for conflict management and low levels of social cohesion. As Dany Rodrik (1998:1) argues, "when social divisions run deep and the institutions of conflict management are weak, the economic cost of exogenous shocks—such as the deteriorations in the terms of trade—are magnified by the distributional conflicts that are triggered." From this perspective, in the 1970s Spain was in a very bad position to confront the shocks and economic slowdown that confronted the entire developed world. At the death of Franco, not only did the political system completely lack legitimacy but also the country still had to wait two years to know, after the first democratic general elections in 1977, where the real political power was located. Obviously, under those circumstances, the main goal of the government was to achieve a peaceful transition to democracy, and not so much to fight the effects of the global economic slowdown. That battle would have demanded the implementation of painful measures that could not be taken in such a delicate political situation.

Just to offer a glimpse of the weakness of the institutions for conflict management, note that free trade unions were illegal until 1977, although they worked undercover, infiltrated the official trade unions, and were highly politicized by the 1970s. Similarly, employers' organizations were in practice nonexistent until the late 1970s; for example, the CEOE, a confederation of employer's associations, was founded in 1977. The combination of weak employers' organizations and vindictive trade unions, during a time of impasse in terms of economic policy, produced, from 1974 to 1978, an increase in real labor costs of more than 30% and triggered inflation, which reached 24% by 1977. Needless to say, the social divisions in the country at the time also ran deep. Taking the distribution of income as an indicator of social division, in 1970 the upper quintile in the distribution of income received 53% of total income.[5] In the sphere of industrial relations, the lack of social cohesion translated into as many as 20 million days lost in strikes in 1977 (figure 7.2), while on the political front it was manifested in the even division of votes between the Left and the Right at a time when the differences between right- and left-wing parties were much more marked than they are today and when those differences reflected serious ideological disagreements over the nature of the project of civil society (figure 7.3).

This lack of appropriate institutions for conflict resolution at a time of change produced a much higher level of uncertainty than was warranted by the economic crisis itself. In Spain, firms were uncertain not only about the evolution of the economy but also about the type of society that was going to be developed in the very near future. This situation translated into what was known at the time as an "investment strike," a strike at least partially politically driven, which led to 10 years (1975–1984) of either stagnant or diminishing investment.[6] This behavior is unique in the modern history of the country. As a result of the Moncloa Pact[7]—a social agreement signed by the government and the major political parties with the backing of the major trade unions and the confederation of employers' organizations—the rate of inflation dropped from 24% in 1977 to 8% in 1985. At the same time there was a deep redistribution of income away

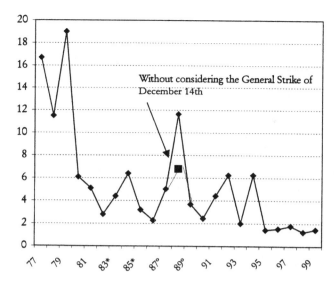

Figure 7.2. Millions of working days lost in strikes, Spain, 1977–1999. Source: Author's analysis of Ministry of Labor data. (* without data for the Basque country; ° without data for Catalonia.)

from wage and salaries and toward profits so as to facilitate the recovery of firms' profits and the relaunching of investment. This redistribution was so intense (also in comparative terms with the EU or the United States) that by 1982 the percentage of national income that went to profits had regained the level enjoyed in 1970 and by 1985 was at the level of 1964.

These are some of the specific features of Spanish recent economic history that should be taken into consideration when dealing with the roots of unemployment in Spain. Other elements, such as the specific regulation of the labor market and the orientation of government economic policy, are considered later in this chapter. But, before doing so, it is important to consider the extent to which the unemployment statistics accurately reflect the situation of the Spanish labor market.

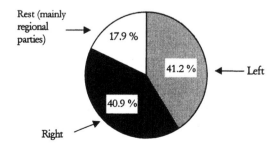

Figure 7.3. Results of the general elections of 1978 (%).

## 7.3 QUESTIONING THE NUMBERS

The coexistence of high unemployment rates, high GDP growth rates, and a reasonable level of social peace has led politicians and public opinion on many occasions during the past two decades to question the relevance of the numbers produced by the Labor Force Survey, arguing that the estimated rates of unemployment were incompatible with the social peace and the feeling of prosperity enjoyed by the country in the 1990s.[8]

One of the more popular explanations for the coexistence of high unemployment and social peace in Spain has been that the figures produced by the Labor Force Survey misinterpret the reality because of the existence of a buoyant underground economy. The underground economy in Spain has been estimated to represent anything from a low of a few percentage points of the GDP to 15–20%, a range so wide that it makes these estimates almost useless.[9] Some of the studies also offer estimates of so-called irregular labor, defined in terms of noncompliance with social security and labor regulations and believed to range from 15% to 22% of overall employment. Most likely, if we could produce a detailed account of all the people employed in both the official and the shadow economy, we would get a picture of higher employment, but this would almost certainly not bring unemployment in Spain down to the levels found in northern Europe. So we still have to explain how it is possible to make high unemployment compatible with social peace and a certain sense of shared national prosperity.

The answer lies in the existence of multiple layers of social protection that introduce a wedge between not having a job and not having a basic income to get by. Among those layers it is important to highlight two: unemployment compensation and the family. Focusing on the latter, as the former is the subject of a detailed analysis later in the chapter, we can say that, to a large extent, through a system of resource pooling and income sharing, the family covers the basic needs of those unemployed. For example, and keeping in mind that a third of the unemployed in Spain are young people (ages 16–24), if we look at the living arrangements of Spanish young people (ages 15–29), we find that 79% are living with their parents, and most of them also live mainly (57%) or partly (17%) on family income (CIS 1997). In Spain, 89% of those ages 20–24 live with their parents, a percentage only matched in Italy (87%). Close behind is Portugal (82%), followed by Germany (55%), France (52%), the Netherlands (47%), and Finland (29%). In terms of income, Italy and Spain are the European countries where family transfers are most important as a source of income, accounting for 67.6% and 62.4% of the income of those ages 20–24, respectively, while public transfers represent a marginal amount (3.4% and 3.6%, respectively). On the other end of the spectrum, in the United Kingdom, income from work (regular and casual) is the major source of income for people ages 20–24, while family transfers play only a marginal role, being the major source of income in only 17% of the cases (IARD 2001).

The major insurance role played by the family in Spain is also shown in a recent study by Bentolila and Ichino (2000), where the authors find that comparable periods of unemployment of male households heads are associated with lower loss in consumption in Spanish and Italian homes than in homes in Germany, Britain, or the United States. This difference, in the opinion of the authors, can be explained only by the existence of extended family networks that provide a fundamental source of insurance against unemployment. In a study of the determinants of the intensity of job search, Garcia and Toharia (2000) show that family income negatively affects the intensity of search.[10] According to the Labor Force Survey, in 1998 19.1% of Spanish households had at least one member of the family unemployed, but only in 7.9% were *all* of the members unemployed.[11] Thus, if family income is used to cover the family needs, regardless of the position of the different members of the family in the labor market, then the redistributive role played by the family could help to explain, at least partially, the coexistence of social peace and massive unemployment.

## 7.4 LABOR MARKET INSTITUTIONS AND EMPLOYMENT PERFORMANCE

In this section we review the situation and the policy measures implemented in Spain in the areas established by the OECD *Jobs Study*, paying special attention to their impact on the evolution of employment and unemployment.

### 7.4.1 Labor Market Reform and Employment in Spain

Since the early 1980s, the orthodox interpretation of the causes of unemployment in Spain has focused on the high degree of "rigidity" of the labor market as a product of (a) low wage flexibility, that is, low response of wages to the condition of the labor market, (b) high employment protection, (c) generous unemployment benefits, and (d) a dysfunctional system of collective agreements. For example, in the OECD 1985–1986 *Economic Survey* of Spain, we can read that "Real wage rigidity was supported by the legal framework and labor market practices" and that "High redundancy payments tended to strengthen workers' bargaining power in collective negotiations" (OECD 1986: 57).

At the same time, it should be recognized that post-Franco Spain inherited a highly regulated labor market, and since the early 1980s the efforts of the Spanish state have been directed toward the "liberalization" or "deregulation" of the labor market. In short, the predemocratic labor system in Spain was characterized by:

1. The prohibition of free trade unions, with the collateral problems of police persecution and the governmental determination that all strikes were illegal and must be suppressed as a matter of public order.
2. The setting of basic wages at a very low level, although there were many kinds of bonuses and commissions, of a selective

nature, negotiated between the firms and the workers under the umbrella of the official trade unions with the purpose of allowing enough flexibility in the wage system so as to create an incentive for productivity.[12] Nevertheless, the overall effect of the system of wage fixing was to impose relatively low wages. For example, while from 1965 to 1969 the GDP rose at an annual rate of 6.8%, the growth of real wage per waged worker was only 2.5%, resulting in a distribution of income much more favorable to profits than in the rest of the European countries (Revenga, 1991).

3. The establishment of a quasi-tenured employment system to compensate for the low level of wages and to help to legitimate the system. A whole set of legal measures was developed to restrict the right of firms to fire employees.[13] Firing was not impossible, but it was bothersome, so jobs for life became the custom in the Spanish labor market of the time.

Although in 1980 a new legal framework for labor relations was approved,[14] the mainstream opinion was that the new set of rules, while increasing the role of the market, was still too restrictive. The rules included, for example, tight limits on the type of labor contracts available and on the power of dismissal. According to the OECD, the hiring and firing regulations were, along with two other features of this law—the role given to the trade union in the process of wage setting and the system of unemployment benefits—the major sources of "rigidity" in the Spanish labor market, and they have consequently been the target of criticism and deregulation proposals. In the terms of the 1996 *OECD Economic Survey* of Spain: "The ... failure of labor market conditions to adapt substantially is due to ... a strict system of employment protection legislation ... that has led to excessive severance payments and low rates of hiring; an inflexible wage bargaining system; and since the 1980's, a relatively generous benefit system"(51–56).

### 7.4.2 Costs of Layoffs

One of the criticisms leveled by the employers' association, CEOE, is the high cost of layoffs, something that in the association's opinion leads to a higher-than-optimal share of workers with temporary contracts. This emphasis on the reduction of employment security provisions is interesting because, from a theoretical point of view, as Nickell (1997) reminds us, laws that raise the cost of dismissal have a double impact on the labor market: a reduction of the outflow to unemployment, resulting from the cost associated with dismissal through redundancy payments and other administrative costs, and a reduction of the inflow of workers from unemployment to work, as the firms wait until they are certain they need one more worker before doing the actual hiring. As a result, "the overall impact on employment is likely to be rather small, as these effects would tend to cancel out" (66).[15] This outcome is consistent with the conclusion

Table 7.2. Regulation of Redundancy Payments

| Type of dismissal | Reason of Dismissal | Redundancy payment | | Maximum |
|---|---|---|---|---|
| Disciplinary | Lack of fulfillment of duties by the worker | None | | |
| Objective or Collective | There are economic, technical, productive, or organizational reasons powerful enough in the opinion of the judge to justify the dismissal | 20 days of wage per year working in the firm | | 12 months |
| | | 45 days of wage per year working in the firm | | 42 months |
| | | The judge can consider the layoff null and require the rehiring of the worker. If the firm does not observe the edict, the redundancy payment can be increased up to 15 more days | | 12 months |
| Unfair | The judge considers that there are no reasons powerful enough to fire the worker | Reform of 2001 | New type of long-term contract for specific groups of workers: 33 days of wage per year working in the firm | 24 months |
| | | | Extension of the reform of 1997 to new groups | 24 months |
| | | Reform of 1997 | Redundancy payment to workers with fixed-term contracts at the end of the term: 8 days of wage per year working in the firm | |

reached by most of the researchers of this topic (see, for example, Buechtemann 1993).[16] More recently, Blanchard and Portugal (2001), in a comparative analysis of the American and Portuguese labor markets, concluded that an increase in employment protection leads to a decrease in flows into unemployment and an increase in its duration, "but the two cancel out when looking at unemployment" (204).

Table 7.2 presents a summary of the regulation on redundancy payments in Spain, including the amendments introduced by the 1997 reform. Redundancy payments fluctuate from 0, in cases of "disciplinary" dismissal, to 45 days per year of work in the firm (subject to a maximum of

3.5 years) in cases of unfair dismissal. In the case of dismissal as a result of "objective" circumstances not related to the worker's performance, the redundancy payment is reduced to 20 days per year and the maximum total quantity to one year.

Although ranking countries according to firing costs is not always an easy task (Malo and Toharia 1999),[17] Spain is usually included in the group of countries that pose greater obstacles to the termination of employment contracts (Emerson 1988; Kuechle 1990; OECD 1999b). According to Segura et al. (1991), the major differences between Spain and other OECD countries are not in the level of redundancy payments in fair dismissal (Spain's are generally in line with the amounts granted in other countries) but in the case of unjust dismissal suits. In the opinion of Toharia and Malo (1997), the problem is that the judges who set the redundancy payment in case of disagreement between firms and workers apply a very narrow interpretation of what constitutes "objective" economic causes to justify the dismissal, while collective dismissal can be used only when the firm is facing losses. Thus, firms, anticipating the likely result of lawsuits, usually resort to disciplinary dismissal (which does not require advance notice). Of course, since the real reason for firing the worker is otherwise, the judge ends up declaring the dismissal unfair and passes sentence accordingly. In the end, the firm pays the redundancy payment equivalent to 45 days per year, the rate originally set to discourage the capricious firing of workers, even if there are economic reasons behind the firing. The data available on the results of dismissal suits taken to court partially backs this argument. In 2001, the verdict was fully or partially favorable to the worker in 32% of the cases, while in only 13% of the suits was it favorable to the firm (in 25% of the cases the parts reached an agreement, and 22% were rejected).[18] Nevertheless, despite the supposed higher level of employment protection in Spain, workers with indefinite contracts experience a dismissal rate similar to those in other countries: from 3% to 4% in the period 1987–1998, excluding the recession years 1992–1994, when it jumped to 4%–6% (Durán 1999). This result is comparable to the dismissal rates of other Western industrialized nations in the 1980s: 4% in West Germany, 3.7% in France (1984–1987), 3.5%–4% in the United Kingdom (1984–1989), 3.1% in Italy (1984), and 4%–5% in the United States.[19]

If the dismissal rate is more or less similar to that of the rest of Europe, then the impact of stricter employment protection legislation in Spain would have to be felt in the cost of labor. According to the *Survey of Labor Cost* (INE 1998), redundancy payments in 1996 amounted to 2.1% of total labor costs.[20] This higher cost, given the lower real unit labor cost of Spain compared with those in most of the European countries with lower employment protection, can hardly account for much of the difference in unemployment rates.[21]

Nevertheless, the Spanish government followed the OECD's advice and introduced two reforms aimed at reducing dismissal costs. In 1994, the Socialist Party (PSOE) reduced the possibilities for nullifying a dismissal and increased the possibilities of dismissal for economic reasons. It also reduced the transaction costs related to layoffs by reducing "transaction wages" (the right of the worker to his or her wage until the end of the process) and by speeding up the administrative process. In 1997, the right-wing government of the People's Party (PP) created a new type of long-term contract with lower redundancy payments in case of dismissal and a reduction in the employer's social security contribution.[22] Finally, in 2002, the PP eliminated the transaction wages. According to Malo (1996), the 1994 reform did not have much impact on the size of the redundancy payments granted. As for the 1997 reform, we can say that it managed to stop the increase in temporary employment (the temporality ratio went from 33.5% in 1997 to 32.7% in 1999), but so far its impact has not been strong enough to produce an important reduction in the size of the contingent workforce. Nevertheless, since its creation, the new long-term contract has become dominant in the Spanish panorama of long-term labor contracts.[23] This result should come as no surprise. Owing to its lower redundancy payments and the temporary reduction in social security costs, this type of contract is not only cheaper than the standard indefinite contract but cheaper even than temporary contracts during the first 24 months.

### 7.4.3 Hiring Flexibility

The first important amendment to the 1980 law aiming to increase the "flexibility" of the labor market came only four years after its approval by the first government led by the Socialist Party.[24] At the time, it was believed that one important reason behind the high rate of unemployment was the high cost of dismissal (through redundancy payments). Faced with the option of reforming the system of redundancy payments or, alternatively, facilitating hiring on fixed-term bases, the government opted for the latter, introducing a new type of temporal contract and eliminating the "causation" principle from the short-term contract.[25] This liberalization of the contract law had a fast and deep impact on the structure of the Spanish labor market: 10 years later, 35% of the waged and salaried workers had fixed-term contracts, compared to around 12% before the reform. That percentage has come down slightly since 1997 as a result of changes in the legislation. Firms quickly adopted the new possibilities of hiring à la carte, turning the once standard indefinite contract into something rare. For example, in 1996, out of the 8.6 million contracts signed (equivalent to having every employee sign a contract), only 4% were indefinite contracts. Not only have temporary contracts become the standard way of hiring for the Spanish firms, but also, as we can see in figure 7.4, most of the contracts have a relatively short duration; 30% are for one month or less. Thus, it is not unusual for firms to have a permanent job carried out by a string of temporary workers (or by the same worker with a string of temporary contracts).[26]

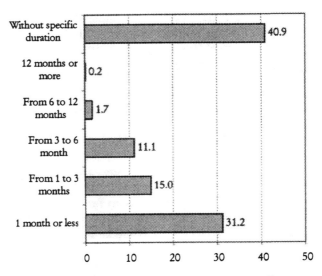

Figure 7.4. Distribution of short-term contracts according to duration (%), Spain, 2000. Source: INEM, *Estadística de contratos registrados*.

Fifteen years after the reform of the hiring system in Spain, the possibility of hiring à la carte has had the following impact on the economy:

1. It has increased the capacity of firms to adjust their workforce to business cycle conditions. The high share of temporary workers in Spanish firms is probably one of the elements to consider when explaining the huge employment impact of the 1992–1993 recession. From 1992 to 1993 the temporary worker share went from 33.5% to 32.3%, absorbing about 60% of the employment reduction. On the other hand, the fact that firms could use temporary contracts would also have increased the employment intensity of the economic recovery, an effect detected by Segura et al. (1991) for the 1986–1990 recovery. So a high temporary share of employment increases the responsiveness of overall employment to cyclical swings in the economy.

2. It has saved firms money. Fixed-term contracts are less costly for firms, since they save redundancy payments in case of downsizing. Furthermore, workers with temporary contracts face a tangible wage gap. In 1996, according to the *Encuesta de Distribución Salarial*, the average worker with a temporary contract had annual earnings equivalent to 45% of the annual earnings of the average worker with an indefinite contract. This wage gap, when calculated according to broad categories of work, varies from a high of 67 percentage points for an administrative worker to a "low" of 40 points

for a construction worker. Evidently, the level of aggregation of the data does not allow us to determine which part of the gap responds to the existence of differences in productivity and which part responds to pure wage discrimination, but the difference is important enough to allow for the existence of discrimination once the rest of the objective differences are taken into account. For example, Bover et al. (2000), after taking into account differences in age, activity, education, and tenure, estimate a wage gap of 10%. Furthermore, because seniority has an important (positive) impact on wages, the lack of job stability also negatively affects earnings growth for temporary workers.

3. There is also indirect evidence that the index of temporality has a negative impact on productivity, as in many cases workers do not stay in the firm long enough to improve their skills or develop a sense of identification with the firm. Specific on-the-job training is also less likely in firms with high temporality ratios.

4. It has social costs. There is evidence of the existence of a positive relation between the degree of temporality and work accidents (Pita y Dominguez 1998). In 1996, Spain, along with Portugal, had the highest accident rate of the EU 15, with more than 6,000 work accidents resulting in more than three days of leave per 100,000 employed workers. Furthermore, according to survey data, the most valuable element of a job is its stability, which is valued much more highly than the interest level of the tasks performed or a good salary.

5. Finally, according to some authors,[27] the explosion in the index of temporary workers has created a dual labor market, a textbook example of an insider-outsider problem. The relevance of this analysis depends on two elements. First, as we have seen, although the adjustment of the workforce to shifts in market demand relies heavily on temporary workers, permanent workers are not entirely safe from the effects of downsizing. Second, as we see later on, the final impact of the dualization of the labor market on wage negotiation depends on the type of trade union and its wage-negotiating strategies.

Altogether, it seems that the final evaluation of this first move toward a freer labor market—deregulating the entry of workers into firms—has to be negative. In fact, this interpretation was by the recent conservative government, as suggested by its first legislative action in labor policy, which was aimed at the reduction of the temporary worker rate through the creation of a new type of contract. If we were to assess the costs and benefits of the fixed-time contract system, we could say that by making use of these types of contracts, the country has managed to create higher employment in times of economic expansion at the price of growing insecurity, lower productivity, reduced job safety, and higher employment loss each time there is an economic recession. It can be seen as a policy with significant social costs but with no clear effect on the secular trend in unemployment.

### 7.4.4 Unemployment Benefits

Because of the unpopularity of proposals to reduce unemployment protection in a country with massive unemployment, the debate over this issue in Spain has hardly ever left the think tanks and reached the political arena.[28] In fact, the changes introduced in the past decade in the system of unemployment protection were more the product of fiscal concerns than the instrument of employment policy. Only the last reform of the unemployment protection system promoted by the conservative government of the PP in May 2002 was not inspired by fiscal considerations. This reform, approved in a period of surplus within the unemployment insurance system, faced strong trade union opposition and led to a general strike. Among other things, it changed the special unemployment assistance to temporary agricultural workers and gave more power to the employment agencies (INEM) to decide when a job is suitable for an unemployed individual.

Unemployment protection in Spain is a two-tier system. The first level is classic unemployment insurance, which covers all employees who work in the industrial, agricultural, or service sectors. In order to qualify for unemployment benefits, a person must (1) have lost the job involuntarily,[29] (2) be able and willing to work, (3) be at the disposal of the employment office, (4) be affiliated with the social security scheme or have equivalent status, and (5) have covered the required contribution period (currently the minimum period is 12 months during the six years immediately preceding the legal status of unemployment).[30] The duration of UI depends on the contribution period and goes from four months up to two years (available to those who have contributed for at least six years). The replacement rate is 70% of previous wages for the first 180 days and 60% afterward. There is a floor of 75% of the minimum wWage (100% if the worker has at least one child under his orher care) and a ceiling of 170% of the minimum wage (220% with two or more children). As we see later on, the minimum wage is set at quite a low level in Spain—30% of the average wage—so this is an important qualification to consider when analyzing the "generosity" of the UI.

After having exhausted their unemployment benefits, unemployed workers can apply for unemployment assistance.[31] The duration of this second level of protection is from 6 to 18 months (an extension of the period is possible in some cases),[32] and the amount granted is from 75% to 125% of the minimum wage, according to the number of dependents.

Given these restrictions, it is hard to recognize the features of the Spanish unemployment protection system in the typical table on UI used in most comparative studies on the subject, such as the one reproduced in table 7.3 and taken from Nickell (1997). As Atkinson and Micklewright (1991) note: "unemployment compensation is not simple to describe and differences between countries are not easy to summarize. But this does

Table 7.3. Comparative Indexes of Unemployment Protection Schemes

| Country | Benefit replacement ratio (%) | Benefit duration (years) | Country | Benefit replacement ratio (%) | Benefit duration (years) |
|---|---|---|---|---|---|
| Austria | 50 | 2.0 | Portugal | 65 | 0.8 |
| Belgium | 60 | 4.0 | Spain | 70 | 3.5 |
| Denmark | 90 | 2.5 | Sweden | 80 | 1.2 |
| Finland | 63 | 2.0 | Switzerland | 70 | 1.0 |
| France | 57 | 3.0 | United Kingdom | 38 | 4.0 |
| Germany | 63 | 4.0 | Canada | 59 | 1.0 |
| Ireland | 37 | 4.0 | United States | 50 | 0.5 |
| Italy | 20 | 0.5 | Japan | 60 | 0.5 |
| Netherlands | 70 | 2.0 | Australia | 36 | 4.0 |
| Norway | 65 | 1.5 | New Zealand | 30 | 4.0 |

Source: Nickell (1997), p. 61.

not ... justify reducing comparisons of actual benefit system to single parameters like the benefit rate or the duration of benefit" (169).

First, the benefit replacement ratio considered in table 7.3 is relevant only for the first year, and even within the first year it does not consider the existence of an upper limit. Second, the 3.5 years of duration considered is the maximum and is both subject to strict eligibility criteria and associated with a much lower benefit replacement ratio. In fact, as we can see in figure 7.5, 43% of those unemployed receiving unemployment compensation have a benefit duration of one year or less. On the other hand, 44% qualify for a benefit duration of from 1.5 to 2 years, logical considering the high rate of long-term unemployment in Spain (46% in 1999). In 2001, the average duration of unemployment compensation was slightly under 15 months, of which only half, 6.7 months, was actually used (CES 2002: 330).

Another interesting feature of the Spanish unemployment protection system has been the progressive substitution of unemployment insurance benefits for unemployment assistance in a process of "welfarization" of the system of unemployment protection. Since the creation of unemployment assistance in 1982, the proportion of those receiving unemployment compensation out of all those receiving unemployment benefits has decreased to around 40% of the total number of people protected.

As is well known, the major charge made against the system of unemployment protection, as presented, for example, in the OECD *Jobs Study* (1994), is that unemployment protection can have a negative impact on intensity of job search, increasing the duration of unemployment. In their own words, unemployment insurance (UI) systems "have drifted towards quasi-permanent income support in many countries, lowering work incentives" (1994: 48). In fact, the three major interventions in Spain

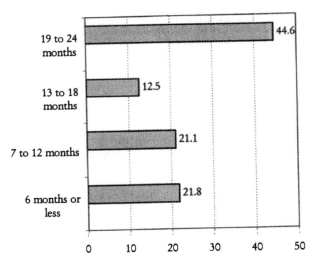

**Figure 7.5. Distribution of duration of unemployment compensation (%). Source: INEM, second quarter, 2000.**

since the consolidation of the unemployment protection system in 1984 have been aimed at making unemployment insurance more difficult to get and less attractive. In 1992, the benefit replacement ratio was reduced from an 80-70-60 scheme (80% during the first six months, 70% during the next six months, and 60% during rest of the period), to a 70-60 scheme (70% for the first six months and 60% for the rest of the qualifying period). At the same time, the number of months of work required to be eligible for UI was increased from 6 to 12. In 1993, unemployment benefits became subject to income tax deductions and social security contributions. At the same time, the minimum benefit was reduced from 100% of minimum wage to 75%. To compensate first for the increase in the duration of unemployment and later on for the growth of groups in the labor force not covered by UI, in 1989 and again in 1994, unemployment assistance was increased. These reforms explain the progressive substitution of the supposedly "generous" unemployment compensation for the more Spartan unemployment assistance. Finally, in 2002, the employment agency, INEM, was given more power to decide whether a job was suitable for those receiving unemployment benefits and given the power to penalize those who refused to accept job offers considered suitable by the employment agency.

There are several studies available that have tried to measure the impact of the system of UI on the behavior of the unemployed who receive unemployment benefits in Spain (see table 7.4). In contrast to the typical cross-country regression of the determinants of employment, as in the classic Layard et al. (1991) and Nickell (1997) studies, these case studies analyze the actual behavior of the unemployed workers, introducing whether they are entitled to UI or not as one of the explanatory variables.

Most of them, drawing on the theory of job search, try to measure the impact of unemployment benefits on the intensity of job search. As is well known in the literature, the existence of UI reduces the opportunity cost of being unemployed, generating a perverse incentive for those unemployed to either stop looking for a job altogether or to reduce the intensity of their job searches. Nevertheless, from another perspective, it is argued that the efficiency of job search may also improve with UI, since workers who receive unemployment benefits have more income to "invest" in the sometimes costly process of job searching, while at the same time the mere existence of UI helps to maintain the worker's connection to the world of work (Jackman et al. 1990).

As we can see from table 7.4, most of the studies surveyed conclude that receiving unemployment benefits is a relevant variable when it comes to explaining the rate of exit from unemployment to employment, although with important caveats. For example, for Alba-Ramirez and Freeman (1990), having UI increases the duration of unemployment but also increases the probability of getting a permanent job and a higher wage, precisely one of the objectives of UI: to allow the unemployed to search for a proper job. Another common result is the concentration of the estimated negative impact on the first few months of unemployment (Cebrian et al. 1995; Bover, Arellano, and Bentolila 1996). Another interesting result is the relatively small role played by UI in explaining the Spanish unemployment problem. According to García Brosa (1996), the increase in the average duration of unemployment associated with receiving UI explains less than half a percentage point of the unemployment rate. Even the paper of Bover et al. (2000), which accords to UI a more prominent role than changes in the economic cycle in explaining the transition from unemployment to employment, admits that "the small estimated difference in the disincentive effects of receiving benefits on the probability of exiting unemployment coupled with the current difference in the levels of unemployment benefits coverage between the two countries cannot explain by itself the big difference in unemployment rates between Portugal and Spain" (405). These results should not come as a surprise. After all, it is only natural that a person without any source of income would be much less choosy when it comes to accepting a job and more eager when it comes to looking for one. In fact, according to the Survey on the Conditions of Life of the Unemployed in Spain, the same behavioral difference is found when we look at the family income of the unemployed: while 75% of those unemployed in families with income under 50,000 Pts. are looking intensively for a job, the percentage goes down to 56% for those in families with income over 300,000 Pts.

But we should be very careful when reading the results obtained from microeconomic evidence in terms of the impact of unemployment insurance on aggregate unemployment.[33] First, in a nontextbook-perfect labor market, a reduction in the rate of exit from unemployment of those with UI as a result of the disincentive effect of the benefit may lead not to an

**Table 7.4. Estimated Impact of Unemployment Insurance on Job Search and Unemployment in Spain: Summary of Major Studies**

| Author | Year | Source | Results |
|---|---|---|---|
| Alba-Ramirez & Freeman (1990) | 1985 Spain | *Encuesta de condiciones de vida y de trabajo* | The duration of unemployment is positively related to the conditions of UI eligibility. Those eligible have a duration of unemployment between 4 and 6 months longer. It also increases the probability of getting a permanent job (12%) and the wage received in the new job (from 3.6 to 5.7% higher). |
| Andrés & García1 (1991) | 1985 Spain | *Encuesta de condiciones de vida y de trabajo* | The negative impact of UI on employment duration holds only in the model with homogeneous workers. The introduction of heterogeneity greatly reduces the impact. |
| Sempere & Ródenas (1996) | 1985–1990 Spain | SIPRE files | Positive nonlinear relation between imputed duration of UI and duration of unemployment (strong for the first 6 months). |
| Cebrian et al. (1995) | 1984–1990 Spain | SIPRE files | The duration of UI has a negative incentive effect on workers eligible for UI of short duration (from 3 to 9+ months). For this group, the rate of exit to employment increases in the months close to the termination of the benefits, although this result could be a product of unobserved characteristics of the individuals. There is no observed relation between the generosity ratio and the probability of exit to employment. |
| García Brosa (1996) | 1990 Catalonia | EPA Sample of 720 people | The expected duration of unemployment in a scenario of no UI would have been between 9.5% to 14.9% lower. The estimated unemployment rate in the absence of UI is from 12.49% to 12.54% compared with an observed rate of 12.7%. |
| Bover, Arellano, & Bentolila (1998) | 1987 (II)–1994(III) Spain | EPA | Receiving UI reduces the probability of exit from unemployment to employment. For example, for a person in his/her third month of unemployment, when the effect is highest, the hazard of leaving unemployment for those not receiving UI is twice the rate of a person receiving UI. From the ninth month on, impact is negligible. |

**Table 7.4.** (*Continued*)

| Author | Year | Source | Results |
|--------|------|--------|---------|
| Bover, García Perea, & Portugal (2000) | 1992–94 Spain Portugal | EPA | After isolating effects of age, schooling, tenure, sector of the previous job, and head of household and seasonal differences, being a recipient of UI reduces the probability of getting a job (in both countries): the chances of exit from unemployment into employment for those without UI is 1.8% higher (1.5% for Portugal). |
| García & Toharia (2000) | 1996 Spain | *Condiciones de vida de los desempleados en España* | Job search is not affected by the fact of receiving unemployment benefits; neither is the intensity of the search nor the number of systems used. Only when it comes to accepting a low wage or a part-time job do those receiving unemployment benefits show less availability. |
| | | Sample of 4658 persons | |
| | 1998 (2nd quarter) Spain | EPA | The relative probability of job search is lower for those unemployed receiving unemployment benefits (1.06) than for those without (1.58). Once the unemployed who are not looking for a job are excluded, there is no difference in job search intensity between the two groups. |

increase in the unemployment rate but to a change in the distribution of exit of those unemployed in favor of those without UI, who are more eager (and needy) to find a job, since they do not have to compete with those receiving UI. The standard account, *ceteris paribus*,[34] would be more likely to take place if there were vacancies waiting to be filled but not taken because of the delay in job search allegedly associated with unemployment benefits, but the contrary is not necessarily true. If this is not the case, the disincentive effect of UI could even be evaluated positively as it might actually, and in an unplanned way, accord priority when it comes to filling vacancies to those more in need of a job (because they do not have an alternative source of income). This aspect is especially relevant in Spain because of the relatively low proportion of unemployed who receive benefits. This factor is seldom mentioned in comparative analyses of the generosity of the unemployment insurance system. In 1999, according to the Labor Force Survey, less than 50% of those unemployed were receiving unemployment benefits or assistance, up from 37% in the years right after the recession of early 1990s. This proportion is lower than in most other European countries, such as Germany, the United Kingdom, and Ireland, and above only those for Greece, Portugal, and Italy.

Once again, it is difficult to consider unemployment protection the culprit behind the high rate of unemployment in Spain when more than half of the unemployed workers are not eligible for UI and when, of those who are eligible, more than half are eligible only for the much less generous (and means-tested) unemployment assistance. Second, the weaker the estimated negative impact of UI, the longer the duration of unemployment, an important consideration in view of the fact that around half of Spanish unemployment is long-term unemployment. These two arguments greatly reduce the reasonable range of estimates of the effects of the unemployment benefits system on aggregate unemployment. After these considerations, I believe we can safely say that the UI aggregate negative impact on unemployment is less than is usually assumed and much of this may be compensated for by its positive effect on job search, its socioeconomic impact as a macroeconomic stabilizer, and its function as a major mechanism for reducing family hardship in case of unemployment.

In any case, and although driven by other concerns, the reforms of UI implemented in the past decade followed the OECD blueprint: tightening of the eligibility requirements leading to an important reduction of the proportion of the unemployed covered by UI, and a reduction in the benefit replacement ratio. Nevertheless, looking at the present distribution of the duration of unemployment—51% of the unemployed had been jobless for more than one year in 1999, the same proportion as in 1991—it does not seem likely that the reform of the Spanish unemployment system has had a major impact on the profile of long-term unemployment.

### 7.4.5 Active Labor Market Policies

Active labor market policies (ALMP) have been, without a doubt, one of the hot topics in the debate on labor policy and labor reform in the 1990s. Just to give an example, the increase in the proportion of expenditure on ALMP was one of the few quantitative goals introduced in the Employment Guidelines approved at the Luxembourg Job Summit of the EU in 1997. From the outside, ALMP has a triple appeal to policy makers. First, in the part that deals with training, it contributes to the deepening of the human capital of the workforce and, therefore, to future productivity increases. Second, it helps to keep the unemployed in touch with the world of work, thereby improving their prospects of finding a job. Last, giving the unemployed an income in exchange for something, be it work in a subsidized work program or attending a training course, fits better with the dominant ideology of market societies than does just putting workers on the dole.

In Spain, these factors are complemented by the relatively lower educational attainment of the Spanish labor force, a product of the late development of the Spanish welfare state. In 1998, 34% of the Spanish workforce ages 25–64 had an educational attainment of primary education or lower, compared with 8% in the Netherlands, 15% in France, and just 1% in Germany. On the other hand, less than half of the Spanish workforce (42%) had upper secondary education or more, in sharp contrast with the rest of the EU (71%), excluding Greece and Portugal, and the United States (89%). This situation is rapidly changing as a result of the universalization of education: the percentage of population neither enrolled in nor having completed upper secondary education is 42% for those ages 25–29, 32% for those ages 20–24, and 20% for those ages 15–19 (OECD 2000b: table C2.4).

Among the current problems of the Spanish education system, I highlight two. First, the slightly lower public expenditure in education, 4.6% of GDP according to Eurostat, compared with the EU average (5%), together with a lower level of GDP (80% of EU income per capita), leads to an expenditure per pupil far below the European average, especially for tertiary education, where the expenditure per student is 69.4% of the EU average (above only that of Greece, at 40.7%). Obviously, the underfinancing of the tertiary system has an impact on the development of high-tech activities, including R&D. Second, Spanish secondary education shows an abnormally high predilection (compared to the rest of the EU) toward general education as opposed to vocational education and training (VET). While in the EU(15) 57.6% of the pupils attend VET programs (71% in Italy, Germany, and Portugal), in Spain the percentage is only 37.5%. In Spain, VET has long been considered second best to general secondary education. Interestingly, while in the rest of the EU those ages 15–29 who have basic education plus VET qualifications have a lower unemployment rate than those in the same age group who do not have such qualifications (9.7% versus 20.5%), the opposite is true in Spain (36.9% versus 32.0%), which probably reflects the lack of connection between the VET and the world of work in Spain. In contrast, this link is strongly present in other countries such as Germany and Denmark, where work-linked training accounts for a majority of students (87% and 66%, respectively).[35]

In this context, ALMPs, mainly those centered on training, acquire more relevance. This is especially true given the background of high youth unemployment, a product, along with other general factors such as the lack of effective demand, of a difficult transition from school to work. As we can see in table 7.5, Spain has followed the EU recommendation, increasing the weight of ALMP both in relative (in relation to total labor market policy expenditure) and absolute (in relation to GDP) terms. So, in a time of reduction of relative expenditure on labor market policies resulting from the economic recovery and the reduction of unemployment, expenditure on ALMP has increased as a proportion of the GDP.[36]

As a general category, ALMP groups together very different employment policies, from administration and job search counseling to training and job subsidization. It is interesting to know what type of policy has been most favored in Spain. In Spain, the increase in the importance of ALMP has occurred almost exclusively in subsidies to private employment. This may be a less than ideal arrangement since "most evaluations

Table 7.5. Distribution of Expenditure on Labor Market Policies

|  | Total expenditure on labor market policies/GDP % | ALMP/ GDP % | ALMP/Total expenditure on labor market policies % |
| --- | --- | --- | --- |
| 1996 | 2.69 | 0.66 | 24.54 |
| 1997 | 2.33 | 0.52 | 22.32 |
| 1998 | 2.24 | 0.68 | 30.36 |
| 1999 | 2.22 | 0.81 | 36.49 |

Source: OECD *Employment Outlook* (2000).

show that subsidies to private sector employment have both large dead-weight and substitution effects. As a result, most such schemes yield small net employment gains, particularly in the short term when aggregate demand and vacancies are fixed" (Martin 2000: 97).

At the same time, the resources dedicated to public employment services, training, and specific youth measures have decreased in relative as well as in absolute real terms. In this respect, it is worth noting that in the EU as a whole, the expenditure profile of ALMP is much less marked than in Spain, while in the OECD it is completely the opposite; in both cases more emphasis is put on employment services and less on employment subsidies.[37] The reduction of expenditures on public employment services is particularly dangerous if we take into consideration that the INEM, the Spanish employment service, is one of the least generously financed employment services in the OECD.[38] In fact, only about 9% of successful job searches[39] are carried out by the INEM, and most of them are for low-quality jobs.[40] These shortcomings of the Spanish employment system should not be overlooked, especially considering that, according to a recent evaluation of ALMP summarized by Martin (2000), in-depth counseling by employment agents was one of the more effective ALMPs.

### 7.4.6 Industrial Relations and Wages

The final issue we review in this section is the impact of the system of industrial relations and labor policy on unemployment. On the basis of comparative statistics on union membership, Spain, with a trade union density of 19% (compared with 83% in Sweden, 51% in Belgium, and 40% in Italy) appears to be a country where the trade union movement has a low presence in the world of work. As we will see, that is far from true.

The trade union movement was one of the major social institutions in the struggle for the Spanish democratic system. Because the new democratic government required their support, trade unions obtained a much more powerful role in the labor market than the affiliation rate would lead one to believe. For example, trade unions participate in the negotiations of collective agreements according to the results obtained in trade union elections every four years. These elections are open to all workers, so in the negotiations of collective agreements or other issues at the national level, trade unions act as representatives of all the workers, legitimized by a general election of those employed. They are not just representatives of their affiliates. As a result, most employees are covered by collective bargaining, which is generally applicable, although its real effect is questionable, since it is often difficult to apply the agreements in a productive structure where small firms are dominant[41] and where temporary workers abound. In 1999, slightly more than 5,000 collective agreements (CAs) were signed, covering 8.8 million workers. Of these CAs, 72% were negotiated at the level of the firm, although they covered only 12% of the workers. Thus, the working conditions and wages of most employees are negotiated at higher levels, most of the time by collective bargaining at the provincial level in negotiation with a specific sector of activity (53%) or at the national level (28%).[42] This proliferation of collective bargaining is considered dysfunctional by trade unions and business organizations, as manifested in the 1997 agreement, where the social partners proposed to transform collective bargaining by sectors of activity at the national level into the core of the collective agreement negotiation. In the terms of the agreement, the intention was to "contribute to the rationalization of the structure of collective bargaining, avoiding the existing atomization," building "an adequate articulation among the different levels of negotiation, leaving some issues to be negotiated at the national level—by sector of activity—while others could be dealt with at lower levels."[43]

According to the analysis developed by Calmfors and Driffil (1988), among others, there are reasons to believe that both highly centralized (national-level) and highly decentralized (firm-level) collective bargaining can lead to a better balance between employment and inflation, since in both cases the labor representatives have reasons to consider the impact of wage increases on employment. In the former case, a large wage increase can lead to an acceleration of inflation, with a corresponding decrease in real wages, and to a reduction in the country's competitiveness and employment. On the other hand, CA negotiators at the firm level will take into consideration the high elasticity in demand and the opportunities for substitution among products in the same sector of productive activity and so will also moderate their wage-raise claims, since otherwise the increase in costs for the firm that result from higher salaries could lead to lower sales and employment,[44] and the resulting reduction in employment would fall on their constituency. If this analysis is correct, Spanish bargaining institutions, which are biased toward bargaining at the industrial level, may be poorly prepared to face the problem of unemployment. Fortunately, as stressed by Calmfors (1993), the outcome of wage bargaining at the industrial level depends also on the existing degree of foreign competition. So, at least for manufacturing, a productive activity that has faced growing foreign competition in Spain over the past two decades, the supposed negative impact of the system of collective bargaining should be greatly checked.

When we look at the differences in outcome of the different levels of collective bargaining in Spain, we see that, as expected, wage increases for collective agreements negotiated at the firm level are lower than those negotiated at the industry level; however, the differences are quite small (an average of 0.4 in the 1990s, with a minimum of 0.2 in 1991 and a maximum of 0.9 in 1993).[45] So, after all, it may be that the bargaining at the industrial level is carried on with concern for the possible impact of wage increases on employment at the national level, that is, with a degree of coordination higher than expected according to the dominant type of wage bargaining. Furthermore, throughout the past decade, real wages arrived at through collective bargaining showed what can be considered moderate behavior, especially when we compare the end of the 1986–1991 growth cycle with the present growth cycle, which started in 1996. This moderation in wage increases plus the growth in productivity allowed a reduction in the aggregate unit labor cost, which in 1999 was 7% lower than in 1991.

This moderate behavior in wage bargaining is especially notable when we consider the huge increase in business profits that characterized the present growth cycle. Thus, according to the Central Balance Sheet Office of the Bank of Spain, in the period 1997–1999, at a moment when real bargained wages were growing at a rate of under 1%, business real profits grew at a rate of 13%.[46] Summing up, we could say that in the 1990s, a potentially dysfunctional structure of collective bargaining does not seem to have done much damage to the process of employment creation, owing to the moderate wage claims made by the trade unions.

So far we have seen how the behavior of Spanish trade unions in the wage bargaining process has permitted wage moderation and a reduction of real unit labor cost, contributing to the increase in employment experienced in the second part of the 1990s. However, there is a further objection leveled against the impact of trade unions on the workings of the labor market: that in the process of wage bargaining, they generate a compression of wages, pricing low-wage jobs out of the market.[47] In the words of Bover et al. (2000): "By preventing wage dispersion from adjusting in the face of changing demand for skills, the Spanish labor market bought lower wage inequality at the price of a much greater incidence of unemployment" (411).[48] But trade unions appear to play a limited role in the determination of wage inequality in Spain. Palacio and Simón (2002), in their study of characteristics of firms and workers as determinants of wages in Spain, conclude that "it does not seem that the structure of collective bargaining is a major determinant by itself of wage differences, as these depend, mainly, on the characteristics of the productive system and of each of the establishments or firms"[49] (184).

Furthermore, although the data are inadequate, the wage inequality appears to have risen over the past two decades. Thus, according to the survey of collective bargaining in big firms carried out annually by the Ministry of Economy, the wage distance between the lowest and the highest category subject to collective bargaining rose from 2.2 in 1977 to 4.4 in 1993. The same conclusion is reached for the 1980s from the analysis of the *Encuesta de salarios*, which shows an increase in the Gini index between 1981 and 1988 (the last year available) of 22% (Muñoz de Bustillo 1990), and from the study of social security records for the period 1980–1987 carried out by Arellano, Bentolila, and Bover (1997), which shows an increase in high-skill real earnings of 1.42% and a reduction of median and low-skill real earnings of 0.22% and 0.37%, respectively. It is also worth noting that, according to data compiled by Eurostat, wage differences in Spain, at a ratio of 3.3, are above the figure for the EU, with an average ratio of 2.8. In this data set, only Italy and Luxembourg had higher wage differences than Spain, while the Netherlands, with 1.9; Denmark, with 2.1; Sweden, with 2.2; and Germany, with 2.5, had significantly lower ratios.[50] Finally, if we look at the standard deviation of the logarithm of wages, Spain, at 0.535, comes third in a list of 12 OECD countries, with standard deviations ranging from 0.583, for the United Kingdom, to 0.274, for Denmark (Palacio and Simon 2002).

So, if Bover et al. are right about the decisive negative impact of the lower wage differentials on employment in Spain, then we should expect to find even bigger employment problems in the rest of Europe. Furthermore, since the beginning of the 1980s, the minimum wage has lost ground in relation to average wage (almost 20% from 1980 to 1999), as well as in real terms (9%), so, in real terms, in 2000 the minimum wage was at the level of 1975 and 23% under its peak level of 1980. This evolution of the minimum wage reflects the position of successive governments in relation to wage policy. The Spanish government tried to influence the process of wage bargaining indirectly by offering admonitions to the negotiating partners, by setting unrealistically low inflation targets, and by approving very low wage increases for public-sector employees. In this respect, according to one of the major Spanish trade unions, UGT, from 1992 to 2000 Spanish civil servants lost 12 percentage points of purchasing power as a result of two wage freezes (1994 and 1997) and several years of wage increases under the inflation rate.[51]

Summing up, we can say that the still relatively low and decreasing real labor cost of the Spanish economy, the moderate wage increases of the second part of the 1990s, even in a period of strong GDP growth and rising profits, and the relatively high and growing wage inequality cast doubts on the relevance of the wage rigidity explanation for Spanish unemployment. In relation to this, it is worth noticing that the opinion of some of the authors mentioned earlier regarding insufficient wage dispersion as an explanation for unemployment in Spain does not seem to be shared by the OECD itself. In fact, in the country-specific recommendations for structural reforms to increase employment addressed to Spain by the OECD (1997), neither facilitating greater wage dispersion nor reducing the minimum wage is recommended.

## 7.5  REGIONAL UNEMPLOYMENT RATES AND INTERREGIONAL MOBILITY

A comprehensive account of the Spanish unemployment problem and its employment policies should consider regional differences in unemployment rates and mobility between regions. In 2000, the region with the lowest unemployment, Navarra, had an unemployment rate of 5.9%, while Andalusia, the region with the highest unemployment rate, had an unemployment rate of 24.5%. These differences, commonly thought to be an example of the lack of flexibility of the labor market, have remained roughly stable throughout the period 1989–1999, although that stability hides a clear countercyclical pattern, with a reduction in the disparity in regional unemployment rates through the recession years 1991–1994 and an increase from that year on as a result of the improvement in the economy.[52] The correlation of the regional unemployment rates in 1989 and 2000 is also quite high, 0.925, showing a relatively high stability in the ranking of the regions according to their employment performance.

These large differences in regional unemployment rates are not a special feature of the Spanish labor market. The only peculiarity shown by Spain in this field is the high level of both the lowest and highest unemployment rates. If we measure the dispersion of regional unemployment rates by the coefficient of variation, Spain ranks eighth after Italy, Germany (including the eastern *Länder*), Belgium, Australia, the United Kingdom, Canada, and the United States (OECD 2000a: 39).

The dispersion of regional unemployment rates and the stability of this dispersion over time reflects a lack of labor mobility that may retard the decline in unemployment. According to the information collected by the OECD from different sources and reproduced in table 7.6, Spain is among the countries with the lowest population mobility. In 1995, only 0.6% of the population changed region of residence over the course of one year. This ratio is not only much lower than that for the United States (2.22%), Japan (2.45%), and Canada (2.15%), countries known for their higher population mobility, but also is well under the ratio of other European countries such as France (1.49%) and Sweden (1.61%). This lack of mobility also appears in the data of interregional commuting, under 2% for Spain, compared with 18.5% in Belgium, 10% in Germany and the United Kingdom, and 8% in Austria and the Netherlands.[53] In 1999, only 25% of these unemployed were willing to change residence, a percentage lower than the percentage of those willing to change occupation (74%), take a job with a lower wage (58%), or accept a job of a lower category than expected (63%).

This lack of spatial labor mobility should certainly come as a surprise in a country, like Spain, where not so long ago emigration (inside as well as outside the country) was a major source of income for regions.[54] Two factors help to explain this apparent anomaly. First, the high rate of unemployment in the would-be receiving regions reduces the attractiveness of moving to other regions in search of work. Of course, the incentives for

Table 7.6. Internal Migration in a Sample of OECD Countries

| | Number of regions | Ratio of gross flows to population[1] | | | | |
|---|---|---|---|---|---|---|
| | | 1980 | 1985 | 1990 | 1995 | 1998 |
| Australia | 8 | 1.85 | 1.86 | 1.93 | 1.93 | 1.96 |
| Belgium | 11 | 0.86 | 0.84 | 0.60 | 1.27 | — |
| Canada | 66 | — | — | 2.50 | 2.15 | — |
| Finland | 5 | 1.28 | 1.30 | 1.29 | 0.92 | — |
| France | 22 | 1.52 | 1.31 | 1.40 | 1.49 | 1.58 |
| Germany | 16 | 1.29 | 1.05 | 1.34 | 1.24 | — |
| Italy | 20 | 0.68 | 0.59 | — | 0.50 | 0.53 |
| Japan | 10 | 2.89 | 2.59 | 2.59 | 2.45 | — |
| Netherlands | 12 | 1.56 | 1.56 | 1.64 | 1.61 | — |
| New Zealand | 12 | — | — | — | 1.99 | — |
| Portugal | 7 | — | 0.19 | 0.54 | — | — |
| Spain | 17 | 0.19 | 0.42 | 0.65 | 0.60 | — |
| Sweden | 8 | 1.30 | 1.44 | 1.54 | 1.61 | — |
| United Kingdom | 12 | — | — | — | — | 2.30 |
| United States | 51 | 2.79 | 3.00 | 3.52 | 2.22 | 2.40 |
| Average | — | 1.47 | 1.47 | 1.76 | 1.54 | — |

1. Gross flows expressed as the total number of people who changed region of residence over one year.
Source: OECD (2000a), p. 53.

moving to a region with an unemployment rate of 10% are much lower than those for moving to a region with a 4% unemployment rate. This is especially true if you cannot rely on the efficiency of the employment office when looking for a job and if moving also means losing the network of relationships informally used when searching for a job.

Second, mobility is further hindered by the high and increasing cost of housing. In the past decade and a half, housing prices in current terms have increased at the same rate as the GDP per capita, although with different timing, rising faster than GDP per capita in the boom years of the second half on the 1980s and at a lower pace since the 1993 recession. But, housing prices increased much faster than wages, especially from 1987 to 1991 and from 1997 to 2000. As a result, the effort index (number of wage years needed to buy a 90-square-meter house) increased by 53%.[55] In Spain, where 79% of the dwellings are owner occupied,[56] this increase in price had a strong impact on the cost of moving and on the mobility of the labor force, since there seems to be a negative relation between interregional mobility and the index of owner-occupied housing. Furthermore, in all the regions with unemployment rates over the national average, housing prices are well under the national average, further hindering the mobility of the population.[57] It is also interesting to note how from 1987 to 2000 the gap in housing prices between those regions with high unemployment and those with low unemployment and/or high employment potential increased notably, from 1.35 to 2.23,[58] making it more difficult for unemployed workers to move to regions where their chances of getting a job are higher.

In sum, the combination of the high and increasing cost of moving, the fact that a large share of the unemployed live in families with other sources of income, the relatively high unemployment rates in the magnet regions, and the prospect of low wages and short-term contracts (i.e., the lack of stability) for those unemployed workers fortunate enough find a job after moving help explain the low mobility of the Spanish labor force.

## 7.6 BEYOND LABOR MARKET DEREGULATION

So far, we have focused on the analysis of the role of labor market regulation and labor market reforms in the employment recovery of the second part of the 1990s, reviewing along the way the importance of the macropolicy followed in the past two decades. But the OECD recommendations cover other important areas of economic policy, which, while often considered of secondary importance, may be crucial for future growth. This section reviews the situation and actions taken in several of these areas: education, research and development, and restrictions on the creation and expansion of firms. The intention of this section is not so much to offer a detailed account of the measures taken in each of these areas as to show how successive governments have concentrated on labor market reforms while neglecting other areas. This emphasis on a specific subset of the recommendations of the OECD, those related to the labor market and income distribution, suggests an ideological bias in Spain's recent economic policy making.

### 7.6.1 Nurturing an Entrepreneurial Climate

An element considered in the OECD *Jobs Study* strategy was, in its own words, the importance "of nurturing the entrepreneurial climate" by developing a business-friendly public administration. This goal can also be found in the EU employment strategy launched in 1998 after the Luxembourg employment summit, where one of the four areas of concern was the promotion of entrepreneurship.[59]

In relation to the existing level of red tape associated with the creation of a firm, Spain, unfortunately, still retains much of the administrative bureaucracy of the old, predemocratic interventionist regime, although there have been numerous attempts to trim the amount of paperwork required to start a business. Currently, in order to start a firm in Spain, an entrepreneur has to complete 13 or 14 different formal application processes, which take from 19 to 28 weeks, although the period can be reduced to one day in the case of nonincorporated firms[60] (OECD 2000a). Nevertheless, according to the index developed by Nicoletti et al. (2000) for the OECD, from a comparative point of view, Spain ranks close to the average in terms of barriers to entrepreneurship. That relatively favorable aggregate outcome is, however, the product of its better-than-average performance in the areas related to barriers to competition and to regulatory and administrative opacity, while its performance in the area dealing with burdens on startups is 50% worse than the average.

In sharp contrast with the entrepreneurship data, Spain is a country with a higher-than-average level of self-employment. While in 1998 in the EU 15 an average 16.6% of workers were self-employed, in Spain the percentage was 23% (versus 7.2% in the United States).[61] Of course, the higher-than-average level of self-employment is explained not by an oversupply of "schumpeterian" entrepreneurs but by the lower level of development of the Spanish economy, as well as by the still higher importance of agriculture, a sector characterized by small family holdings (nonagricultural self-employment accounts for 17.6% of nonagricultural civilian employment). In fact, the level of self-employment has been decreasing since employment statistics first became available: in 1955, the proportion of self-employment was 45%; 10 years later, it was 37%. Nevertheless, the fact remains that in Spain an abnormally high percentage of workers are self-employed.

Recently, there has been a renewed interest in the nature and characteristics of self-employment, an interest probably explained, as pointed out by Blanchflower (2000), more by the "belief that businesses are essential to the growth of the capitalist economy" than because of self-employment's relationship to overall employment, a relationship subject to many caveats. Blanchflower's study, and chapter 5 of the *Employment Outlook 2000* (OECD 2000a), titled "The Partial Renaissance of Self-Employment," are two good examples of this concern. In this respect, the behavior of self-employment in Spain follows a clear anticyclical pattern, with the rate of self-employment having negative values for the last two periods of GDP and employment growth (1985–1991 and 1998–1998), pointing to the fact that, at least partially, self-employment is a second choice taken when there is not enough labor demand in the economy. On the other hand, it should be noted that most surveys show a higher level of job satisfaction among the self-employed.[62] Although only a very small proportion of unemployed find employment through self-employment,[63] the Spanish government has developed special programs targeted at the self-employed, aimed at facilitating the startup of businesses and improving their likelihood of survival.

### 7.6.2 Investment in Research and Development

The OECD *Jobs Study* stressed the importance of enhancing the creation and diffusion of technological know-how. In this respect, the recent Spanish experience could not be more dismal. In a period when R&D has increased in importance as a way to outdistance the competition, Spain is at the bottom of the EU in terms of expenditure in R&D, both public and private.

Spain was never a country much oriented to innovation. As a Catholic country, Spain for a long time (although long ago) looked upon commercial activity with disdain, and also scientific activity related to material production. The contributions of Spain to the list of famous people is long in the fields of painting, poetry, and literature, but not in science or technology. Nevertheless, the second half of the twentieth century saw an important increase in R&D, which rose from 0.2% of GDP in 1970 to 0.5% in 1985, reaching a maximum of almost 1% in 1991. Unfortunately, from that year on, the priority given to the fulfillment of the convergence criteria (reduction of public deficit) for joining the European Monetary Union and the economic downturn forced a change in the policy of increasing the amount of resources devoted to R&D. Only after the recovery of the Spanish economy and the reduction of its deficit did public expenditures in this area regain the level reached at the beginning of the 1990s. The break in the progressive increase in R&D expenditures is especially important if we consider that Spanish expenditure in R&D in relative terms is half the EU 15 average, one-third that of the United States, and slightly more than one-fourth that of Japan (Laafia 2001).[64]

This historical legacy of public and private underinvestment in research and development shows in almost every indicator related to the field: a lower percentage of employment in high-tech sectors (7.1% in Spain versus 13.6% in Germany and 10.7% in France),[65] low penetration by the Internet (13% in Spain, versus 23% in the EU14 and 51% in the United States),[66] a growing deficit in the royalties and license fees subbalance in the balance of payments (in 1999 the income generated by royalties and license fees covered only 18.83% of the payments under this rubric),[67] and low digital literacy. The emphasis on labor market deregulation policies in this context of long-term neglect of R&D could lead to the specialization of the Spanish economy in low-value-added goods and services, a highly dangerous strategy of growth in the mid-term, especially in an expanded EU with the former countries of the East bloc paying wages only a fraction of those paid in Spain.

## 7.7 MACROECONOMIC POLICY AND EMPLOYMENT IN SPAIN

Two elements stand out when we review the evolution of macroeconomic policy in Spain over the past two decades: a permanent fiscal deficit and a relatively strict monetary policy, at least until the 1990s, when the recession and then the takeover of monetary policy by the European Central Bank (until then in the hands of the Banco de España) led to a reduction in interest rates. This relaxation was probably not as extensive as the conditions of the Spanish economy required because of the intensity of the recession of 1992–1993 and therefore deepened the recession's impact on unemployment. In this section we will review the role played by these factors in explaining Spanish unemployment.

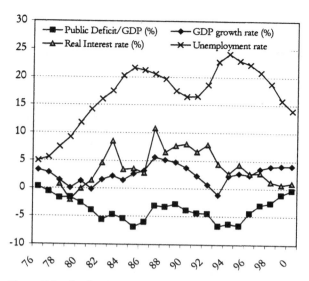

Figure 7.6. Fiscal policy, monetary policy, unemployment rate, and GDP growth (%), Spain, 1976–2000. Source: Author's analysis of INE and Banco de España data.

As we can see in figure 7.6, from 1977 to 1999, despite oscillations, Spain had a continual public deficit, a deficit that resulted more from the late construction of the welfare state, from the assumption by the state of much of the cost of the restructuring of the industrial and financial sectors, and from the existence of an underdeveloped tax system than from a specific anticyclical fiscal policy designed to combat the economic crisis. In the words of Carlos Solchaga (1997), secretary of industry and energy first and later secretary of finance of the Socialist Party from 1982 to 1993, "This increase in public expenditure was, in a sense, the bill we had to pay in order to get popular backing for the transition to democracy. Having all the attention on the task of dismantling the previous regime and consolidating the new made it very difficult to maintain orthodox and unpopular positions in relation to industrial policy or in relation to the financial crisis of all sorts of firms (including banks)" (290).

In fact, by the end of the 1980s, the minister of finance presented the elimination of the deficit as a policy goal to be met by the early 1990s; however, first social pressures in 1988 and later the unexpected recession of 1992–1993 made it impossible to reach such a goal. It is interesting to note that, in terms of the share of public expenditure in the GDP, the highest increase in public expenditure, mainly social expenditure, took place in the years before the Socialist Party came to power, while during the successive PSOE governments' expenditure increased only as a result of popular pressure (e.g., after the 1988 general strike of December 14) or as result of the 1992–1993 recession.

In contrast, since the early 1980s, the monetary authorities have practiced a very restrictive monetary policy, even in times of decreasing inflation and growing unemployment, as in the 1980s. For example, in 1987, with decreasing inflation and an unemployment rate of 20%, the real interest rate was set at more than 10%. Spain's acceptance of the exchange rate mechanism of the European Monetary System while the peseta was overvalued[68] put further pressure on the monetary policy. High interest rates were used as a means to maintain the national currency within the agreed fluctuation range at a time when the Spanish economy was growing at a rate above the EU average. The devaluation of the peseta three times in the five months between September 1992 and January 1993 allowed the Spanish government to rely less on monetary policy as a means of achieving currency stability, but the Maastricht Agreement and the declared goal of the government to join the European Monetary Union kept the anti-inflationary role of tight monetary policy high on the policy agenda.

A discussion of the monetary policy followed in Spain (and in Europe, since the existence of an agreed-upon relatively narrow range of exchange fluctuation made it difficult for a single country to follow an independent monetary policy) is important for two different reasons. First, the inadequate performance of the European economy in terms of employment creation could very well have been at least partially the result of the extreme strictness of the monetary policy applied by the European countries obsessed with meeting the Maastricht conditions by 1997 in a time of recession all across Europe. In this respect, it was after 1992 that the difference between the unemployment rate on both sides of the Atlantic increased. Second, and more important, following the analysis presented by Ball (1999), the Spanish history of restrictive monetary policy not only could very well have had an impact on the short-run level of unemployment (which was higher than it would have been under a more lax monetary policy) but could also explain, at least partially, the difficulties faced by the country at the end of the recession in its attempts to bring the unemployment rate quickly back to prerecession rates. According to Ball, in countries "where unemployment rose only temporarily, it did so because of strongly counter-cyclical policy: after tight policy produced a recession to disinflate the economy, policy lifted toward expansion" (190).

The inability to relax monetary policy once the process of disinflation has started, or to tighten monetary policy either to meet anti-inflationary goals or to support currency policies, can lead to a permanent increase in unemployment through the generation of hysteresis and the subsequent increase in the NAIRU. This interpretation fits the Spanish case quite well. If we look at the different estimates of the NAIRU for the Spanish economy in table 7.7, two things catch our attention: (a) the wide range of the estimates (reflecting the sensitivity of the results to the method of estimation used and to the different specification of the models), which suggests that they should be used with extreme caution, and (b) the important growth in

Table 7.7. Range of Estimates of the NAIRU. Spain, 1960–1995

| Period | 1960–71 | 1972–79 | 1980–85 | 1986–90 | 1991–95 |
|---|---|---|---|---|---|
| NAIRU | 0.9–6.7 | 2.9–10.1 | 11.27–16 | 10.8–18.21 | 17.25–20.5 |
| Unemployment (U) | 2.53 | 4.84 | 16.6 | 18.62 | 20.94 |
| Number of estimates | 7 | 7 | 7 | 5 | 3 |

Source: Gómez and Usabiaga (2000), p. 30.

the NAIRU, from 11% to 17%, or from 16 to 20%, between the late 1980s and the late 1990s, depending on whether we use the low or the high estimates. The increase is difficult to explain in the absence of hysteresis, given that the labor policy followed since the late 1980s, as we saw, was intended to deregulate the market, and so it should have had, if anything, the opposite impact on the NAIRU. Furthermore, it is difficult to square the OECD's 19.4% NAIRU for 1997 (IMF 1999: 91) with the actual unemployment rate of 13% and stable inflation just three years later (2000).

Summing up, I think it is reasonable to assume that an overly strict monetary policy was one of the elements that contributed to the increase in unemployment to a point that made it very difficult for the unemployed to be absorbed in the two recent periods of rapid economic growth (1986–1991 and since 1994).[69] It is also important to note that the significant increase in employment in the second half of the 1990s coexisted with the lowest real interest rates since 1981 (see figure 7.6).

## 7.8 SUMMARY AND CONCLUSIONS

This chapter started with a short summary of the specific characteristics of recent Spanish economic history that could explain, at least partially, the massive unemployment generated during the second half of the 1970s and the first part of the 1980s, an increase in unemployment that has proven very difficult to reduce. With that background, and after a brief discussion about the reliability of the existing unemployment estimates and the compatibility of social peace and massive unemployment, the chapter reviewed the economic policies adopted to meet the challenge of unemployment, using as a guide the OECD *Jobs Study* recommendations.

A key OECD policy recommendation has been to enhance flexibility by reducing the strength of employment protection legislation (EPL). Following the OECD's lead, the Spanish Employers' Confederation has had as its battle cry a call for a reduction in employment protection, and this has been a major source of disagreement between it and the trade unions. The confrontation between labor and management over this issue could easily lead to the deterioration of the labor relations environment, which in turn could undermine the struggle to reduce unemployment. In fact, the view that employment protection legislation (EPL) has significant negative employment effects has remarkably little empirical support in the cross-country data (see chapter 3) and appears to have a weak empirical basis in Spain, as well. In fact, as Bertola et al. (2000) remind us, the effects of employment protection legislation "are difficult to study in practice because of the complex and elusive nature of available information, and of the EPL concept itself." On these grounds, the authors propose that all "policy recommendations should be formulated with caution, and should not be based on any of the indicators available to date" (9). Given the lack of empirical support for the negative effects of EPL, the stubbornness shown by government and Employers' Associations on this issue may be misplaced or may simply reflect an attempt to increase the leverage of firms over their workers.

According to chapter 3 of this volume, the cross-country evidence shows no simple association between standard measures of unemployment benefit generosity and unemployment, especially once Spain is taken out of the sample of countries, where it is an outlier. In this chapter it was shown that it is also difficult to blame the unemployment insurance system for high unemployment in Spain. When properly understood, Spanish unemployment benefits (UB) are not as generous as usually believed. First, there is a ceiling of 170% of the minimum wage (which amounts to 30% of the average wage, one of the lowest in the EU). Second, and more important, it is difficult to consider unemployment benefits the culprit behind the high rate of unemployment in Spain when more than half of the unemployed workers are not eligible for unemployment insurance and when, of those who are eligible, more than half are eligible only for the much less generous (and means-tested) unemployment assistance. Finally, the longer the duration of unemployment, the weaker the estimated negative impact of UB, an important caveat considering that around half of Spanish unemployment is long-term unemployment. These arguments greatly reduce the reasonable range of estimates of effects of the unemployment benefits system on aggregate unemployment. In any case, it is important to stress that the benefits system was not designed to minimize unemployment but to serve as a mechanism to reduce the income hardship and social stress traditionally associated with unemployment.

Consistent with the OECD's view, the reform of the wage bargaining process (mainly through decentralization of collective bargaining) is high on the Spanish government's agenda. But Spain's experience in the 1990s shows that the existing system of collective bargaining is compatible with wage moderation, even in a context of growing business profits and increasing employment. Indeed, the growth in real wages has been compatible with a reduction in real labor unit costs, leading to a significant reduction of the share of wages in total income. Moreover, Spain has a relatively high level of wage dispersion. So, at least from a comparative perspective, wage compression does not appear to be the driving factor behind the massive unemployment in Spain.

The increase in the contingent labor force in Spain, a result of the easing of temporary contracts, is probably one of the factors behind the rise in the rate of employment creation associated with a given rate of GDP growth experienced through the second half of the 1990s. However, that very same policy is also probably responsible for the dramatic increase in unemployment associated with the 1992–1994 recession. Furthermore, the growth of temporary employment has many other negative implications, ranging from reductions in workers' welfare and job mobility to increases in work injuries. Taking all these elements into consideration, we can say that this pattern of "flexibilization" of the labor force may be less beneficial for employment performance than the conventional view suggests.

In sum, it is very difficult to explain the Spanish unemployment problem by relying on the OECD-IMF orthodoxy. The core of the problem does not appear to be the Spanish welfare state, with its panoply of labor, social, and redistribution policies. In the context of the EU, Spain has a relatively low level of public social expenditure, with only Ireland ranking lower. At the same time, Spain has a high dispersion of wages and income, with an index of income inequality similar to that of the United Kingdom and the United States. These differences are big enough to show how unconvincing the orthodox rigidity view is in the Spanish case. This is not to say that Spanish labor and social policy cannot be improved, or that they have had no negative impact whatsoever on the working of the labor market. But the evidence surveyed in this chapter does not suggest that employment-unfriendly labor market institutions are the main source of Spanish unemployment.

Rather, it seems more likely that that a key culprit can be found in the disinflationary policies followed by the Spanish government since the early 1980s. These policies worsened the impact on unemployment both of unfavorable changes in the structure of economic activity and of the high rate of labor force growth. The late process of deruralization of the Spanish economy in a time of economic crisis (the 1970s), the lack of sound political institutions, and the impact of demographic shifts should also be considered as part of the explanation for the high unemployment in Spain. On the other hand, the reduction in the size of the potential labor force in the 1990s contributed to the dramatic reduction in the unemployment rate in the second part of the past decade.

Nevertheless, the orthodox view remains that the solution must be labor market deregulation. This can be a particularly harmful policy prescription, not just for the workers directly affected but for the long-term growth path. Such a process of deregulation, as is well known, could lead to a change in the distribution of income away from wages and toward profits, reducing the pressure on firms to push for productivity improvements. In this respect, as stressed by Gough et al. (1991), there are two different paths to high international competitiveness. One path is characterized by low wages, low social benefits, and low productivity, the other by high wages, high social benefits, and high productivity. While the results in terms of competitiveness are indistinguishable in the short run, it is clear that they are quite different in terms of workers' well-being and of income distribution. A glance at the different experiences of employment in Europe and in the United States shows that countries, even in an open world, still have plenty of autonomy in labor and social policy. If anything is clear after decades of reforms, it is that there are many viable models for market economies, with different priorities in terms of social protection and income distribution, different tradeoffs in terms of growth and income generation, and different emphases on the responsibilities of the market and of the public sector for the generation of well-being.

This review of the evidence suggests that policy makers ought to shift their focus from labor market deregulation to other, much more important structural bottlenecks, such as excessive product market regulation, the shortcomings of vocational training, and inadequate research and development spending. This shift away from orthodox prescriptions is particularly important, given that further efforts to reduce employment protection, cut back unemployment benefits, and decentralize wage bargaining could very well lead to a deterioration in relations among government, business organizations, and trade unions. This, in turn, could undermine the continuation of wage moderation and productivity growth, which will be critical to maintaining the current downward trajectory of unemployment in Spain.

*Acknowledgment* I would like to thank Kevin Hearle for his help in turning this chapter into something (that I hope is) readable.

## Notes

1. In 1999, social expenditure as percentage of GDP was 20.0% in Spain and 27.6% in the EU (15). Of the 15 member states of the EU, only Ireland (14.7%) had a lower social expenditure as a percentage of GDP (Abramovici 2002: 2).

2. In this respect, Marimon and Zilibotti (1996) simulated what would have been the evolution of unemployment in Spain had Spain had, in 1974, only 10.4% (the French percentage) of its workforce employed in agriculture, with the remainder divided between the industrial and the service sectors according to their relative employment at the time. The result, supposing the same rate of employment growth for the last two sectors and the French agricultural employment rate of growth for the agricultural sector, is that in 1992 the unemployment rate would have been 8.2%, ten percentage points less than the observed unemployment rate.

3. As a matter of fact, by the beginning of the 1970s, even before the economic crisis was felt throughout most of Europe, Spanish emigration to Europe had already practically stopped as a result of Spanish economic development during the 1960s (the average growth rate from 1960 to 1972 was 7%) and of the tightening of immigration requirements by the host countries. For example, the Spanish

resident population in France peaked in 1968, in West Germany in 1973, and in Switzerland in 1974 (Izquierdo 1992).

4. *Anuario de Migraciones 2000* (Madrid: Ministerio de Trabajo y Asuntos Sociales).

5. Compare this with the 37% for Austria and Finland, the 36% for Germany, the 45% for Italy, or the 40% for the United Kingdom in 1970. In fact, only Ireland and France show a similar or higher figure for the participation of the top quintile in the national income (Atkinson, Rainwater, and Smeeding [1995]).

6. A behavior matched by no other country in the EU. From 1975 to 1984 the share of gross fixed capital formation in GDP in Spain fell by 8 percentage points. Only Belgium and Luxembourg, in both cases due to their orientation toward heavy industries that were hit hard by the energy crisis, came close. In Germany the loss was 0.4 points, and in France, 4.8 points.

7. This was the first of a series of social agreements that acted as the backbone of the anti-inflationary policy of the late 1970s and early 1980s.

8. The importance of the issue is shown, for example, by the inclusion of an ad hoc chapter on the reliability of Spanish employment statistics in the 1994 report on the socioeconomic situation of Spain published by the Economic and Social Committee (CES).

9. A review of the different estimates of the Spanish shadow economy can be found in Serrano et al. (1998). For a comparative analysis of the size and causes of the shadow economy in various countries, including Spain, see Schneider and Enste (2000).

10. If we measure the intensity of search by the number of methods of job search used, the relative probability of using more methods (up to six) of job search shows a quadratic behavior, increasing with family income from 1.22 methods for families with an income under 50,000 pts. to 1.41 for families with an income from 150,000–200,000 pts., then decreasing to 0.95 for families with an income of 300,000 pts. or more.

11. Using a slightly different index for comparison, according to Eurostat, in 2000, the percentage of households where no one worked in Spain was 12%, a figure lower than that for Germany (13%), France (14%), Belgium and Greece (15%), the United Kingdom (17%), or Ireland (20%) (Eurostat, *Statistics in Focus, Population and Social Conditions*, Theme 3-15/2002).

12. The ratio of total to minimum legally set wages has been estimated for the period 1958–1960 from 1.16 to 1.88 (Serrano and Malo de Molina 1979).

13. In the words of the president of the Supreme Court of the time (1968): "If we allow the free dismissal of workers we would have to approve also, without limitation, the right to strike, things that would lead us right away to the class struggle, which brings such bad memories to all of us" (quoted in Serrano and Malo de Molina 1979: 70).

14. This was the *Estatuto de los Trabajadores*, or Worker's Statute, which regulates labor relations in Spain. Approved in 1980, it has been amended several times since.

15. In fact, in his paper on the determinants of unemployment in Europe, when Nickell adds labor standards to the unemployment regression he gets a negligible and insignificant coefficient, a result consistent with the conclusions reached by Bertola (1990) after studying the impact of dismissal costs on labor demand: "by themselves, job security provisions . . . neither bias the firm's labor demand

towards lower average employment at given wages, nor bias wage determination towards higher wages and lower employment" (870).

16. In fact, after reviewing the existing literature on the issue, Buechtemann (1993) is able to quote only an empirical study (Lazear 1990), which concludes that employment security policies had a strong negative impact on employment.

17. These authors, after a detailed study of dismissal costs in a set of European countries using up to nine different indexes, arrived at the following conclusion: "our recommendation (based on the information supplied in this section) is to be careful when using apparently simple comparisons based on monetary estimates, because they hide an important number of assumptions and problems of measurement and comparability not always made explicit" (51).

18. "Asuntos Judiciales Sociales," *Boletín de Estadísticas Laborales* (Madrid: Ministerio de Trabajo y Asuntos Sociales).

19. Buechtemann (1993), p. 21.

20. In 1988, a year of higher growth (5% versus 2.3%), the dismissal cost amounted to 0.72 of total labor cost, while in 1992, when the growth rate was 1%, it was 1.61.

21. According to textbook economics, the higher labor cost should lead to lower employment—although, again, this result is maintained only if the firm is not able to pass on the extra cost of employment protection (Schellhass 1993). Furthermore, its impact on employment would be mediated by the elasticity of employment to wages. For example, taking as valid the higher-than-usual elasticity of employment of $-0.68$ estimated by Segura et al. (1991), the 2.1% reduction in total labor cost from the full elimination of dismissal costs would lead to an increase of employment of 1.4% ($-0.68 \times 0.021 \times 100$), equivalent to 177,015 new jobs in 1996 (12.39 million workers $\times$ 0.1428) and to a reduction in the unemployment rate from 22.2 to 21.1% (3.54 million unemployed $-177,015$ now employed = 3.36 million, divided by a labor force of 15.9 million = 21.1%), hardly a radical reduction considering the assumptions made: total elimination of dismissal costs and a relatively high elasticity.

22. Up to 60% for some specific groups of workers. This contract was supposed to be available until 2001. After this period of four years, the social partners were supposed to evaluate its impact and decide whether to maintain it as it was or change it. In fact, after a few months of negotiations by the social partners, the government decided unilaterally to maintain the existing legislation with few changes.

23. This type of contract can be used only when hiring workers who belong to specific population groups characterized by their below-average employment performance—unemployed young people ages 18–19, the long-term unemployed, the unemployed who are 45 years old or older, the handicapped, the socially excluded, and those with short-term contracts.

24. This is not the only time the PSOE confronted the trade unions during its first mandate. In 1985, as a result of the reform of the pension system promoted by the PSOE, the leader of the UGT, the major trade union, who was also a Socialist member of Parliament, resigned his seat in the Parliament, starting an era of strained relations between the Socialist union and the Socialist Party.

25. The causation principle, compulsory before the reform, meant that a fixed-duration contract could be used to deal only with temporary productive activities (e.g., harvesting, Christmas sales).

26. For example, almost 40% of the contracts signed between January and August of 2000 were signed by persons already known as workers to the firm,

while one-third of temporary workers had been working for more time than that specified in the contract. The analysis of job creation and job destruction also shows that most of the mobility of temporary workers involves movement to and from jobs already existing in the economy. According to García Serrano (1996), from 1993 to 1994, only 20% of the mobility of temporary workers was explained by the destruction and creation of jobs, while for the rest of workers the percentage reached 60%.

27. See Bentolila and Dolado (1993), for example.

28. For example, when writing these pages, a conservative think tank of businessmen, *El Círculo de Empresarios*, proposed the reduction of unemployment benefits for those over 45 years old (*El País*, November 30, 2000).

29. In case of dismissal for fault, there is a waiting period of three months.

30. Until the 2002 reform, temporary agricultural workers in Extremadura and Andalusia, two of the poorest regions of Spain, could profit from a special complementary unemployment benefit with lower eligibility criteria under specific conditions. During the second quarter of 2000, almost a quarter of a million people profited from this special program (75% of minimum wage for a maximum of 180 days—and up to 360 days for workers more than 52 years old).

31. Unemployment assistance is available to those unemployed ages 18–65 with family responsibilities and who have exhausted their entitlement to contributory benefit or who are not entitled to allowances but have paid contributions for three months. It is also available to those unemployed who are older than 45 without family responsibilities; those who have exhausted their entitlement to an unemployment allowance for at least 12 months; and those who are not entitled to contribution-related allowances but who have paid contributions for six months. Other covered groups are the unemployed over age 52 who have fulfilled all conditions for receiving a retirement pension but who are still below the age requirement; returning emigrants; ex-convicts for six months after their release; and disability pension claimants whose pensions have been suspended because their health condition has improved or because the claimant has been recognized as capable of work. In addition, the law covers those registered at an employment office who have exhausted the entitlement to contributory unemployment, have failed to find work for 30 days subsequent to exhausting entitlement to contributory benefit, and have no other sources of income that exceed the minimum wage.

32. Up to 24 months for unemployed workers 42 years old or over, and until retirement for unemployed workers more than 51 years of age. A full account of the casuistry involved can be found at: http://www.inem.es/ciudadano/p_desempleo.html.

33. A review of some of the problems associated with the extrapolation of microrelationships to the macro realm can be found in Summers and Clark (1983): 222–225.

34. The *ceteris paribus* condition is necessary because we are not counting the effective demand impact of UI; the elimination of UI could lead to a decrease in effective demand, compensating, totally or partially, for the incentive effect of the measure on job search.

35. Eurostat, Education and Culture News Release, no. 60/2000.

36. In 1985, ALMP absorbed just 11% of the labor market policy expenditure.

37. In 1997, the expenditure on employment services was of 18% of total ALMP in the EU and 23% in the OECD, while in Spain it was 14% (7.5% in 1999).

38. According to Jackman et al. (1990), of the 20 OECD countries, Spain's expenditure in employment services and administration per unemployed as a percentage of the average production per person in 1988 was 0.4, the lowest after Turkey, while Germany had an index of 3.5.

39. Lucía Abellán, "El Inem gestiona solo el 15% de todas las colocaciones en España," El País, December 9, 2000: 64.

40. To give an example of the shortcoming of the present system of employment information, at this writing (January 2001), the databases of the employment offices of seven regions with competencies in employment policy were not connected to the database of the national employment institute, so some job offers are not known outside the region where they occur. According to the INEM, the problem was to be solved in 2001.

41. In 1999, of the firms with employees, 57% had only one or two, and 20% had from two to five. Thus, fewer than a quarter of the firms had more than five employees.

42. Estadística de Convenios Colectivos de Trabajo (Madrid: Ministerios de Trabajo y Asuntos Sociales, 2002.

43. A summary of the major developments in industrial relations in Spain in 1999 can be found on the web page of the European Foundation for the Improvement of Living Conditions, http://www.eiro.eurofound.ie/1999/12/features/ES9912100F.html.

44. On top of this, the capacity of trade unions to negotiate at the firm level might be reduced as a result of a higher level of "personalizing" of the bargaining and the lack of bargaining skills among trade union representatives.

45. Estadística de Convenios Colectivos de Trabajo (Madrid: Ministerio de Trabajoy Asuntos Sociales).

46. Excluding financial firms, which, on average, experienced much higher increases in profit rates.

47. An impact increased by the design of social contributions, which are not strictly proportional to wages.

48. This statement is made in the context of a comparative analysis of the Spanish and Portuguese labor markets undertaken by the authors. For full-time workers, the ratio of D9 to D1 is 20% higher in Portugal (4.3 versus 3.6). It is interesting to note that the higher dispersion in Portugal is explained by its "longer and fatter" upper tail; the bottom 50% is more compressed in Portugal than in Spain. In fact, the Portuguese minimum wage in 1999 was set at 57% of average earnings, while in Spain it amounted to only 34% (Eurostat, Statistics in Focus, theme 3-2/2001). Furthermore, according to Eurostat, the D5/D1 ratio is higher in Spain, 1.9, than in Portugal, 1.5, and the percentage of low wage employees twice as high (12% in Spain and 6% in Portugal). This result does not fit particularly well with the idea that low-skilled jobs are priced out of the market—either by elimination of the job itself or by a change in the productive technology—due to the existence of a high wage floor.

49. In fact, the characteristics of the firm (plus the combined impact of the worker's and the firm's characteristics) explain more than 60% of the variance of wages, more or less the same percentage as in Portugal, and more than in other countries such as the United States, where the characteristics of the firms by themselves explain around 19% of the variance (Groshen 1989), compared with 27% in Spain.

50. Defined as best-paid occupation/worst-paid occupation, 1995. figures for Greece include only the industrial sector; figures for France are for 1994, and those for Germany exclude the new *Länder*; the corresponding figure for the old GDR is 2.17 (Eurostat, *Statistics in Focus*, theme 3-8/1998).

51. In 2000 alone, public-sector workers lost more than two points of purchasing power as their wages rose 2% while the inflation rate rose over 4%.

52. As measured by the coefficient of variation and the ratio of the unemployment rate of the region with the highest unemployment rate to the unemployment rate of the region with the lowest.

53. European Commission, *Employment in Europe* 1997, p. 72.

54. This puzzle is shared by Italy, for example, where we can find a fall in internal migration and a substantial increase in regional unemployment disparities. For more details on the Italian case see Faini et al. (1997).

55. Author's analysis from data from the *Anuario del Ministerio de Fomento* (2001) and the *Encuesta de Salarios*.

56. The European average for 1994 was 59%. Of the countries considered in the first wave of the ECHP, only Ireland had a higher percentage of owner-occupied houses, with 81%; on the other end was Germany, with 41%.

57. For an analysis of the relation between the housing and the labor markets in the United Kingdom in the 1980s, see Bover and Muellbauer (1998) and Layard (1986).

58. Average price of housing in Baleares, Madrid, Catalonia, and the Basque Country, divided by the average price of housing in Extremadura, Galicia, Murcia, and Andalusia.

59. In the words of the Commission, "there is an urgent need for all Member States to make considerable, concerted efforts to create an environment in which enterprises can flourish and which encourages individuals to become entrepreneurs in order to apply their ideas and hence to create new jobs. The action should: make it easier to start up and run businesses by providing a clear, stable, predictable and simplified set of rules; develop the markets for venture capital, thereby mobilizing Europe's wealth behind entrepreneurs and innovators: a pan-European secondary capital market should be established by the year 2000; make the taxation system more employment-friendly by reversing the long-term trend towards higher taxes and charges on labor, while maintaining budget neutrality" (Commission Communication of October 1, 1997, Proposal for Guidelines for Member States' Employment Policies, 1998).

60. The different steps can be found at http://www.ipyme.org/Indexnetscape.htm.

61. In fact, only Greece, with 43%; Italy, with 28%; and Portugal, with 29%, have higher proportions of self-employed workers.

62. Although the difference in the levels of job satisfaction between those who work for somebody else and the self-employed is quite small in Spain, 3%, in sharp contrast with the United States, where the difference is 19% (Blanchflower 2000).

63. In Spain, in the period 1990–1997, of those unemployed the previous year only 1.8% were self-employed, while 26.9% were employees, 63.6% were still unemployed, and 7.2% were out of the labor force (OECD [2000a]: 167).

64. We should not be misguided by the data in table 7.6 that refer to employment in R&D, software, and other corporate activities, since the bulk of the increase is in the administrative and logistics tasks.

65. European Commission (2000): 59.
66. *The European Internet Report*. Morgan, Stanley, Dean Witter June 1999. http://www.morganstanley.com/institutional/techresearch/euroinet.html?page=research
67. Banco de España (2001).
68. To have an idea of the overvaluation of the Spanish currency at the time, Spain joined the EMS in 1989 with a central exchange rate of 64 pesetas per DM. Eight years later, the fixed Euro-peseta exchange rate (supposedly the equilibrium rate) was set at 85 pesetas per DM, roughly one-third lower.
69. The importance of disinflationary policies is also emphasized by Dolado and Jimeno (1997) in their analysis of Spanish unemployment from a structural VAR approach.

## References

Abramovici, G. 2002. *Social Protection in Europe. Statistics in Focus.* Theme 3-1/2002. Brussels: Eurostat.

Alba-Ramirez, A., and R. Freeman. 1990. "Job Finding and Wages When Long-Run Unemployment Is Really Long: The Case of Spain." NBER Working Paper 3409.

Andrés, J., and J. García. 1993. "Los determinantes de la probabilidad de abandonar el desempleo: evidencia empírica para el caso español." Mimeografiado. Universidad de Valencia.

Arellano, M., M. Bentolila, and O. Bover. 1997. "The Distribution of Earnings in Spain during the 80's: The Effects of Skill, Unemployment, and Union Power." CEPR/IEEG Workshop on Rising Inequalities. A Coruña. February 14–15.

Atkinson, A. B., and J. Micklewright. 1991. "Unemployment Compensation and Labour Markets Transitions: A Critical Review." *Journal of Economic Literature* 29: 1679–1727.

Atkinson, A. B., L. Rainwater, and T. M. Smeeding. 1995. *Income Distribution in OECD Countries*. Paris: OECD.

Ball, L. 1999. "Aggregate Demand and Long-Run Unemployment." *Brookings Papers on Economic Activity* 2: 189–251.

Banco de España. 2001. *The Spanish Balance of Payments 1999*. Madrid: Banco de España.

Bentolila, S., and J. Dolado. 1993. "Who Are the Insiders? Wage Setting in Spanish Manufacturing Firms." CEPR Discussion Paper No. 754.

Bentolila, S., and A. Ichino. 2000. "Unemployment and Consumption: Are Job Losses Less Painful near the Mediterranean?" CESifo Working Paper 392. Available at ftp://129.187.96.124/CESifo_WP/372.pdf.

Bertola, B. 1990. "Job Security, Employment, and Wages." *European Economic Review* 34(4): 851–886.

Bertola, G., T. Boeri, and S. Cazes. 2000. "Employment Protection in Industrialized Countries: the Case for New Indicators." Paper presented at the Workshop on Concepts and Measurements of European Labor Markets Flexibility/Adaptability Indexes, Brussels, October 26–27. Available at http://europa.eu.int/comm/employment_social/empl&esf/docs/agenda18.pdf.

Blanchard, O., and P. Portugal. 2001. "What Hides behind an Unemployment Rate: Comparing Portuguese and U.S. Labor Markets." *American Economic Review* 91 (1): 187–207.

Blanchflower, D. G. 2000. "Self-Employment in OECD countries." *Labour Economics* 7: 471–505.

Bover, O., and J. Muellbauer. 1988. "Housing, Wages and U.K. Labour Markets." CEPR Discussion Paper No. 268, London.

Bover, O., M. Arellano, and S. Bentolila. 1996. "Duración del desempleo, duración de las prestaciones y ciclo económico." *Estudios económicos* No. 57, Banco de España.

Bover, O., P. García-Perea, and P. Portugal. 2000. "Iberian Labor Markets: Why Spain and Portugal Are OECD Outliers." *Economic Policy* 15(31):381–428.

Buechteman, C. F. (ed). 1993. *Employment Security and Labor Market Behavior.* Ithaca, N.Y.: ILR Press.

Calmfors, L. 1993. "Centralization of Wage Bargaining and Macroeconomic Performance—A Survey." *OECD Economic Studies* 21 (Winter): 161–191.

Calmfors, L., and J. Driffil. 1988. "Bargaining Structure, Corporatism, and Macroeconomic Performance." *Economic Policy* 3(6): 13–62.

Cebrian, I., C. García, J. Muro, L. Toharia, and E. Villagomez. 1995. *Protección social y acceso al desempleo.* Madrid: CES.

Consejo Económico y Social (CES). 2002. *España 2001. Memoria sobre la situación socioeconómica y laboral.* Madrid: CES.

Centro de Investigaciones Sociológicas (CIS). 1997. *Juventud y entorno familiar.* Estudio 2262. Madrid. Octubre.

Clark, K. B., and L. W. Summers. 1990. "Unemployment Insurance and Labour Market Transitions." In *Understanding Unemployment*, edited by L. W. Summers. Cambridge, Mass.: MIT Press.

Dolado, J. J., and J. F. Jimeno. 1997. "The Causes of Spanish Unemployment: A Structural VAR Approach." *European Economic Review* 41: 1281–1307.

Durán, A. 1999. "Costes de despido económico: Efectos económicos y bienestar colectivo." *Documentación laboral* No. 58: 29–54.

Emerson, M. 1988. "Regulation or Deregulation of the Labour Market: Policy Regimes for Recruitment and Dismissal in the Industrialised Countries." *European Economic Review* 31(4): 775–817.

European Commission. 2000. *Employment in Europe 2000.* Brussels: European Commission.

Faini, R., G. Galli, P. Gennari, and F. Rossi. 1997. "An Empirical Puzzle: Falling Migration and Growing Unemployment Differential among Italian Regions." *European Economic Review* 41: 571–579.

García, I., and L. Toharia. 2000. "Prestaciones por desempleo y búsqueda de empleo." *Revista de economía aplicada* 8(23) (Otoño): 5–34.

García, J., P. J. Hernández, and A. López. 1997. "Diferencias salariales entre sector público y sector privado en España." *Papeles de economía española* No. 72: 261–269.

García Brosa, E. 1996. *Prestaciones por desempleo y duración del paro.* Madrid: CES.

García Serrano, C. 1996. "On Worker and Job Turnover." *Working Papers of the ESRC Research Center on Micro-Social Change* Paper 96-17, University of Exeter.

Gómez, F., and C. Usabiaga. 2000. "Las estimaciones de la NAIRU: Una valoración de conjunto." EEE31. Madrid: FEDEA.

Gough, I., A. Pfaller, and G. Therborn. 1991. *Can the Welfare State Compete?* London: Macmillan.

IARD. 2001. *Study on the State of Young People and Youth Policy in Europe. Final Reports.* Milan: IARD.

International Monetary Fund (IMF). 1999. *World Economic Outlook 1999.* Washington, D.C.: IMF.

Instituto Nacional de Estadística (INE). 1998. *Encuesta de coste de la mano de obra.* Madrid: INE.

Izquierdo Escribano, A. 1992. *La inmigración en España.* Madrid: Ministerio de Trabajo y Seguridad Social.

Jackman, R., C. Pissarides, and S. Savouri. 1990. "Unemployment Policies." *Economic Policy* 5(11): 449–490.

Krueger, A. B., and J-S. Pischke. 1997. "Observations and Conjectures on the U.S. Employment Miracle." NBER Working Paper 6146, Cambridge, Mass.

Kuechle, H. 1990. "Kuendigungsvorschriften im europaeischen Vergleich." *WSI-Mitteilungen* 43: 392–400.

Laafia, I. 2001. "R & D Expenditure and Personnel in Europe and Its Regions." *Statistics in Focus.* Theme 9-3/2001. Brussels: Eurostat.

Layard, R.1986. *How to Beat Unemployment.* Oxford: Oxford University Press.

Layard, R., S. Nickell, and R. Jackman. 1991. *Unemployment: Macroeconomic Performance and the Labour Market.* Oxford: Oxford University Press.

Lazear, E. P. 1979. "Job Security Provisions and Employment." *Quarterly Journal of Economics* 105: 699–726.

Malo, M. A. 1996. "La negociación de los despidos en España: una aproximación desde la Teoría de Juegos." Ph.D. diss., Universidad de Alcalá de Henares.

Malo, M. A., and L. Toharia. 1999. *Costes de despido y creación de empleo.* Madrid: Ministerio de Trabajo y Asuntos Sociales.

Marimon, R., and F. Zilibotti. 1996. "¿Por que hay menos empleo en Espana?" In *La economia espanola: Una vision diferente,* edited by R. Marimon. Barcelona: Antoni Bosch Editorial.

Martin, J. P. 2000. "What Works among Active Labour Market Policies: Evidence from OECD Countries Experiences." *OECD Economic Studies* no. 30: 79–113.

Ministerio de Fomento. 2000.*Anuario del Ministerio de Fomento.* Madrid: Ministerio de Fomento.

Ministerio de Trabajo y Asuntos Sociales. 2002. *Estadística de convenios colectivos de trabajo.* Madrid: Ministerio de Trabajo y Asuntos Sociales.

———. 2000. *Annuario de Migraciones.* Madrid: Ministerio de Trabajo y Asuntos Sociales.

Muñoz de Bustillo, R. 1990. "En 'Distribución de la Renta." In J. Albarracin et al. eds., *Reflexiones sobre Política Económica.* Madrid: Editorial Popular.

Nicoletti, G., S. Scarpetta, and O. Bolyaud. 2000. *Summary Indicators for Product Market Regulation with an Extension to Employment Protection Legislation.* Economic Department Working Paper No. 26. Paris: OECD.

Nickell, S. 1997. "Unemployment and Labour Market Rigidities: Europe versus North America." *Economic Perspectives* 11(3): 37–54.

Organization for Economic Cooperation and Development (OECD). 2002. *Employment Outlook.* Paris: OECD.

———. 2000a. *Employment Outlook.* Paris: OECD.

———. 2000b. *Education at Glance.* Paris: OECD.

———. 2000c. *Regulatory Reform in Spain.* Paris: OECD.

————. 1999a. *Social Expenditure Database 1980–1996*. Paris: OECD.

————. 1999b. *Employment Outlook 1999*. Paris: OECD.

————. 1997. *Implementing the OECD Jobs Strategy—Lessons from Member Countries' Experience*. Paris: OECD.

————. 1996. Economic Surveys: Spain. Paris: OECD.

————. 1994. *The OECD Jobs Study*. Paris: OECD.

————. 1986. *Economic Surveys. Spain 1985/86*. Paris: OECD.

Palacio, J. I., and H. Simón. 2002. "Dispersión salarial y negociación colectiva en España." *Cuadernos de relaciones laborales* 20(1): 169–187.

Pita, C., and B. Dominguez. 1998. "Los accidentes laborales en España: La importancia de la temporalidad." *Documentación laboral* No. 55: 37–64.

Revenga, A. 1991. "La liberalización económica y la distribución de la renta: La experiencia española." *Moneda y crédito* no. 193: 179–223.

Rodrik, D. 1998. "Where Did All the Growth Go? External Shocks, Social Conflict and Growth Collapses." CEPR Discussion Paper No. 1789.

Schellhaas, H. 1993. "The Economics of Employment Protection: A Comment to Daniel S. Hamermesh,", in *Employment Security and Labor Market Behavior*, edited by C. F. Buechteman (Ithaca, N.Y.: ILR Press, 1993).

Schneider, F., and D. Enste. 2000. "Shadow Economies: Size, Causes, and Consequences." *Journal of Economic Literature* 38 (March): 77–114.

Segura, J., F. Durán, L. Toharia, and S. Bentolila. 1991. *Análisis de la contratación temporal en España*. Madrid: Ministerio de Trabajo y Seguridad Social.

Serrano, A., and J. L. Malo de Molina. 1979. *Salarios y mercado de trabajo en España*. Madrid: Blume.

Serrano, J. M., et al. 1998. *Desigualdades territoriales en la economía sumergida*. Zaragoza: IAF.

Solchaga, C. 1997. *El fin de la edad dorada*. Madrid: Taurus.

Toharia, L., and M. A. Malo. 1997. "Las indemnizaciones por despido: Su origen, sus determinantes y las enseñanzas de la reforma de 1994." *Documentación laboral* No. 51: 13–32.

# 8

## Is Labor Market Regulation at the Root of European Unemployment?: The Case of Germany and the Netherlands

RONALD SCHETTKAT

### 8.1 INTRODUCTION: WELFARE STATE INSTITUTIONS AND EMPLOYMENT

The difference in employment performance between the United States and Europe has attracted much attention, and indeed the differences are striking: in the 1960s and early 1970s, the United States had a much higher unemployment rate than most European countries, but U.S. unemployment then remained—with cyclical fluctuations—at that level, whereas unemployment rates in many European countries rose with every recession and remained at ever higher levels (table 8.1). Intercountry differences in economic performance have always led economists to investigate institutions as a possible explanation for this phenomenon. In the 1960s and 1970s, the economic advisers of the U.S. president sought to understand which European institutions were responsible for such low unemployment rates (e.g., Council of Economic Advisers 1962). Increasingly, influential Europeans are proposing American-type institutions as a cure to high European unemployment.

Peering across the Atlantic, many European economists have concluded that the minimalist welfare state and less strictly regulated labor markets of the United States must be the cause of its superior employment performance. In what Solow (2000) calls a "prototype article," Horst Siebert (1997) argues:

> most importantly, a whole set of measures raised the reservation wage: the duration of unemployment benefits was partly increased; it was made easier to obtain such benefits; the conditions under which the unemployed were expected to accept jobs were interpreted more generously; governmental

Table 8.1. Unemployment Rates, approximated U.S. Concept

| Years | France | Germany | Italy | Netherlands | Sweden | U.K. | EU mean[1] | Canada | U.S.A. | Japan | Australia |
|---|---|---|---|---|---|---|---|---|---|---|---|
| 1961–70 | 1.8 | 0.6 | 3.2 | — | 1.7 | | 1.8 | 4.7 | 4.7 | 1.3 | 2.0 |
| 1971–80 | 4.3 | 2.3 | 3.8 | 4.8 | 2.1 | 5.0 | 3.7 | 6.9 | 6.4 | 1.8 | 4.4 |
| 1981–90 | 9.5 | 6.1 | 6.6 | 9.2 | 2.5 | 10.1 | 7.3 | 9.4 | 7.1 | 2.5 | 7.7 |
| 1991–98 | 11.6 | 8.1 | 10.6 | 6.0 | 8.1 | 8.7 | 8.8 | 10.0 | 6.0 | 3.0 | 9.3 |
| 2000 | 9.4 | 8.1 | 10.7 | 3.0 | 5.8 | 5.5 | 7.1 | 6.1 | 4.0 | 4.8 | 6.3 |

1. EU mean = unweighted average of the unemployment rates of the listed countries.
Source: Computations based on BLS international comparative labor force database.

schemes for the unemployed were extended; the relative distance between the lowest wage in the labor market and non-working income in welfare programs became more narrow; and the minimum wage, which is applied in some countries, was raised.[1]

The Organization for Economic Cooperation and Development (OECD) and the International Monetary Fund (IMF) also argue that the "generosity" of unemployment payments and related welfare benefits increases the natural rate of unemployment and reduces the speed of readjustment to equilibrium following shocks (Martin 1996; OECD 1999; IMF 1999). Consequently, the OECD has recommended that Germany, for example, should lower unemployment benefit replacement rates, cut the duration of benefits, strengthen the work availability conditions, and tighten eligibility conditions and employment-dependent transfers in order to encourage people to take low-paid jobs (OECD 1997).

The Netherlands and Germany are particularly interesting cases because both are highly developed welfare states with similar institutional structures but diverging employment trends. Since the mid-1990s, the Netherlands experienced strong employment growth and a sharp fall in the unemployment rate, whereas employment and unemployment have been roughly stagnant in Germany. At the same time, the Netherlands implemented many policy reforms and is identified by many authors as the country experience that exemplifies the orthodox view that labor market deregulation in Europe is a necessary condition for employment expansion. In addition, the Netherlands gave up an independent monetary policy in 1983 when the Dutch Central Bank pegged the guilder to the mark and thus followed the Bundesbank's decisions. Both the Netherlands and Germany suffered from the same tight, price-stability-oriented monetary policy of the Bundesbank, but obviously with very different labor market outcomes.

This chapter shows that the Netherlands deregulated from a very high regulatory level, and these reforms moved Dutch institutions in the direction of German institutions. In almost every relevant respect, by the late 1990s, Dutch institutional arrangements were more restrictive (e.g., dismissal protection) or more generous (e.g., unemployment benefits) than the comparable arrangements in Germany. Thus, given the strong claims for the negative employment impact of welfare state institutions,[2] the Dutch-German case is a puzzle. How is it possible that the less regulated economy does less well in employment terms if regulation is the prime cause for high unemployment?

I suggest that the micro view on the incentive structure produced by welfare state institutions is insufficient and that one has to look into macroeconomic effects, as well. I argue that the German welfare state institutions would in principle have allowed for an employment expansion similar to that in the Netherlands but that, in contrast to the Netherlands, macro-economic policy was contradictory in Germany.[3] In the Netherlands, employers and unions, as well as the government, have regular consultations about economic trends and policy (institutionalized in the SER [Social Economic Council] and the Stichting van de Arbeid [Labor Foundation]). The main function of these institutions is to enable convergence of expectations and to promote a mutual reinforcing mix of monetary, fiscal, and wage policies. In contrast, these major macroeconomic policies were uncoordinated—to put it mildly—in Germany.

In what follows, I focus on the impact of labor market regulations and welfare state institutions on the functioning of labor markets in the Netherlands and in Germany. I first give a broad overview of some institutional features and discuss their relationships with economic performance, that is, labor market performance. The empirical evidence is largely based on broad indicators and comparisons across countries, although reference is made as well to some detailed studies that have compared the Netherlands and Germany. Reference is also made to U.S. trends, both because they may facilitate an understanding of the Dutch-German differences and because the United States has become the benchmark in discussions of European employment performance.

## 8.2 ANALYZING THE IMPACT OF INSTITUTIONS ON LABOR MARKET PERFORMANCE

Consistent with the recommendations of both the OECD and the IMF, "Labor market rigidities are at the root of European unemployment" became by far the most popular hypothesis for the explanation of the differences in employment and unemployment between the United States and Europe. The European Central Bank (ECB), which is primarily responsible for keeping inflation low,[4] takes a "sit back and relax" attitude and claims that the European economy operates at its NAIRU. If there is an unemployment problem in Europe, governments must deregulate their labor markets. According to this view, expansionary monetary policy cannot improve employment. Given the institutional setting, the European economies are in equilibrium, understood as the optimal position the economy can reach given the institutional environment. In such a situation, any expansionary policy will lead to inflation, rather than to higher employment.

It is true, of course, that overly rigid labor markets may create unemployment and may, therefore, be quite costly to society. High unemployment can be disastrous for the welfare state, as well as for the unemployed, because it tends to mean that transfer payments must increase from a tax base that has declined. But it is difficult to determine what the impact of welfare state institutions on employment actually is. The strength of the OECD-IMF orthodoxy is theoretical rather than empirical. The empirical evidence for Siebert's claims is, to put it mildly, not very strong. The problem with this approach is that it identifies welfare state measures as deviations from the perfect-market model (a model that assumes perfect information, no mobility costs, and so on). As such, these interventions distort the working of the price mechanism. Siebert sees the more favorable employment trends in the deregulated U.S. economy in the 1990s as evidence that policies against the perfect-market model cannot be successful.

Indeed, many welfare state regulations may look unnecessary and inefficient when compared with the perfect-market model. A good example of an argument based on the perfect-market model was provided by the German *Monopolkommission* under the leadership of Professor Carl-Christian von Weiszäcker. The committee classified collective bargaining as a bilateral monopoly in which the union—the monopolist on the supply side of the labor market—has three possible ways of setting wages. If the union sets wages at the equilibrium level, then collective bargaining is unnecessary because this would also, according to the *Monopolkommission*, be the market result. If the union sets wages below the equilibrium level, firms will pay higher wages (wage drift). In these two cases, the union will do no harm but will be unnecessary. However, the *Monopolkommission's* report argued that the incentive structure for union officials is such that they need to create a premium for their members and that wages are for this reason set above the equilibrium level, reducing demand and welfare and creating unemployment. The *Monopolkommission* provided no empirical evidence on union wage setting but instead concluded from its theoretical model that wages will (so long as unions exist) be too high and therefore cause unemployment. The Weizsäcker commission started from observed unemployment and then simply assumed that this could be interpreted as evidence for its conclusions that wages are too high.

Institutions such as wage bargaining arrangements may be evaluated differently when the presence of market imperfections is recognized (e.g., Blank and Freeman 1994; Buttler, Franz, Schettkat, and Soskice 1996; Krueger 2000; Stiglitz 2000). Regulations clearly limit *ceteris paribus* the scope for discretionary decisions by employers, but only in the perfect-market model are they necessarily inefficient. In a less perfect environment, they may well create opportunities. It has been shown that small deviations from the perfect-market assumption can lead to very different results and that market processes can create suboptimal outcomes. Individual rational behavior may create macro results that do not fit the preferences of any (!) individual (Schelling 1978). In this situation, regulations are necessary to achieve the social and individual optimum. For example, works councils may not only constrain managerial decisions but also give workers a voice and thus improve decision making (Hirschman 1970; Freeman and Medoff 1984). Furthermore, there is usually more than one way to do things, and some instruments may actually facilitate adjustments (e.g., the reduced working hours subsidy, which provides a short-term alternative to dismissals).

Although European economies are almost all highly developed welfare states, they show a great diversity of labor market performance: job creation in the Netherlands, relatively speaking, outstripped that in the United States in the 1990s; in the 1970s, Denmark achieved an employment-population rate that was not achieved by the United States until the mid-1990s; and Austria's unemployment rate has consistently been below the U.S. rate. Even the west German unemployment rate was always below that of the United States until 1993 (OECD 2002, Statistical Annex Table A).

The evidence on the impact of welfare state institutions on labor market performance is much less clear than the conventional wisdom suggests. For instance, for those advocating OECD-style flexibility, the real world trends in the European Tiger economies—Denmark, the Netherlands, Austria, and Ireland—must be especially puzzling. These countries are undeniably generous welfare states, with the probable exception of Ireland, which is more an industrializing country (Schettkat 1999). To take just one prominent indicator, their unemployment replacement rates are among the highest in the world, and Denmark, the Netherlands, and Austria rank very high on the OECD's scale of unemployment benefit generosity.[5] Denmark and the Netherlands are also among the countries with the lowest degree of wage inequality, and their total tax wedges, the difference between and gross and net income, are among the highest in OECD countries. Not long ago, the Netherlands was characterized as "the sick man of Europe" (by former Prime Minister Lubbers), but now it is the shining star of European and international summits, celebrated as a prime example of the "third way," combining strong employment growth with one of the most developed welfare states in the world. However, the Netherlands also serves as an example for deregulation: replacement rates have been reduced but are still exceptionally high (see later discussion), and employment protection has been eased, albeit from a level unthinkable in many other countries (Schettkat and Reijnders 2000). So, while it is true that the Netherlands has practiced substantial deregulation, it is still far from being a deregulated economy. Even so, it is experiencing enormous employment growth.

Many welfare state institutions have been introduced to shelter workers from the harmful effects of competitive labor markets. Unemployment insurance, of course, is intended to prevent wages falling below a certain level. This may increase unemployment, but very low wage levels may be harmful to society in other ways. Furthermore, if skilled workers accept jobs far below their proper skill (and pay) levels, it is not only their individual incomes that will suffer: the output of the economy may do so, as well. In fact, it may be more efficient to allow unemployed workers a longer search period in order to achieve a better worker-job match and thus higher productivity (Acemoglu and Shimer 2000). This is just one example of a welfare state regulation that may look unnecessary and inefficient when compared with the perfect-market model but that may prove to be the opposite when market imperfections are taken into account.

This may also be the case in some other areas of social insurance. In any case, even if welfare state measures reduce efficiency, this may be a price that society is prepared to pay in order to achieve certain goals in other spheres (Blank and Freeman 1994; Krueger 2000; Stiglitz 2000). Many things carry a positive price tag, yet we demand them. However, to determine the impact of specific institutional arrangements on employment, it seems more promising to compare the outcomes of actually implemented measures than to compare them with the perfect-market model, which relies on extreme assumptions.

International comparisons can potentially produce evidence on the impact of institutions. Unfortunately, however, the model used in international comparisons is often overly simple: a difference in an indicator for economic performance is often related to a certain institutional difference, and if the results fit our (theoretical) priors, we are too easily willing to be convinced of the "evidence."[6] Actually, countries usually differ in many respects, and this makes it extremely difficult to identify the impact of specific institutional features. Problems range from "trivial" measurement issues to the difficulty of achieving a deep understanding of the formal and actual working of institutions. No wonder that public discussions suffer from exaggerations of the success of countries, often judged by the development of a single economic variable and explained by reference to a specific institution. In this way, we admire Japanese institutions while Japan is economically successful and switch 180 degrees to the "American model" when the U.S. employment performance is superior.[7]

## 8.3 COMPARATIVE INSTITUTIONAL ANALYSIS: THE NETHERLANDS AND GERMANY

Welfare state institutions are expected to have an impact on labor markets in several areas:

- Employment flexibility
- Wage flexibility (wage inequality)
- Reservation wages and the incentive to work

The institutions involved are employment protection measures, wage-bargaining institutions, unemployment insurance, taxes and contributions, and other transfers.[8]

### 8.3.1 Employment Protection

The orthodox argument is that dismissal protection and severance payments increase labor costs and thus make employers reluctant to hire (Flanagan 1989; Schellhaass 1989). But, while these factors may reduce hiring in an upswing, they also discourage dismissals in a downturn. Relaxing dismissal protection may therefore have two opposing effects, and in the end it may affect the variation of employment over the business cycle more than the average level of employment. Whether dismissal protection actually raises labor costs depends on the wage level in the absence of this regulation. If employees pay for job security by a wage reduction (insurance premium)—that is, if the wage with dismissal protection is lower than it would otherwise be—the effect on employment is not so clearcut (Bertola 1992). If workers paid an actuarially fair insurance premium for job security, deregulation of employment protection would have no employment effect at all.

In Germany as in the Netherlands, regular employment contracts are generally assumed to be permanent,[9] and dismissal requires advance notice of at least four weeks.[10] In both countries, the law defines the minimum in this respect, and collective agreements can specify more generous periods of advance notice. The actual dismissal procedure, however, is far more restrictive in the Netherlands, where dismissals have to be confirmed by the employment office, and this is a lengthy procedure. Somewhat quicker but more costly dismissal procedures have been made available through labor courts (Hassink 1999).

Table 8.2 lists the OECD estimates for the strictness of employment protection, distinguishing between regular and temporary employment. The higher the value of the indicator, the stricter the employment protection. According to this indicator (column 1), the Netherlands has the strictest regulations for regular employment, stricter than those in Germany and far above the U.S. value. As column 2 indicates, between the 1980s and the 1990s, no deregulation of regular employment has occurred

**Table 8.2. Employment Protection**

|  | Strictness of employment protection | | | |
|---|---|---|---|---|
|  | Regular employment | | Temporary employment | |
|  | Late 1990s | 1990s–1980s | Late 1990s | 1990s–1980s |
|  | 1 | 2 | 3 | 4 |
| Germany | 2.8 | 0.1 | 2.3 | −1.5 |
| Netherlands | 3.1 | 0.0 | 1.2 | −1.2 |
| United States | 0.2 | 0.0 | 0.3 | 0.0 |

Source: OECD *Employment Outlook* (June 1999).

in the Netherlands, and for Germany the OECD even indicates a slight increase in employment protection.

Deregulation has taken place for temporary employment in both countries, but the OECD puts the strictness of employment protection for temporary employment more than 1 point higher for Germany than for the Netherlands; however, the regulations that govern these contracts seem to be very similar in both countries. The "flex-wet" (flexibility law) of 1999 provides that the fourth fixed-term contract in a row must legally be regarded as a permanent contract of employment (with some exceptions for temporary-work agencies).

In Germany, the major step in relaxing the conditions concerning fixed-term employment contracts was the introduction of the Employment Promotion Act (*Beschäftigungsförderungsgesetz*) in 1985.[11] The law provided unconditional freedom for the conclusion of fixed-term contracts up to 18 months in duration. Highly controversial when first introduced, the law was initially limited to a period of four and a half years ending January 1, 1990, and its introduction was accompanied by extensive research (Büchtemann and Höland 1989). Since then, the law has been extended several times with slight modifications (see Fuchs and Schettkat [2000] for an overview).

The evaluation took place from May 1985 to April 1987, a period in which the German economy was recovering from recession and therefore exactly the kind of period in which such a law would be expected to have the strongest impact. The researchers found that fixed-term contracts were used mainly in small and medium-size companies, which typically have a large proportion of low-skilled labor. This is, of course, not an argument against the law, but it does show that the relevance of short-term contracts is limited to that segment of the labor market in which neither workers nor employers invest much in the relationship. A major motive for fixed-term contracts was selection (cited by 40% of the firms that used them). Employers used the fixed term as an extended probationary period in order to overcome information asymmetries. Once employers have confidence in the skills of workers, they are obviously interested in long-term relationships, because hiring is costly, even at the low-skill end of the jobs market.[12]

A second evaluation of the extended Employment Promotion Act (Bielenski, Kohler, and Schreiber-Kittl 1994) comes to conclusions similar to those of Büchtemann and Höland. No increase in the use of fixed-term contracts was observed between 1985 and 1994: the share remained at 5%–6% of all new contracts. Most surprising of all, the share of fixed-term contracts did not vary over the business cycle (Bielenski 1997; also Kraft 1994). This shows that the Employment Promotion Act had no significant employment effects, even in periods when it might have been expected to have the strongest impact.

One may conclude that the empirical evidence on this "natural experiment" gives orthodox deregulators no reason to be euphoric. But neither does it support those critics who predicted the collapse of industrial relations in Germany if employers were allowed to conclude fixed-term contracts. It provides confirmation of the arguments of neither side. Indeed, it may be that both sides view the labor market from an overly narrow theoretical perspective: deregulators rely too heavily on the perfect-market assumption, while critics place too much emphasis on balances of power. Obviously, reality, with all its uncertainties and imperfections, is more complex than extreme models suggest.

### 8.3.2 Wage Bargaining

Countries can choose to organize collective bargaining in different ways. Probably the most important decision identified in research to date is the level at which bargaining occurs. At one extreme, collective bargaining is entirely decentralized, with unions and employers bargaining at the plant (or equivalent) level. At the other extreme, bargaining is entirely centralized, with a large union (or confederation of unions) negotiating with an employers' federation over a single contract that effectively covers every worker in the country. Theory and much empirical evidence suggest that the choice of bargaining method can have an important impact on national employment outcomes. Centralized ("coordinated" or "corporatist") bargaining affects employment in two countervailing ways: (1) greater centralization increases union bargaining power, which may lead unions to set wages "too high," leading to unemployment; and (2) greater centralization may internalize the externalities (job loss) involved in wage bargaining, tempering wage demands relative to decentralized bargaining and thereby increasing employment.

Some empirical analysis that has attempted to measure the relative importance of these two competing effects has concluded that employment follows a U-shaped pattern as centralization rises, with employment high at low levels of centralization (where union power is weakest), low at mid-levels of centralization, and high again at high levels of centralization (where union power is strong but restrained by concerns for potentially unemployed union members) (Calmfors and Driffill 1988). Other studies have failed to find a U-shaped relationship, concluding instead that employment rises directly with the degree of centralization (Bruno and Sachs 1985; Nickell 1988; Layard, Nickell, and Jackman 1991; Soskice 1990).

The Dutch wage bargaining system converged with the German system during the 1980s and 1990s. In the 1960s and 1970s, the Dutch government could intervene in wage bargaining, but wage indexation made it impossible to break up the price-wage-price spiral. In this respect, the Netherlands had more in common with Italy than with Germany. Since 1969, the Netherlands has had a statutory minimum wage derived from a defined social minimum, first under the assumption of one-earner households but later related to individuals.[13] In real terms, the Dutch minimum wage declined (see Salverda 1998 for details) but was in 1995 still at about 58% of the mean wage. Germany does not have a statutory minimum wage, but the transfer system creates a reservation wage, which amounts to about 32% of the mean German wage, roughly the same proportion represented by the U.S. minimum wage (Freeman and Schettkat 1998).

In both the Netherlands and Germany, bargaining takes place essentially at the industry level (although in the Netherlands without a regional component); collective agreements can be extended to cover firms that do not participate in employers' associations, but both countries also allow firm-specific contracts. In the Netherlands and in Germany, most of the workers covered by collective agreements (about 90% in Germany and 76% in the Netherlands) come under an industry agreement. This was increasingly the case in the 1990s (see Hartog 2000). If the survival of the firm is at risk, escape clauses permit deviations from collective agreements. In both countries, these two bargaining systems produce similar levels of wage dispersion, which is comparatively low by international standards, and both countries have a similar underlying skill structure. If a compressed wage structure was the cause for high Dutch unemployment as claimed by the wage compression hypothesis, one would expect wage dispersion to rise with increasing employment (or decreasing unemployment). This, however, is not observed (see chapter 2).

What stands out is the difference in real wage trends since the mid-1980s. In the famous Wassenaar agreement of 1982, the Dutch unions agreed on a policy of wage restraint, working time reductions, and "active labor market policies" designed to boost employment by basically following the suggestions of a SER commission (the Commission Wagner of the Social Economic Council).[14] The core unions agreed to follow a moderate wage policy to improve employment.[15] In the late 1970s, unemployment rose as real wages declined, but this was the result of high nominal wage growth and even higher inflation, driven by the surge in energy costs. After Wassenaar, the Dutch unions followed a policy of nominal wage moderation, and real wages roughly stagnated, with declining rates of inflation. In the 1980s and 1990s, real wages in manufacturing grew by about .4% per year as compared to about 1.5% in Germany. Since wage growth was lower than productivity increases, the labor share declined. Thus, the Dutch unions accepted claims for higher profits in order to prevent inflationary pressure and negative employment effects given the tight monetary policy of the Bundesbank, which the Nederlandsche Bank followed without exception. As is argued later, the acceptance of the dominant monetary policy and the wage response are key elements of the Dutch employment miracle.

Without doubt, the raw wage distribution is more compressed in both the Netherlands and Germany than in the United States. The D9/D5 ratios (the 90th to the 50th percentile in the wage distribution) were about 1.6 and 1.7 in Germany and the Netherlands, but 2.1 in the United States. Similarly the D5/D1 ratios were 1.4, 1.6 and 2.1, respectively (see table 8.3).[16]

However, the raw wage distribution is inadequate to judge whether the European wage distributions are more compressed than the U.S. wage distribution. If low-skilled workers in Europe have higher skills than low-skilled American workers, part of the lower wage dispersion is related to the low skill dispersion. Indeed, skills differ substantially between the United States and the continental European countries, as the International Adult Literacy Survey (IALS) has revealed (OECD 1997). Years of schooling, the most common skill measure, hide these differences and can produce misleading results (Freeman and Schettkat 2000).

The raw wage distributions differ between the United States and the two European countries, but the skill distributions are also very different, especially at the low-skill end. Table 8.3 displays the literacy scores for the employed, the unemployed, and those not in the labor force. Columns 1, 3, and 5 show the D1, the median, and the D9 literacy scores for the three groups. The median and the D9 do not differ much between the countries in all employment status categories (columns 3, 5). For those in the middle

**Table 8.3. Literacy Score by Employment Status, Wage Deciles**

| | Skills | | | | | | Wages | | | |
|---|---|---|---|---|---|---|---|---|---|---|
| | D1 | % | Median | % | D9 | % | D9/D5 | D5/D1 | D9/D5 | D5/D1 |
| | 1 | 2 | 3 | 4 | 5 | 6 | 7 | 8 | 9 | 10 |
| **Germany** | | | | | | | | | | |
| Employed | 239.4 | 100.0 | 291.3 | 100.0 | 342.7 | 100.0 | 1.2 | 1.2 | 1.6 | 1.4 |
| Unemployed | 208.9 | 87.3 | 275.9 | 94.7 | 333.0 | 97.2 | | | | |
| Not in labor force | 214.8 | 89.8 | 277.7 | 95.3 | 331.6 | 96.8 | | | | |
| D5$_{employed}$/D1$_{unemployed}$ | | | | | | | | 1.4 | | |
| **Netherlands** | | | | | | | | | | |
| Employed | 242.9 | 100.0 | 299.5 | 100.0 | 339.5 | 100.0 | 1.1 | 1.2 | 1.7 | 1.6 |
| Unemployed | 201.4 | 82.9 | 289.0 | 96.5 | 323.6 | 95.3 | | | | |
| Not in labor force | 204.4 | 84.2 | 274.2 | 91.5 | 322.5 | 95.0 | | | | |
| D5$_{employed}$/D1$_{unemployed}$ | | | | | | | | 1.5 | | |
| **United States** | | | | | | | | | | |
| Employed | 207.1 | 100.0 | 291.6 | 100.0 | 352.0 | 100.0 | 1.2 | 1.4 | 2.1 | 2.1 |
| Unemployed | 118.4 | 57.2 | 256.6 | 88.0 | 328.1 | 93.2 | | | | |
| Not in labor force | 136.3 | 65.8 | 263.7 | 90.4 | 331.6 | 94.2 | | | | |
| D5$_{employed}$/D1$_{unemployed}$ | | | | | | | | 2.5 | | |

Source: Computations based on IALS for skills, OECD *Employment Outlook* (1999: 62) for wage deciles.

and top of the literacy distribution (the median and the D9), the unemployed and those not in the labor force test nearly as well as the employed (90%–96% as well) in all three countries (columns 4, 6). However, at lower skill levels, the literacy scores differ substantially between Germany and the Netherlands on the one hand and the United States on the other. First, the literacy scores for the D1 are substantially lower in the United States (column 1). Second, among the least literate, the scores of the unemployed and those not in the labor force are much lower relative to the scores of the employed in the United States than in the two European countries (column 2)—at the bottom of the skill distribution, there is a sizable skill gap between the literacy levels of those with and without jobs in the United States, but not in Germany and the Netherlands.

Another way to look at this is to compare the full range of skills at the bottom of the skill distribution by dividing the skill scores of the median employed worker by the D1 score of the unemployed (see last row in the country blocks). The values for the $D5_{employed}/D1_{unemployed}$ literacy score ratios show values 0.2 and 0.3 points higher than the ratio for the employed ($D5_{employed}/D1_{employed}$) in Germany and the Netherlands, but in the United States the difference is 0.9 points (column 9). The least skilled 10% among the unemployed reach 87% of the skill level of the least skilled 10% employed in Germany and 83% of the skill level of the least skilled 10% in the Netherlands and are roughly at the same skill level as the least skilled employed in the United States. In contrast, in the United States, the least skilled 10% among the unemployed reach only 57% of the skill level of the least skilled with jobs.

This is a remarkable result and appears to directly contradict the wage compression hypothesis, which states that downwardly inflexible wages in Europe exclude the least skilled from employment, whereas the flexibility in U.S. wage setting allows the labor market to integrate the less skilled into employment. According to this view, the United States has to pay for skill-biased demand shocks against the less skilled with inequality, but Europe pays with high unemployment (see also chapter 2). If this is true, one would expect the unemployed to have skill levels roughly similar to those of the employed in the United States, but in Europe a substantial skill gap should occur because here the low-skill unemployed are supposed to be excluded from employment through the wage mechanism.[17] In fact, the reverse of this orthodox hypothesis seems to be revealed by the data. The skill difference between the employed and the unemployed is especially high in the United States but much narrower in the Netherlands and in Germany. These data appear to directly contradict the wage compression hypothesis (a similar conclusion is reached with different data in chapters 2 and 5).

If we compare the skill differentials with the wage differentials, another surprising result emerges. The comparison between the D5-D1 ratios for skills (column 8) with those for wages (column 10) provides at least an impression of the wage spread in relation to the skill spread. Although skill scores may not be proportional to productivity (this relation is unknown actually), we expect the D5-D1 ratio for wages $(D5-D1)_{wages}$, which refers to the employed only, to be roughly similar to the skill score of the D5 of the employed $(D5_{employed})$ divided by the skill score of the D1 of the unemployed $(D1_{unemployed})$ if downwardly flexible wages integrate the low-skilled unemployed into employment. This computing exercise, however, produces values of $(D5/D1)_{wages}$ divided by $[(D5_{employed}/D1_{unemployed})_{skills}]$ of .85 for the United States but 1.04 for Germany and 1.05 for the Netherlands. In other words, the wage spread is less than the skill spread in the United States but greater than the skill spread in these welfare state countries. By this metric, wages at the low end of the labor market are not more compressed in Europe. This confirms a result Freeman and Schettkat (2000) get from a regression analysis on a totally different data set.[18]

### 8.3.3 Tax Wedges and Work Incentives

Pecuniary incentives to work depend on the difference between net transfers (transfers net of taxes) and the net wage.[19] Wages, taxes, contributions, and benefits all influence this so-called tax wedge. Table 8.4 displays the average and marginal taxes for a minimum wage earner, an average

**Table 8.4. Taxes and Net Income as % of Transfers**

|  | Germany | New York | Texas | Canada | Netherlands |
|---|---|---|---|---|---|
| Taxes (including contributions) by wage level | | | | | |
| Average | | | | | |
|   Minimum wages | 20.1 | 18.7 | 17.0 | 18.4 | 31.9 |
|   APW | 41.4 | 37.3 | 31.8 | 33.3 | 44.0 |
|   2 * APW | 41.7 | 40.7 | 32.7 | 36.1 | 48.4 |
| Marginal | | | | | |
|   Minimum wages | 49.9 | 41.6 | 37.4 | 38.3 | 58.6 |
|   APW | 52.6 | 39.1 | 29.7 | 33.4 | 53.9 |
|   2 * APW | 35.6 | 51.0 | 39.9 | 46.8 | 59.7 |
| Net income as % of net transfers | | | | | |
| Single with: | | | | | |
|   Statutory minimum wage. | n.a. | 145 | 591 | 164 | 117 |
|   Lowest collective wage | 127 | 145 | 498 | 164 | 126 |
|   APW | 266 | 345 | 503 | 405 | 184 |
| Single-earner household, 2 children, with: | | | | | |
|   Statutory minimum wage | n.a. | 109 | 210 | 109 | 100 |
|   Lowest collective wage | 89 | 109 | 188 | 109 | 105 |
|   APW | 158 | 177 | 366 | 188 | 134 |

Source: CPB 1995. Taxes include employers' and employees' contributions, income tax, family and rent subsidies.

production worker (APW), and an employee who earns twice as much as the average production worker (2 * APW). Because earned income reduces benefits, actual marginal tax rates can be very high for those on low wages and may actually decline as income increases. In Germany, marginal taxes for minimum-wage earners are in fact higher than for those who earn twice the wage of an average production worker (APW). In all cases, however, average and marginal tax rates (including contributions) in the Netherlands are higher than those in Germany. It is surprising that the average tax rates in the State of New York are comparable to the German rates, although taxes in Texas and California are clearly below the European rates. However, the differences between Europe and the United States occur mainly in the higher wage classes and are much lower for the minimum-wage earners, where the strongest disincentive to work is thought to exist.

Does it pay to work rather than receive transfers? The lower panel of table 8.4 displays net earned income as a percentage of transfers. Again, it is important to distinguish between household types, because transfers as well as taxes are often influenced by the family status and the number of children. Since Germany does not have a statutory minimum wage, the lowest collectively agreed wage is used as a category in table 8.4. For a single person earning the lowest collectively agreed wage, the net earned income as a percentage of transfers is similar in Germany and in the Netherlands. For the average production worker (APW), however, Germany provides a much higher incentive to work than the Netherlands, although the earned net income is still 84% higher than the transfer in the Netherlands.

For a single-earner couple with two children earning the lowest collectively agreed wage, the CPB study has identified a clear disincentive to work in Germany. For this household, the net earned income would be about 11% lower than the net transfers, whereas a similar household in the Netherlands would improve its net income by 5% if one member were to work. For the average production worker, the incentive to work would again be higher in Germany than in the Netherlands. The comparative figures for three U.S. states show much higher ratios of net wages to transfers. Since the tax rates are not very different (see table 8.4, upper panel), the higher ratios in the United States must be caused by lower transfers.

### 8.3.4 Unemployment Benefits

In both the Netherlands and Germany, the duration of eligibility for unemployment benefit depends on the individual's working record. The initial period (available after 12 months of employment) is extended as a function of employment and age. In both countries, unemployment assistance is unlimited. The job acceptance criteria, however, have been tightened in both economies.

Unemployment insurance is designed to reduce the economic pressure on workers who have lost their jobs; inevitably, therefore, it reduces the search intensity of the unemployed. Higher replacement rates and longer eligibility periods tend to reduce search intensities, and countries with more generous unemployment insurance systems (or transfer systems in general) should therefore observe higher rates of equilibrium unemployment. Steve Nickell (1998) found that the unemployment patterns across countries are consistent with this thesis, but he also mentions that the longitudinal evidence within countries does not support it. Also, detailed econometric studies based on micro data find that replacement rates have either no effect or very mixed effects on unemployment.[20]

What does seem to have a major effect on unemployment duration is the eligibility period, but it is unclear whether longer eligibility causes longer duration or whether longer eligibility periods have been introduced because of the increasing difficulty of finding jobs (e.g., eligibility periods have been extended for older workers in response to the labor market situation). Hazard rates also show astonishing peaks when eligibility periods end. Nevertheless, most spells of unemployment are very short, and workers may have other very good reasons to search hard and to try to return to employment quickly; for example, lengthy unemployment may both decay their human capital and signal a "lemon" to potential employers (Schettkat 1996). Also, the possible indirect effects of long-term unemployment (the fact that longer search duration may well improve matches and thus raise productivity) have been almost completely ignored (Acemoglu and Shimer 2000).

Net replacement rates for different types of households and periods of unemployment in the Netherlands can be compared to the German replacement rates. There is only one household type for which the German system provides higher replacement rates than the Dutch systems: the single-earner couple with two children earning a minimum wage. At least with reference to this measure of generosity, the unemployment insurance system cannot provide a plausible explanation for the higher rate of unemployment in Germany compared to the Netherlands.[21]

## 8.4 COORDINATION OF MACROECONOMIC POLICIES

The Dutch guilder has been pegged to the DM since 1983 as part of an effort by the Nederlandsche Bank to reduce inflation and to gain credibility. Thus, both the German and the Dutch economies have been operating under the same monetary policy constraints. However, the coordination of the other two major macroeconomic tools—fiscal policy and wage policy— has been much more successful in the Netherlands due to institutions that have facilitated coordination.

The moderate wage policy of the Netherlands was supported by fiscal policy that lowered the tax burden, especially at the lower-wage end. Per capita income in the Dutch economy grew at a higher rate than real wages (and productivity) because an increasing share of the population was integrated into the labor market. In this respect, the development of the Netherlands is similar to that of the United States (see Schettkat 1999).

Despite the nominally fixed guilder–DM exchange rate and roughly similar productivity trends in tradable goods, the very moderate wage increase in the Netherlands led to a declining price level relative to Germany. In other words, the Dutch guilder depreciated in real terms against the DM, which boosted net exports. Increases in net export create multiplier effects, but these tend to be very limited in a small open economy. A "back-of-an-envelope" calculation suggests that the consumption multiplier for the Dutch economy should not be higher than 1.5.[22]

Although exports are, as everywhere, concentrated in manufacturing, employment growth has occurred in services, where part-time jobs represent a substantial proportion of new employment, even when measured in full-time equivalents. In 1980, the Dutch rate of employment in services was close to that of Germany (33.8% and 33.1%, respectively), but by the end of the 1990s, about 49% of the Dutch working-age population was employed in services, compared to only 38% of the German (see Freeman and Schettkat 2000). Service expansion was facilitated by the existence of part-time jobs, which allow employers to adjust the provision of services as demand varies (over the day, for example). The use of part-time workers, concentrated in services (see Schettkat and Reijnders 2000), gives employers the flexibility to adjust the number of workers across peak and off-peak periods and thus reduces costs. In this way, part-time work may have reduced the effect of Baumol's cost disease in services in the Netherlands. Indeed, some studies show that the expansion of part-time work in the Netherlands is strongly related to the requirements of business, although it may fit the needs of the households as well (see Schettkat and Yocarini 2000).

In Germany, the situation after unification was almost the reverse of the relative harmony that characterized the Dutch situation.[23] Unification was promoted as a "win-win" situation that involved no costs for the West Germans and huge gains for the East Germans. Since the Kohl government was committed to keeping taxes unchanged, unification raised both the public debt and contributions to social security. Rising public debt was heavily and openly opposed by the Bundesbank, which threatened to impose tight monetary policy in an effort to force a shift in government policies. At the same time, unions and employers' associations agreed, in the early 1990s, to raise East German wages to West German level. In just a few years during the unification boom, wages rose substantially in West Germany (see Fuchs and Schettkat 2000 for details). Rising contributions, shared by employees and employers, put upward pressure on wages and labor costs. Thus, in Germany, the three major macroeconomic policies (monetary, fiscal, and wage policies) were inconsistent, with labor costs allowed to rise in the context of tight monetary policy (constraining demand) and loose fiscal policy (raising public deficits). The result has been disappointing employment growth.

## 8.5 CONCLUSION

According to the OECD-IMF orthodoxy, welfare state institutions influence labor markets mainly through their negative effects on employment and wage flexibility. The major institutions related to these two areas are employment protection laws, wage bargaining institutions, taxes, unemployment insurance, and other income transfer programs (like social assistance). If the orthodox view is right, in almost every relevant respect, the Dutch institutional arrangements should promote higher unemployment levels than the system in Germany because they are either more restrictive (e.g., dismissal protection) or more generous (e.g., unemployment benefits) than the comparable regulations in Germany. Thus, given the strong claims on the negative employment impact of welfare state institutions, the Dutch-German case is a puzzle.

With respect to wage inequality, the two countries are very similar and present a sharp contrast to the United States. Taking skills into account, the differences in the wage distributions between the European and the United States look much less severe than the raw wage distributions suggest. In contrast to the orthodox wage compression hypothesis, the skill level of the average low-skill unemployed worker is substantially lower than that of the low-skill employed worker in the United States, but not in Germany or the Netherlands.

A remarkable difference between the German and the Dutch economies is the trend in real wages. In the Netherlands, wage and fiscal policies were designed in a way that was consistent with the tight monetary policy imposed by the German Bundesbank. Tax reductions supported the moderate wage policy, and rising employment reduced the pressure on public budgets. In the Netherlands, the coordination of the major macroeconomic policies produced a real depreciation of the guilder and a net export boom. Booming net exports did not lead to a nominal appreciation of the guilder, which is probably related to the smallness of the economy. Rising net exports were a major source of the Dutch employment miracle. In the Netherlands, transfers are more generous than in Germany, taxes are higher, and employment protection is stronger, but employment growth has been much higher than in Germany. This offers little support for the "labor market rigidities are at the root of unemployment" hypothesis.

*Notes*

1. Siebert's claims, however, cannot be confirmed. On the contrary, with rising unemployment, the conditions for benefits have been tightened, replacement rates

lowered, and so on. Professor Solow's comments on lists like the one from Siebert: "timing is wrong" (Solow 2000).

2. The phrase "welfare state institutions" is used as a shortcut for a variety of institutional arrangements such as employment protection, social security provisions, and wage bargaining arrangements.

3. Actually, in response to the unification boom in the 1990–1991, employment in West Germany rose substantially and even helped to integrate the long-term unemployed.

4. See Protocol on the Statute of the European System of Central Banks and of the European Central Bank, Constitution of the ECB, Chapter II, Article 2. The obligation of the ECB are therefore much narrower than those of the Fed (Blinder 1998).

5. Tax rates, social security contributions, and so on show a similar picture.

6. For a discussion on methods of international comparative analysis see Schettkat 1989.

7. These shifts in opinion not only occur in business but also among academics.

8. This fits the list of institutions that Siebert identifies as the cause of rigidities: (1) high replacement rates, (2) employment protection legislation, (3) overly high minimum wages, (4) wage compression, (5) union power, and (6) the higher rate of payroll taxes in Europe.

9. This does not apply to apprenticeship agreements in Germany, which are generally of limited duration.

10. Before 1993, the period of advance notice was six weeks for white-collar workers and only two weeks for blue-collar workers in Germany. Since 1993, it has been the same for blue- and white-collar workers, but collective labor agreements may define longer periods, usually increasing with seniority in Germany (compare Schettkat and Yocarini 2000).

11. Fixed-term contracts had been possible before, but the employer had to show good reason for them.

12. The evidence presented is based on Büchtemann and Höland (1989).

13. This "individualization" affected all transfers and lowered the transfer for individuals.

14. For details see Visser and Hemerijk (1997)

15. Other elements were working-time reductions and an active labor market policy in an attempt to increase employment.

16. These differences in inequality occur also with other measures. Child poverty, the share of children living in households with 50% or less of the median income, is 11% in Germany and 8% in the Netherlands but 23% in the United States (*Economist* [2000]).

17. The same logic should produce similar unemployment rates across skill groups in the United States and greater relative unemployment among the less skilled in welfare state countries. In chapter 5, Schmitt and Wadsworth show that there is no empirical support for this prediction.

18. However, if the comparison is limited to employed workers, Table 3 indicates that the bottom of the U.S. wage distribution is much more unequal relative to the skill distribution than it is for the Netherlands or Germany (see the first row of columns 8 and 10 for each country). The U.S. wage inequality to skill inequality ratio is 2.1/1.4, which compares to the much narrower 1.6/1.2 and 1.4/1.2 ratios for the Netherlands and Germany.

19. Transfers are difficult to compare internationally because in some countries transfers are taxed (the Netherlands, for example), whereas in others they are untaxed (Germany, for example).

20. For a detailed econometric analysis of this issue see, for example, Hunt 1995; Steiner 1997; Zimmermann 1993. What does seem to have a strong effect on unemployment duration is the eligibility period (Steiner 1997).

21. The data are after-tax replacement rates from the OECD (1999). The difference in net replacement rates between Germany and the Netherlands varies there with the household type, as well, but for all household types it is more generous in the Netherlands (OECD 1999: 34).

22. A marginal rate of consumption of .6 and a marginal propensity of imports of .4 would result in a consumption multiplier of 1.25.

23. This refers to the major macroeconomic policies. In other areas, such as pension reforms, there were severe conflicts in the Netherlands (see Visser and Hemerijk 1997).

*References*

Acemoglu, D., and R. Shimer. 2000. "Productivity Gains from Unemployment Insurance." *European Economic Review* 44: 1195–1224.

Appelbaum, E., and R. Schettkat. 1998. "Institutions and Employment Performance in Different Growth Regimes." In *Employment, Technology, and Economic Needs: Theory, Evidence and Public Policy*, edited by J. Michie and A. Reati. Cheltenham: Edward Elgar. pp. 67–87. To be reprinted in G. Hodgson, ed., *A Modern Reader in Institutional and Evolutionary Economics*. Cheltenham: Edward Elgar, 2001.

Bertola, G. 1992. "Labor Turnover Costs and Average Labor Demand." *Journal of Labor Economics* 4.

Bielenski, H. 1997. "Degegulierung des Rechts Befristeter Arbeitsvertrage: Entauschte Hoffnungen, Unbedrundete Befurchtungen." *WSI-Mitteillunen* 50(8): 537–37.

Bielenski, H., B. Kohler, and M. Schrieber-kittl. 1994. "Befristete Beschaftigung und Arbeitsmarkt: Empirische Untersuchung uber Befristete Arbeitsvertrage nach dem BesuchFG." Forschungsbericht 242 des Bundesmunsteriums fur Arbeit und Sozialordung.

Blanchard, O. 1986. "The Wage–Price Spiral." *Quarterly Journal of Economics* 104: 699–718.

Blanchard, O., and J. Wolfers. 2000. "The Role of Shocks and Institutions in the Rise of European Unemployment: The Aggregate Evidence." *Economic Journal* 110 (March): c1–c33.

Blank, R. M., and R. B. Freeman. 1994. "Evaluating the Connection Between Social Protection and Economic Flexibility." In R. M. Bland, ed., *Social Protection versus Economic Flexibility*. Chicago: University of Chicago Press: 21–41.

Blinder, A. S. 1998. *Central Banking in Theory and Practice*. Cambridge, Mass.: Harvard University Press.

Blinder, A., and R. Solow. 1973. "Does Fiscal Policy Matter?" *Journal of Public Economics* 2: 329–337.

Bruno, M., and J. Sachs. 1985. *Economics of Worldwide Stagflation*. Cambridge, Mass.: Harvard University Press.

Büchtemann, C. F., and A. Höland. 1989. *Befristete Arbeitsverträge nach dem Beschäftigungsförderungsgesetz 1985, Forschungsberichte Band 183.* Bonn: Bundesminister für Arbeit und Sozialordnung.

Bureau of Labor Statistics. 1997. *Comparative Civilian Labor Force Statistics, Ten Countries.* Washington, D.C.: BLS.

Buttler, F., W. Franz, R. Schettkat, and D. Soskice. 1996. *Institutional Frameworks and Labor Market Performance.* London: Routledge.

Calmfors, L., and J. Driffill. 1988. "Bargaining Structure, Corporatism and Macroeconomic Performance." *Economic Policy* 6: 14–61.

Carlin, W., and D. Soskice. 1990. *Macroeconomics and the Wage Bargain: A Modern Approach to Employment, Inflation and the Exchange Rate.* New York: Oxford University Press.

Central Planning Bureau (CPB). 1995. *Replacement Rates.* The Hague: Central Planning Bureau.

Chadwick, L., J. Volkert, and D. Woods. 2000. "Welfare-to-Work Financial Incentives: How Strong Do They Have to Be to Encourage Work Effort? U.S.-American Models for a German Context." Paper prepared for GAAC Summer Institute, July 10–21, Berlin, Wissenschaftszentrum.

*Economist.* 2000. "Child Poverty," June 17, p. 132.

Freeman, R. 2000. "Single-Peaked vs. Diversified Capitalism: The Relation between Economic Institutions and Outcomes." NBER Working Paper No. 7556, National Bureau of Economic Research, Cambridge, Mass.

Freeman, R. B. 1988. "Evaluating the European View That the United States Has No Unemployment Problem." *American Economic Review* 78 (May): 294–299.

Freeman, R. B., and R. Schettkat. 1998. "From McDonald's to McKinsey: Comparing German and U.S. Employment and Wage Structures." Leverhulme II conference, "Labor Market: Stocks and Flows," September 28–29, 1998, Institute of Economics and Statistics, Oxford.

———. 2000. "Skill Compression, Wage Differentials and Employment: Germany vs. the U.S." National Bureau of Economic Research Working Paper 7610. Forthcoming in *Oxford Economic Papers.*

Fuchs, S., and R. Schettkat. 2000. "Germany: A Regulated Flexibility." In *Why Deregulate Labor Markets?* edited by G. Esping-Andersen and M. Regini. Oxford: Oxford University Press. Pp. 211–244.

Gregg, P., and A. Manning. 1997. "Labor Market Regulation and Unemployment." In *Unemployment Policy: Government Options for the Labor Market,* edited by D. J. Snower and G. de la Dehesa. Cambridge: Cambridge University Press.

Hartog, J. 2000. "The Dutch Way." Paper presented at the international conference "Ways and Means of Increasing Employment," September 5, EXPO, Hannover.

Hassink, W. 1999. "De rol van de leeftijd bij de ontslagbeslissing." *Economisch Statistische Berichten* 84 (December): 947–949.

Hunt, J. 1995. "The Effects of Unemployment Compensation on Unemployment Duration in Germany." *Journal of Labor Economics* 13: 88–120.

International Monetary Fund (IMF). 1999. "Chronic Unemployment in the Euro Area: Causes and Cures." Chapter 4 in *World Economic Outlook* (May): Washington, D.C.: IMF.

Krueger, A. 2000. "From Bismarck to Maastricht." *Labor Economics* 7: 1–26.

Layard, R., and S. Nickell. 1985. "The Causes of British Unemployment." *National Institute Economic Review* 111: 62–85.

Layard, R. S. Nickell, and R. Jackman. 1991. *Unemployment: Macroeconomic Performance and the Labour Market*. Oxford: Oxford University Press.

Martin, J. P. 1996. "Measures of Replacement Rates for the Purpose on International Comparisons: A Note." *OECD Economic Studies* 26: 100–115.

Nickell, S. 1998. "Unemployment: Questions and Some Answers." *Economic Journal* 108: 802–826.

Nickell, S. J., and B. Bell. 1996. "Changes in the Distribution of Wages and Unemployment in the OECD countries." *American Economic Review* (Papers and Proceedings) 86(5): 302–308.

Olson, M. 1982. *The Rise and Decline of Nations: Economic Growth, Stagnation and Social Rigidities*. New Haven: Yale University Press.

Organization for Economic Cooperation and Development (OECD). 1995. *Taxation, Employment and Unemployment: The OECD Jobs Study*. Paris: OECD.

———. 1997. *Literacy Skills for the Knowledge Society, International Adult Literacy Survey*. Paris: OECD.

———. 1998. *Employment Outlook*. Paris: OECD.

———. 1999. *Benefit Systems and Work Incentives*. Paris: OECD.

———. 1999. *Implementing the OECD Jobs Strategy: Assessing Performance and Policy*. Paris: OECD.

Reinberger, G. 2000. "Flexible Production Is Planned at Chrysler." *Financial Times*, November 24, p. 19.

Rowthorn, R. 1992. "Centralisation, Employment and Wage Dispersion." *Economic Journal* 102: 506–523.

Salverda, W. 1998. "Incidence and Evolution of Low-Wage Employment in the Netherlands and the U.S., 1979–1989." In *Low Wage Employment in Europe*, edited by S. Bazen, M. Gregory, and W. Salverda. Cheltenham: Edward Elgar. pp. 25–62.

Schettkat, R. 1989. "The Impact of Taxes on Female Labour Supply." *International Review of Applied Economics* 3(1): 1–24.

———. 1996. "Labor Market Flows over the Business Cycle: An Asymmetric Hiring Cost Explanation." *Journal of Theoretical and Institutional Economics* 152(4): 641–653.

———. 1999. "Small Economy Macroeconomics: The Economic Success of Ireland, Denmark, Austria, and the Netherlands Compared." *Intereconomics* 34(4): 159–169.

Schettkat, R., and J. Reijnders. 2000. *The Disease That Became a Model*. Washington, D.C.: Economic Policy Institute.

Schettkat, R., and L. Yocarini. 2000. "Institutional Arrangements in Germany and the Netherlands." Working Paper, Faculty of Social Sciences, Department of Economics, Utrecht University.

SER. 1997. "Ruud Lubbers en de hete adem van een nooit voorgelezen regeringsverklaring." SER Bulletin, 37e jaargang: 4–5.

Siebert, H. 1997. "Labor Market Rigidities: At the Root of Unemployment in Europe." *Journal of Economic Perspectives* 11(3): 37–54.

Solow, R. 2000. "The European Unemployment Problem." *CESIFO Forum* (Spring): 3–5.

Soskice, D. 1990. "Wage Determination: The Changing Role of Institutions in Advanced Industrialized Countries." *Oxford Review of Economic Policy* 6(4): 36–61.

Steiner, V. 1997. "Extended Benefit-Entitlement Periods and the Duration of Un-
    employment in West Germany." Discussion Paper #14, Center for European
    Research.
Stiglitz, J. 2000. "Democratic Development as the Fruits of Labor." Keynote
    address, Industrial Relations Research Association, Boston (January).
Visser, J., and A. Hemerijk. 1997. *A Dutch Miracle*. Amsterdam: Amsterdam
    University Press.
Zimmerman, K. F. 1993. "Labour Responses to Taxes and Benefits in Germany."
    In A. B. Atkinson and G. V. Morgensen, eds., *Welfare and Work Incentives*.
    Oxford: Clarendon Press.

# 9

## Labor Market Policy, Flexibility, and Employment Performance: Denmark and Sweden in the 1990s

PETER PLOUGMANN
PER KONGSHØJ MADSEN

### 9.1 INTRODUCTION

The comparative employment performance of Denmark and Sweden in the 1990s has been widely viewed as telling a tale of contrast between success and failure within the Scandinavian welfare state model. Denmark's success at "curbing structural unemployment and improving overall labor market conditions" has been attributed by the Organization for Economic Cooperation and Development (OECD) to the fact that it is "amongst the most determined in implementing the Jobs Strategy" (OECD 1999: 54). Similarly, the International Monetary Fund (IMF) celebrates Denmark's procompetitive "reform efforts in the early 1990's" (IMF 1999: 113). On the other hand, Sweden has exemplified the collapse of the Scandinavian welfare state model, particularly for proponents of procompetitive, neoliberal economic policy.[1] In a prominent survey of the state of the Swedish model in the mid-1990s, Assar Lindbeck (1997: 1315), concluded by asking whether, with 65% of the electorate receiving nearly all their income from the public sector (as employees or through redistribution), Sweden had hit "a point of no return."

A closer look, however, reveals a more complex picture. Sweden has actually done better than its popular reputation suggests, and the employment performance of Denmark might be viewed as overrated, particularly if employment growth, rather than unemployment, is the main criterion. But the most telling fact is that both have dramatically improved their employment performance while maintaining a strong commitment to a universalistic welfare state with high levels of social protection. Indeed, according to the OECD, in the second quarter of 2002, Denmark's unemployment rate was just 4.2% and Sweden's 5%, well under the U.S. rate of 5.9%.[2]

In fact, these two countries are quite similar in many respects that may help explain their impressive recent employment performance. The macroeconomic environment in Denmark and Sweden has been characterized by low inflation, low interest rates, moderate wage growth, and consolidated government budgets. The improvements in labor market conditions in the late 1990s have taken place without significant increases in wage and income differentials and without major changes in the benefits systems (unemployment benefits and social security). Both countries are in the process of turning themselves into knowledge-intensive economies. In both countries there has been much public and private attention paid to the education and training of the labor force with an emphasis on lifelong learning and focus on broad competencies developed by all employed and job seekers alike. And, closely related, both countries are well known for their strong commitment to active labor market policy (ALMP).

In this chapter, we argue that a strong and flexible ALMP helps explain the ability of both countries to combine low unemployment and positive real wage increases with a low rate of inflation and a relatively high unemployment compensation rate. We begin by describing the development of the labor market in the two countries and discuss the application of the recommendations of the OECD *Jobs Study* (1994) to Denmark and Sweden. We then turn to our main task, a discussion of the significant national features of ALMP. The dynamics behind the positive employment developments recently observed in both countries are briefly discussed. Finally, we look ahead and pinpoint some future problems in the Swedish and Danish national labor markets.

## 9.2 MAIN CHARACTERISTICS OF THE LABOR MARKETS IN THE TWO COUNTRIES

Both Denmark and Sweden experienced high levels of unemployment in the beginning of the 1990s. However, since 1993–1994, Denmark has experienced a remarkable recovery. The same has been the case for Sweden since 1997. For both countries, the outcome in recent years has been high levels of labor force participation rates and a low level of official unemployment.

### 9.2.1 Unemployment and Employment Rates

As shown in figure 9.1, unemployment in Denmark and Sweden is considerably lower than the average in the EU 15. Unemployment in Denmark has been more than halved in just five years and is currently among the lowest in Europe, coming close to the level of the United States.[3]

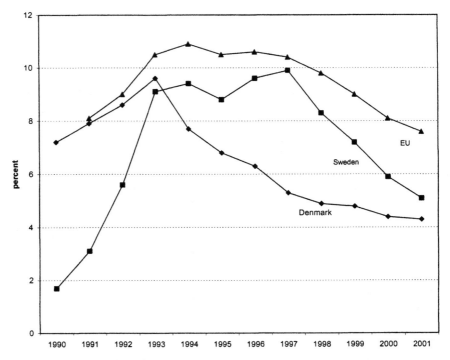

Figure 9.1. Standardized unemployment rates in Denmark, Sweden, and the European Union, 1990–2001. Source: OECD, *Employment Outlook* (2001, 2002) Statistical Annex, table A.

Especially impressive by international standards are the reduction in youth unemployment and the reduction in the long-term unemployment. Unemployment trends in Sweden have been more turbulent, moving from 2.5%–3% before 1991 to a peak of approximately 10% in 1997 and then decreasing to 4.9% in 2001. As figure 9.2 shows, concurrent with the decline in general unemployment, both countries have succeeded in reducing the level of long-term unemployment. Denmark succeeded earlier than Sweden, which had to go through a rough period of readjustments before being able to combat long-term unemployment effectively.

The employment rates of both Denmark and Sweden are currently among the highest in the EU (table 9.2). In Denmark, the labor force participation rate and the employment rate are among the highest in the world, indicating a strong utilization of the existing and the potential labor force, particularly among women.

Sweden did indeed lose some of its economic strength in the early 1990s, mainly because of both macroeconomic shocks and structural weaknesses in the Swedish economy.[4] In the years following 1991, Sweden

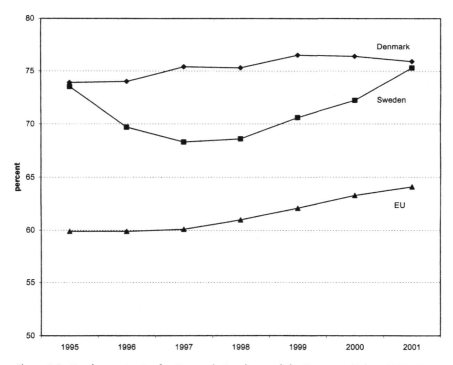

Figure 9.2. Employment rates for Denmark, Sweden, and the European Union, 1995–2001.
Source: OECD, *Employment Outlook* (2000, 2001, 2002), Statistical Annex, table A.

lost more than 600,000 jobs. Labor force participation has traditionally been high in Sweden, but it no longer stands out internationally in this respect. A reduction in hours worked and increased absenteeism have reduced the effective utilization of labor by 17% over the past three decades. The employment growth rates fluctuated greatly in both countries in the 1990s, especially in Sweden. However, since 1997, Sweden has experienced strong growth rates in employment, allowing it to surpass Denmark and the EU 15 in 1999. Job growth in Sweden tended to stay strong in 2000 and 2001, despite the downturn in 2001 in the high-technology sectors, which resulted in numerous job cuts.

Job growth in Denmark has been lower than the OECD average. Even if the reduction in unemployment in Denmark has been impressive, it does not reflect an equally impressive growth in employment. The increase in new jobs has been lower than what is apparent in other OECD countries.[5] On average, between 1997 and 2002 there has been a net job increase of 1.4% in Denmark. The average for 21 OECD countries has been 1.5% in the same period. Countries such as the Netherlands (2.7%), Ireland (5.5%), and Spain (2.8%) have achieved much larger increases.

Since the mid-1990s, Sweden has had a more impressive job growth record than Denmark. According to the labor market authorities, in Sweden the development of the labor market is exceptionally positive, and jobs are being created more quickly than since the end of the Second World War. During 1998 and 1999, employment increased by a total of 146,000 jobs, and for 2000 and 2001 the labor market authorities predict an increase of 86,000 and 77,000, respectively, which means a total increase of 309,000 jobs over four years. This means that almost 60% of the jobs lost at the beginning of the 1990s have been regained. Employment has increased particularly strongly in the private service sector in recent years, accounting for about 70% of the total increase in jobs in the country.

The low level of unemployment and the high level of employment in both countries imply that any additional growth in employment will have to be based on a net increase in the number of people entering the labor force. Because of the demographic constraints of a negative reproduction rate and a general graying population, immigrants must supply an increasing share of employment, which is highly controversial in both countries.

## 9.3 MACROECONOMIC DEVELOPMENTS

As has been shown, both Denmark and Sweden have made impressive recoveries in recent years. Unemployment has declined to half its former level in recent years, and employment rates for both men and women are among the highest in Europe. Most astonishing is the sharp drop in unemployment and the rise in employment that has taken place without increasing wage inflation, which could be expected based on historical experience. Figures 9.3 and 9.4 show the relationships between unemployment and wage inflation (the traditional Phillips curve) in recent years for Denmark and Sweden.[6,7]

When the record for Denmark is examined (figure 9.3), the pattern of wage inflation and unemployment in the years from 1961 to 2001 can be divided into four distinct subperiods. During phase 1, from 1961 to 1970, unemployment was low, and wage inflation tended to increase slowly from the first to the second half of the decade while remaining below 15%. During phase 2, from 1972 to 1975, wage increases reached about 20% per year, while the unemployment rate at the same time increased from 2% to 6%. An important institutional factor behind this development was the automatic indexation of wages to price inflation, which was then part of Danish wage agreements. The outburst of inflation in relation to the first oil crisis automatically spilled over into rising nominal wages. This form of regulation was restricted somewhat in 1975 and finally suspended in 1983.

The third phase can be identified from 1975 to 1994. What may be interpreted as a new, rather stable Phillips curve appears; wage increases during the upswing from 1984 to 1988 tended to reach levels seen at the

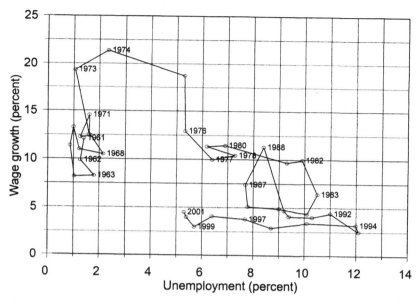

Figure 9.3.  Denmark: Unemployment and nominal wage growth, 1961–2001.
Source: OECD, *Economic Outlook* (various issues).

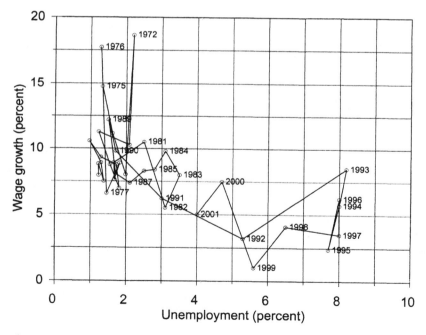

Figure 9.4.  Sweden: Unemployment and nominal wage growth, 1961–2001.
Source: OECD, *Economic Outlook* (various issues).

same level of unemployment around 1980. Finally, the fourth phase is represented by the observations for the period from 1993 to 2001. During this period, open unemployment in Denmark was cut in half. This was mainly a result of a sharp increase in effective demand, while the level of wage inflation remained below 5%.

Several explanations have been offered for this exceptional recent development. One focuses on a changed climate in wage negotiation, with organizations on both sides becoming increasingly aware of the potential damages for employment caused by high nominal wages in a situation where the Danish currency has been firmly linked first to the German mark and then to the euro. A second explanation points to the contribution of the Danish labor market reform of 1994 in reducing imbalances in the labor market during the upswing.[8] Finally, a third approach has been to focus on the artificial reduction in registered unemployment caused by the rising number of persons in labor market programs and leave schemes. However, even though there was an increase in the use of such programs in 1994–1995, the fall in unemployment since then cannot be attributed to so-called bookkeeping effects. If one calculates the "gross rate of unemployment," including persons in all sorts of active labor market programs and labor market–related benefit schemes, this rate was at a level of 20% to 21% during 1994 but then started to decline and reached 14.9% in 2000.[9] Among transfer recipients, the reduction in the number of those involuntary unemployed has been particularly pronounced, with the number dropping from 360,000 in 1994 to less than 150,000 in early 2000. Over the same period, an additional 40,000 people accepted voluntary schemes such as early retirement or leave. Long-term unemployment has dropped a great deal, from 160,000 persons to less than 40,000 over that same period. The number of long-term unemployed in activation schemes on top of that has been almost unvarying, at 70,000 to 80,000 persons.[10]

Sweden also shows a configuration of unemployment and wage inflation that during some subperiods may be interpreted along the lines of a traditional Phillips curve (figure 9.4). Most of the observations from the first 30 years are located in a cluster, in which unemployment lies in the interval from 1% to 3% and wages increase by between 7% and 11% per year. The main exceptions are again found in the early 1970s, when the inflationary push of the first oil crisis made Swedish wages increase by up to 19% per year. Apart from that, it is tempting to interpret these three decades as the golden years of the Swedish model, where low unemployment and moderate wage inflation went hand in hand. After this long first phase, a second period can be identified covering the 1990s. Here unemployment rapidly increased to 8%. At the same time, wage growth declined to a level of 3% to 6% per year. It is especially notable that the recent Swedish recovery, which has lowered unemployment to around 4%–5%, has not yet been accompanied by a new rise in wage inflation. For Sweden—and also for Denmark, as noted—this presents a remarkable change in the pattern of nominal wage formation.

## 9.4 LABOR MARKET POLICY AND EMPLOYMENT PERFORMANCE

### 9.4.1 The Scandinavian Model

Both Denmark and Sweden represent welfare state models that differ significantly from the models of the United States, the United Kingdom, and other continental European countries. Most important, they have remained committed to maintaining universal social coverage in case of unemployment, based on an assumption of the individual rights and needs of the labor force.

Gallie and Paugam (2000) have developed an interesting taxonomy of different welfare state models, using three criteria for "unemployment welfare regimes": (1) the share of the unemployed entitled to receive unemployment insurance benefits, (2) the level and duration of the benefits, and (3) the scope of ALMP. On the basis of these indicators, it is possible to identify four different welfare state regimes, which are shown in table 9.5.

Denmark and Sweden are both classified as universalistic welfare state regimes. It is important to have this taxonomy in mind when the recommendations of the OECD are discussed. Being committed to a strong, comprehensive welfare state, during the 1990s policy makers in Denmark and Sweden made no serious attempt to follow the OECD recommendations for reducing the replacement rate or for changing the eligibility criteria for unemployment benefits.

However, some changes in policy have taken place in both countries. When describing the policy changes in the 1990s, Casey and Gold (2000) point out that the Netherlands, Sweden, and Ireland all performed better in the recent period and add:

Each of these countries displays neo-corporatist traits. However, each of them has been moving toward supply-side corporatism, which places a

Table 9.1. Four Different Welfare State Regimes as Defined by the Situation of the Unemployed

| Regime | Unemployment Benefit Eligibility | Benefit Generosity | ALMP | Examples |
|---|---|---|---|---|
| Subprotective | Very incomplete | Extremely limited | Generally not existing | Greece, Italy, Portugal, Spain |
| Liberal (minimum protection) | Limited | Limited | Weakly developed | United Kingdom, Ireland |
| Employment-centered | Variable (depends heavily on the employability of the person in question) | Unequal | Extensive | France, Germany, Netherlands |
| Universalistic | Comprehensive coverage | High, generous | Very extensive | Denmark, Sweden |

Source: Adapted from Gallie and Pauham (2000), table 1.9 and pp. 9–11.

considerable premium upon decentralisation, ordered deregulation and a respect for the role of the market. The first two countries have also taken substantial steps to modify and adapt their systems of social protection. (99)

One may see changes in the form of industrial relations governance in Sweden as a decline of corporatism, leading to greater decentralization. This has not happened in Denmark in the 1990s, at least not as significantly as in Sweden, although some critics claim that the trend toward a new regime is evident. In order to investigate this claim, the labor market policy of both countries is examined more closely.

### 9.4.2 Benefits and Unemployment

The unemployment benefit system is in the core of all discussion of ALMP. The Danish and the Swedish unemployment insurance benefit systems have often been criticized for being too generous, thereby creating rigidities in the labor market by failing to create effective incentives for increasing the job search behavior of the unemployed or for increasing geographic mobility and thus damaging the process of job creation.

The Danish Economic Council (DØR) might serve as an example of this kind of orthodoxy when it argues that "at present a large proportion of the unemployed would gain only very little extra income from getting a job. More than 40% of persons with a long history of unemployment have an unemployment compensation rate that exceeds 90%. Thus their economic incentive to find a job is virtually zero."[11] The DØR has often, with references to OECD studies, suggested a reduction in unemployment benefits. Analysis by DØR suggests that a reduction in unemployment by 25,000 persons could be obtained by reducing unemployment benefits by 8%.[12] In the past two decades, there have been some adjustments in the unemployment benefits replacement rate in Denmark. For the eligible unemployed, the maximum duration of benefits and participation in activation programs has been reduced from approximately nine years to five years (from 1999). However, the level of replacement is, as in Sweden, still relatively high by international standards (see table 1.2). Yet, as we argue, the labor markets of Denmark and Sweden show a high level of flexibility.

### 9.4.3 The Flexibility of the Labor Market

Labor market flexibility is essential to the long-term success of national economies. However, it is necessary to understand the concept of flexibility properly (see also chapter 4). All too often, the demand for flexibility takes only the short-term interests of the employers in flexible labor costs into account, leaving out the long-term collective interest in achieving a high level of both numerical and functional flexibility. We have already mentioned that long-term unemployment has decreased significantly in both countries. If we turn to the other indicators, data from Denmark clearly give the impression of a very flexible labor market, while the picture for Sweden is more mixed.

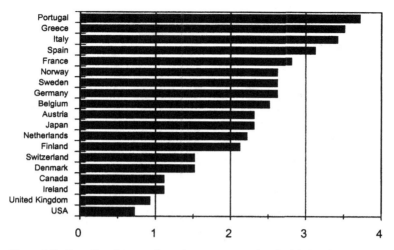

Figure 9.5. Overall strictness of employment protection legislation (EPL) in the late 1990s (average indicator for regular contracts, temporary contracts, and collective dismissals). Source: OECD (1999), table 2.5.

As is evident from figure 9.5, Denmark shows a low level of employment protection compared to most other industrialized countries—and much lower than those of the other Nordic countries, including Sweden. It must be noted that both Denmark and Sweden have made adjustments in the employment protection law during the past decade.

The low level of employment protection in Denmark is associated with a high level of numerical flexibility, measured by labor turnover of more than 20% per year. International statistics on labor turnover are not available, but recent studies from the OECD and the International Labor Organization (ILO) show that average job tenure in Denmark is among the lowest in Europe and is on the same level as that found in the United Kingdom, as shown in figure 9.6. Again, Sweden is located at the other end of the scale, with a level of job tenure similar to those for Japan and Greece. More detailed studies show that the high level of labor mobility in Denmark seems to be a phenomenon that is widespread across sectors, including the public sector (Bingley et al. 1999).

A high level of mobility of employees among workplaces and industries is an indicator of a flexible labor market. High mobility can reduce the capacity problems of industrial production by reducing mismatch problems. High mobility also may reduce the level of structural unemployment if increased job openings give unemployed persons greater opportunities to find new jobs. On the other hand, it must be recognized that increased mobility can also take the form of forced, nonvoluntary job change. However, the majority of all job turnovers have in recent years

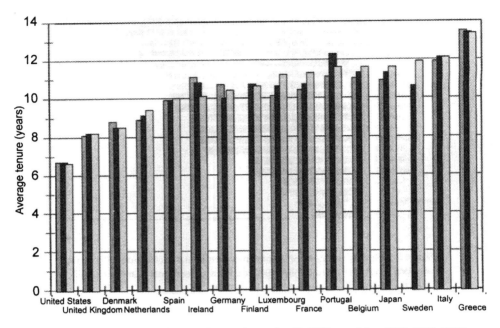

Figure 9.6. Average tenure in years for employees for 16 OECD countries, 1992, 1995, 1998.
Source: Auer and Casez (2000).

been voluntary, reflecting the wishes of the employees to pursue new opportunities in an expanding labor market.[13]

In the period from 1980 to 1998, geographic mobility gradually increased in Denmark. People looking for work tended to commute greater distances in 1998 than in 1980 (an increase of 50%). One effect of this is a potential better match between vacancies and the competencies of job seekers. This changing behavior also has an impact on reducing structural unemployment. Statistics show that unemployed persons who find new employment are generally more mobile than persons coming from another job. Those unemployed with a degree of 0.5 or more of annual unemployment[14] have increased their commuting distance relatively more than other groups of unemployed and already employed persons.[15]

This kind of indicator seems to show that the generosity of the Danish unemployment benefit system is not creating rigidities in the labor market. The criticism of the benefit systems lacks substantial empirical support. On the contrary, the data show that the effect of the unemployment benefit system is a much more positive one: it actually helps facilitate a high level of labor market flexibility by facilitating the matching of workers with jobs.

Another interesting aspect of labor market flexibility is perceived job security among employees. Empirical evidence from the European Foundation for the Improvement of Living and Working Conditions reported remarkably low job insecurity among Danish workers, despite relatively weak employment protection regulations.[16] Less than 1 in 10 employees in Denmark (9%) is afraid of losing his or her current job. That is the lowest level in the EU, where one out of three workers expresses this fear. Employees in countries such as Germany and Italy are far less secure than Danish workers. But, like those in Denmark, employees who live and work in Scandinavia generally express a high level of employment confidence. Sweden is ranked seventh among EU countries, with 20% of the employees feeling insecure. Norway and Finland fall between Denmark and Sweden in the ranking.

There is a close relationship between a high level of concern and a high level of present unemployment, as is the case in, for example, Greece and Spain, where two of three workers express doubts about their future employment opportunities. However, other societal factors seem to play a role when it comes to perceived job security. Austria, for example, with an unemployment level lower than Denmark's, has more employees who are concerned about job security (23%).

The high flexibility of the Danish labor market seems to be the main reason for the high rating by Danish employees. According to the European Foundation (2000), 68% of all Danish employees think it will be easy for them to find another job if they lose their current job. On average in the EU, only 35% of employees believe it to be easy to find a suitable job, whereas 48% expect it to be difficult. Only 25% of the Danes think it might be difficult to find a new job that matches their preferences.

This potential contradiction between a high labor turnover and a perception of easy employability among Danish employees might be explained in two ways that supplement each other. First, the Danish industrial structure, which includes many small firms and almost no large, nationally dominant corporations, creates a very open local labor market with many entry and exit opportunities. In contrast, labor markets dominated by large corporations that create an internal labor market tend to leave relatively few job openings for outsiders. That explanation might be the reason that the European Foundation study finds a sizable difference between Denmark and Sweden on this indicator: Sweden is much more dependent on large corporations than Denmark. The second explanation is the generous unemployment benefit system, which makes high mobility and a perception of relative economic security possible at the same time. In contrast to the OECD-IMF orthodoxy, the Danish model shows how a generous social protection system can promote labor market flexibility and efficiency.

## 9.5 THE "BALANCE" STRATEGY

The political strategy behind this achievement is the combination of an effective macroeconomic policy, a policy of wage moderation, and a labor market reform carried out jointly by the social partners (unions and

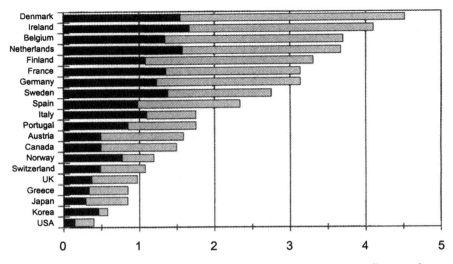

Figure 9.7. Expenditure on active (black) and passive (gray) labor market policy as a share of GDP (2000 or latest year). Source: OECD (2000, 2001), table H.

employers associations) and the government. This balanced strategy is one of the main reasons for the Danish success. An active labor market, along with education and training policy supporting labor market mobility, is an additional factor that explains the Danish labor market revival in the 1990s. Both Denmark and Sweden are high spenders when it comes to labor market policy, as figure 9.7 shows. Indeed, Denmark ranks at the top of the OECD ranking, with the highest passive (income support) spending and nearly the highest active spending as a share of GDP.

Allan Larsson, the former director of EU's DG5 (the directorate responsible for employment) has been a firm advocate of the Danish ALMP. He summarized why politicians should pay attention to what has happened in Denmark:

> Over the past few years, Denmark has implemented many of the elements of what is now being pursued as the European Employment strategy: employability, entrepreneurship, adaptability and equal opportunities. Denmark has done this with impressive results. That is why policymakers in many Member States now look to Denmark as an inspiration for the development of labour market policies in the EU. (Larsson 1999)

One interpretation of the success of the Danish employment system that has become popular in recent years has been that of the "Golden Triangle," which summarizes three important characteristics of the Danish labor market (Madsen 2002):

- A high level of mobility and flexibility combined with a low level of formal job protection

- A generous public unemployment insurance benefit system that absorbs the bulk of the social costs of high flexibility
- A strong ALMP with an emphasis on the rights and obligations of participants

These three elements of the "golden triangle" make it socially acceptable for companies to adjust the use of their staff very flexibly. Dismissed workers rely on the flexible labor market for rapid entry to new jobs and rely equally on the high level of compensation of the unemployment insurance benefit system in case of a short period of unemployment. Persons who find it difficult to obtain employment enter training programs as part of ALMP and in this way gain skills that enable them to exploit the available job opportunities.

This Danish model therefore is a totally different employment system from the one found in southern Europe, for example, but it also differs somewhat from the system in Sweden. As described earlier, job protection measures in Sweden place a great deal of restriction on the companies when it comes to dismissing labor. The price for this institutional setup is obvious—low flexibility in the labor market and a high premium on hiring new staff. Managers of companies tend to think twice before hiring. This also creates an environment in which less competitive labor is easily bypassed, thus increasing the risk of long-term unemployment. The fact that the Swedish labor market recovered so quickly under these institutional conditions makes the recovery that much more impressive.

While some differences between the Danish and the Swedish employment systems may be observed when it comes to regulating the employment relation between the employer and the individual employees, the ability of both countries to recover rapidly from the deep economic crisis of the early 1990s indicates that these differences should not be exaggerated. Thus, their common traits with respect to the overall active profile of labor market policy and strong growth in the demand for labor, combined with a successful restructuring of the economy, must be taken into account. In the following sections we therefore deal with these two subjects in more detail.

## 9.6 ACTIVE LABOR MARKET POLICIES, 1994–2000

### 9.6.1 The Danish ALMP 1994–2000

So how has the Danish ALMP evolved in recent years? ALMPs appear to have facilitated the integration of unemployed people into the labor market quite effectively. The approach focuses on both motivation and qualification. Job seekers are motivated to search for jobs more effectively. An individual action plan must be drawn up for all unemployed persons before they reach 12 months of unemployment. First, the action plan forms the basis for the continued measures and is drawn up in cooperation between the unemployed and the Public Employment Service (the motivation effect). Second, the employability of job seekers is improved through participation in training programs (the qualification effect).

In order to realize this strategy, the Danish labor market policy has undergone rather drastic changes in recent years:

- The share of active expenditures has increased.
- The formation and implementation of policy have been decentralized (the steering reform).
- At the same time, the use of instruments and programs has been changed (the activation reform).
- For the unemployed who are insured, the maximum duration of benefits and of participation in activation programs has been reduced from approximately nine years to five years (from 1999).
- Emphasis is now put on an obligation to full-time activation after only one year of unemployment. For some groups, activation takes place at an even earlier time.

One of the most important reforms has been a *steering reform*, which involves a decentralization of responsibility for policy implementation to regional labor market authorities, which were empowered to design activation programs in line with local needs. One has to bear in mind the smallness of Denmark. Nevertheless, the decentralization process placed the responsibility for implementing ALMP at the county level. The integration of the social partners at the county level is essential to the success of this steering model. The outcome thus relies heavily on the existing social capital in the local area.

Another part of the reform contained an *activation reform* with the following elements:

- The creation of a two-period benefit system for the insured unemployed with strong emphasis on activation during the second period
- A change in the assistance to the long-term unemployed from a rule-based system to a system based on a needs assessment of the individual unemployed and of the local labor market (introducing the so-called individual action plan)
- The removal of the connection between job training and the unemployment benefit system, which meant that participating in job training would no longer extend the right to unemployment benefits if a person became unemployed after the training period

These reforms may be seen as initiatives that comply with some of the key recommendations of the OECD *Jobs Study*, especially the recommendation that points to the need for strengthening the emphasis on active labor market policies and for reinforcing their effectiveness. Furthermore, the 1995 initiative to intensify the supervision of availability (and employability) might appear to comply with the OECD recommendations. However, these policy initiatives were taken in 1993–1994 and have been adopted within the framework of the Danish welfare regime, a regime that aims at universal and generous social coverage. Thus, the social effects of the reforms were not the kind the OECD had in mind.

The programs directed at the younger unemployed (those under 25 years of age) involved the imposition of stronger obligations to undergo education and a reduction in unemployment benefits after six months of unemployment. These changes have proved to be a success in the sense that most of the young unemployed in the target group left unemployment either to take an ordinary job or to begin an education.[17] Both changes contributed to reducing open youth unemployment. In 1999, the rights and obligations of activation were applied to young people after six months of unemployment, thereby increasing the effectiveness of ALMP even further.[18]

The ALMP reform of 1994 also changed the way the programs are financed. From a system where unemployment insurance benefits, vocational training, and similar programs were financed by the state through taxes and via payments from insured members of the unions, ALMP is now generally financed by a direct tax on all employed and self-employed persons (8% of gross income). The employers also contributed by paying a total of 0.6% of the wage sum of all employed in a company—a so-called labor market contribution. These changes in the financing model make all costs of ALMP more visible to both policy makers and the public in general.

Finally, a number of paid-leave schemes were introduced, which were not in line with OECD thinking. In 1994, paid leave schemes encouraging both employed and unemployed people to take a leave of absence were introduced. These schemes served two aims. First, they increased the number of vacancies for the unemployed to fill; second, they provided the employed part of the labor force with a new welfare service. A third aim, which was related only to the job rotation scheme, was to enhance the competence of the employed and at the same time to provide the unemployed with job experiences that they could not obtain otherwise. These paid leave schemes were very successful—actually, too successful—and the incentive structure was changed several times over the following years to reduce the number of people taking advantage of them. In recent years, the paid-leave schemes have been integrated into other pieces of legislation concerning adult education and maternity leave and are no longer in existence as separate programs.

Evaluations of the reform demonstrate that the activation reforms in many respects have been successful, although not without problems. A study by the Danish National Institute of Social Research summarizes the findings of the large-scale evaluation program of the 1994 labor market reforms.[19] The general question raised is whether the labor market reforms and the subsequent adjustments in labor market policy have had a positive impact on the functioning of the labor market. The evaluation findings concerning the importance of the activation strategy may be summarized as follows.[20]

- The employment goals specified in the individual action plans indicate that there is a *considerable planned mobility* among the unemployed.
- The labor market policy seems to function effectively in the sense that the planned mobility among the unemployed is *greater* in areas where the need for mobility is highest (due to threats of bottlenecks).
- There are *significant positive employment effects* of both vocational training and education for the unemployed.
- The *effective supply of labor among the insured unemployed seems to have increased* between 1994 and 1997, probably because of the stricter demands made on the unemployed during the second phase of the reform (for instance, the increased demands on the young unemployed).

With regard to the measures directed at firms, there are indications that the reforms have contributed to the absence of bottlenecks since 1994. There is some indication that the quality of the services provided by employment services to firms has improved since the reform in terms of meeting the need for skilled labor (although there are also examples of short-term labor shortages). In addition, the introduction of new forms of placement services (in the form of open self-service placements), together with monitoring activities and regular contacts with employers, has led to an increase in the transparency of the labor market, thereby improving its functioning as a system for matching labor supply and demand.

Whether these effects of the reforms have led to an improvement in the general functioning of the labor market, measured by its ability to adapt to external shocks and to allocate labor efficiently, is hard to evaluate. The lack of significant shortages of labor since 1994, in spite of the fall in unemployment and the strong growth in employment, could indicate that the functioning of the labor market has improved.

A specific feature of ALMP in both countries is the focus on competence development and training. The Danish system may serve as an illustration. The most important aspects of the Danish education and training system are these:

- The public system for both basic and adult vocational education and training operates under strong influence from the social partners (unions and employers associations).
- The training and education system is targeted at the workforce in general (on the basis of the concept of life-long learning) and not solely at the unemployed.

In Denmark, this system has functioned for more than 40 years. The 1994 labor market reform allows for a more flexible use of adult education and training. Another important part of the reform was the fact that the integration of the unemployed using training and education partly took place through job rotation and paid-leave schemes. However, these schemes have been abandoned or severely reduced in effect in recent years.

The Danish government introduced a new reform of the adult and continuing education system in January 2000, a reform that in many ways marks a change of strategy and incentive structure from a market-driven to a public-policy approach and that leaves more responsibility for education and training to the social partners. The goal of the reform is to give all adults access to lifelong learning opportunities. The government intent is to focus education and training activities on adults with low educational and skill levels. Firms have been given a larger financial responsibility for improving the skills and education of higher-educated employees and are responsible for financing the continued education of their higher-skilled workers (e.g., via company-related vocational training courses).

### 9.6.2 The Swedish ALMP in the 1990s

There are many similarities between the Danish and the Swedish ALMP. Sweden has a long tradition of ALMP, but during the recession of the 1990s, the volume of such programs reached an unprecedented level, encompassing almost 5% of the labor force in 1994.

Swedish labor market programs can, like those in Denmark, be divided into active and passive components. The active component is directed partly toward matching employees and employers (the placement service) and partly to running training and work experience programs and to providing employment subsidies. The passive part consists mainly of providing unemployment benefits for the unemployed. Compared to most European countries, as already mentioned, Sweden spends a large percentage on active labor market programs.

The basic features of Swedish labor market policy emerged in the late 1950s and the 1960s, but the focus of labor market programs has changed over the years. Originally, the main purpose was to promote an efficient allocation of labor, but later, in the 1970s, policy concentrated on keeping down registered unemployment. In the late 1990s, the focus changed to competence development and the securing of a sufficient supply of labor.[21] Different programs have been aimed at influencing the demand for labor; these include employment development, recruitment subsidies, relief work, educational leave replacements, start-up grants, and workplace introductions. Other programs attempt to influence the supply of labor. There are initiatives like employment training, in-house employment training, and employment institutes, which aim to improve the level of skills in the labor force and to facilitate occupational mobility. Employment training has during the years been by far the largest of these programs.

In recent years, the aim of Swedish ALMP has been:

- The promotion of investments in vocational training based on the principle of life-long learning and access to continued training for all

Table 9.2. Development of the Labor Market and Number of Participants in Employment Policy Programs in Sweden, 1996–2001 (per thousand persons)

|  | 1996 | 1997 | 1998 | 1999 | 2000 (est.) | 2001 (est.) |
|---|---|---|---|---|---|---|
| Labor | 4,310 | 4,264 | 4,255 | 4,309 | 4,358 | 4,404 |
| Employed | 3,963 | 3,922 | 3,979 | 4,068 | 4,154 | 4,231 |
| Unemployed | 347 | 342 | 276 | 241 | 204 | 173 |
| % of LF | 8.1 | 8.0 | 6.5 | 5.6 | 4.7 | 3.9 |
| Employment policy programs | 202 | 191 | 173 | 142 | 113 | 115 |
| % of LF | 4.7 | 4.5 | 4.1 | 3.3 | 2.6 | 2.6 |
| Imbalance in % of LF | 12.7 | 12.5 | 10.6 | 8.9 | 7.3 | 6.5 |

- The promotion of flexible working arrangements, wage restraint, and the creation of new job opportunities, for example, in the environmental and social services spheres
- Improvements in the effectiveness of labor market policy
- Employment measures targeted at groups particularly hard hit by unemployment, especially young people, the long-term unemployed, older employees, and unemployed women[22]

During the 1990s, ALMP reached a level of activity no one had ever expected. A total of 630 billion SKR were spent, and 2.9 million people were in contact with the Public Labor Market Authorities in some way or other during the 1990s. Every year, as many as 200,000 persons participated in public employment programs, a substantial share of the Swedish working-age population.[23]

Table 9.2 shows that in 1996, employment programs involved approximately 4.7% of the labor force, while the open unemployment was 8.1%, amounting to an imbalance of 12.7% in 1996. This picture has changed since then. It is estimated that the number of persons in ALMP programs in Sweden totaled 113,000 in 2000 and 115,000 in 2001, representing approximately 2.6% of the labor force. This means that the unemployed and program participants tother accounted for 7.3% of the labor force in 2000, a figure that was expected to decline to 6.5% in 2001. Counted as numbers of people, this represents a reduction from 383,000 persons in 1999 to 288,000 in 2001. In other words, there is still a large number of unemployed, but the situation has definitely changed for the better since 1996.[24]

### 9.6.3 Assessment: The Effectiveness of ALMP

There is an intense debate on the effectiveness of ALMP in general and in Denmark and Sweden in specific. The net effects of ALMP may be difficult to identify because of their interaction with other policies. As discussed in more detail by the OECD,[25] the positive development with respect to the unemployment rate reflects the impressive economic performance of the Swedish economy, which has been characterized by its recovery from thesevere recession of the early 1990s. While the reduction in unemployment can be explained by the growth in demand and by the increased rate of increase in GDP, the dispute concerns whether the continuing low level of inflation, which has also characterized this period, can be attributed to strong ALMP. In our view, the main contribution of ALMP has been to allow for a rapid reduction in unemployment without an increase in strong inflationary pressures.[26]

While ALMP is, therefore, an important candidate when it comes to explaining the low rates of inflation in the Danish and the Swedish economies in recent years, one should be aware of other factors that also may have played an important role. One such factor is an increase in the number of hours worked by employees.[27] The increased availability of working hours might, at least for some time, compensate for the high level of employment and help limit wage inflation. Another factor is the changing patterns of wage formation, in which still more decentralized models of wage negotiations have become widespread. Together with the falling level of international inflation and the increasing integration of both the Danish and the Swedish economies into the stable exchange rate system of the European Union, this has probably created a new "regime" of wage formation in which both trade unions and employers' organizations are becoming increasingly aware of the risks associated with strong nominal wage increases. However, an important precondition for the survival of such a regime is, of course, that it not be hindered by severe shortages of labor. Here ALMP has played an important role.

In sum, there seems to be a strong case in favor of maintaining ALMP in order to ensure strong economic development and a high employment level in the future. We now turn to a short discussion of what challenges ALMP might face.

## 9.7 THE "JOB CREATION MACHINE" IN DENMARK AND SWEDEN

As stressed in the previous section, ALMP can deliver respectable results only if the economy in general is doing well. So what are the dynamics behind the positive employment development in both countries? In short, the dynamics can be identified as a robust "job creation machine" that has taken advantage of the possibilities of the so-called New Economy.

Both Denmark and Sweden have traditionally relied on manufactured exports for most of their growth. Sweden has historically been dominated by large corporations operating in the global market to a greater extent than has Denmark. In the 1990s, both countries deregulated industries such as telecommunications, airlines, and banking, as recommended by the OECD. The results have been strong growth in the ICT sector, involving many megamergers, heavy layoffs, and major restructuring of whole industries, while adapting to the demands of the global competition.

Both governments have focused on fostering a more entrepreneurial culture in order to help new companies and high technology flourish. This policy has been particularly successful in Sweden, where much of the growth is currently coming from businesses that did not exist 10 years ago. This policy has also been pursued in Denmark, but with less success than in Sweden.

In Sweden, information technology and service companies are now the main source of new jobs, not the traditional manufacturers. Sweden has invested a larger part of its gross domestic product in "knowledge"— research, development, training, and education—than has any other country in the world in recent years.[28]

Denmark has been a bit slower to catch up with the possibilities presented by the global market and new technologies. However, the growth of the mobile telecommunication industries, as well as new biotech businesses, has taken root in the greater metropolitan area of Copenhagen. The different traditional industrial sectors of the national economies have been quick to adapt to the new circumstances and opportunities created by the "new economy."[29] An indicator of this is the widespread access to the Internet among companies of all sizes: in 2000, close to 9 out of 10 enterprises had access to the Internet, and even among small firms close to 80% had access in Sweden and Denmark. Available indicators of ICT usages show a business environment in both Sweden and Denmark that has utilized many of the possibilities of the New Economy.

Another important indicator is the long-term development of productivity. According to ILO figures (ILO 1999), labor productivity grew by 39 points in Sweden and in Denmark by 34 points in the years 1980–1997, placing Sweden and Denmark among a group of high-growth countries and surpassing countries like France and Germany during this period.

Many of the companies in the old traditional industries have incorporated the best from the New Economy companies in terms of flexibility, innovations, and a new work culture.[30] This has generated new international market opportunities and allowed for the utilization of new technologies. This also puts pressure on human resource management that spills over into ALMP. The cornerstone of this development is the focus on competence development and the realization of new forms of work organization. The managements of an increasing number of firms and organizations have acknowledged the effectiveness of mobilizing the tacit knowledge of the employees. Changes in management forms toward high-skill and high-trust organizational and management models are becoming still more widespread in order to generate efficiency in all parts of the production process.[31,32] This development has been endorsed by the trade unions, which view these changes as a road to better, higher-paying, and higher-skill jobs.

## 9.8 THE FUTURE OF THE DANISH AND SWEDISH
## LABOR MARKET MODELS

Finally, we consider the future of the Danish and Swedish labor market models. The dangers are already becoming obvious. In the case of a continuous high-growth scenario, the demand for qualified labor will increase faster than the supply. According to the National Action Plan (NAP) for Denmark and Sweden, the economies face challenges in the short term as well as in the long sterm:

> In the short-term perspective, it is important to continue a balanced development; this means, among other things, avoiding the development of bottlenecks and a too high growth in prices and wages. The strong reduction in unemployment since 1994 has led to a certain tightening of labour market. . . .
> In a more long-term perspective, it is of decisive importance to increase the labour force and to continue the reduction in public debts.[33]

The bottlenecks in the labor market are already a problem in Sweden. In 2000, unemployment was down to 4.7%, and the employment rate among 20- to 64-year-olds was back to the level achieved before 1993 (78%). The Stockholm area has experienced shortages of computer specialists, sales representatives, and teachers, even caterers. The public employment service's most recent analysis shows shortages in several dozen job categories and acute shortages in many others, including car mechanics, taxi drivers, and nurses. Labor force reserves are also becoming scarce, especially in Denmark,[34] and the demographics of both countries, which are creating an increasingly "gray" labor market, are threatening to become a major obstacle for the continuation of the "job machine."

The main risk is, of course, increasing wage inflation. Even if the Phillips curve shown earlier was more or less flat in the 1990s, increasing wages in some segments of the labor market are now a fact. The continuous high demand for labor over the past several years has been reflected in wage increases in Denmark, with hourly earnings in private industry rising by an average of 3.75% in 2000 and by 4.25% in the following year. Compared to the development of hourly wages in the euro area, Danish industry has lost some of its advantage in terms of wage competitiveness since 1997.[35]

At the same time, the group of marginalized persons in the labor market is still a major social and labor market problem. The handicapped, older workers with inadequate formal skills, and immigrants are facing employment problems. Immigrants have huge difficulties getting jobs. In particular, immigrants coming to Denmark without adequate education find it difficult to get jobs. Few manage to obtain an education after arriving, and many have difficulties learning the language and the culture. The high level of unemployment among immigrants is not only a result of immigrants' low level of formal education. Discrimination is also likely to be a factor.[36] This is a problem that needs to be addressed as part of a future ALMP in order to increase the supply of labor in the years to come.[37]

The major challenge facing ALMP in both Sweden and Denmark is the need to modernize the programs and incentives once more. The future focus of ALMP should be not only on combating long-term unemployment but on increasing the size of the labor force and on enhancing the qualifications of the labor force. This includes:

- Getting the nonactive part of the population mobilized and motivated to enter the labor force
- Integrating immigrants into all parts of the labor market by fighting discrimination
- Establishing a structure in the labor market that will increase the possibilities for older workers to find flexible, part-time employment
- Reducing absenteeism and improving the quality of the working life
- Reforming the unemployment insurance benefit system in order to accommodate a labor market with more job changing and more self-employed[38]

Should there be a new economic recession, both countries are in danger of encountering heavy mismatch problems in the labor market, that is, increasing long-term unemployment among low-skilled labor coexisting with increasing demand for specialized qualified labor. This will be a real challenge for future ALMP in the welfare regimes of Denmark and Sweden.

## 9.9 CONCLUSION

This chapter's assessment of the recent employment performance in Denmark and in Sweden has highlighted the use of active labor market policies to help reduce unemployment and to prepare the workforce for the "new economy" of the future, while remaining committed to social consensus and relatively high social-protection spending and regulation. There is no doubt that flexibility in the labor market, numerical as well as functional, is essential to the future of the employment in countries like Sweden and Denmark, and ALMP plays a crucial role in achieving it.

During the 1990s, both countries managed to make the transition from high unemployment to their current, much stronger employment performances, but they also face increasing mismatch problems in the labor market. Both countries have also integrated elements of the recommendations of the OECD *Jobs Study*, but they have done so without abandoning the universalistic welfare state. In this way, Sweden and Denmark point to the limits of the "one size fits all" recipe of labor market deregulation prescribed by orthodox economic theory. The recent success of the Scandinavian model clearly demonstrates that it is not necessary to embrace the U.S. model for good employment performance.

## Notes

1. See Assar Lindbeck, "The Swedish Experiment," *Journal of Economic Literature* 35 (September 1997): 1273–1319.
2. See figure 1.3 in the Introduction to this volume.
3. Benchmark report, *International Employment Ranking 2000*.
4. See Lindbeck, "The Swedish Experiment," p. 1312.
5. Bertelsmann Foundation, *International Employment Ranking 2000*.
6. This trend in the 1990s of the Phillips curve can also be found at the EU level. See European Commission (2001).
7. The figures are based on OECD data. A more detailed analysis of institutions and wage formation in Denmark and Sweden can be found in Boje and Kongshøj Madsen (2002).
8. P. Kongshøj Madsen (1999).
9. For a more detailed discussion, see P. K. Madsen (1999), chapter 3.
10. Danish Ministry of Finance (2000).
11. Danish Economic Council, "Danish Economy" (Autumn 1997).
12. Ibid.
13. Nina Smith, "Det effective, rummelige og trygge danske arbejdsmarked?," i *Arbejdsmarkedspolitisk Årbog* 1997: 102–119, referring to analysis by Danish Economic Council, "Danish Economy" (Autumn 1997).
14. Persons unemployed for six months or more.
15. Dansk Teknologisk Institut, Erhvervsanalyser,'Mobilitetsundersøgelse i AF region Ringkøbing amt og Storstrøm, Tåstrup, juni 1996.
16. Dublin Institute (2000).
17. Mogens Nord-Larsen, *Ungeindsatsen—1½ år efter*, Servicerapport, Socialforskningsinstituttet, 1998.
18. From 2003, this change in incentives will be further broadened to apply to the unemployed up to the age of 30. Also, from 2003, a number of other adjustments will take place with respect to Danish labor market policy.
19. Larsen and Langager (1998).
20. Ibid., pp. 34–36.
21. See Nordisk Ministerråd, "Arbejdsudbudet I Norden," Nord (2000), København, p. 20.
22. See, for example, European Parliament, Directorate General for Research, "Social and Labour Market Policy in Sweden," Working Document Social Affairs Series, 1997.
23. Ackum Agell et al. (2000).
24. For a detailed account of the Swedish ALMP, see "Arbetsmarknadspolitiska program—årsrapport 2001 Prora" (2002): 3.
25. OECD (2001a, 2002).
26. See Forslund Anders and Ann-Sofie Kolm, "Active Labour Market Policies and Real-Wage Determination—Swedish Evidence," Working Paper 2000, IFAU, p. 7.
27. Peter Plougmann et al. (2001).
28. An illustration of this development is the expansion of Kiska Science Park, which started in the early 1970s outside Stockholm. Kiska is now a complex of more than 600 technology companies employing approximately 27,000 workers.
29. Nordic Council (2001).

30. "Danish Industry in the New Economy," Danish Technological Institute, October 2000. ("Dansk Industri i den ny økonomi," Teknologisk Institut, oktober 2000.)

31. Different Danish studies have concluded that approximately 25% of all companies (particularly in the industrial sector and in knowledge-intensive business services) are experiencing a development in the direction of an increasingly comprehensive, flexible form of work organization. See, for example, Erhvervsudviklingsrådet (1997).

32. See European Observatory (2001).

33. National Action Plan (NAP), Denmark 2001. The same considerations are stressed in the NAP for Sweden 2001.

34. Ploughman et al. 2001.

35. Bertelsman Foundation 2000.

36. Danish Economic Council, "Danish Economy," Spring 2000.

37. Danich Finance Ministry (Finansministeriet), 2002.

38. Danish Federation of Trade Unions (LO), "Udfordringer til arbejdsmarkedet, Dokumentation" (Challenges to Labor Market Documentation), 2002, prepared jointly by LO and Oxford Infight A/S.

## References

Ackum Agell, Susanne, Anders Forslund, Anders Harkman, Eva Johansson, Martin Lundin, Sara Martinson och Kristian Persson. 2000. *Erfarenheter av nittiotalets arbetsmarknadspolitik.* Institutet för arbetsmarknadspolitisk utvärdering (IFAU).

Auer, Peter. 2000. "Employment Revival in Europe, Small Countries on the Way to Success." Geneva: International Labor Organization.

Auer, Peter and Cazes, Sandrine. 2000. "Stable or Unstable Jobs: Untangling and Interpreting the Evidence in Industrialized Countries." Working Paper. Geneva: International Labor Organization.

Bertelsmann Foundation. 2000. *International Employment Ranking 2000.*

Bingley, Paul, Tor Eriksson, Axel Werwatz and Niels Westergård-Nielsen. 1999. "Beyond "Manucentrism"—Some Fresh Facts About Job and Worker Flows." Centre for Labour Market and Social Research. Working Paper 99-0. Århus (www.cls.dk).

Boje, Thomas P; Åberg Rune. 1999. "Den nya danska arbetsmarknadspolitiken." *Arbetsmarknad & Arbetsliv.* 5(1): 5–26.

Boje, Thomas P, Madsen, Per Kongshøj. 2003. "Wage Formation, Institutions and Unemployment." In Thomas P. Boje and Bengt Furåker, eds., *Post-industrial Labour Markets: Profiles of North America and Scandinavia.* New Yok: Routledge.

Casey, Bernard and Michael Gold. 2000. *"Social Partnership and Economic Performance, the case of Europe."* Cheltenham. Edward Elgar.

Danish Ministry of Finance. 2000. *Finansredegørelse 2000* (Annual Medium Term Economic Survey), København.

Dublin Institute. 2000. *Employment Options of the Future.*

Erhvervsudviklingsrådet. 1997. "Den fleksible virksomhed." Disko-rapport 1, Copenhagen.

European Commission. 2001. "The EU Economy 2001 Review, Investing in the Future." European Economy. No. 73 DG Economic and Financial Affairs.

European Observatory. 2001. "Business Practices in Skills-based Management." Danish Case studies, prepared by Oxford Insight A/S on behalf of the Danish Employers Association and MEDEF. Paris.

Gallie, Duncan and Serge Paugam. 2000. *Welfare Regimes and the Experience of Unemployment in Europe.* Oxford: Oxford University Press.

International Labor Organization (ILO). *Key Indicators of the Labour Market 1999.* Geneva: ILO.

Larsen, M. and Langager, K. 1998. *Arbejdsmarkedsreformen og arbejdsmarkedet* 98: 13, Socialforskningsinstituttet, Copenhagen.

Larsson, Allan. 1999. "What Can We Learn from Denmark?" Wissenshaft Zentrum Symposium. February 10, 1999. Berlin.

Lindbeck, Assar. 1997. "The Swedish Experiment." *Journal of Economic Literature* 35: 1273–1319.

Landsorganisationen i Danmark (LO). 2001. *Udfordringer og muligheder på arbejdsmarkede.* København: LO.

Madsen, P. Kongshøj. 1999. *Denmark: Flexibility, Security and Labour Market Success,* Employment and Training Papers No. 53. Geneva. ILO. Available at http://www.ilo.org/public/english/employment/strat/publ/etp53.htm

———. 2002. "The Danish Model of *Flexicurity*: A Paradise—with Some Snakes." In Hedva Sarfati and Giuliano Bonoli, eds., *Labour Market and Social Protections Reforms in International Perspective: Parallel or Converging Tracks?* Ashgate Publishing Company: 243–265.

National Action Plan (NAP). 2001. Denmark.

National Action Plan (NAP). 2001. Sweden.

Nordic Council. 2001. "Use of ICT in Nordic enterprises 1999/2000." Copenhagen.

Organization for Economic Cooperation and Development (OECD). 1999. *Employment Outlook.* Paris: OECD.

——— 2000. *Employment Outlook.* Paris: OECD.

——— 2001a. *Employment Outlook.* Paris: OECD.

——— 2001b. *Economic Surveys. Sweden 2001.* Paris: OECD.

——— 2002. *Economic Surveys. Sweden 2002.* Paris: OECD.

——— 2002a. *OECD Employment Outlook.* Paris: OECD.

Plougmann, Peter et al. 2001. "Are the Labour Reserves being Depleted?" Report to the Danish Department of Labour. Oxford Insight A/S.

# 10

## Unemployment and Labor Market Institutions: An Assessment

DAVID R. HOWELL

Though it remains widely accepted that high unemployment is a "European" problem, just a glance at the data will confirm that over the past two decades the standardized unemployment rate has varied widely, both across the developed world and within Europe. Equally significant, the mix of high- and low-unemployment countries also changed markedly over this brief period. Denmark, the Netherlands, and Ireland switched from high- to low-unemployment countries between the 1980s and the 1990s, Sweden and Germany did just the opposite, and the United States went from the middle of the pack in the early 1980s to being one of the best performers in the mid-1990s and then slid back to the middle as the developed world edged into recession in 2001–2002. Often overlooked in the 1990s in the rush to embrace market fundamentalism and to applaud the American model was the fact that several European countries with strong welfare states have consistently reported unemployment rates well below that of the United States (Austria and Norway). At the same time, other European welfare states, characterized by some of the lowest levels of wage inequality and the highest levels of social protection in the developed world, experienced substantial declines in unemployment over the 1990s, reaching levels that are now below that of the United States (e.g., Denmark, the Netherlands, and Sweden). The United Kingdom and Ireland also currently report lower rates than the United States, and, while still high, unemployment rates for Canada, Spain, and France have declined sharply, resulting in substantial convergence toward U.S. levels. Still, a serious unemployment problem remains. Four large European countries—France,

Germany, Italy, and Spain—reported unemployment rates between 8.6% and 11.3% in 2003 (OECD 2004: Statistical Annex, Table A).

The market fundamentalists, led by the Organization for Economic Cooperation and Development (OECD) (1997, 1999) and the International Monetary Fund (IMF) (1999, 2003), have claimed that these dramatic differences in performance in the 1990s are explained by differences in the rigidity of national labor markets and that these differences in turn reflect mainly the willingness of the "success stories" to take the "bitter medicine" prescribed by the OECD's Jobs Strategy (see table 1.1) and the unwillingness of the "failures" to curb the power of "insider" interests. As the IMF has recently pointed out, the leading international institutions— the IMF, OECD, and the European Commission—have long argued that "the causes of unemployment can be found in labor market institutions. Accordingly, countries with high unemployment have been repeatedly urged to undertake comprehensive structural reforms to reduce 'labor market rigidities'" (IMF 2003: 129). Indeed, the OECD-IMF orthodoxy goes even further, arguing that there is really only one solution: "high and persistent unemployment can only be solved through structural reforms" (IMF 2002: fn 8, 133).

The dominance of the OECD-IMF orthodoxy reflects a sharp ideological swing to the right after the energy and productivity shocks of the 1970s, exemplified by the coming into political power of conservative parties by the mid-1980s in the United States, the United Kingdom, and Germany. In the "New Economy" of the late twentieth century, the market was to replace the welfare state programs and regulations that had been established in earlier generations to mitigate the most harmful effects of the capitalist economy on workers—to reduce the risk of job loss, to limit earnings inequality, to provide access to health care, and to provide a poverty floor below which no family could fall. The economics profession experienced its own shift to the right a bit earlier (it was already in full gear by the 1970s) and played a central role in the policy shift, with research and popular pronouncements on the inherent superiority of market solutions. Applying core textbook principles, economists, politicians, and pundits alike announced that the solution for poor employment performance was a freer, more competitive labor market.

The essays in this volume contest this free-market orthodoxy. The cross-country analyses in chapters 2–4 conclude that there is no compelling evidence of tradeoffs between inequality (the degree of "wage compression") and employment performance. Chapter 3 showed that recent statistical tests of labor market institutions produce quite mixed results and are decidedly unrobust to minor changes in number of countries, time period, variable specification, and econometric method. Although a number of these statistical studies have been highly influential, it is increasingly recognized that it would be imprudent, to say the least, to base major policy decisions on such evidence.[1] This is particularly so since this body of research—including the reports of the major "independent" international organizations (e.g., the OECD and the IMF)—has made little effort to take into account the *costs* of dismantling existing networks of protective labor market institutions.

The largely uncritical acceptance of these statistical results as compelling evidence in support of the OECD-IMF orthodoxy can be explained by the widely accepted presumption among economists that an unhindered market will nearly always be the most efficient arrangement and that, as a result, almost any move toward deregulation will improve economic (and employment) performance. In this regard, the policy prescriptions of "economic science" in the current period have been little different from those Keynes challenged in the 1930s—the orthodox (or, as Keynes put it, the "classical") view that downwardly "sticky wages" explain persistent high unemployment. At the heart of this orthodoxy, as Gregg and Manning (1997) have pointed out, is the *faith* that deregulation will move the economy toward the perfectly competitive world of the elementary textbook, and not toward one marked by even more market imperfection—imperfect information, imperfect mobility, and extensive monopoly/monopsony power. By underscoring the complexity of the relationship between employment performance and labor market institutions in real-world economies, the country case studies (chapters 4–9) point to the potential efficiency gains that are possible with the right combination of labor market institutions, which varies from one country to another. Although these gains are well established in the academic literature (Barr 1998; Agell 1999; Hall and Soskice 2001), this "varieties of capitalism" perspective has been no match for the much simpler orthodox view in the policy debate.

In this concluding chapter, I make use of evidence from the earlier chapters in this volume, from other recent country case studies, and from some additional data on labor costs and profit shares, to critically assess the OECD-IMF orthodoxy. This also provides an opportunity to consider briefly some dimensions of the French, Italian, Belgian, and Austrian experiences, countries not covered in our case studies. I conclude by noting an unfortunate consequence of the dominance of the OECD-IMF orthodoxy for research—the failure to focus research on other prime suspects.

## 10.1 UNEMPLOYMENT TRENDS FOR LOW AND HIGH UNEMPLOYMENT COUNTRIES

The OECD has pointed to Denmark, the Netherlands, Ireland, the United Kingdom, and New Zealand as the "success stories" of the late 1990s and has attributed their improved labor market performance to a political willingness to swallow the "bitter medicine" of structural reform and to implement the recommendations of the Jobs Strategy (Elmeskov et al. 1998; OECD 1999). Our case studies have focused on all five of these countries and highlight the difficulty of generalizing about the correct "recipe" for achieving low unemployment. Both Glyn (Ireland and New Zealand) and Schmitt and Wadsworth (the United Kingdom) conclude that the lesson of these cases is that labor market reform has been neither necessary nor sufficient for good employment performance. The same can be said for Denmark and the Netherlands (see chapters 8 and 9), two countries that have clearly maintained their commitment to a universalistic welfare state.

The limits of the OECD-IMF orthodoxy can be illustrated by comparing two sets of countries with the United States, which has been explicitly identified as the "right" labor market model by the OECD and IMF. To keep the discussion manageable (and the figures comprehensible), in this chapter the United States is set against three low- and three high-unemployment countries, using unemployment rates relative to the United States in 2002 as the criterion. The "low" group includes two continental countries, Austria, with a history of extremely low unemployment, and the Netherlands, a country that has managed to move from "Dutch Disease" status to an "official" OECD success story. This low unemployment group also includes Sweden, a Nordic, social democratic model that, between 1975 and 2003, experienced higher unemployment rates than the United States

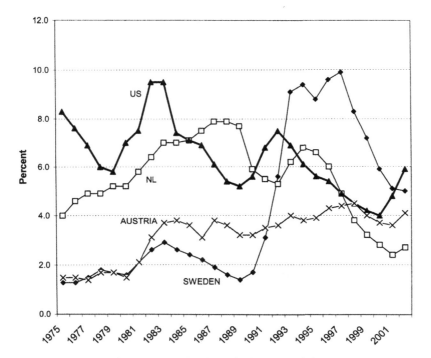

Figure 10.1. Unemployment rates for the United States and three low-unemployment countries, 1975–2002. Source: OECD *Employment Outlook*, Statistical Annex, table A (various issues).

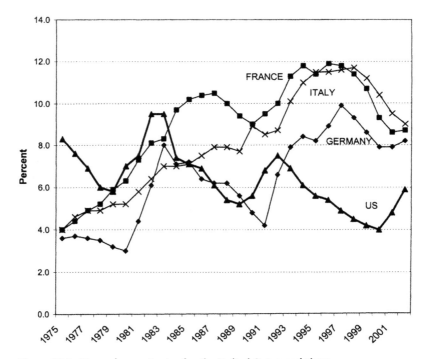

Figure 10.2. Unemployment rates for the United States and three
high-unemployment countries, 1975–2002. Source: OECD *Employment Outlook*,
Statistical Annex, table A (various issues).

for just eight years (1993–1999). Figure 10.1 shows that Austria has consistently outperformed the United States, while the Netherlands outperformed the United States before 1985 and after 1997 and had roughly
similar unemployment rates for 1985–1997.

In sharp contrast are three relatively large country "failures" that have
been hounded by the OECD and IMF for not pursuing major structural
(labor market) reforms—Germany, France, and Italy. Figure 10.2 shows
that the United States has shown far superior employment performance to
France and Italy since the mid-1980s, and to Germany since 1993.

## 10.2 SOCIAL SPENDING, LABOR MARKET INSTITUTIONS, AND UNEMPLOYMENT

In nearly all cases, labor market institutions, regulations, and taxes can be
reformed to make them more "employment-friendly." It is another matter
entirely to make a convincing case that the design of these social interventions, much less modest changes in them, can explain major differences
in aggregate employment performance over time and across countries. As

Schettkat points out in his Netherlands-Germany study (chapter 8), while Holland did introduce liberal reforms in the 1990s, it continues to ranked at the top of nearly all the standard "rigidity" indicators. If the orthodox view is right, European countries need to transform their institutions so that they are no more interventionist than their counterparts in the United States. It is absolute *levels* that should matter. As the IMF explains, "Across a range of structural indicators, the EU labor market continues to compare unfavorably to more competitive labor markets. For example, EU unemployment benefits and marginal effective tax rates on additional income are about twice as high as U.S. levels" (IMF 2003: 139). According to the OECD-IMF orthodoxy, it is level of labor market regulation relative to the United States that is the yardstick.

Table 10.1 (the same as table 1.2) presents some of these key structural indicators—standard measures of some of the most frequently identified sources of labor market rigidity. It is immediately apparent that our three low-unemployment countries have outperformed the United States without adopting the U.S. model, or even moving much toward it. The first two columns show different measures of the kind of social spending that can raise reservation wages and reduce work incentives. Compared to the U.S. level of cash transfers to the nonelderly population of 3.7% in the early 1990s, Austria spent 8.9%, the Netherlands 14.1%, and Sweden 13.8%. The broader general measure of social spending presented in column 2 puts the United States at 16.5% of GDP for 1997, far below the generosity levels of the three low-unemployment welfare states (26.2%, 25.9%, and 33.7%, respectively).

And the high-unemployment countries? Two of the three, France and Italy, show much lower rates of social spending than Holland and Sweden (10.7% and 7% compared to 14.1% and 13.8%), while the third, Germany, spends slightly less than low-unemployment Austria (8.4% and 8.9%, respectively). It is notable that even the United Kingdom, whose unemployment rate has converged to the U.S. level recently, also shows substantially more generous social spending rates than the United States. No obvious link between labor market success and failure appears in the cross-country social spending data.

The remaining indicators in table 10.1 measure regulation of the labor market. The IMF (2003: 137) contends, on the basis of cross-country regression tests conducted by IMF staff and other researchers, such as Nickell et al. (2003), that "greater unionization is found to be associated with greater unemployment." But the raw data in table 10.1 for our three low-unemployment and three high-unemployment countries do not support this view. Column 3 shows that the share of workers covered by collective bargaining (1994) in Austria, the Netherlands, and Sweden was 98%, 81%, and 89%, respectively, compared to just 18% for the United States. The collective bargaining rates for the three "failures" are similar to those for the three "successes" (France at 95%, Germany at 92%, and

Table 10.1. Selected Measures of Social Protection for OECD Member Countries, 1980–1995

| | Nonelderly Cash Transfers Share of GDP[1] (%) | Social Spending Share of GDP[2] (%) | Collective Bargaining Coverage[3] (%) | Collective Bargaining Structure Index[4] | Unemployment Benefit Replacement Rate[5] (%) | | Unemployment Benefit Duration Index[5] | | Employment Protection Law Strictness Index[5] | |
|---|---|---|---|---|---|---|---|---|---|---|
| | 1992–95 | 1997 | 1994 | 1994 | 1980–84 | 1995–99 | 1980–84 | 1995–99 | 1980–84 | 1995–99 |
| Australia | 6.2 | — | 80 | 3 | 22.3 | 26.7 | 1.02 | 1.02 | 0.5 | 0.5 |
| Austria | 8.9 | 26.2 | 98 | 5.25 | 33.2 | 31.0 | 0.75 | 0.75 | 1.25 | 1.3 |
| Belgium | 12.1 | 25.1 | 90 | 4.25 | 50.6 | 46.2 | 0.80 | 0.76 | 1.55 | 1.19 |
| Canada | 8 | 16.9 | 36 | 2 | 56.6 | 57.8 | 0.24 | 0.21 | 0.30 | 0.30 |
| Denmark | 12.4 | 30.8 | 69 | 4.25 | 69.0 | 60.8 | 0.62 | 1.00 | 1.10 | 0.74 |
| Finland | 15.3 | 29.5 | 95 | 4.5 | 32.5 | 58.6 | 0.66 | 0.54 | 1.20 | 1.08 |
| France | 10.7 | 29.6 | 95 | 4 | 62.5 | 57.9 | 0.32 | 0.51 | 1.30 | 1.50 |
| Germany | 8.4 | 27.7 | 92 | 5 | 38.8 | 36.3 | 0.62 | 0.60 | 1.65 | 1.41 |
| Ireland | — | 17.9 | — | — | 51.1 | 31.6 | 0.38 | 0.75 | 0.50 | 0.54 |
| Italy | 7 | 26.9 | 82 | 4.5 | 0 | 43.5 | 0.00 | 0.20 | 2.00 | 1.78 |
| Japan | 1.9 | 14.8 | 21 | 4 | 27.6 | 30.6 | 0.00 | 0.00 | 1.40 | 1.40 |
| Netherlands | 14.1 | 25.9 | 81 | 4 | 66.5 | 70.0 | 0.64 | 0.50 | 1.35 | 1.23 |
| New Zealand | — | — | 31 | 2 | 29.9 | 26.4 | 1.04 | 1.04 | 0.80 | 0.80 |
| Norway | 10.1 | 26.5 | 74 | 4.75 | 52.1 | 61.5 | 0.49 | 0.51 | 1.55 | 1.39 |
| Portugal | — | 19.1 | 71 | 4 | 34.3 | 65.0 | 0.02 | 0.38 | 1.93 | 1.91 |
| Spain | 6.8 | 20.9 | 78 | 4 | 76.9 | 65.0 | 0.19 | 0.28 | 1.91 | 1.62 |
| Sweden | 13.8 | 33.7 | 89 | 4 | 67.8 | 68.5 | 0.05 | 0.04 | 1.80 | 1.32 |
| Switzerland | — | 27.2 | 50 | 4.25 | 41.7 | 62.6 | 0.00 | 0.16 | 0.55 | 0.55 |
| United Kingdom | 9.4 | 21.9 | 47 | 2.5 | 27.6 | 21.6 | 0.70 | 0.73 | 0.35 | 0.35 |
| United States | 3.7 | 16.5 | 18 | 2 | 32.9 | 26.9 | 0.15 | 0.16 | 0.10 | 0.10 |

1. Smeeding et al., table 5a.2, in Danziger and Haveman (2001).
2. Public and mandatory private social expenditure as % of GDP; OECD Social Expenditure database.
3. OECD (1997: table 3.3).
4. OECD (1997: table 3.3). This is a sum of the OECD's Centralization and Coordination indices.
   Each ranges from 1–3, and includes estimates of 1.5, 2.5, and 2+.
   The latter are given a value of 2.25.

Italy at 82%). As in the case of social spending, the United Kingdom, at 47%, falls between the continental welfare states and the United States. The IMF position is also challenged by the OECD's own state-of-the-art chapter on collective bargaining, which concludes that unionization, whether measured by collective bargaining coverage or by union density (the share of union members), is not statistically linked to employment performance across the OECD (OECD 1997). Baker et al. (chapter 3) confirm this conclusion. The IMF position on collective bargaining effects is not supported by the balance of the available evidence.

It seems clear that it is less the share of unionized workers or the share under collective bargaining than how well the industrial relations bargaining system works that matters most for employment performance. Hall and Soskice (2001) make the useful distinction between "liberal" and "coordinated" market economies. In the former, the market does most of the coordination required for responding to changed circumstances (and particularly to shocks), while in the latter, coordination is the responsibility of negotiations between employer and trade union groups, often with a guiding or supporting role played by the state. In sharp contrast to the free-market orthodoxy,[2] the evidence indicates that a decentralized system with many independent unions and firms bargaining in an atomistic fashion is not a necessary condition for good or improved employment performance. As table 10.1 shows, the strong welfare state countries (Austria, Denmark, the Netherlands, Germany, Norway, and Sweden) have coordination/centralization scores of 4–5.5, far above the 2–2.5 scores of the United States, New Zealand, and the United Kingdom, but all of these countries outperformed the latter over much of the 1980–2002 period. Cross-country econometric studies of unemployment since the early 1990s have usually found that bargaining coordination is associated with *lower* unemployment. As even the OECD concludes from its own econometric tests of unemployment and employment rates, "the only statistically significant result is that centralized/co-ordinated countries have lower unemployment rates" (OECD 1997: 77; see also chapter 3). This is a particularly striking finding, not only because it sharply challenges the decentralization (free-market) view but because it is perhaps the most robust of all the findings in the cross-country regression literature on institutions and unemployment. It should also be noted that, along with the positive effect of coordination/centralization on employment performance, there is a well-established positive association between decentralized, atomistic bargaining and high and rising earnings inequality (OECD 1997).

Country case studies have produced convincing evidence that effective coordination of wage bargaining with social and macroeconomic policy depends upon strong associations of employers and unions in a relatively stable, conflict-free political context. An important part of any explanation for the poor employment performance of France since the late 1970s is the "fundamental instability" of French politics and social policy

(Levy 2000: 312). "*Dirigiste* policymaking concentrated power in a 'strong,' centralized state at the expense of societal and local associations that were deemed too self-serving and particularistic to be trusted. . . . The relative isolation of policymakers has lent a peculiar character to French welfare reform: the plight of proposed changes is determined less by bargaining among political and corporatist elites than by unmediated exchanges between state and citizen, either through the ballot box or in the streets" (331). This model is the mirror opposite of that developed since the late 1970s by the Netherlands, in which successful coordination and bargaining among Dutch employers, unions, and the government in the 1980s helped produce an enormous improvement in employment outcomes in the 1990s (chapter 8; Hemerijck, Unger, and Visser 2000). Indeed, it might be argued that a big part of France's inability to produce effective long-term coordination among industrial relations bargaining, social policy, and macro policy (as in the Dutch, Austrian, and Irish success stories) was the *weakness* of the French labor movement. It seems fair to conclude that the free-market model—decentralized unions (firms) bargaining without coordination with other unions (firms)—better characterizes the "failure" countries than the success stories.

Perhaps the leading culprit for the OECD-IMF orthodoxy is the generosity of the unemployment benefits system. Columns 4–5 show the replacement rate for the first year of benefits. Columns 6–7 present a measure of the generosity of benefits over long periods—the share of benefits in years 2–5 as a share of the first year's benefits. Both dimensions are important for judging the generosity of the system, as are the eligibility requirements for benefits in the first place (which is much harder to measure consistently across countries and not currently available for cross-country statistical tests). Predictably, the United States scores among the lowest of all OECD countries on both indicators. The three low-unemployment countries are all much more generous than the United States, and not particularly less generous than the high-unemployment countries. Austria's generosity is roughly similar to Germany's (though with slightly more generous long-term benefits); the low-unemployment Dutch show more generous first-year replacement rates and similar longer-term generosity than the supposedly sclerotic French system. And, in the first year, the Swedes are far more generous than the Italians.

Italy and France are illustrative of the limited role played by unemployment benefits in accounting for persistent high unemployment. Italy is characterized by dramatic regional productivity and unemployment differentials. In 1998, the unemployment rate for men in the north was about 4% but over 17% in the south. For women the disparity was also huge: about 10% in the north and 30% in the south (Bertola and Garibaldi 2002: figures 3–4). If the orthodox view is right that the direction of causation runs from the level of institutional intervention to economic and employment performance, this is an anomalous result, since the system applies to the nation as a whole. Alternatively, this might be viewed as a perfect example of the setting of wage floors by national labor market institutions that are too high for low-productivity regions. This may have been a factor, but at least as far as the unemployment benefit system goes, table 10.1 indicates that Italy is among the least generous in Europe.

Equally important, it should be recognized that a large part of the unemployment problem in the south—and throughout the country—is among youth. While the unemployment rate for those ages 25–54 are nearly identical for Italy and for OECD Europe in 1999 (8.3 and 8.0%, respectively), Italy's youth (ages 15–24) unemployment rate is almost twice as high: 31.1% compared to 17.7 for OECD Europe (OECD 2002a: table C). This is important because these youth are generally ineligible for unemployment benefits. According to a recent OECD report on long-term unemployment, "Greece, Italy and Spain are among the four countries with the highest incidence of very-long-term youth unemployment, yet benefits are not generally available to unemployed youths in these countries" (OECD 2002a: 203). Indeed, Bertola and Garibaldi (2002: 16) contend that "conventional unemployment insurance is not an important labor market institution in Italy." If high reservation wages are the culprit for Italy's high unemployment rate, the fault does not appear to lie with the generosity of the benefits system.

In sharp contrast to the figures for Italy, table 10.1 shows that France offers relatively generous unemployment benefits. But a critical dimension of generosity is eligibility, and, as in Italy (and Spain), eligibility in the French system is limited. According to the OECD's country study for France, "the unemployment compensation system also provides incentives to return to work. Eligibility criteria are relatively strict, less than half of job seekers receive an allowance. Allowances are degressive and therefore encourage recipients to return to work after an initial period" (OECD 2001: 91). But the current system is still deemed too generous by the OECD authors, and, while they offer no evidence regarding the sensitivity of unemployment levels to the generosity of the benefits program, they recommend "a gradual decrease in unemployment benefit" (table 5, p. 74).

While the recent cross-country regression literature generally supports a negative effect of unemployment benefit generosity on unemployment (see table 3.5), Baker et al. report no evidence of such effects (see table 3.6). At least with reference to our three low- and three high-unemployment countries, the unemployment benefits data provide no sure guide to success and failure in national employment performance.

Finally, if flexibility in hiring and firing is considered critical to good employment performance, the strictness of employment protection laws should help explain the pattern of unemployment across countries. The IMF and OECD have both stressed the importance of moving towards American practice in this area. The final column shows a U.S. score of just .1 for both the early 1980s and the late 1990s, which is far below that of every other nation in the table. How do the three high-unemployment countries compare to our three success stories? France (1.5), Germany

(1.41), and Italy (1.78) all had high scores, but so did Austria (1.3), the Netherlands (1.23), and Sweden (1.32). Perhaps the lower scores for the successful countries help explain their success, but one can ask: if this is such a key determinant of employment performance, why have Austria, Sweden, and the Netherlands (and Norway) outperformed the United States throughout most of the past three decades? It is true that some of the cross-country literature has found that strict employment protection laws have a positive effect on unemployment (table 3.5), but again Baker et al. regression results do not support this conclusion (table 3.6). Interestingly, neither does the OECD's own chapter on employment protection: "This analysis strengthens the conclusion that EPL strictness has little or no effect on overall unemployment" (OECD 1999: 88).

## 10.3 LABOR COSTS AND UNEMPLOYMENT

Much of the upward effect of labor market institutions on unemployment is supposed to take place through labor costs. In his account of German unemployment, Heckman (2003: 361) explains that "Higher wages achieved by unions or by minimum wage statues must lead to substitution against labor—fewer jobs—if firms are to remain competitive." This may manifest itself in the form of wage compression, in which low-skill workers are priced out of the labor market and account for the high unemployment rate. Or, more generally, overregulation may cause a general rise in labor costs, spreading unemployment across large parts of the workforce as national competitiveness declines.

### 10.3.1 Wage Compression

The wage compression account has been highlighted as a key source of the European employment crisis (Siebert 1997). Wages that are too high for less-skilled workers reduce both employer demand for them and the incentive for these workers to take (low) paid employment seriously. Union bargaining power and high minimum wages are cited as the main culprits (Heckman 2003). This amounts to a call for greater inequality, and assumes a tradeoff between high levels of earnings inequality (the United States) and high unemployment ("Europe"). This is a direct application of the simple textbook model to entire national labor markets, and this simplicity surely helps to explain its popularity, since the empirical evidence for such inequality-unemployment tradeoffs is remarkably weak.

Howell and Huebler (chapter 2) try numerous alternative measures of employment performance and earnings inequality and find little or no support for the wage compression prediction. Similarly, Schmitt and Wadsworth, in chapter 5, demonstrate that the predicted better relative outcomes for less-skilled U.S. and U.K. workers fails to show up in the data. Further, as Schettkat, in chapter 8, points out, the sizable gap in employment performance between the Netherlands and Germany cannot be explained by greater wage compression in the latter. In a direct test of the wage rigidity thesis for Germany, Beissinger and Moeller (1998: 16) conclude that "relative demand shocks in combination with rigid relative wages are not the main cause of the German unemployment problem" (see also Steiner and Wagner 1997). Bustillo (chapter 7) also finds that this argument does not explain Spain's high unemployment, since Spain's wage inequality has been high (and increasing) relative to European standards.

The same can be said for France and Italy. France has a level of earnings inequality below that of the United States and Canada, but far above that of its continental European neighbors, such as Denmark, the Netherlands, Germany, and Austria (see chapter 2, figures 2.3 and 2.4). Yet, all these neighboring countries have reported lower unemployment than France since the 1970s. An important study by Card, Lemieux, and Kramarz (1999) challenges the view that rigid wages in France can explain employment rate differences by skill group with Canada and the United States (see later discussion). Nor does the problem of low-skill workers getting priced out of the labor market appear to apply to the Italian case. According to Bertola and Garibaldi (2002: 4–5), "the structure of unemployment in Italy is only very mildly related to skill differentials as measured by formal education . . . to be protected from unemployment in Italy it is much more important to be old than to be well educated."

Heckman (2003) points to high minimum wages as a key culprit (with centralized bargaining) for the poor employment performance of both Germany and France (in Germany the minimum wage is not legislated and is effectively enforced through collective bargaining). But Schettkat (chapter 8) points out that minimum wages cannot account for the gap between Dutch and German unemployment rates (indeed, Heckman reproduces a table, from Dorado [1996], that shows the minimum wage for *both* countries at .55 of the average production worker wage). As for France, two studies by Abowd et al. (1998, 1999), relied upon by Heckman for empirical evidence, find statistically significant employment effects, particularly for youth. But the authors (Abowd et al. 1997: 24) point out that the magnitude of the impact on the unemployment levels of French adults is probably quite limited.

In another minimum-wage study that compares France and the United States, three French economists concluded that neither the minimum wage nor unemployment benefits appears to produce a higher "reservation wage" for French workers (Cohen, Lefranc, and Saint-Paul 1997). As they put it, "minimum wage regulations are not relatively more important in one country than in another when it comes to analyzing the reentry of displaced workers into the job market . . . the difference between France and the USA does not originate from a lower (job) acceptance rate in France, be it the outcome of unemployment benefits or minimum wage regulations" (1997: 278). Compared to the United States, France has been characterized by much lower hiring and separation rates, dating back at least to the 1970s, when France typically had an unemployment rate half that of the United States. It should also be recalled that the magnitude of this effect is not likely to be large, since the share of the unemployed in the French youth population is actually quite small (see figures 1.6 and 1.7). In any case, it is worth noting that if a relatively high minimum wage does in fact threaten low-skill employment opportunities, a solution is to reduce employers' social contributions (payroll taxes) and thereby reduce employer labor costs. This has, indeed, been French policy since the early 1990s (OECD 2001; Levy 2000).

If the minimum wage played an important role in employment performance across the OECD, we should observe dramatically different employment rates by skill level. But Card, Kramarz, and Lemieux (1999) found no support for the conventional view that French employment performance for the less skilled can be traced to wage rigidity:

> Consistent with the view that French labor market institutions restrict relative wage flexibility, we find that wage differentials between skill groups held constant or narrowed slightly over the 1980s. As in Canada, however, we find little evidence that this apparent rigidity in relative wages translated into greater employment losses for less-skilled workers. Indeed, the pattern of employment-population growth rates across age-education cells in France is almost identical to the pattern in the United States. Taking the evidence for the United States, Canada, and France as a whole, we conclude that it is very difficult to maintain the hypothesis that the wage inflexibility in Canada and France translated into greater relative employment losses for less-skilled workers in these countries. (3)

In sum, it seems fair to say that above a certain threshold, the minimum wage is likely to produce negative employment effects, such as those the Abowd studies found. But even if that threshold has been reached in France—and the evidence is mixed—there is no evidence that the magnitude of the effect on the overall French unemployment rate has been anything but negligible. I am aware of no credible study that claims to show that reductions in, or even the elimination of, the legislated minimum wage across the OECD would have more than marginal effects on the level or pattern of unemployment rates. This is, indeed, the position taken by the OECD's own *Employment Outlook* chapter on minimum wages (OECD 1998). There are a number of reasons not to be surprised by this inconsequential result: the extremely low (nonbinding) levels in some countries (the United States), the tendency of low-skill workers to drop out of the formal labor market when faced with very low wages, and the egalitarian social norms in most European countries that would prevent the payment of very low wages. The continued focus on minimum-wage regulations in the European unemployment debate appears to be fueled as much by ideological predispositions as by the evidence.[3]

### 10.3.2 Labor Costs

If not wage compression, it may be that overall labor costs are the key to the unemployment problem. This more general position holds that labor market institutions undermine the competitiveness of large parts of the economy. A key to economic survival for small trade-dependent nations like Ireland and the Netherlands is wage moderation—a thriving export sector has been important for both (see chapters 6 and 8). Did France, Germany, and Italy become high-unemployment countries because of out-of-control labor costs? The orthodox explanation is that highly protective labor market institutions stood in the way of the downward wage flexibility needed to confront the shocks of the 1970s and early 1980s (Blanchard and Wolfers 2000; Heckman, 2003).[4]

To assess this labor cost argument, the United States can be compared to our three low-unemployment and three high-unemployment countries for four related measures: trends in hourly labor compensation costs, the social insurance (payroll tax) share of those labor compensation costs, gross profits shares, and an index of relative unit labor costs—all for manufacturing. While manufacturing is an increasingly small part of the overall economy, it is the only sector for which these measures are available. There is no reason to believe that they do not provide a useful guide to economywide differences and trends across countries. And, to the extent that trade plays a key role in employment performance, manufacturing is particularly important.

Figures 10.3 and 10.4 show total hourly employer labor compensation costs for the United States, the Netherlands, Austria, and Sweden. These data are produced by the U.S. Bureau of Labor Statistics expressly for international comparisons. It should be noted, however, that these are not per unit costs, so productivity differences affect the ability of employers to bear them. Hourly compensation costs for all three low-unemployment countries (figure 10.3) moved closely together over the 1975–2001 period and were substantially higher than U.S. costs for the entire decade of the 1990s. From this figure, it would be impossible to predict the actual pattern of unemployment: Austria was consistently well below the United States; the Netherlands roughly tracked U.S. unemployment rates; and Sweden outperformed the United States except for the 1993–1999 period.

Figure 10.4 shows that compensation trends for France, Italy, and Germany have moved together since 1975. But, while compensation in Italy and France rose to U.S. levels in the late 1980s and then fell below U.S. costs after 1996, Germany showed a spectacular increase in labor costs, reaching $30 in the mid-1990s, almost twice the average hourly cost of U.S. manufacturing workers. Germany's higher labor costs may be related to its recent rise in unemployment, but the relationship is far from perfect—labor costs took off in the mid-1980s, well before unification; unemployment took off in the mid-1990s, a decade later and just after

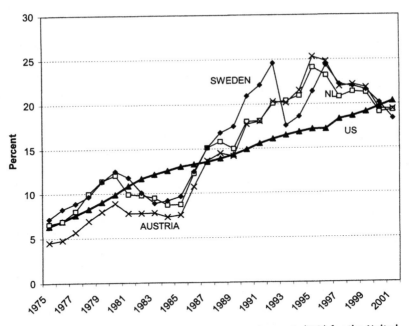

Figure 10.3. Hourly manufacturing labor compensation costs (U.S.) for the United States and three low-unemployment countries, 1975–2002. Source: U.S. Bureau of Labor Statistics, September 2002 (table 2, downloaded from ftp://ftp.bls.gov/pub/special.requests/ForeignLabor/supptab.txt, June 18, 2003).

unification. On the other hand, these data provide even less support for a labor cost story for Italy and France.

Both the OECD and the IMF have called for lower social security (payroll) taxes to spur employment creation. To the extent that employers bear the burden of the tax, they incur higher costs, reducing their demand for labor. To the extent that they can pass along these costs, workers are paid lower wages, which may reduce their incentive to work, lead to more turnover, and increase the time workers spend searching for better jobs (and possibly collecting unemployment benefits in the process). Figure 10.5 shows, not surprisingly, that the United States has much lower social security payroll costs than either Austria or Sweden. Nonlabor costs for the Netherlands and the United States were similar for a few years in the early 1990s, but Dutch costs have risen relative to those in the United States over the past decade, just as Dutch unemployment fell below U.S. levels. Again, it should be noted that, despite much higher payroll costs, Austria has had an unemployment rate consistently below that of the United States. Figure 10.6 shows that tax costs have been much higher in France and Italy (28–32% since 1993) than in Germany (24–25%) or the United States (21–22%). But, returning to the previous figure, they are only moderately above Austrian levels (about 28%). As figure 10.4 showed,

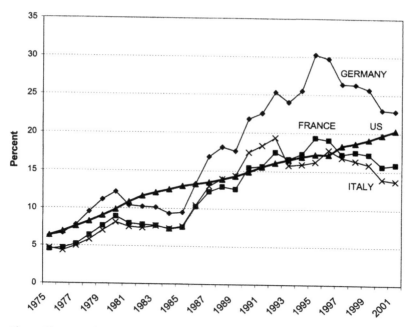

Figure 10.4. Hourly manufacturing labor compensation costs (U.S. $) for the United States and three high-unemployment countries, 1975–2002. Source: U.S. Bureau of Labor Statistics, September 2002 (table 2, downloaded from ftp://ftp.bls.gov/pub/special.requests/ForeignLabor/supptab.txt, June 18, 2003).

despite these high nonwage labor costs, French and Italian hourly compensation costs have been similar to or below those for the United States. The upshot seems to be that the social payments portion of hourly compensation costs is substantially higher in countries with *both* lower and higher unemployment rates than the United States.

Gross profit shares are presented in figures 10.7 and 10.8. These provide a measure of relative competitiveness, particularly in an increasingly global financial world in which capital can migrate with increasing ease. Profit shares reflect not only labor costs (and the social insurance component of them) but also productivity levels and exchange rates. Figure 10.7 indicates that, apart from the large downward swings for Sweden, first in the late 1970s and then again during the crisis of the early 1990s, profit shares for the three low-unemployment welfare states and the United States have shown similar trends since 1975. While Austria's profit share was almost identical to that of the United States from the early 1980s to 1997, Dutch profits have consistently been higher since 1984. It is worth noting the takeoff of Dutch profits after the Wassenaar agreement of 1982 (see chapter 8; Hemerijck, Unger, and Visser, 2000).

What about the high unemployment countries? Figure 10.8 shows that, like the hourly compensation trends, the profit shares for the United

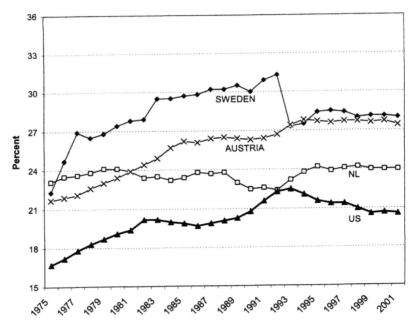

Figure 10.5. Social insurance costs as a share of total hourly compensation in manufacturing for the United States and three low-unemployment countries, 1975–2002. Source: U.S. Bureau of Labor Statistics, September 2002 (table 13, downloaded from ftp://ftp.bls.gov/

States and France tracked each other closely throughout the period, at least until French profits moved *higher* in 1998. Italy actually outperformed the United States on this measure from the late 1970s to about 1990 and has closely tracked U.S. profit shares since. And, again, echoing the pattern for the labor compensation figures, Germany is the outlier: slightly lower than the others in the late 1980s and then much lower after 1991 (21–24% compared to U.S., French, and Italian rates that were between 30% and 38%). The timing of the downturn in German profit share points directly to the role played by reunification.

Another measure of competitiveness is relative unit labor costs. Figure 10.9 presents OECD estimates of the trends in these costs, measured as an index of total hourly compensation in U.S. dollars (so exchange rate changes affect the trends). Consistent with its unemployment record, Austria showed steadily declining relative unit labor costs during the years measured. Similarly, France showed gradual declining relative unit costs from 1986 to 2000, a pattern that does not suggest that French workers' total compensation became increasingly uncompetitive, as many have assumed, given that country's poor unemployment record. The United States did well between the mid-1980s and 1995, after which relative unit

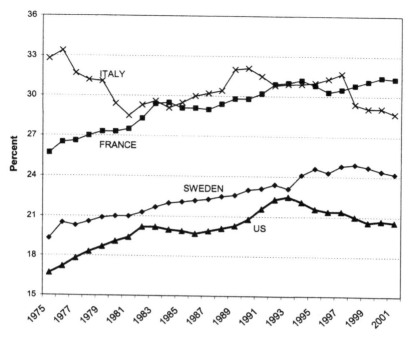

Figure 10.6. Social insurance costs as a share of total hourly compensation in manufacturing for the United States and three high-unemployment countries, 1975–2003. Source: U.S. Bureau of Labor Statistics, September 2002 (table 13, downloaded from ftp://ftp.bls.gov/pub/special.requests/ForeignLabor/supptab.txt, June 18, 2003).

costs started to rise. Sweden's rising costs (declining productivity) in the late 1980s anticipated that nation's early 1990s crisis, a pattern that is strikingly similar to Italy's.

Finally, Germany's rising relative labor costs between 1991 and 1995 probably reflected the incorporation of the East. But the figure shows a steady decline since 1995, and figure 10.8 shows that over the same post-1995 period, the profit share gained almost 5 percentage points. While the manufacturing sector shrank, as it did across the developed world, high productivity levels (low unit labor costs) helped Germany remain an exporting power. As Manow and Seils (2000: 264) put it, "German industry's outstanding export performance has apparently not been hurt by the generous German welfare state's high spending levels." According to Manow and Seils, the explanation for continued high unemployment can be found in the failure of the policy response to unification, the unexpectedly high costs, and the failure of the German economy to generate service jobs. These are closely linked: policy failures raised costs, which led to the need to increase nonwage labor costs (see figure 10.6), which were difficult to absorb in low-productivity sectors. This is precisely why

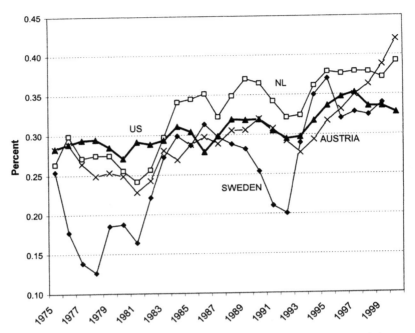

**Figure 10.7. Gross profit shares in manufacturing for the United States and three low-unemployment countries, 1975–2000. Source: Andrew Glyn, from OECD data.**

the French scaled back payroll costs for low-wage jobs (OECD 2001). The links among nonwage labor costs, the availability of part-time jobs, female participation, and the proliferation of low-skill service jobs across countries deserves much more study (see Esping-Andersen 1999).

## 10.4 BEYOND THE OECD-IMF ORTHODOXY

The essays in this volume, and the evidence just presented, call into question simple labor market rigidity explanations for poor employment performance. Differences in labor market institutions (or their change over time) do a poor job of accounting for the vast differences in levels and trends across developed countries. It greatly exaggerates the distinctiveness of the U.S. unemployment record as a "success story" by not taking a longer-term perspective, one that should now include the recent strong convergence across the OECD toward U.S. unemployment levels since 1999. It relies on a "collapsing demand for the less-skilled" thesis in the face of the evidence on unemployment and employment rates by skill (which shows that where unemployment rates have risen they have done so for all skill groups). It points to wage rigidity, despite the lack of any cross-national association between unemployment levels and measures of wage compression (inequality) and labor costs. It attributes the pattern of

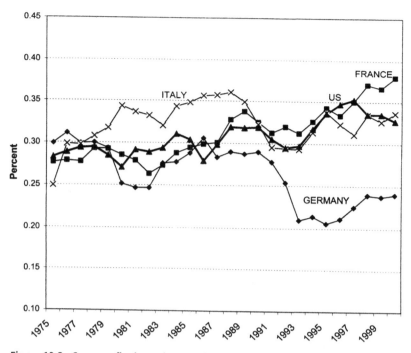

Figure 10.8. Gross profit shares in manufacturing for the United States and three high-unemployment countries, 1975–2000. Source: Andrew Glyn, from OECD data.

unemployment across countries to specific "employment-unfriendly" labor market institutions on the basis of, at best, mixed evidence from remarkably unreliable statistical tests.

A comprehensive and convincing account of the high unemployment that has afflicted much of the developed world since the early 1980s has yet to be written, but it is certainly more complex than the OECD-IMF orthodoxy would have us believe. There were several major country-specific crises in the early 1990s (German unification, Finland's exposure to the Soviet collapse, and Sweden's fiscal crisis). The timing of the postwar baby boom, rapidly increasing female labor market participation, and the overlapping of deruralization and deindustrialization were a particularly difficult mix of developments, particularly for Spain and Italy (chapter 7; Esping-Andersen 1999). In addition, particularly in this context of rapid economic restructuring and of increasing price competition associated with globalization, product market regulations and high start-up costs for new firms may have constrained employment growth (Pissardes 2003; OECD 2002: chapter 5). It may also be the case that high nonwage labor costs and social norms that discourage female employment have worked together to limit the growth of low-productivity service sector jobs—a possibility that can help explain the rapid growth of U.S.

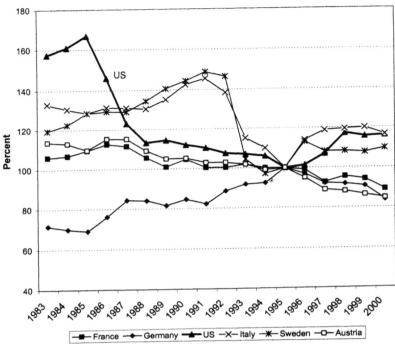

**Figure 10.9.** Relative unit labor costs for manufacturing, 1983–2000 (1995 = 100).
Source: OECD, *Economic Outlook* (no. 68, December 2000), Annex table 44.

employment and the recent employment stagnation in Germany (Esping-Andersen 1999; Manow and Seils 2000).

But, more generally, the case study evidence points to the critical role of macroeconomic policy, institutional coordination, and the political environment. In contrast to the recent conventional wisdom in macroeconomic theory, the effects of fiscal and monetary policies on aggregate demand seem to matter a great deal for long-run trends in unemployment (Ball 1999; Akerlof 2002; Blanchard 2003).[5] And maintaining strong aggregate demand appears to be particularly effective if tax, spending, and monetary policies are closely coordinated with both wage bargaining and social policy. This, in turn, requires high levels of social consensus and a stable political environment, features that characterize the countries that showed the best employment performance in late 1990s—from the United States, the United Kingdom, and Ireland to Austria, Norway, and the Netherlands.

In the orthodox view, a country's "natural rate" of unemployment, or NAIRU (the nonaccelerating inflation rate of unemployment, which is the unemployment rate that can be maintained without triggering rising inflation), is determined only by the flexibility of the labor market, not by aggregate demand. So, for example, extremely tight monetary policy of the sort practiced by the German Bundesband and the European Central Bank in the 1980s and 1990s (but not by the U.S. Federal Reserve) cannot be blamed for *persistent* high unemployment—such policy decisions can push the unemployment rate above the NAIRU for perhaps some years at a time, but flexible labor markets will ultimately ensure the return of unemployment to its "natural" rate. As the banks, the OECD, and the IMF continually point out, the real problem is persistence, and this is explained by sclerotic labor markets.

Increasingly, this conventional wisdom is cracking. Laurence Ball (1999: 189) puts the matter simply: "this conventional view is wrong. Monetary policy and other determinants of aggregate demand have strong effects on long-run as well as short-run movements in unemployment." Similarly, Olivier Blanchard (2003: 4) argues that, in contrast to what he terms the "traditional literature," "monetary policy can and does affect the natural rate of unemployment." And in his Nobel lecture, George Akerlof makes the same case (see footnote 4). In this alternative view, real-world aggregate demand matters, and there is much more to the unemployment story than simply labor market rigidities. An alternative to the OECD-IMF consensus runs as follows: with the productivity and energy price shocks of the 1970s, and faced with rising inflation, countries responded with tight fiscal and monetary policies, which in turn contributed to the high unemployment experienced by nearly all OECD countries in the early 1980s. As Lawrence Ball (1999: 189) puts it:

> In some countries, such as the United States, the rise in unemployment was transitory; in others, including many European countries, the NAIRU rose and unemployment has remained high ever since. I argue that the reactions of policymakers to the early-1980s recessions largely explain these differences. In countries where unemployment rose only temporarily, it did so because of strongly counter-cyclical policy.... In countries where unemployment rose permanently, it did so because policy remained tight in the face of the 1980s recessions ... labor market policies are not important cases of the unemployment successes and failures since 1985." (190–191)

Decisions were made to use monetary policy to increase unemployment above the "natural rate" for extended periods of time—to minimize the threat of inflation and perhaps also to reduce worker bargaining power and increase profitability. Over time, "hysteresis" effects may tend to raise the NAIRU for various reasons (e.g., the long-term unemployed lose skills or access to job search networks). Ball identifies six "failure countries" whose tight and poorly timed monetary policies contributed to rising unemployment that persisted for long periods—Belgium, Denmark, France, Italy, Canada, and Spain. He shows that the first four of these failure countries "saw sharp increases in rates that occurred largely after the mild runups in inflation, when inflation was stable or falling.... In the success countries, by contrast, tightenings occurred only when inflation was rising substantially" (225). Ball cites "historical accounts" (mainly the OECD's country surveys) to make the case that both Canada and Spain pursued "highly contractionary policies" right through the early 1990s recession. The importance of tight monetary policy for Canada's poor employment performance appears well established (chapter 4; Fortin 1996; Riddell and Sharpe 1998). Ball's conclusion for Spain is supported by Bustillo's case study (chapter 7). And, as the home bastion of tight monetary policy, Germany could be added to the list (see chapter 8), but in this case the effects on employment growth may have been felt less at the level of aggregate demand than in the low-productivity service sector. As Manow and Seils (2000: 288, 301) put it, "Even in the face of such an extraordinary challenge as unification, the Bundesbank continued to follow its hard money policy. . . . The government's fiscal austerity in the service of monetary rigor came partly at the expense of social insurance, where contribution rates were forced up even higher."

The statistical evidence for this aggregate demand story is admittedly limited. Studies by Ball (1999) and Blanchard and Wolfers (2000) offer some empirical support for aggregate demand effects. Part of the problem with demonstrating these effects may be simply technical. As Fitoussi (2003: 438) points out, the difficulty of fully representing the effects of monetary policy with a single variable makes it difficult to statistically link monetary policy to unemployment in cross-country analyses. Despite this, the evidence is highly suggestive. As Fitoussi (2003: 438) asks, "how can we believe that the course of unemployment in Europe has been unaffected by the fact that the short-term real rate of interest has been higher than 5% in a period (1991–1995) in which the rate of growth was about 1%?"

While the effects of restrictive monetary policy on aggregate demand are probably quite an important part of the U.S.-Canada and U.S.-Europe unemployment gaps, the country case studies in this volume and elsewhere suggest an even more complicated story. The key to good employment performance is not just expansionary macroeconomic policy but coordinated policy making that reflects high levels of social consensus and political stability. As just discussed, Germany offers a good example of *poor* coordination (chapter 8). Tight monetary policy was tied to tight fiscal policy, which led to across-the-board increases in nonwage labor costs, and these costs appear to be a big part of the reason Germany lags so far behind in low-wage service employment (Manow and Seils 2000).

France provides another example of the importance of coordinated and consensual decision making and illustrates as well how difficult it is to apply "one size fits all" explanations—in this case, that expanding labor market protections is always and everywhere the source of persistent high unemployment. France developed a unique *dirigiste* model of economic development, in which the state (in Paris) played an active, leading role, generally promoting employer interests but without close institutional connection to either business or labor. According to Levy

(2000: 316), "France's dirigiste model was conceived as a way of creating a modern capitalist economy in the absence of a modern capitalist class . . . (employers') preference for stability over growth and aversion to risk-taking was widely blamed for having left France ill-equipped to face the Nazi war machine. In the postwar period, therefore, a directive, interventionist state would take the economy where timorous employers feared to tread." The result was a great deal of state ownership and regulation but a limited welfare state, since for "state technocrats, social spending represented a cost to be contained, a drain on 'productive' investment" (308). But the exclusion of organized interests—business and labor in particular—from the centralized policy-making apparatus produced decisions that lacked social consensus and nourished political instability.

The French government's probusiness policy orientation fractured after the 1968 protests, giving way to an expansion of social spending (e.g., the minimum wage and unemployment benefits) that reflected "the contested political environment of the 1970s" more than a coherent social agenda. As Levy (2000: 320) puts it, "French leaders would become extraordinarily conflict-averse, often backing down at the first sign of street resistance—whether from shopkeepers, farmers, or workers." Faced with rising un-employment following the shocks of the 1970s, the state first swung to the left under Mitterand, pursuing "a sweeping program of nationalizations, covering twelve leading industrial conglomerates and some 38 banks" that required enormous subsidies (Levy 2000: 321). In 1983, with unemploy-ment rising and budget and trade deficits exploding, the French government sharply reversed course and "accepted the logic of the EMS [European Monetary System] with a vengeance." With the developed world still in recession, "redistributive Keynesianism gave way to austerity budgets, wage indexation was abandoned, and most important, monetary policy was tightened, with real interest rates ranging from 5% to 8% for over a decade" (Levy 2000: 324). It is worth noting again that this was just the reverse of the expansionary policy adopted by the United States in the early to mid-1980s.

A second component of this U-turn in policy was the dismantling of the dirigiste model through privatization. But this threatened workers in the nationalized firms with job loss and lower wages in an economy that was already in recession. Despite the promarket policy shift, French unem-ployment rates continued to rise, and, in response to political protests, "the authorities expanded social spending to help protect workers from dislocation and to undercut resistance to measures of economic liber-alization" (Levy 2003: 309). The OECD-IMF orthodoxy, in contrast, would simply apply the free-market formula: ignore the context, target the in-crease in spending (even if selective and minor), and blame it for high and rising unemployment (see IMF 2003: 141). Clearly, the real story is more complex, as more generous unemployment benefits and stricter employ-ment protection followed, rather than precipitated, rising insecurity and unemployment. And these upward adjustments reflected the need to make the broader promarket policy shifts politically palatable.

It was not until the late 1990s that French unemployment rates began to fall, an improvement that can be explained partly by a demand expansion that was experienced across Europe. But it may also have reflected the greater coherence of reforms since the early to mid-1990s. These included a continued focus on budget austerity. But they also included the implementation of several innovative social policies: lower social security charges on low-wage jobs, which facilitated the expansion of low-skill service jobs (OECD: 2001); the creation of a universal guaranteed minimum income (RMI); the establishment of a large youth employment program (PEJ), which almost certainly more than offset any negative employment effect of the minimum wage; and the 35-hour work week (Levy 2000, Pisani-Ferry 2003).

France may be, as the conventional wisdom contends, the quintessential example of "Eurosclerosis," but, even if there is some merit to this conclusion, it does not appear to rest on an the presence of an exceptionally rigid labor market. This brief account suggests several lessons. First, despite taking the orthodox medicine from 1983 and 1995—fiscal austerity, extreme monetary restraint, and business-friendly policies that kept labor costs stable and the profit share rising (see our earlier discussion)—French unemployment remained extremely high. Second, while the orthodoxy has focused on the failure of France to deregulate its labor market, the reality is that on most standard measures of labor market institutions, France is not more highly regulated than its neighbors, and recent increases in benefits and protections were in part a *response* to the hardship imposed on workers by the 1983–1995 neoliberal program of fiscal austerity, monetary tightness, and privatization. And, third, the poor employment performance experienced by France since the 1970s appears to reflect a highly contested political system that has failed to produce a coherent economic development program that has broad legitimacy across French society, as demonstrated by the swings from the policy opportunism of the 1970s to the Mitterand experiment in the early 1980s, to the U-turn toward aggressive neoliberalism from 1983 to 1995. An adequate account of persistent high French unemployment must address the lack of strong institutions that can help craft compromises between major interest groups that both make economic sense and have social support—a failure that reflects the legacy of France's *dirigisme* model.

Perhaps more than any other single factor, countries with the best unemployment records have been characterized by high levels of social consensus and political stability. This in turn has facilitated long-term commitments to a single, coherent economic development program, whether it means taking the free market road (the United States and, more recently, the United Kingdom) or the more coordinated and regulated route (the Netherlands, Austria, Norway, and, more recently, Ireland). A recent case study of Austria, the Netherlands, and Belgium powerfully illustrates the importance of consensus and coordination (Hemerijck, Unger, and Visser 2000). These are small continental European countries in close physical proximity with strong welfare states and highly regulated labor markets. As the authors point out, "The three countries reveal similar trends in terms of total government outlays, resources spent on social expenditure, the share of social transfers, the financial basis of the welfare state, and taxation.... The non-wage share of total labor costs is around the average of all OECD countries" (188). Yet, their unemployment experiences are dramatically different. Austria has reported extremely low unemployment since the 1960s, consistently outperforming even the United States; the Netherlands performed poorly (the "Dutch disease") in the 1970s and early 1980s but had among the lowest unemployment rates in the OECD in the 1990s, outperforming the United States in recent years; Belgium has been, with France, among the OECD countries with the highest unemployment rates since the late 1970s.

What accounts for such divergent unemployment patterns? Hemerijck et al. argue that the key lies in the "relationship between the state and social partners," which ranges from "a very stable, uncontested, and consensual pattern in Austria, through a narrower, and variable though (in major areas) renewed cooperative style in the Netherlands, to a troubled and conflictual mode in Belgium" (2000: 193). Austria responded to the economic crisis of the 1980s by spurring demand (public-sector employment grew substantially) and by restricting supply (sending foreign workers home). Wage moderation was not a problem, either: "The homogeneity of policy priorities is most prominently demonstrated by the amazing fact that income inequality was never a major topic in Austria, while wage moderation proved much easier to maintain than in Belgium and the Netherlands" (251). In the Netherlands, a series of agreements (the most prominent being the Wassenaar Agreement in 1982) between Dutch employers and workers, with state involvement, has provided the basis for economic policy in the Netherlands since the early 1980s (see also chapter 8).

Belgium, on the other hand, faced political conflict, partly driven by linguistic divisions, which made a coherent and consensual response to the economic crisis of the 1970s and early 1980s impossible. Hemerijck et al. (2000: 250) argue that

> organized actors in Belgium—inside and outside the government—failed to agree on the causes of the job crisis and its therapies, and ... continued to work at cross-purposes.... The upshot was that Belgian governments had to impose conditions on trade unions and firms that were mutually negotiated in the Netherlands.... In the ten crucial years between 1972 and 1982, when two major economic shocks needed a response, Belgium had no less than thirteen governments (compared to five in the Netherlands and only three in Austria). The weakening of the state was compounded by the partisan use of the state, with recruitment practices not based on merit but on party membership and the right combination of language and region.

Part of the problem can also be traced to public finance. Political dysfunction contributed to large budget deficits and to the need for severe fiscal austerity. This in turn closed off a key element of the Dutch solution. "Unlike the Netherlands, Belgium was unable to support wage moderation in the 1990s with tax rebates" (Hemerijck 2000: 254).

The rapid rise in German and Swedish unemployment rates in the 1990s can also be traced to mistaken and uncoordinated policy making that produced fiscal crises. In the German case, the unification process was determined by a "political logic" that turned out to be much more costly than the Kohl government had projected. In combination with conservative tax reforms that led to a collapse in individual and corporate tax receipts (despite rising company profits), the federal budget deficit soared. At the same time, as the German economy (with the rest of Europe) slid into recession, the Bundesbank "raised the bank rate to record postwar levels," which further contributed to declining tax receipts and the budget crisis (Manow and Seils 2000: 288). This suggests that it was tight monetary policy and policy mistakes, not labor market rigidity (much less the welfare state in general) that led to the employment crisis. Indeed, as in the French case, the OECD-IMF orthodoxy has the causation reversed: increased social insurance taxes—which later in the 1990s probably did have negative employment effects—were a perverse consequence of a fiscal crisis that had its roots in unification, tax, and bank policy:

> The failure of proper coordination among fiscal, monetary, and wage policy resulted in a labor market catastrophe for eastern Germany and a dramatic decline in employment in the west. At the end of the day, the brunt of adjustment had to be borne by the welfare state.... At a time when the government had to rule out higher deficits, could not rely on corporate and personal income taxes, and found it impossible to reduce expenditures for the east, it was tempting to finance unification via social insurance. This is exactly what happened. (Manow and Seils 2000: 292, 290)

The recent Swedish experience also highlights the role of policy mistakes. While the OECD-IMF orthodoxy jumped on Sweden's employment crisis in 1991–1993 as evidence of the bankruptcy of the Swedish model, the story is not so simple. Brenner and Vad (2000: 455) argue that, while the Swedish economy required adjustments in the 1980s to cope with a changing international environment, "the problems confronting the Swedish economy between 1985 and 1990 were solved in the wrong order." Making matters worse, the 1991–1993 crisis "elicited only weak and uncoordinated responses" (456) from government and bank authorities. Indeed, the lack of coordination can be traced to a decision to replace the centralized approach to economic policy making, which characterized the 1950s and 1960s, with a decentralized model (456). Interestingly, the immediate source of the crisis was the decision by the Swedish central bank—without coordination with government fiscal policy—to follow the lead of the United States and the United Kingdom with regard to financial deregulation. With the post-1986 reduction in oil prices, this helped produce a speculative boom in the home market in the late 1980s. With rising inflation, wage demands rose. The overheated Swedish economy was then crushed by tax reform (in 1990) and tightened monetary policy just as the developed world headed into recession. Decentralized policy making produced a series of uncoordinated and untimely decisions that proved disastrous. As Brenner and Vad put it, between 1985 and 1993 "the economy was stimulated when it was in need of cooling and put on ice when it needed a modest degree of stimulation" (456).

In sum, the past two decades have posed particularly tough challenges for those responsible for making economic policy in countries committed to limiting economic insecurity and social inequality. In the face of tight monetary policy imposed first by the Bundesbank and then by the European Central Bank, and with increasingly open borders and competitive product markets, it has been essential to keep wages moderate and budget deficits limited. With domestic demand severely constrained, many European countries experienced particularly poor employment growth in the mid-1990s. The options for both macroeconomic policy and social policy at the country level may now be more limited than in the "golden age" of the 1960s and early 1970s. But the country case study evidence strongly suggests that good employment outcomes in this new economic environment can still be achieved with a variety of combinations of labor market institutions, with social spending far more generous in some countries than others. This position has been argued recently by a number of leading labor market specialists (Freeman 2000; Hall and Soskice 2001). There is no particular level of social spending and regulation that is the "right one." Rather, successful employment performance appears to require well-timed macro policies that are effectively coordinated with social policies and the wage bargaining system—an achievement that appears to require both strong employer and union associations and a relatively stable and consensual political environment.

## 10.5 CONCLUDING REMARKS

If the empirical basis of the OECD-IMF orthodoxy is so limited, why does it remain the conventional wisdom? Economists know well that only in perfectly competitive labor markets is there an a priori case for deregulation (e.g., see Blau and Kahn 2002). But since such markets exist only in the first chapters of economics textbooks, the real-world employment effects of labor market institutions designed to shelter workers from the harmful effects of the competitive market is an empirical question. Indeed, many welfare state programs and regulations were implemented over the course of the past century precisely to compensate for market failure—the provision of insurance to reduce the risk of unemployment is a classic example, as is the need for collective bargaining and workplace safeguards to compensate for the inadequate information and weak bargaining power of individual workers.

Yet it would be hard to deny that most economists are wedded to what Richard Freeman (2000: 2) calls the "single peak capitalist economic model"—that there is one single best way to run a capitalist economy, and that is the one that most closely resembles the free-market textbook version. U.S. employment growth trends since the 1970s and unemployment performance in the 1990s certainly lend some support to this view. But the negative side of the U.S. employment "miracle" is that American workers enjoy far less leisure time and face much greater insecurity than their European counterparts. Indeed, U.S. families must work even more hours today to achieve the standard of living their predecessors achieved 30 years ago. As Freeman (2000: 9) notes, "the U.S. advantage in living standards actually eroded over the last twenty or so years."

Despite the continued adulation of the American model, the fact is that productivity levels (output per hour) at the end of the twentieth century were about the same in France, Germany, and other northern European countries as in the United States. The response of *The Economist* (quoted by Freeman 2000: 8) exemplifies the OECD-IMF orthodoxy: "if Germany and Japan can grow as fast (faster in the actual data) as America even when their incentives are blunted by an inflexible model, imagine what they might do were their economies to be set free." But perhaps their impressive economic performance is actually a reflection of the institutional "thickness" of these coordinated market economies (Hall and Soskice 2001). Indeed, given their institutional histories and cultural norms, setting these economies "free" might be a recipe for economic disaster. As discussed earlier, the European "success story" countries have been characterized by centralization, coordination, and social consensus, not by radical shifts toward the free market model. It is instructive that even the strong push toward the U.S. model in the 1980s and 1990s by America's Anglo-Saxon cousins, the United Kingdom and New Zealand, resulted in mixed outcomes—among OECD countries, the United Kingdom fell from sixteenth to eighteenth in per capita income, while New Zealand remained in last place, and its per capita income fell from 14% below Australia's to 19% below (Freeman 2000: 10–11).

So the question remains: why are so many economists so convinced that persistent high unemployment can be explained only as a consequence of the rigidities imposed by labor market institutions? Part of the answer must lie in the way economists are trained to see the world and in the elegant simplicity of the basic textbook model. All the messiness of institutions, nonrational behavior, habits, social norms and, above all, power, can be swept aside. Joseph Schumpeter's insight on the centrality of ideology in social science may be helpful here: "Analytic work begins with material provided by our vision of things, and this vision is ideological almost by definition ... the way in which we see things can hardly be distinguished from the way we wish to see them."[6] It is also the case that, with the dramatic post-1970s ideological swing to the right, challenges to market fundamentalism have been muted. In this ideological context, the orthodox economist's "vision of things" will have a powerful influence on the business press, political pundits, and politicians, particularly if that vision emanates from politically powerful international financial and research organizations like the IMF and the OECD.

It is also apparent that the influence of free-market prescriptions will be that much more influential the more in line they are with the economic interests of politically powerful groups. Thus, low wages in the United States can be blamed on technological changes in the workplace and on the failure of workers to upgrade their skills, not on political and managerial decisions that promote low-wage strategies in the interests of firms and higher-income consumers (and voters). And in Europe, with financial interests favoring tight monetary policy, the strong preference of employers for rolling back social spending and protective regulations, and a continued widespread public fear of returning to past episodes of runaway inflation, it may be convenient for European policy makers to agree to a regime of monetary tightness and fiscal austerity, while blaming the resulting unemployment on labor market rigidities imposed by the welfare state—a kind of "free lunch" in policy making for those not themselves threatened with unemployment or low wages. The pressure on policy makers to adopt free-market policy prescriptions has been enormous.

But the empirical evidence remains. The data simply do not support the OECD-IMF orthodoxy. The cross-country statistical evidence is mixed and unreliable, and the evidence from country case studies overwhelmingly supports a much more nuanced and complicated story that often puts the direction of causality in reverse—regulations and spending follow rising unemployment and the turbulence of promarket policies. Stepping outside the confines of a simple demand-supply framework, it is possible to imagine that much more is at work in countries with poor employment performance than inflexible labor markets. There is a less elegant but more convincing story to be told about the declining economic well-being of the less skilled in developed countries, a story in which low-skilled workers have borne the brunt of weak aggregate demand, massive economic and demographic shifts, and, of course, labor market deregulation.

### Notes

1. According to chapter 5 of the OECD's *Employment Outlook* (OECD 2002: 247), "the estimated coefficients for reduced-form regression equations may not provide reliable estimates of the causal impact of policies on economic performance." In tests of the effects of labor market institutions on employment performance, "the findings are only partly consistent with" the results of other prominent recent studies, and this is "most likely in part due to differences in country coverage and

sample period and the choice of the dependent variables, as well as data revisions. Furthermore, the significance of individual policy and institutional variables often depends on model specification" (252).

2. For example, according to James Heckman (2003: 370): "The high level of centralized wage bargaining thwarts the ability of workers and firms to act on local conditions and to bargain flexibly." Heckman supports this position with references to several pre-1997 econometric studies that report a positive link between decentralized unionism and productivity growth—not a positive link between decentralized unionism and employment growth, much less a negative one with unemployment.

3. For example, the OECD country study for France (OECD 2001) states that "It is now generally accepted that the cost of labour at the SMIC (minimum wage) rate thus has a strong and swift impact on the demand for labour and hence on workers' employment prospects," citing Pisani-Ferry (2000). This suggests that the minimum wage is a big part of the French unemployment problem. But what the Pisani-Ferry report makes clear is that this impact refers to the "relevant workforce" (which raises the question of the magnitude of the employment effect). And it is the "cost of labor," not the minimum wage itself, that is at issue. In context, the point of the Pisani-Ferry passage is only that the reduction in the substantial social contributions made by employers on workers paid the minimum since 1992 has had a beneficial effect on less-skilled workers. The Pisani-Ferry report does not recommend cutting the SMIC. Actually, despite the implications of its language, neither does the OECD country study, which recommends only revising the indexing formula.

Similarly, Heckman (2003: 373) implies that the magnitude of the employment losses from the minimum wage are substantial and help explain the high French unemployment rate. But his evidence, only from Abowd (1998), does not in fact demonstrate this. A "significant disemployment effect" does not necessarily translate into an unemployment effect, much less a significant one, as Abowd et al. suggest when they point out that the "at-risk" populations are quite small. Language and selective references also point to the dominance of ideology over evidence. Heckman dismisses Card and Krueger's work, which generally finds weak or zero employment effects, by citing only their 1995 book. He then points out that this study "has been challenged in the professional journals." It goes unstated that Card and Krueger published the core chapters of the book in these same journals and have rebutted the challenges in them as well!

4. This "shocks" argument relies on the notion that since the 1970s we live in a fundamentally more turbulent world than existed in the past. As Heckman (2003: 360) writes, "We live in an age of creative destruction." But Schumpeter said exactly the same a half century ago to describe capitalism and, parenthetically, to critique the simple, perfect competition model on which textbook economics—and the OECD-IMF orthodoxy—is based. Interestingly, it is Olivier Blanchard, perhaps the economist most responsible for making the shocks-to-institutions explanation part of the conventional wisdom, who has pointed out that there is actually little empirical support for the presumed uniqueness of the post-1980 period. With reference to several plausible measures, he concludes that, for both the United States and France, "there is no evidence of an increase in turbulence" (2003: 353).

5. As George Akerlof explains, "A central proposition of the New Classical economics is that monetary policy, as long as it is full perceived, can have no effect on output or employment ... This New Classical hypothesis conflicts, however,

with empirical evidence on the impact of monetary policy and the widespread popular belief in the power of central banks to affect economic performance" (2002: 416).

6. Quoted by Robert Heilbroner and William S. Milberg, *The Crisis of Vision in Modern Economic Thought* (New York: Cambridge University Press, 1995), p. 16.

## References

Abowd, John M., Francis Kramarz, and David N. Margolis. 1999. "Minimum Wages and Employment in France and the United States." NBER Working Paper 6996, March.

Abowd, John M., Francis Kramarz, Thomas Lemieux, and David N. Margolis. 1997. "Minimum Wages and Youth Employment in France and the United States." NBER Working Paper 6111, July.

Agell, Jonas. 1999. "On the Benefits from Rigid Labour Markets: Norms, Market Failures, and Social Insurance." *Economic Journal* 109: F143–F164.

Akerlof, George A. 2002. "Behavioral Macroeconomics and Macroeconomic Behavior." *American Economic Review* 92(3) (June): 411–433.

Baker, Dean, and John Schmittt. 1998. "The Macroeconomic Roots of High European Unemployment: The Impact of Foreign Growth." Economic Policy Institute (October).

Ball, Laurence. 1999. "Aggregate Demand and Long-Run Unemployment." *Brookings Papers on Economic Activity* 2: 189–236.

Barr, Nicholas 1998. *The Economics of the Welfare State*. Stanford: Stanford University Press.

Beissinger, Thomas, and Joachim Moeller. 1998. "Wage Inequality and the Employment Performance of Different Skill Groups in Germany." Manuscript, University of Regensburg, July.

Benner, Mats, and Torben Bundgaard Vad. 2000. "Sweden and Denmark: Defending the Welfare State." In *Welfare and Work in the Open Economy, Vol. II: Diverse Responses to Common Challenges*, edited by Fritz W. Scharpf and Vivien A. Schmidt. Oxford: Oxford University Press. pp. 399–466.

Bertola, Giuseppe and Pietro Garibaldi. 2002. "The Structure and History of Italian Unemployment." Paper prepared for the Yrjo Jahnsson Foundation, November.

Blanchard, Olivier J. 2003. "Comments on Ljungqvist and Sargent." In *Knowledge, Information, and Expectations in Modern Macroeconomics: In Honor of Edmund S. Phelps*, edited by Philippe Aghion, Roman Frydman, Joseph Stiglitz, and Michael Woodford. Princeton: Princeton University Press. pp. 351–356.

———. 2003. "Monetary Policy and Unemployment." Remarks at the conference "Monetary Policy and the Labor Market," New School University, November 2002.

Blau, Francine D., and Lawrence M. Kahn. 2002. *At Home and Abroad: U.S. Labor Market Performance in International Perspective*. New York: Russell Sage Foundation.

Card, David, Francis Kramarz, and Thomas Lemieux. 1999. "Changes in the Relative Structure of Wages and Employment: A Comparison of the United States, Canada, and France." *Canadian Journal of Economics* 4: 843–877.

Cohen, Daniel, Arnaud Lefranc, and Gilles Saint-Paul. 1997. "French Unemployment: A Transatlantic Perspective." *Economic Policy* 25 (October): 267–291.

Elmeskov, J., J. Martin, and S. Scarpetta. 1998. "Key Lessons for Labor Market Reforms: Evidence from OECD Countries' Experience." *Swedish Economic Policy Review* 5(2): 205–252.

Esping-Andersen, Gosta. 1999. *Social Foundations of Postindustrial Economics.* Oxford: Oxford University Press.

Ferrara, Maurizio, and Elisabetta Gualmini. 2000. "Italy: Rescue from Without?" In *Welfare and Work in the Open Economy, Vol. II: Diverse Responses to Common Challenges*, edited by Fritz W. Scharpf and Vivien A. Schmidt.Oxford: Oxford University Press. pp. 351–398.

Fitoussi, Jean-Paul. 2003. "Comments on Nickell, Nunziata, Ochel, and Quintini." In *Knowledge, Information, and Expectations in Modern Macroeconomics: In Honor of Edmund S. Phelps*, edited by Philippe Aghion, Roman Frydman, Joseph Stiglitz, and Michael Woodford. Princeton: Princeton University Press. pp. 432–440.

Fortin, Pierrs. 1996. "The Great Canadian Slump." *Canadian Journal of Economics* 29(4): 761–787.

Freeman, Richard B. 2000. "The U.S. economic Model at Y2K: Lodestar for Advanced Capitalism?" NBER Working Paper 7757, June.

Greg, Paul, and Alan Manning. 1997. "Labour Market Regulation and Unemployment." In *Unemployment Policy: Government Options for the Labour Market*, edited by Dennis J. Snower and Guillermo de la Dehesa. Cambridge: Cambridge University Press.

Hall, Peter A. and David Soskice, eds. 2001. "An Introduction to Varieties of Capitalism." In *Varieties of Capitalism: The Institutional Foundations of Comparative Advantage*, edited by Peter A. Hall and David Soskice. Oxford: Oxford University Press. pp. 1–67.

Heckman, James J. 2003. "Flexibility and Job Creation: Lessons from Germany." In *Knowledge, Information, and Expectations in Modern Macroeconomics: In Honor of Edmund S. Phelps*, edited by Philippe Aghion, Roman Frydman, Joseph Stiglitz, and Michael Woodford. Princeton: Princeton University Press. pp. 357–393.

Hemerijck, Anton, Brigitte Unger, and Jelle Visser. 2000. "How Small Countries Negotiate Change: Twenty-Five Years of Policy Adjustment in Austria, the Netherlands, and Belgium." In *Welfare and Work in the Open Economy, Vol. II: Diverse Responses to Common Challenges*, edited by Fritz W. Scharpf and Vivien A. Schmidt. Oxford: Oxford University Press. pp. 175–263.

International Monetary Fund (IMF). 1999. "Chronic Unemployment in the Euro Area: Causes and Cures." Chapter 4 in *World Economic Outlook* (May). Washington, D.C.: IMF.

———. 2003. "Unemployment and Labor Market Institutions: Why Reforms Pay Off." Chapter 4 in *World Economic Outlook* (May). Washington, D.C.: IMF.

Levy, Jonah D. 2000. "France: Directing Adjustment?" In *Welfare and Work in the Open Economy, Vol. II: Diverse Responses to Common Challenges*, edited by Fritz W. Scharpf and Vivien A. Schmidt. Oxford: Oxford University Press. pp. 308–350.

Manow, Philip, and Eric Seils. 2000. "Adjusting Badly: The German Welfare State, Structural Change, and the Open Economy." In *Welfare and Work in the Open Economy, Vol. II: Diverse Responses to Common Challenges*, edited by

Fritz W. Scharpf and Vivien A. Schmidt. Oxford: Oxford University Press. pp. 264–307.

Nickell, Stephen, Luca Nunziata, Wolfgang Ochel, and Glenda Quintini. 2003. "The Beveridge Curve, Unemployment, and Wages in the OECD from the 1960s to the 1990s." In *Knowledge, Information, and Expectations in Modern Macroeconomics: In Honor of Edmund S. Phelps*, edited by Philippe Aghion, Roman Frydman, Joseph Stiglitz, and Michael Woodford. Princeton: Princeton University Press. pp. 394–431.

Organization for Economic Cooperation and Development (OECD). 1997. "Economic Performance and the Structure of Collective Bargaining." *OECD Employment Outlook* (July).

———. 1998. "Making the Most of the Minimum: Statutory Minimum Wages, Employment and Poverty." *OECD Employment Outlook* (June). Paris: OECD.

———. 1999. "Employment Protection and Labor Market Perfomance." *OECD Employment Outlook* (June). Paris: OECD.

———. 2001. *OECD Economic Surveys: France*. Paris: OECD.

———. 2002. "And the Twain Shall Meet: Cross-Market Effects of Labour and Product Market Policies." *OECD Employment Outlook* (July). Paris: OECD.

———. 2004. *OECD Employment Outlook*. Paris: OECD.

Pisani-Ferry, Jean. 2000. "Plein Emploi." Rapport du Conseil d'Analyse Économique, Paris (http://www.premier-ministre.gouv.fr).

———. 2003. "The Surprising French Employment Performance: What Lessons?" Paper prepared for the CESifo Conference, Munich (December 2002).

Pissarides, Christopher A. 2003. "Company Start-Up Costs and Employment." In *Knowledge, Information, and Expectations in Modern Macroeconomics: In Honor of Edmund S. Phelps*, edited by Philippe Aghion, Roman Frydman, Joseph Stiglitz, and Michael Woodford. Princeton: Princeton University Press. pp. 309–325.

Riddell, W. Craig, and Andrew Sharpe, eds. 1998. "CERF/CSLR Conference on the Canada-U.S. Unemployment Rate Gap."*Canadian Public Policy* 24 (Supp.) (February).

Scharpf, Fritz W., and Vivien A. Schmidt. 2000. "Introduction." In *Welfare and Work in the Open Economy, Vol. II: Diverse Responses to Common Challenges*, edited by Fritz W. Scharpf and Vivien A. Schmidt. Oxford: Oxford University Press. pp. 1–18.

Siebert, Horst. 1997. "Labor Market Rigidities: At the Root of Unemployment in Europe." *Journal of Economic Perspectives* 11(3) (Summer): 37–54.

Smeeding, Timothy M., Lee Rainwater, and Gary Burtless 2001. "U.S. Poverty in a Cross-national Context." In *Understanding Poverty*, Sheldon H. Danziger and Robert H. Haveman, eds. Cambridge, Harvard University Press.

Steiner, Viktor, and Kersten Wagner. 1997. "Relative Earnings and the Demand for Unskilled Labor in West German Manufacturing." Discussion Paper No. 97-17, Centre for European Economic Research, June.

# Index